AF304913

EAST LONDON PHOTO STORIES

WE ARE 5

This book was released on the 5th anniversary
of the start of Hoxton Mini Press. Thanks to all who
have supported us on the way, thanks to all our
lovely photographers, thanks to you for reading this,
thanks to our staff, to our dogs, thanks to our daughters
Olive and Hazel, thanks to East London, thanks
to Fred our main designer, thanks to our profreeders,
thanks to the internet for making physical books
more precious, thanks to Gwyneth's Oscar speech
for inspiring this text. It's been fun. We love it.
You let us do it. Here's to the next 5,000 years.
Use paper, not plastic!

All of these photography projects are available as full individual books.
To order copies, including collector's editions, please go to:

www.hoxtonminipress.com

EAST LONDON PHOTO STORIES

ONE NEIGHBOURHOOD
14 PHOTOGRAPHERS

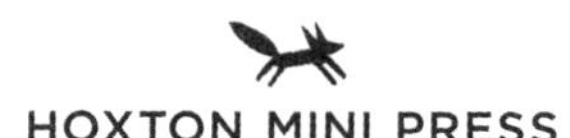

HOXTON MINI PRESS

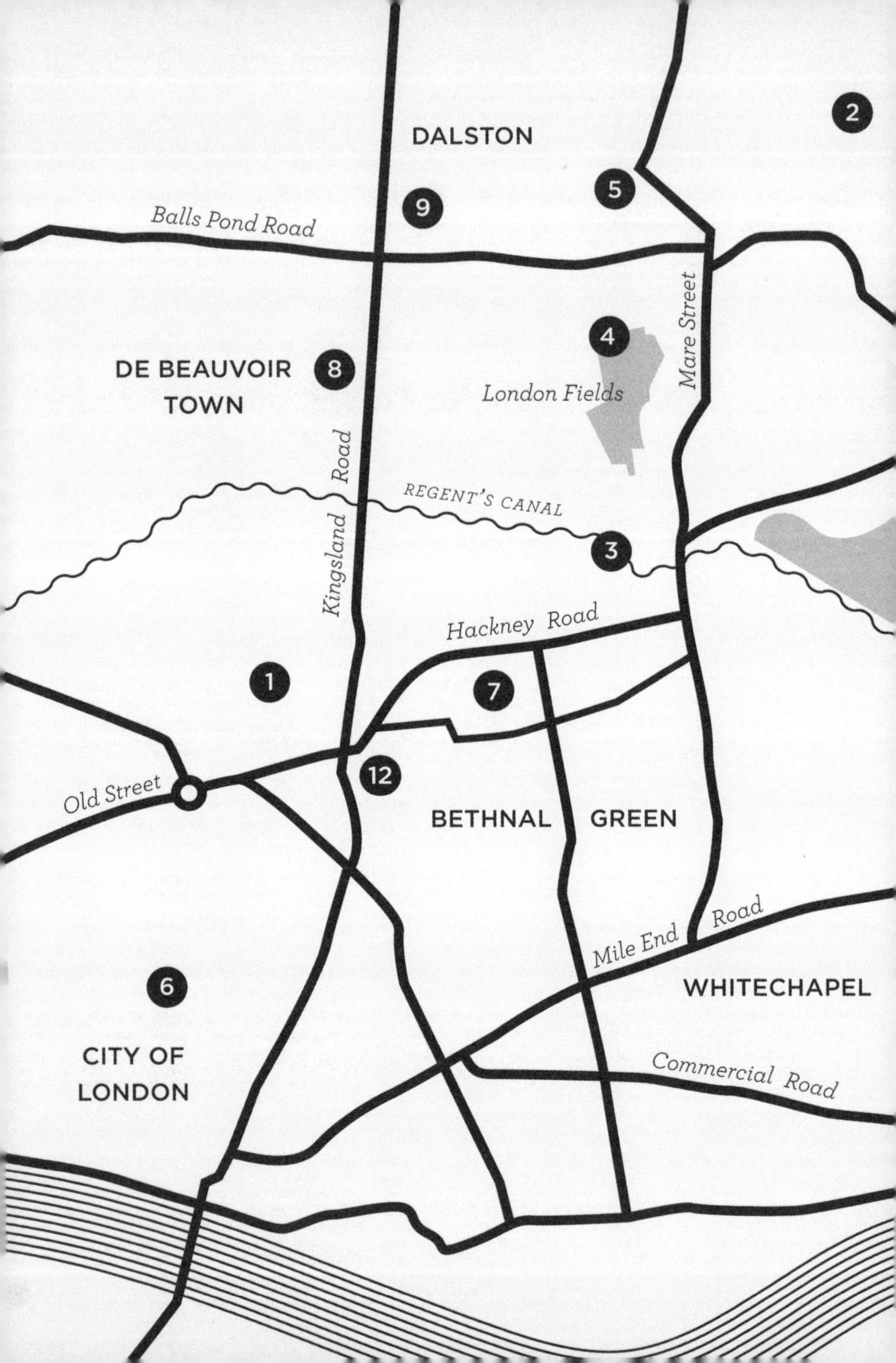

DALSTON
2
5
9
Balls Pond Road
4
London Fields
Mare Street
DE BEAUVOIR
TOWN
8
Kingsland Road
REGENT'S CANAL
3
Hackney Road
1
7
12
Old Street
BETHNAL GREEN
Mile End Road
6
WHITECHAPEL
CITY OF
LONDON
Commercial Road

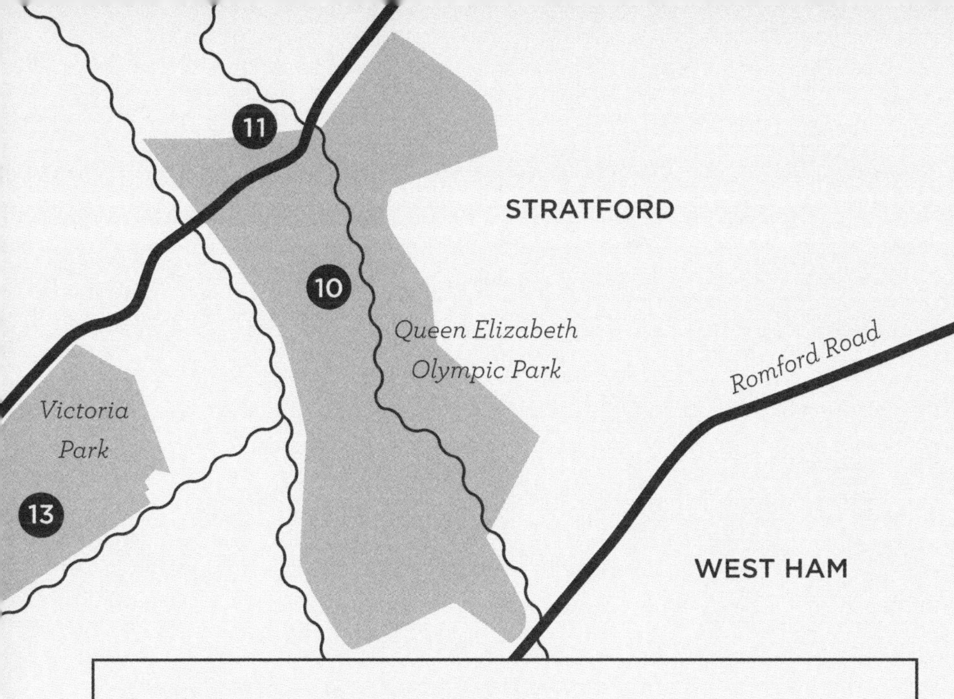

A MAP OF EAST LONDON

(Showing the area in which each project was photographed)

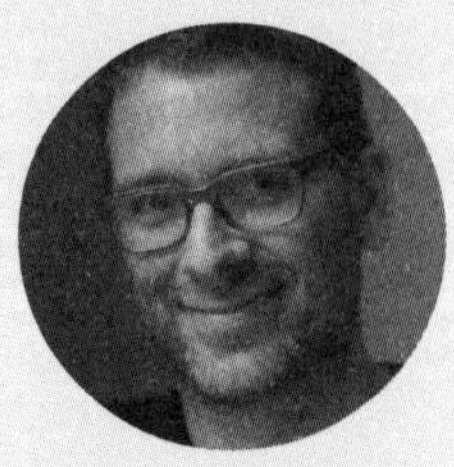

MARTIN USBORNE *I've Lived in East London for 86 ½ Years*
After meeting an old man in Hoxton in 2007, Martin turned the story of their friendship into a book (p.17), which lead to starting Hoxton Mini Press with his wife, Ann, which lead to publishing all the books below, which lead to you reading this.

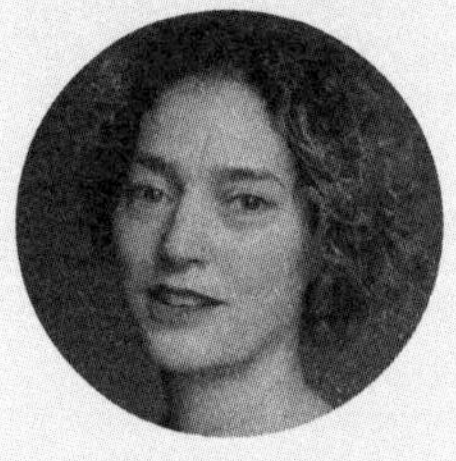

JENNY LEWIS *One Day Young*
Since moving to Hackney over 20 years ago Jenny has made her living as an editorial photographer but it's her personal work that centres on her experience of living and working in East London. She has had two books published by Hoxton Mini Press, the above (p.45) and *Hackney Studios*.

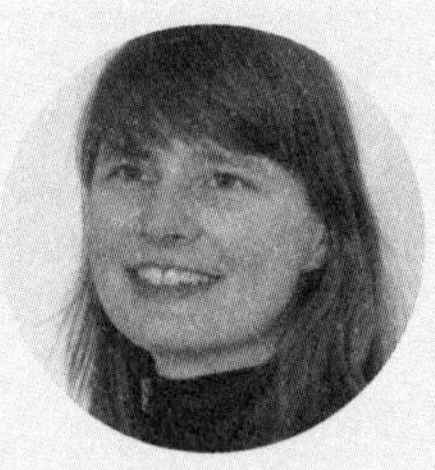

FREYA NAJADE *Along the Hackney Canal*
German photographer Freya made Hackney her home in 2007 and fell in love with the canals that meander through its landscape. Her documentary work has appeared in the *Guardian* and *British Journal of Photography*, and her book (p.69) won *Creative Review*'s Best in Book award in 2016.

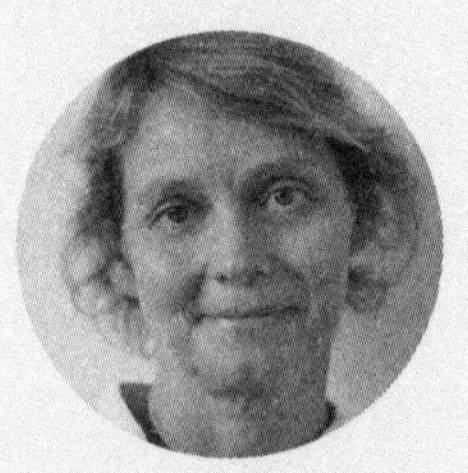

MADELEINE WALLER *East London Swimmers*
Orginally from Australia, Madeleine came to London in 1987 and loved it so much she never left. She lives in Hackney with her husband and three children, and enjoys taking them to the London Fields Lido where these portraits were taken (p.93).

A Portrait of Hackney **ZED NELSON**
From Israel to South Sudan, Zed's lens has touched some of the most troubled areas of the world, but in this book he captures familiar territory. Growing up in Hackney from age three, Zed has witnessed and photographed the area's rapid transformation (p.115).

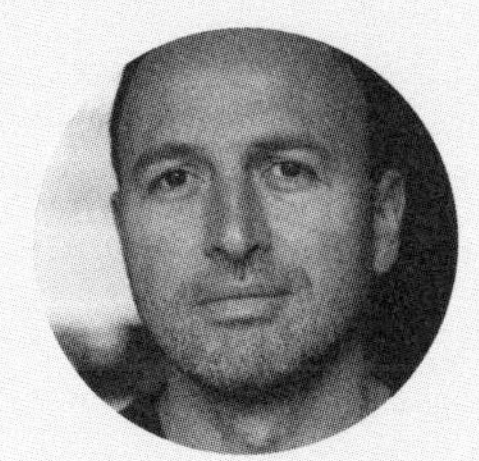

Lost in the City **NICHOLAS SACK**
After drumming in rock bands and gaining a master's in journalism, Nicholas took up photography in his 20s and spent 30 years freelancing for magazines. He now concentrates on personal projects shot on black and white film on long walks, sometimes around London's Square Mile (p.139).

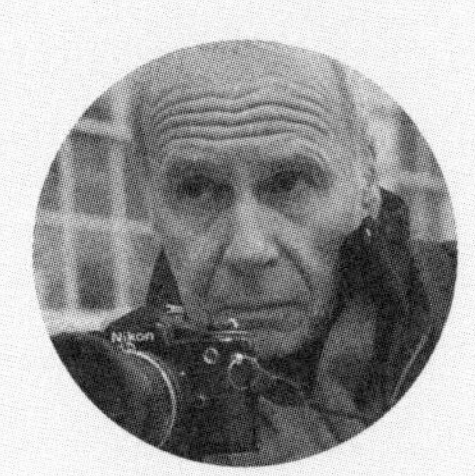

Columbia Road **JOHANNA NEURATH**
Johanna has been a Hackney citizen for all of her adult life. Design director at an international art book publisher, she is a self-confessed image junkie, type nerd and bibliophile. Johanna is also fond of flowers, whether arranged in vases or strewn on Columbia Road's pavements (p.161).

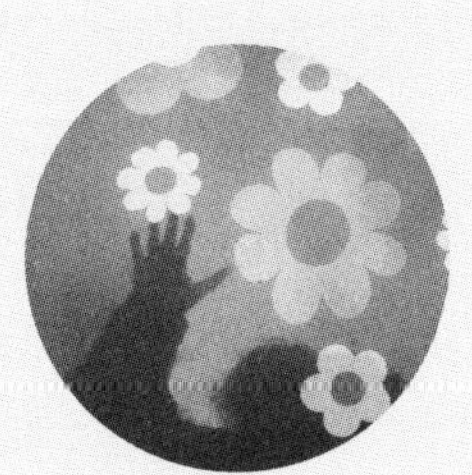

Drivers in the 1980s **CHRIS DORLEY-BROWN**
Chris' family has lived in Hackney and Bethnal Green for nearly 200 years, and though he wasn't born in the East End himself, we still think he's a diamond geezer. His images in this book (p.183) are from the first five rolls of colour film he ever shot. We're glad he continued to shoot.

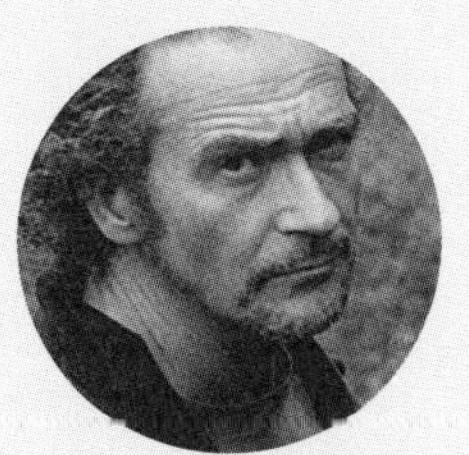

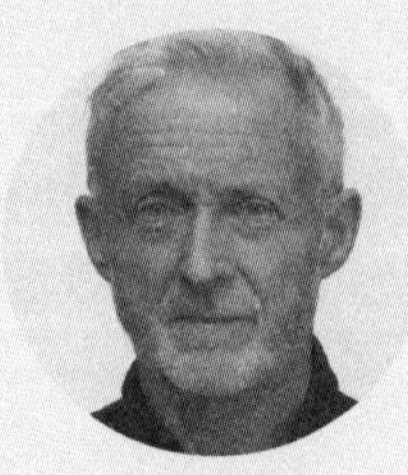

ANDREW HOLLIGAN *Dalston in the 80s*
Andrew has worked in far flung places as a photographer, from the Alaskan Tundra to Australian deserts. He arrived in Dalston in 1984 (p.201) and spent almost 15 years in Hackney, on-and-off. He now lives in the countryside but enjoys coming back to London, with a camera of course.

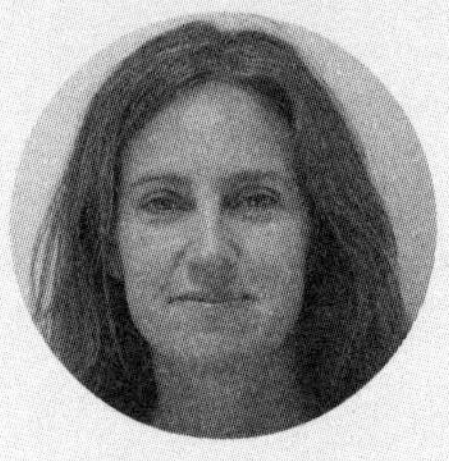

POLLY BRADEN *Adventures in the Lea Valley*
Human relationships are at the heart of Polly's photography. She works on long term projects, such as this book (p.225), shot with David Campany, as well as taking photographs for the *Guardian* and the *Saturday Telegraph*. She has had three photography books published … and counting.

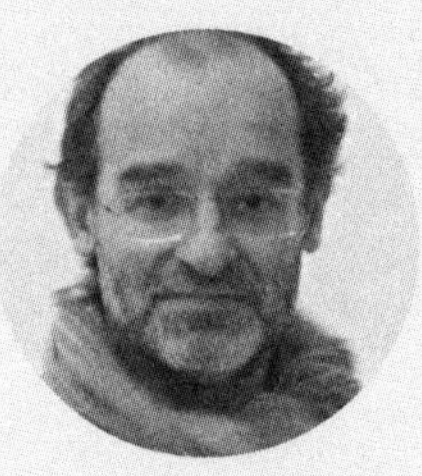

DAVID CAMPANY *Adventures in the Lea Valley*
Curator, photographer and writer of many books – David has an impressive array of guises, though they are all photographic in one way or another. He describes the Lea Valley as 'strange, exciting, ugly, beautiful and unaccountably mysterious'. See for yourself on p.225.

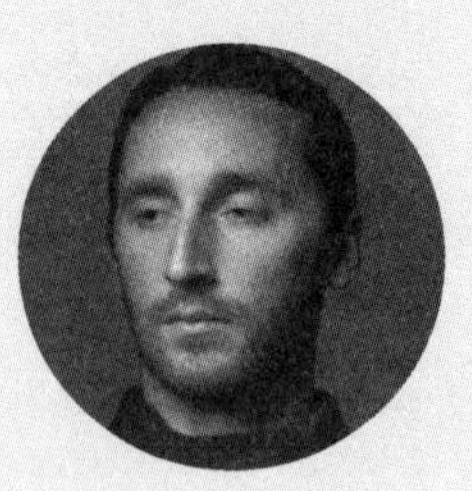

CHRIS BAKER *Sunday Football*
After one too many injuries, Chris decided to get on the safe side of the sidelines and began a two-year documentation of football on the Hackney Marshes (p.249). Prior to his obsession with photography, he worked for an independent record label. He is also co-founder of WeMove magazine.

Shoreditch Wild Life **DOUGIE WALLACE**
After getting a degree in sport and studying photojournalism, Dougie took to the streets with his camera and adopted a distinct, direct style that has had him recognised across the globe. He still takes photos in Shoreditch, even though the night-life isn't as wild as the early noughties (p.273).

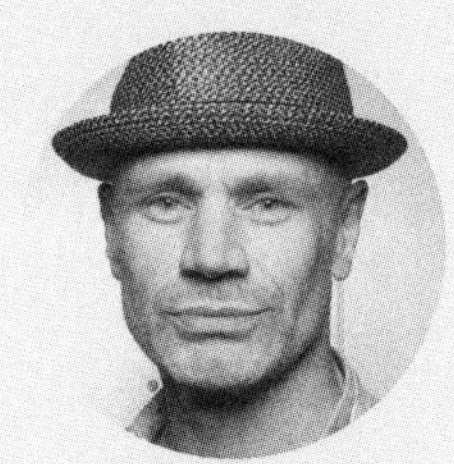

Hackney by Night **DAVID GEORGE**
Long dog walks after dark led David to reveal the unexpected beauty of Hackney at night (p.297). He has been taking pictures for nearly 40 years and lives and works in East London. His photography examines social and political narratives that can be found in British urban landscapes.

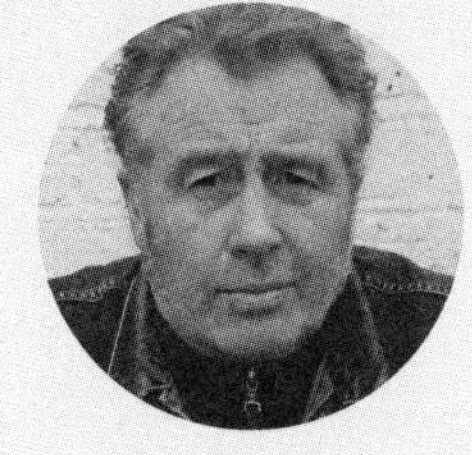

INTRODUCTION

East London's streets are paved with stories. This corner of the capital fuels the imagination like no other – and always has done. In the 19th century, self-styled 'urban explorers' would head here in disguise and write up accounts of what they'd seen: a wretched landscape of cramped houses, shabby slums riddled with violence, poverty, disease and misery. This was Jack the Ripper's stomping ground, a seedy place where most respectable people wouldn't venture. Visiting in 1902, American writer Jack London called it 'the abyss'.

Over the 20th century a more cheerful mythology took hold. Cockney culture with its music halls, pub knees-ups, jellied eels, pearly kings and tough-guy gangsters came to represent East London. Fast forward to the present. An influx of artists, which began in the 90s when they were attracted to the area's cheap and plentiful studio space, and more recently the redevelopment brought by the 2012 Olympics have changed the script again. The shoeless waif and cockney geezer have been usurped by a new character: the hipster. East London has been crowned a centre of cool but for how long? Many of the creative types who made it cool initially have been priced out by rising rents.

The reality, of course, is complicated. Though historically poor, East London has developed through its industries: the docks, the railways, the garment industry, finance in the City, artists and the tech companies of Silicon Roundabout. Cockneys are just one strand of a varied lineage: French Huguenot silk weavers, Irish labourers, Jewish anarchists and Bangladeshi businessmen. Alongside gentrification, 21st century East London has given us Grime – one of our most original homegrown music genres. While it's true that the East End has become pricier, you'll still find incredible creativity and cultural diversity here, especially further out east.

As soon as you think you've got East London figured out, it surprises you. It was precisely that aspect of their neighbourhood that prompted husband and wife Martin Usborne and Ann Waldvogel to set up Hoxton Mini Press in 2013. Their story began with a project by Usborne about Joseph Markovitch, an elderly man he'd noticed out of his Hoxton Square studio window, at odds with the young trendies around him. At first, the photographer thought he'd got Markovitch sussed. He was wrong. 'I planned to make a book about the history of the rich and diverse area around East London. But Joe wanted to talk about action movies, tall Scandinavian women, Nicolas Cage, the catarrh congesting his chest and how technology might blow up the world.'

The book sold out and ignited a passion for publishing that had lain dormant in Usborne, the son of a publisher. His unlikely friendship with Markovitch had shown him that there were many more sides to East London than met the eye. 'It's one of the most exciting, colourful, infuriating, fascinating, historical, ever-changing parts of town,' he explains in the company's Kickstarter video. 'There are so many stories here to tell and so many people that can tell the stories.' Following a storming crowdfunding campaign, Hoxton Mini Press launched with their first two books about East London.

In the five years since then, they've continued to publish books in a number of different series. One collection, 'Tales from the City', taps into urban experiences in London and further afield, from dirt biking to glasshouses to the waterways of New York. There've been other books on coffee culture, startup businesses, artists' studios, hidden London, bubblegum, hand models. Even dogs – the first installation in an ongoing collaboration with Penguin Random House. Across these seemingly varied subjects there's been a common thread. Each one shows you something unique, taking you somewhere you couldn't anticipate. That spirit originates in East London.

This book brings together a selection of pictures from each of the first 13 'East London Photo Stories' titles. In doing so it takes us right to the core of what Hoxton Mini Press is all about. Many of the stories here topple previously-held perceptions about their subjects. *One Day Young* pays tribute to brand new motherhood, not just as a time of sleep-deprivation and selfless devotion, but as an accomplishment, a moment of glory for a woman. *A Portrait of Hackney* takes us beyond the stylish haunts that the photographer's home borough is now known for, and reveals other sides of Hackney life, from kids in hoods to nesting swans.

In some, we see how the photographers themselves set out in one direction and end up somewhere else, pulled along by East London's artistic currents. Like Martin Usborne with Joe Markovitch, Chris Dorley-Brown started with an agenda in mind but his pictures of drivers in the 1980s don't just talk about the day Rolls Royce was sold off, they thrust us right back into a particular era. When Andrew Holligan moved to Dalston, also in the 1980s, from swish New York, the area seemed like a let-down. But he discovered a whole world in microcosm on those bustling streets around Ridley Road. And Johanna Neurath, drawn to the famous Columbia Road, found the photogenic flower market became a mere aside to far more beautiful images hiding in the gutter.

Elsewhere, the East London we think we know is unrecognisable. *Hackney at Night* lifts us like sleeping babes into a fairytale land that exists when darkness falls. *Along the Hackney Canal* gives us East London inside out, through sometimes abstract, watery visions. What comes across in these and projects like *Adventures in the Lea Valley* is how verdant, how ripe with nature, how wild this area is, with its canals and green spaces that reach out, escaping the city. East London isn't just smart warehouse renovations and Olympic villages. It's those nesting swans, it's bleary-eyed footballers on Hackney Marshes. It's something that defies categories, refuses to be contained.

The same could be said for Hoxton Mini Press. Born into a time when the death of print had been declared, they've thrived. True to their East London origins, they have an international appeal – stocked as far afield as Japan and Dubai. On a mission to make art photography accessible and affordable but with books that are never less than gorgeous, immaculately-presented, collectable objects. It's these attributes that have gained them prestigious industry awards and a fiercely devoted following. For the past five years Hoxton Mini Press have consistently done things their way, the East London way. Who knows where the next five years will take them.

Rachel Segal Hamilton
London, 2018

I'VE LIVED IN EAST LONDON FOR 86½ YEARS

MARTIN USBORNE
WITH JOSEPH MARKOVITCH

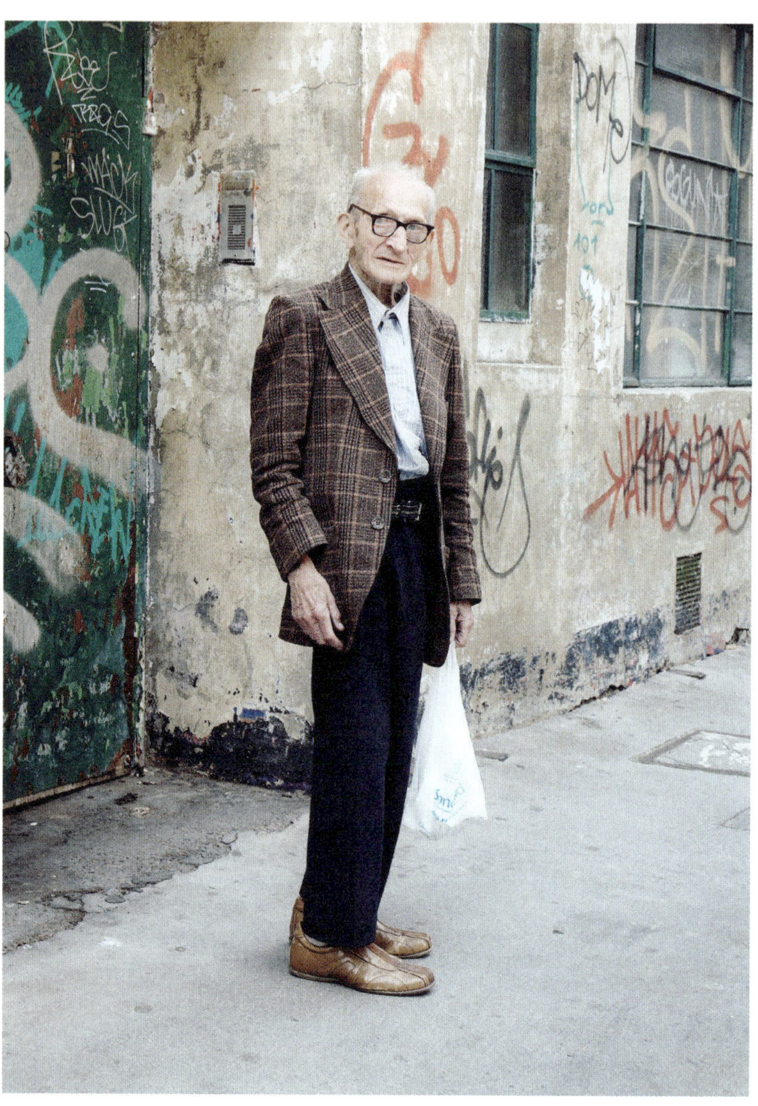

*A poignant study of lifelong East London local
and all-round gent, Joseph Markovitch.*

This is the tale of two men. One, born in 1927 into a Hoxton of raucous music halls and grinding poverty, represents the old East London. The other, photographer and Hoxton Mini Press co-founder, Martin Usborne, the new – all coffee shops and creative buzz. It began by chance in 2007 when Usborne spied Markovitch from the window of his photographic studio. The elderly man cut an incongruous figure, ambling across Hoxton Square with a tatty plastic bag in hand.

Many of the pictures Usborne shot over the following months highlight this contrast. Markovitch fraternises with street artists or with shellsuit-sporting fashionistas, inspects a gold Nike high-top trainer or walks in the imposing shadow of the Olympic Stadium. But in each one, Markovitch seems at ease. He's cheered by the colourful street art that now adorns the walls around where he lives, inspired by the diversity of his new neighbours, amused by the local hipsters.

'A good photographic portrait always captures two people: the subject and the person taking the picture,' writes Usborne. Through the course of shooting the series he learnt much about himself, as well as about Markovitch. A pamphlet of these pictures became a book, which became a publishing company. This story isn't a simple case of then and now, them and us. It's about two lives overlapping and evolving. And it's a perfect metaphor for ever-changing East London.

ON CHILDHOOD

I was born right by Old Street roundabout on January 1st,
1927. Some of the kids used to beat me up – but in a
friendly way. Hoxton was full of characters in those days.
The Mayor was called Mr. Brooks and he was also a
chimney sweep. Guess what? Before the Coronation,
he was putting up decorations and he fell off a ladder
and got killed. Well, it happens. Then there was a
six-foot-tall girl, she was really massive. She used to attack
people and put them in police vans. Maria was her name.
Then there was Brotsky who used to kill chickens
with a long stick. His son's name was Monty.
That's not a common one is it? 'Monty Brotsky'.

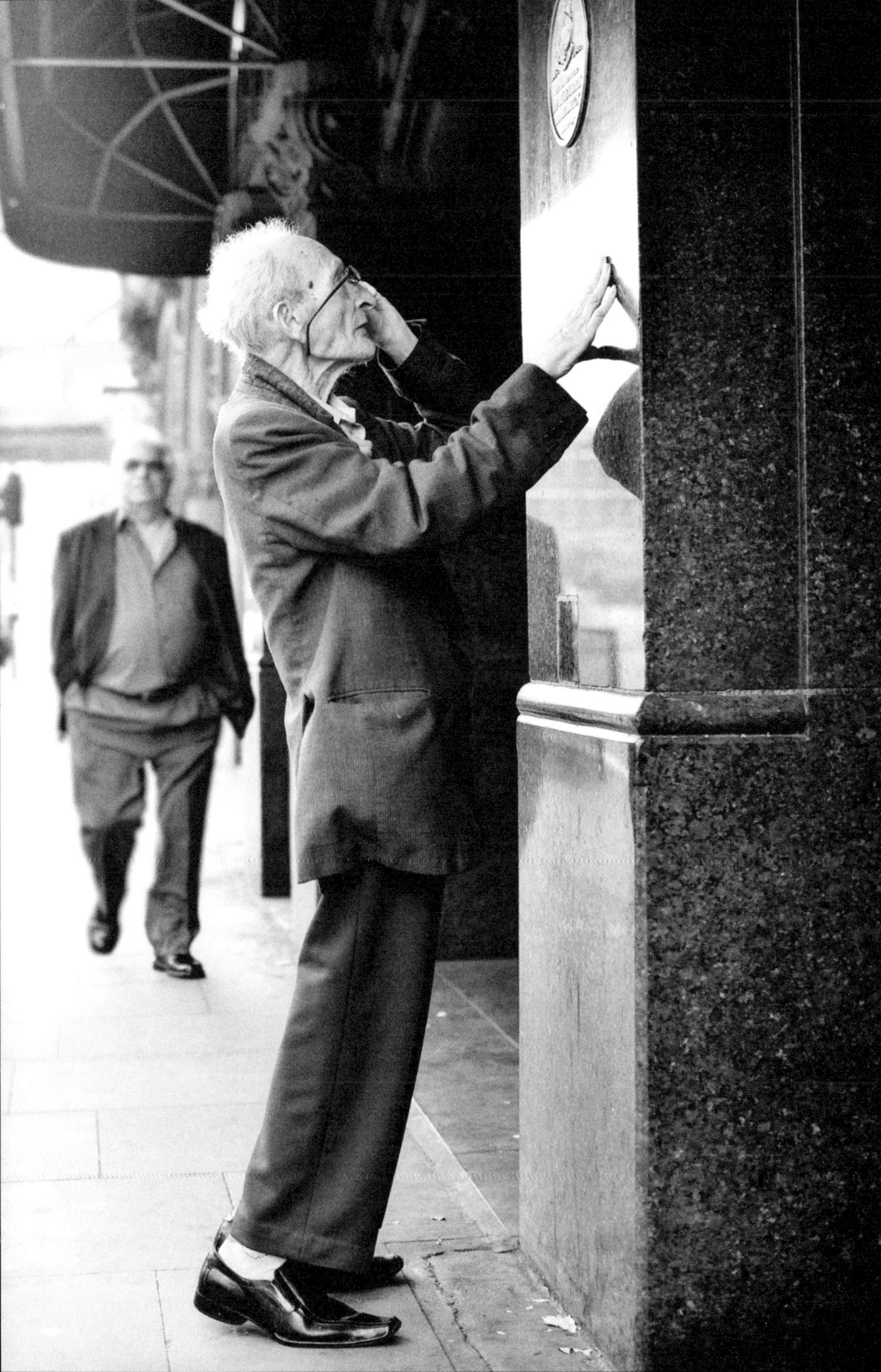

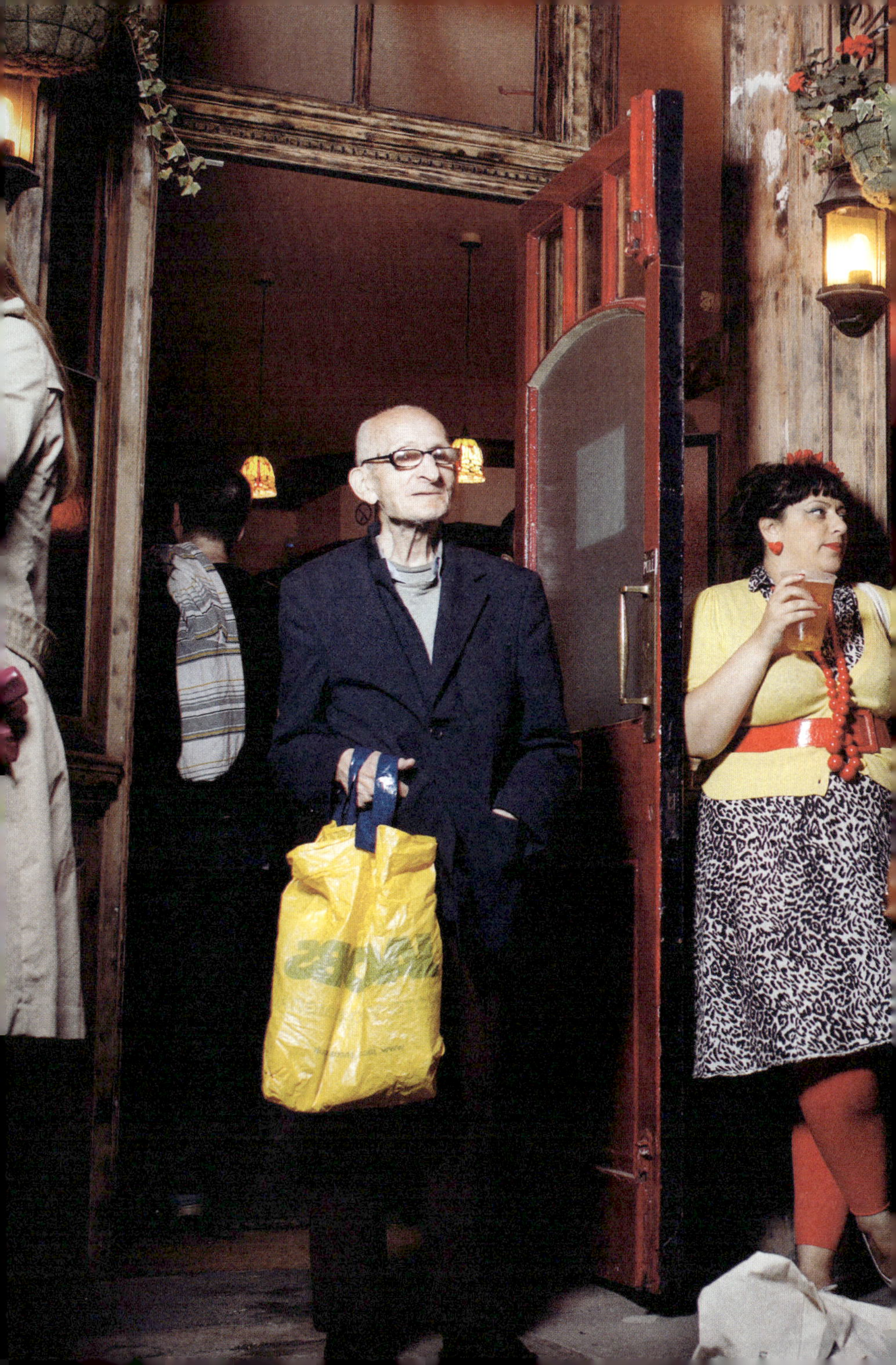

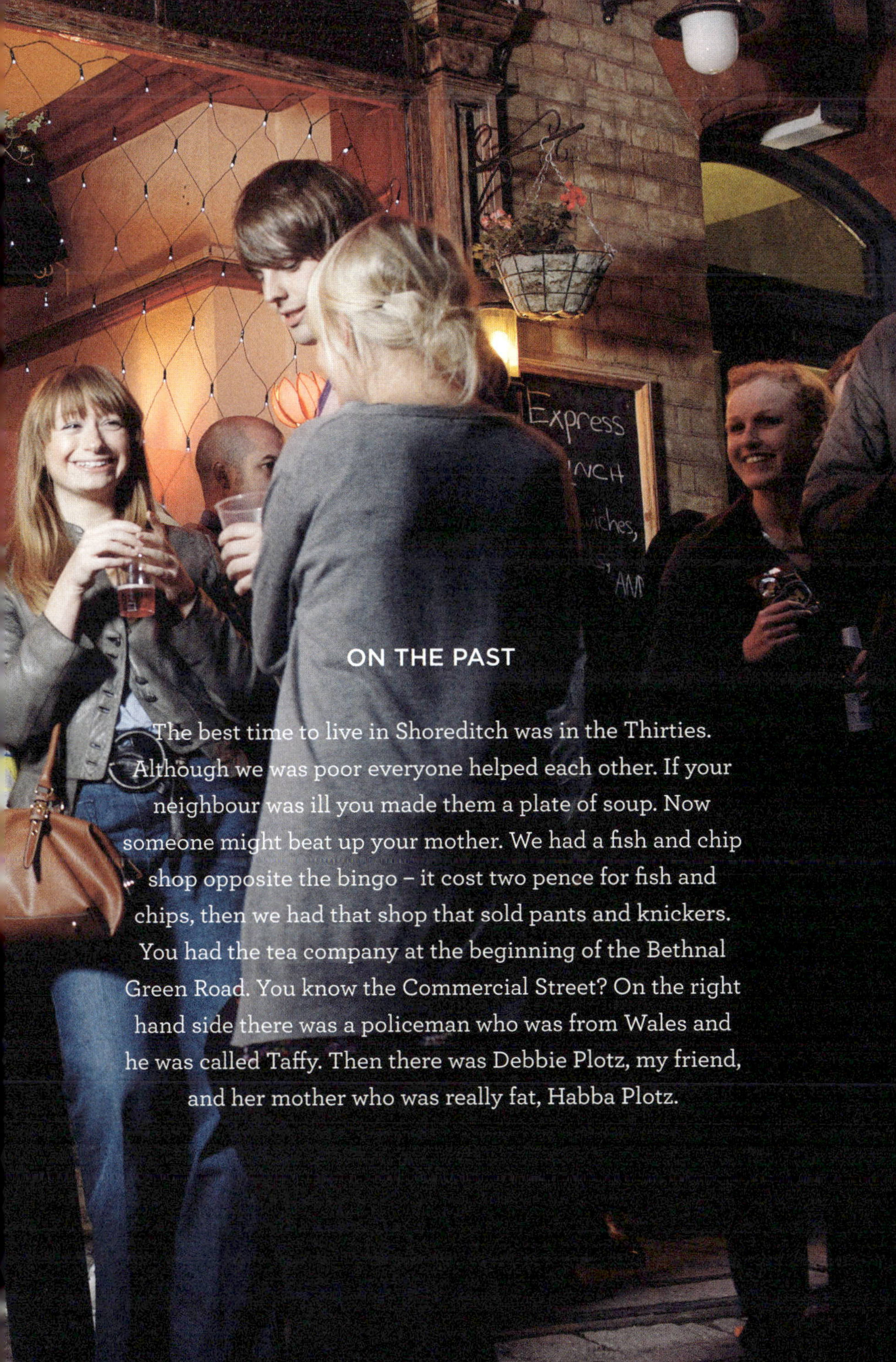

ON THE PAST

The best time to live in Shoreditch was in the Thirties. Although we was poor everyone helped each other. If your neighbour was ill you made them a plate of soup. Now someone might beat up your mother. We had a fish and chip shop opposite the bingo – it cost two pence for fish and chips, then we had that shop that sold pants and knickers. You had the tea company at the beginning of the Bethnal Green Road. You know the Commercial Street? On the right hand side there was a policeman who was from Wales and he was called Taffy. Then there was Debbie Plotz, my friend, and her mother who was really fat, Habba Plotz.

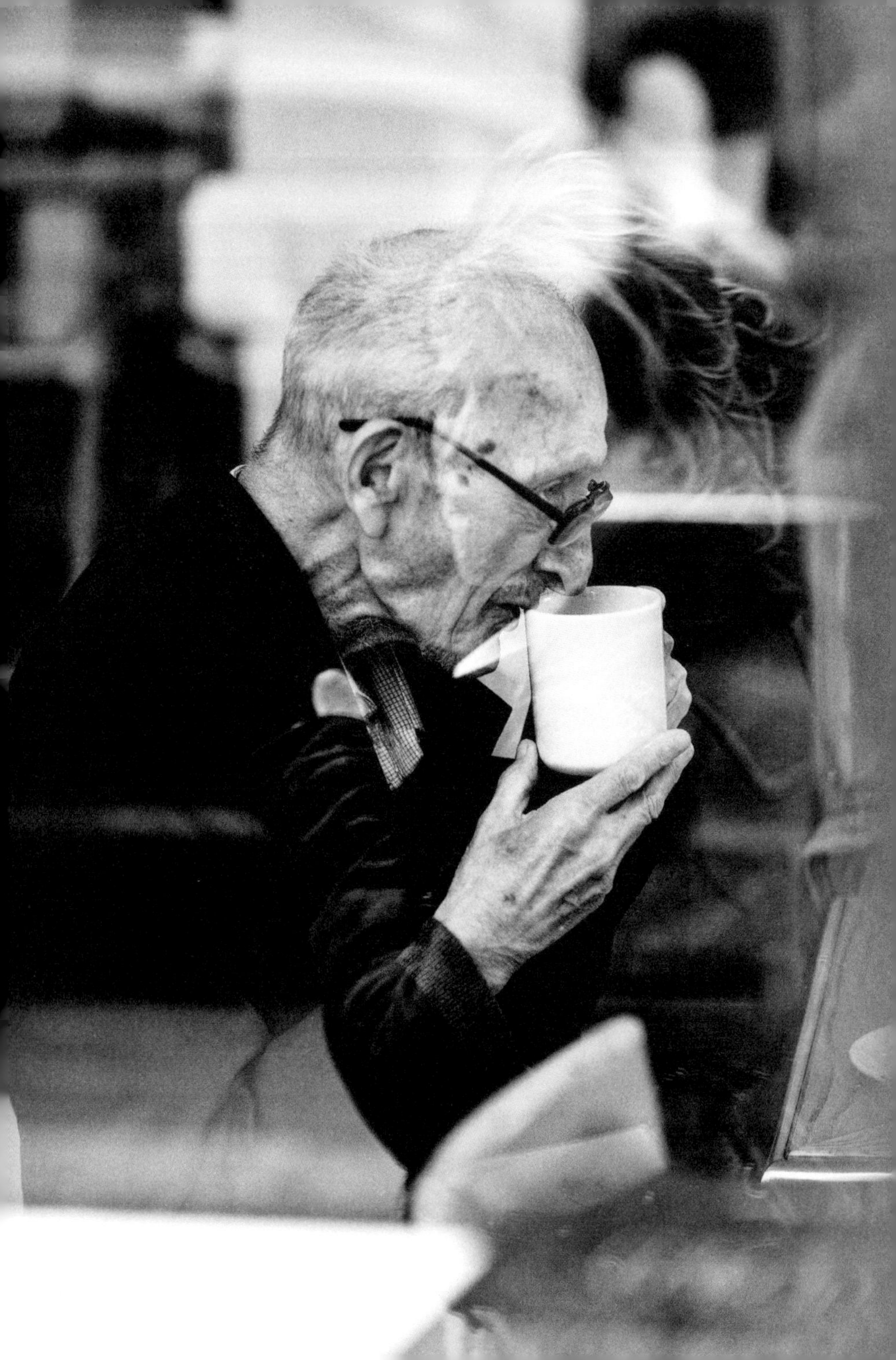

ON RELATIONSHIPS

I've never had a girlfriend. It's better that way. I've always
had very bad catarrh so it wasn't possible. And I had to care
for my mother. Anyway, if I was married I would have been
domineered all my life by a girl and that ain't good for
nobody's health. You know that Bernie Ecclestone, from
Formula One, he is really, really small. He was married to
a Serbian girl who was six-foot-one. I say 'lucky Bernie'.
People always say that dark-haired girls like millionaires.
My preference is very tall blonde Scandinavians. If they are
Hispanic and really tall then I might just like them with
dark hair. I would have liked to have had a girlfriend
but its OK. I've seen the horse and cart, I've seen the
camera invented, I've seen the projector. I never starved,
that's the main thing.

ON FASHION

In the old days, when a man went to see the opera he had
on a bowler hat. If you were a man and you walked in the
street without a hat on your head you were a lost soul.
People don't wear hats any more... but they wear
everything else, don't they?

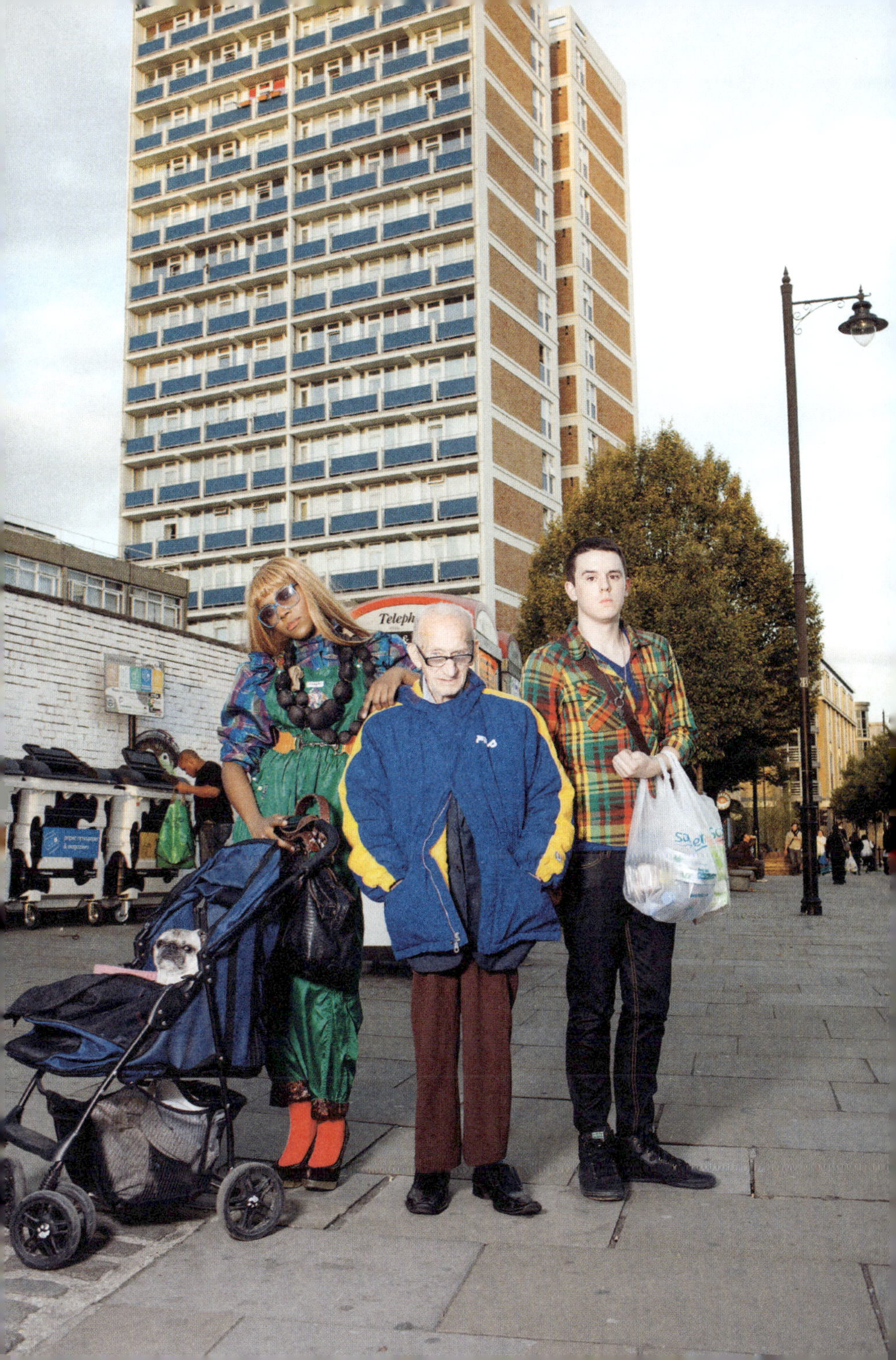

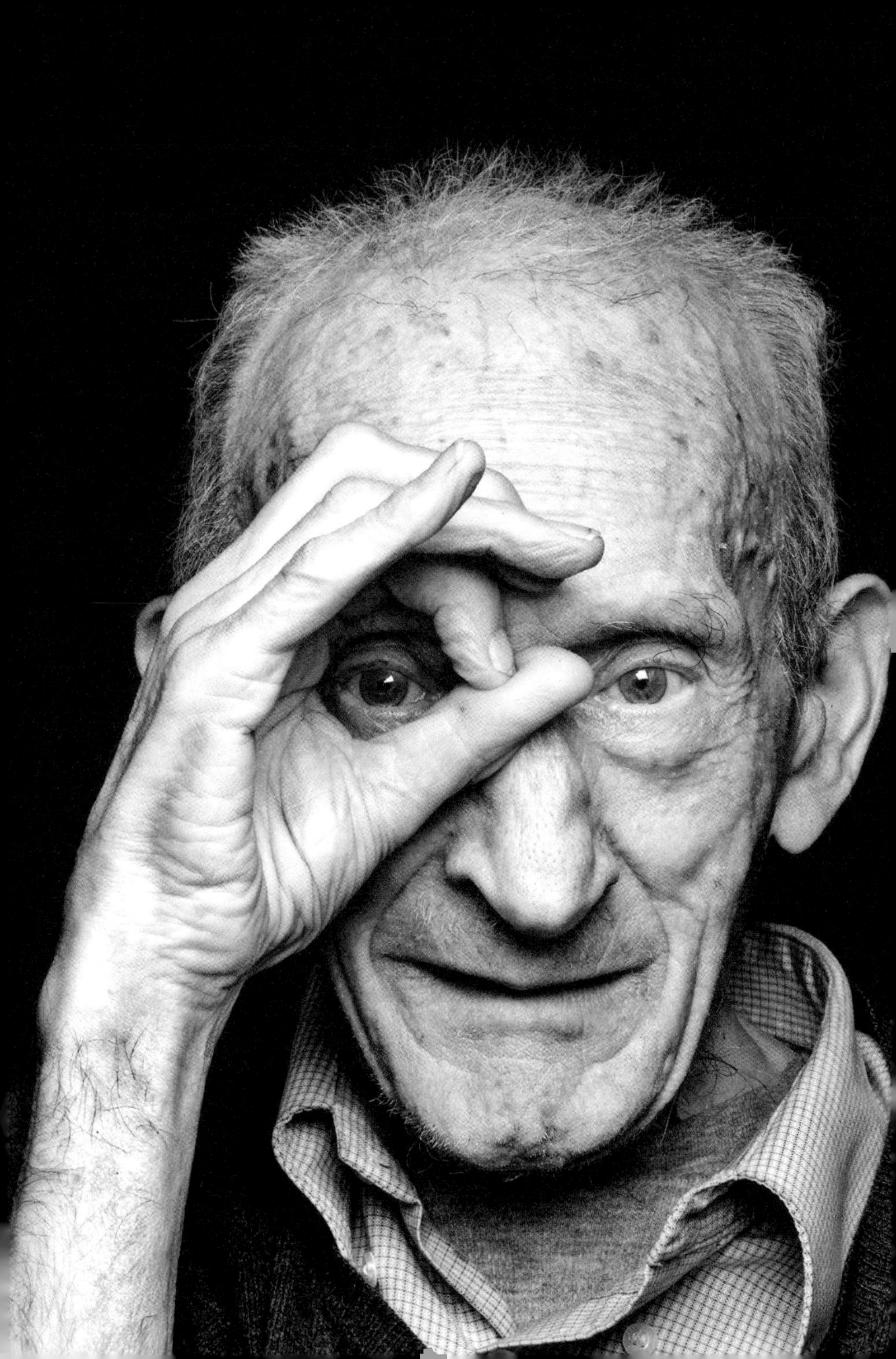

ON THE UNIVERSE

What about those people that study the stars? That's a
very good job. I'm interested in the universe. It's more
interesting than rivets. If we sent a camera far enough into
space we might see people with mouths in their necks and
hearts in their heads. But the universe is a mystery, ain't it?
How did silver happen, how did copper happen, how did
coffee begin? No one knows. The first thing that brought
light was candles. Hey, if a meteor landed in Hoxton square
you think anyone could survive? Probably not.

ON JENNIFER LOPEZ

What about that singer? That Lopez girl. She's
Puerto Rican. She can't be English with a name like Lopez.
If she was born in Hoxton she would be called Jennifer
Smith and that wouldn't be right. I think it's great that
people are all mixed up. The most important thing is
to be kind to each other.

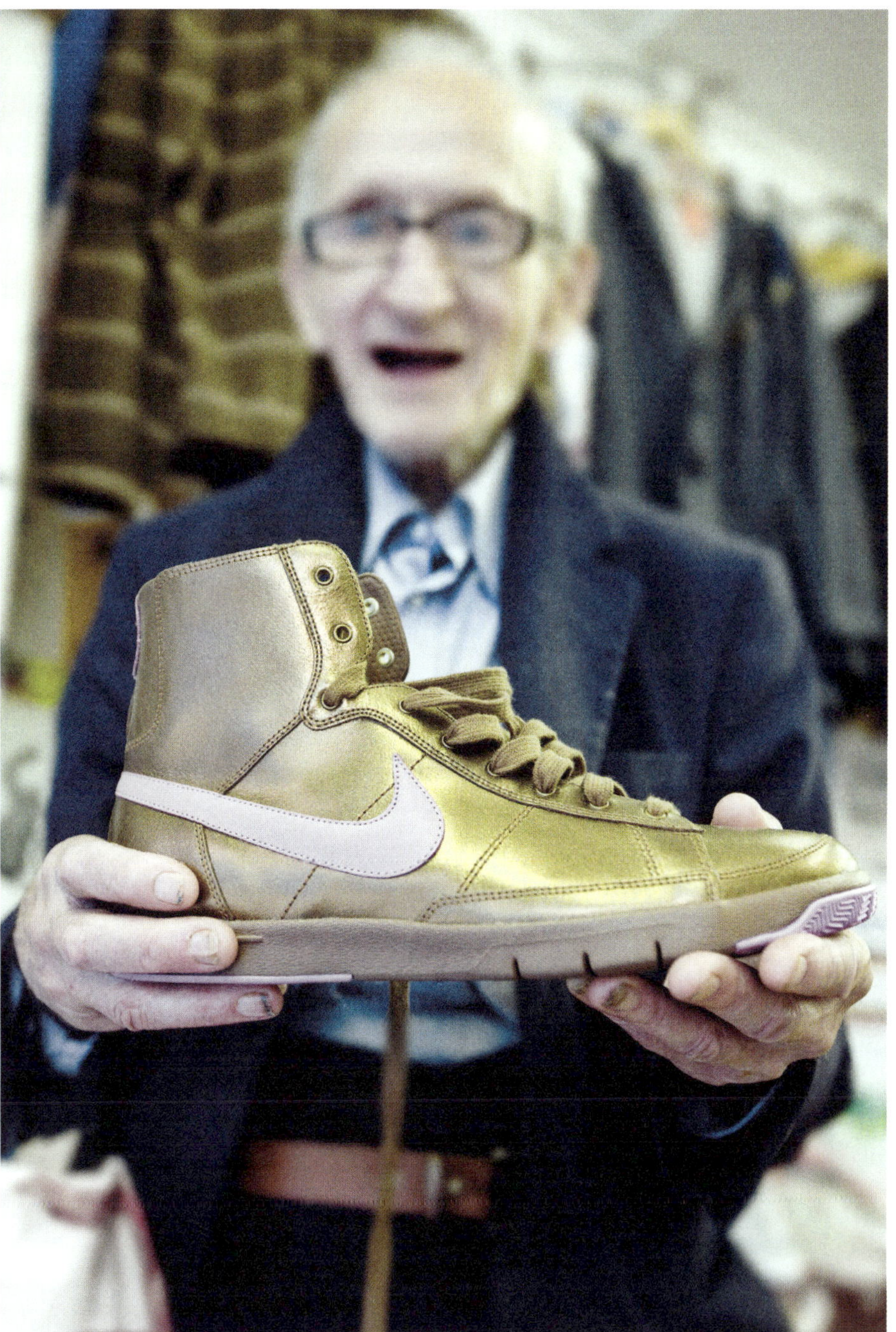

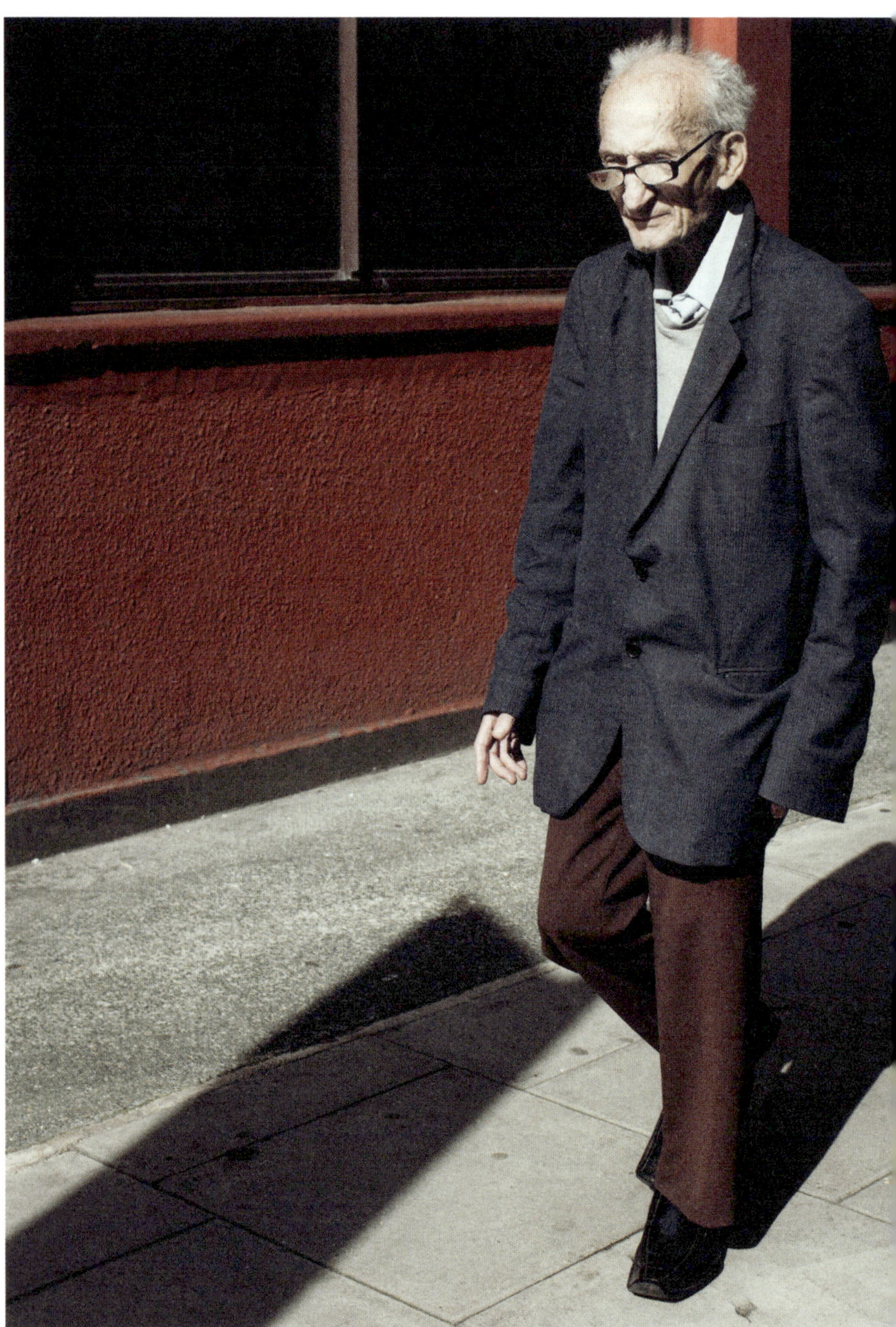

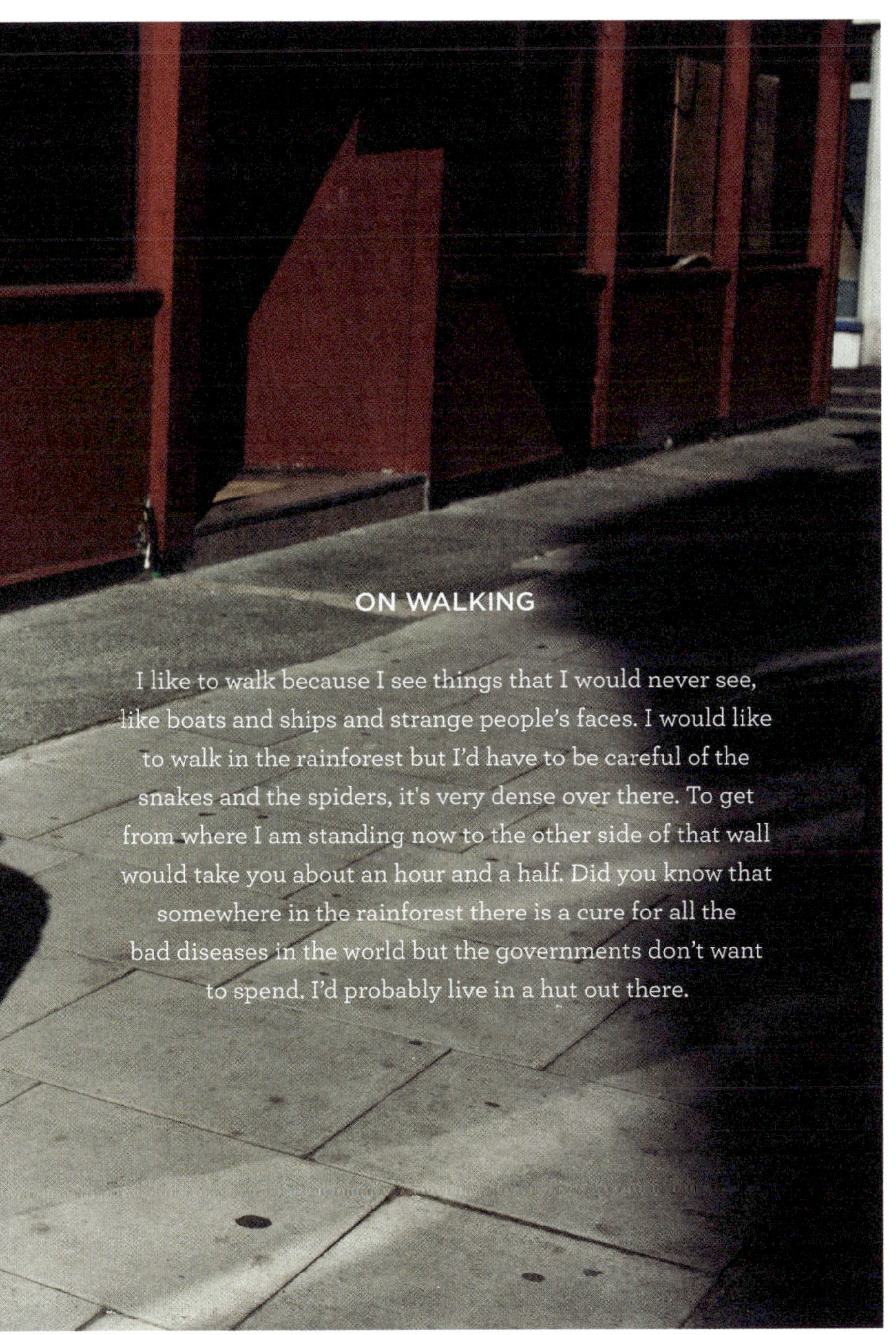

ON WALKING

I like to walk because I see things that I would never see,
like boats and ships and strange people's faces. I would like
to walk in the rainforest but I'd have to be careful of the
snakes and the spiders, it's very dense over there. To get
from where I am standing now to the other side of that wall
would take you about an hour and a half. Did you know that
somewhere in the rainforest there is a cure for all the
bad diseases in the world but the governments don't want
to spend. I'd probably live in a hut out there.

ON MONEY

I don't know what I would do if I won the lottery. There is
that children's charity, what's it called? I wouldn't help them
because they say the money goes straight to the terrorists.
If I won a small amount of money I would give it to the
Synagogue Burial Society – because I've got to pay for
my own funeral. I've been paying into it for 35 years
but every year they raise the prices. I could have
buried a football team by now.

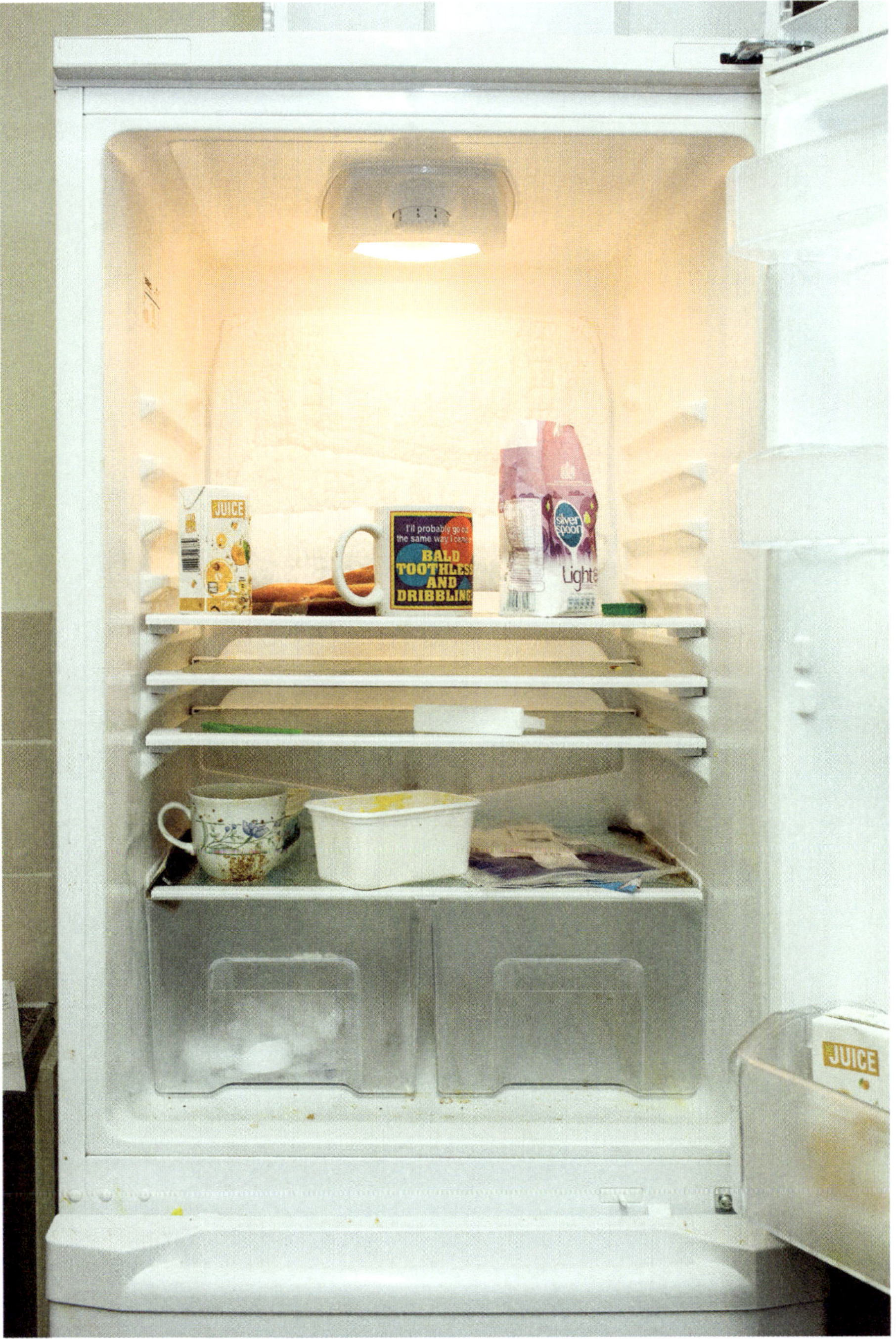

JUICE
I'll probably go the same way I came
BALD TOOTHLESS AND DRIBBLING
silver spoon
Light
JUICE

ON HUMOUR

Lots of things make me laugh. Fruit makes me laugh.
To see a dog talking makes me laugh. I like to see monkeys
throwing coconuts on men's heads, that's funny. When you
see a man going on to a desert island and he is stranded
the monkeys are always friendly. You think the monkey
is throwing things at your head but really he is
throwing the coconuts for you to eat.

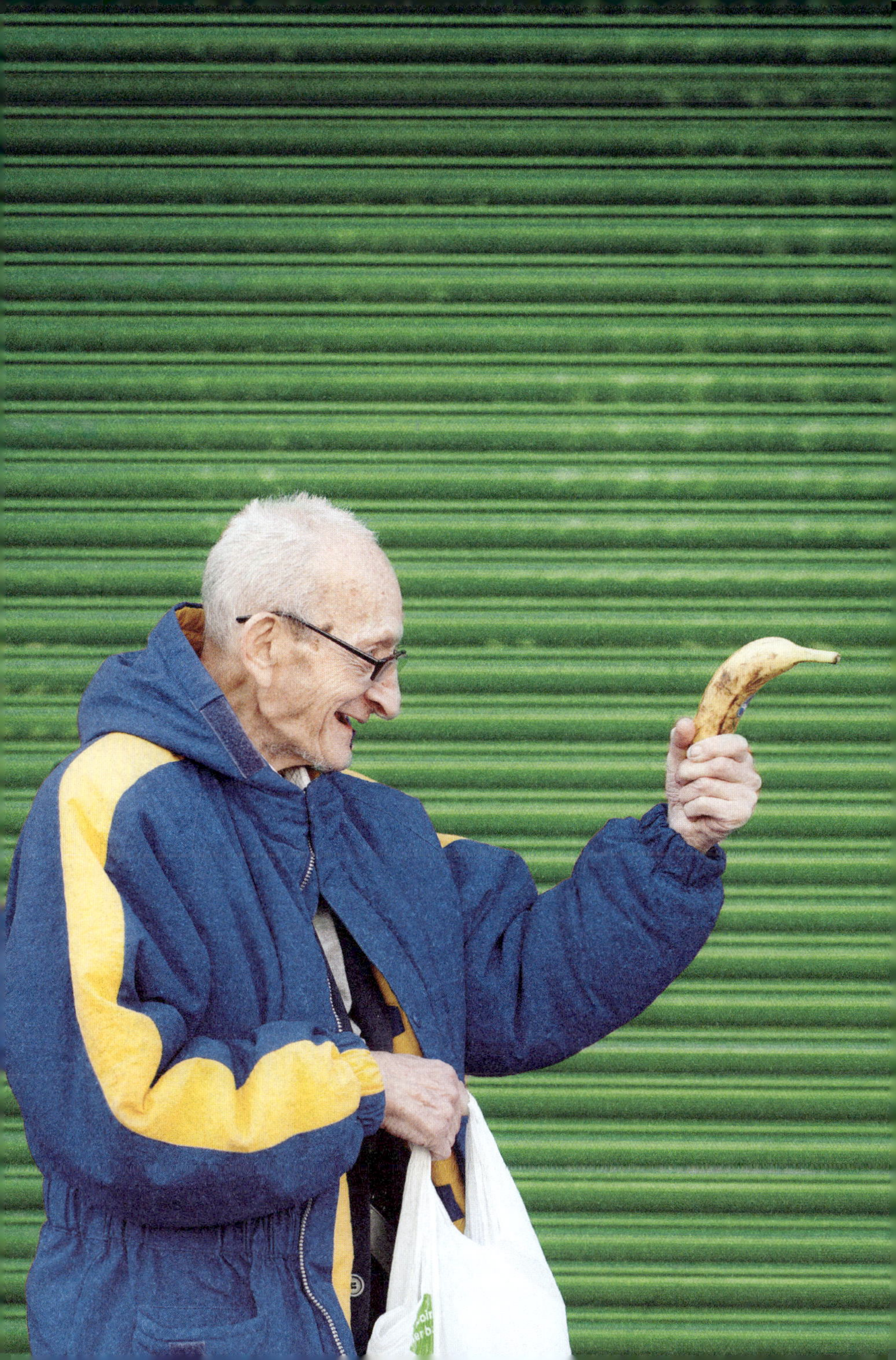

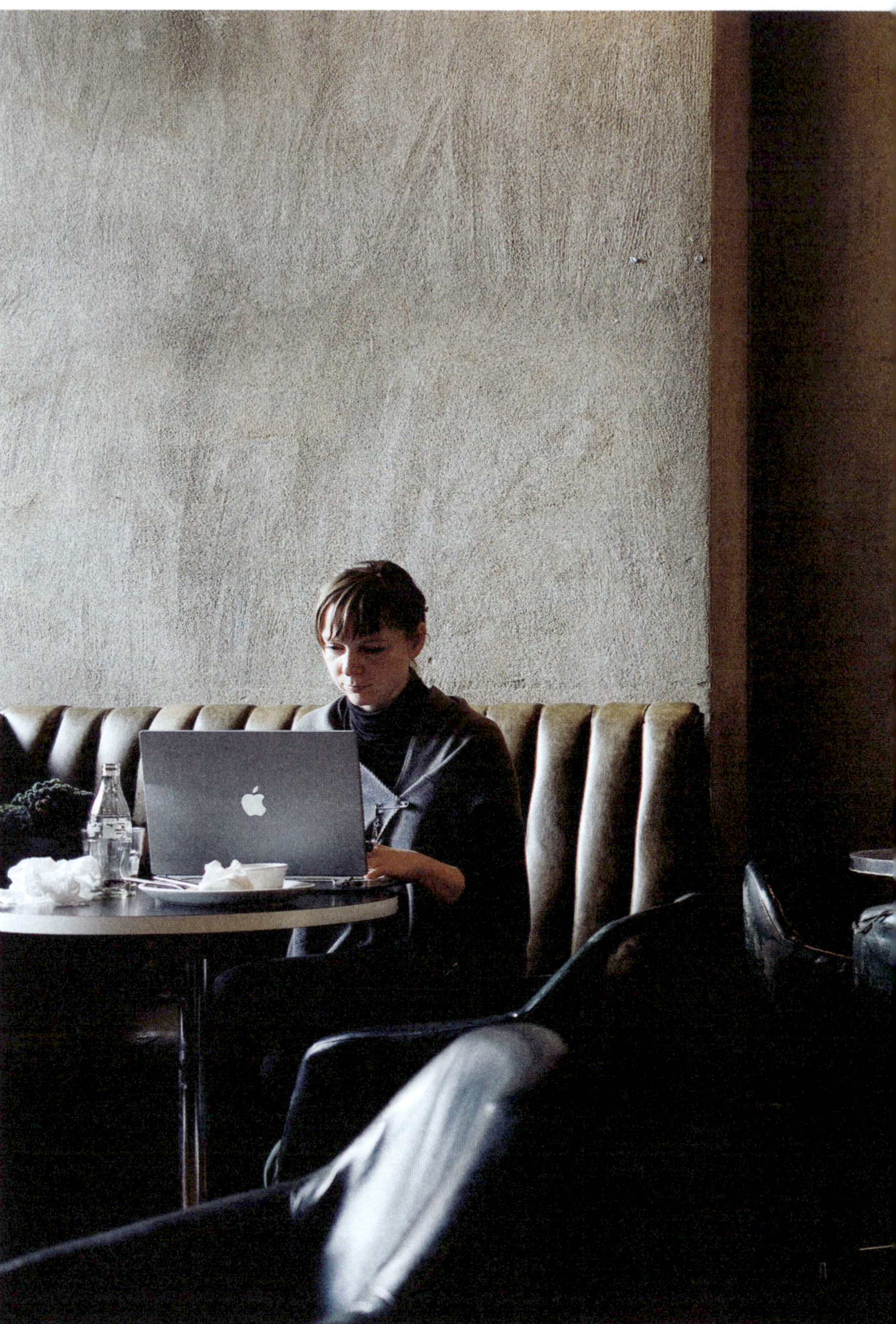

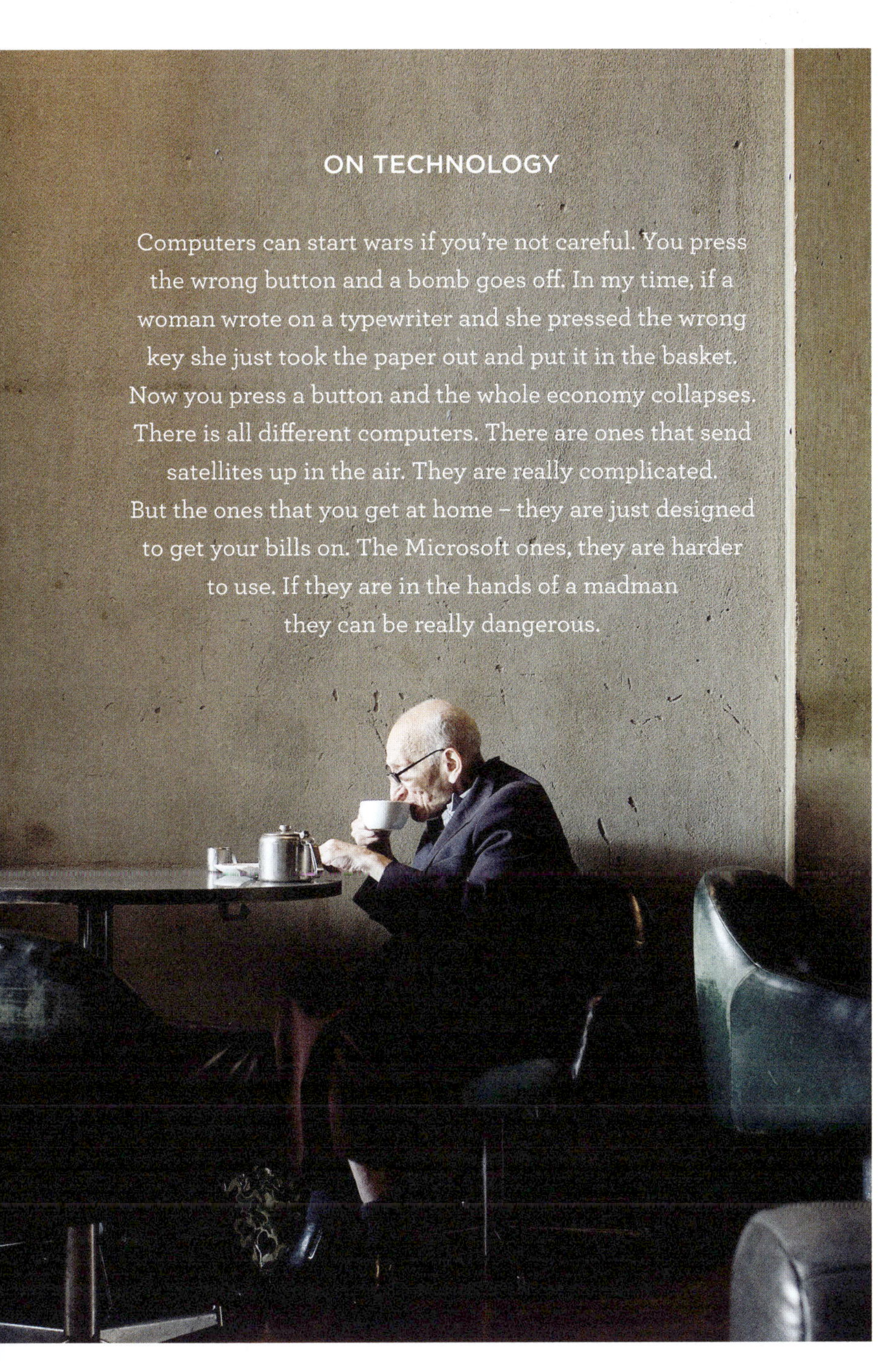

ON TECHNOLOGY

Computers can start wars if you're not careful. You press
the wrong button and a bomb goes off. In my time, if a
woman wrote on a typewriter and she pressed the wrong
key she just took the paper out and put it in the basket.
Now you press a button and the whole economy collapses.
There is all different computers. There are ones that send
satellites up in the air. They are really complicated.
But the ones that you get at home – they are just designed
to get your bills on. The Microsoft ones, they are harder
to use. If they are in the hands of a madman
they can be really dangerous.

ON HIS MOTHER

My mother was a good cook. She made bread pudding.
It was the best pudding you could have. She was called
Janie and I lived with her until she died. I wasn't going to
let her into a home. Your mother should be your best friend.
Our best memories were going on a Sunday to Hampstead
Heath fair. There was a parrot there who used to swear at
me. I once had a locket with a photo in it of my mother.
I had to move house a few times and it went missing.
There's no photos of her anymore. This is the shape
of her locket, it was almost round.

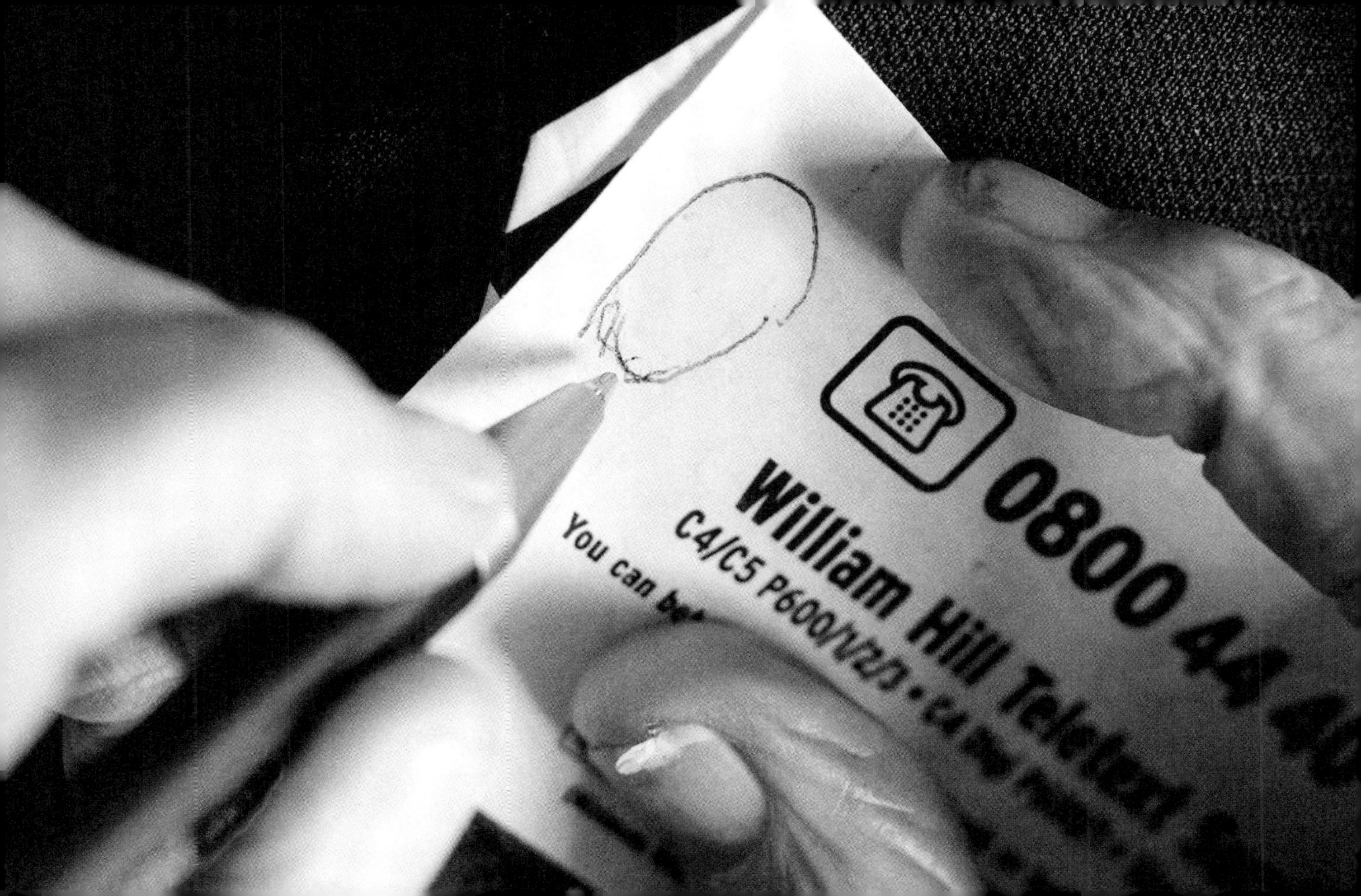

0800 44 4
William Hill Teletext
C4/C5 P600/V223
You can b

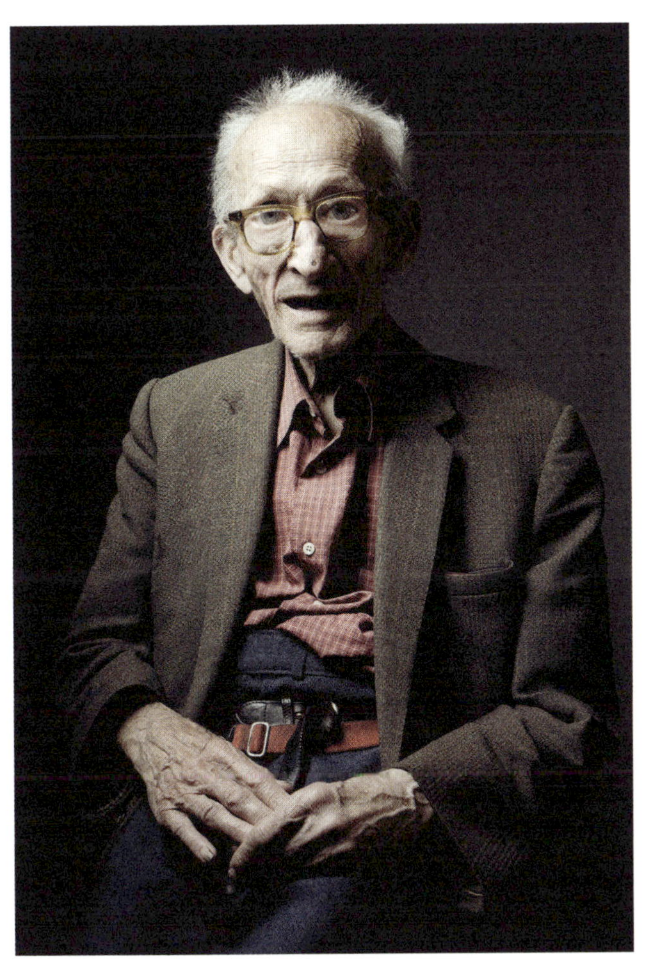

JOSEPH MARKOVITCH

01.01.1927 – 26.12.2013

ONE DAY YOUNG

JENNY LEWIS

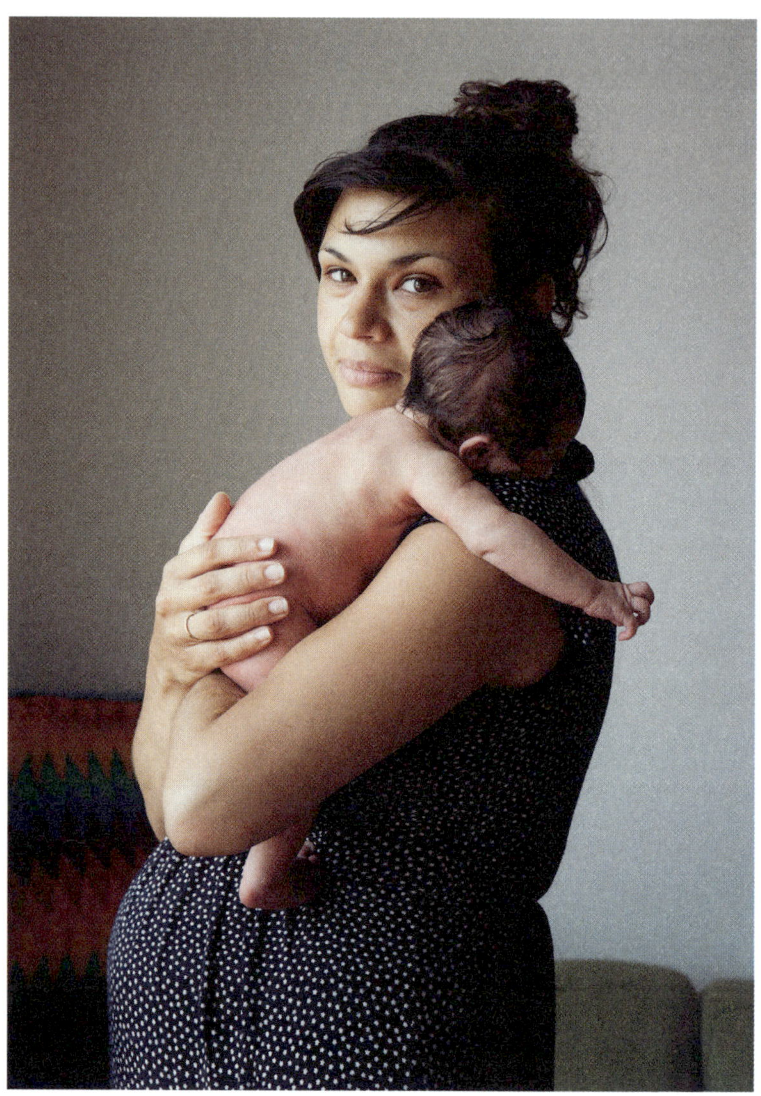

Motherhood is often presented as something that happens to you, not something you do. Women submit to the pain of labour, then to the whims of a tiny, wailing new life. They give up their figures, their work, their identities... But Jenny Lewis tells another story – about the 'triumphant victory' felt by every new mother, fresh from the frontline of their own revolution.

Over five years, Lewis took portraits of women and babies within 24 hours of birth across Hackney, where the Essex-born editorial photographer has lived for more than two decades. She posted leaflets in shops, hairdressers, chippies to which women replied with their name, address and a due date. When the time came, she'd leap on her bike and pedal round to their home where she'd capture them in natural light, 'straight from the battlefield', as Lewis puts it.

Some mothers gaze intently at the magnetic bundle of flesh that hours before was still part of their body, but many look directly into the camera (like Hazel, opposite, with baby Rudy). Their newly vacant bellies are still rounded, though softer now, hair tousled and exhaustion around the edges of their eyes. There's something childlike about their expressions, as though they can't quite take in what they've achieved. And something ferocious too, that says: 'I did it'.

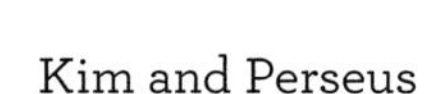
Kim and Perseus

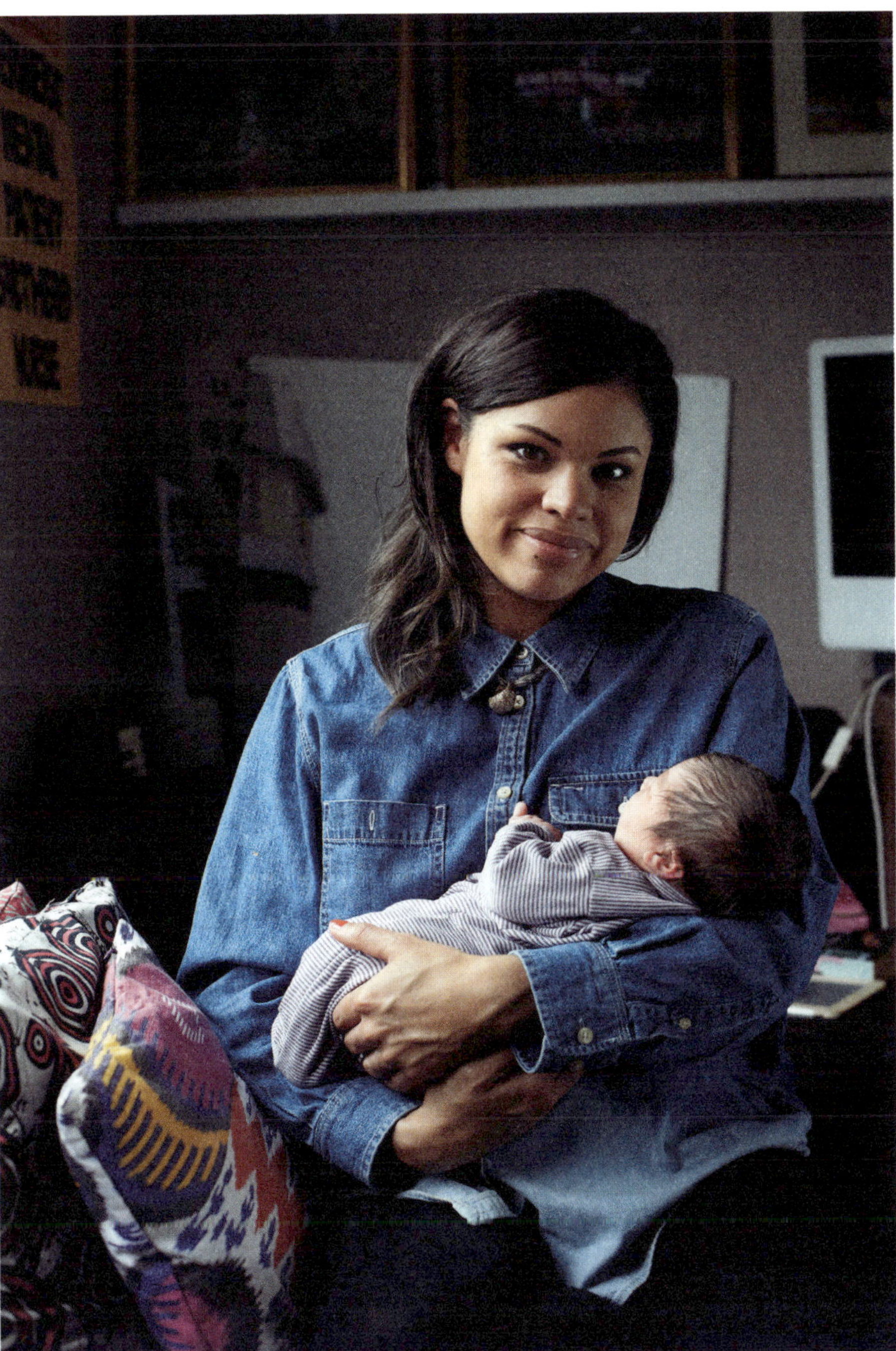

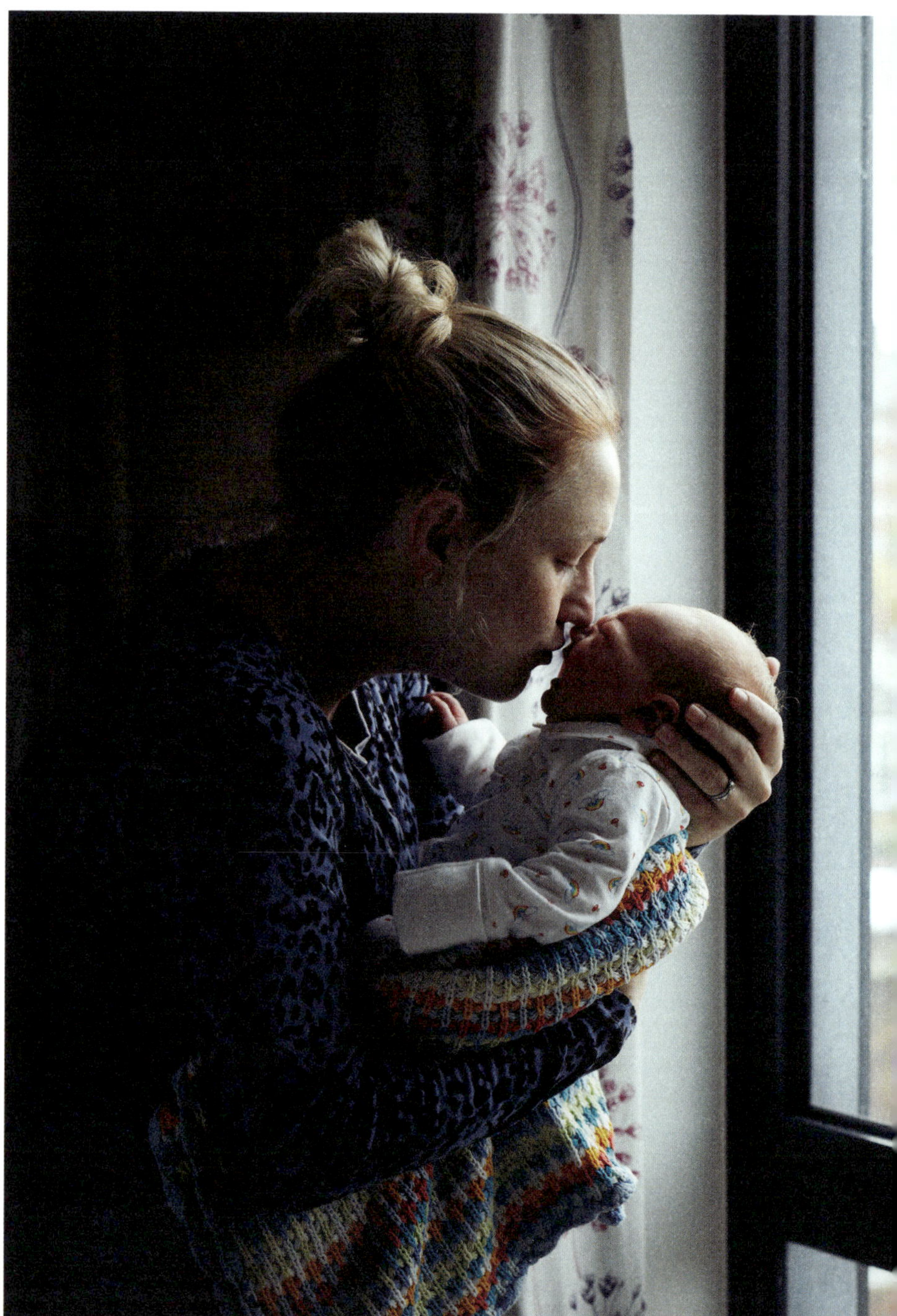

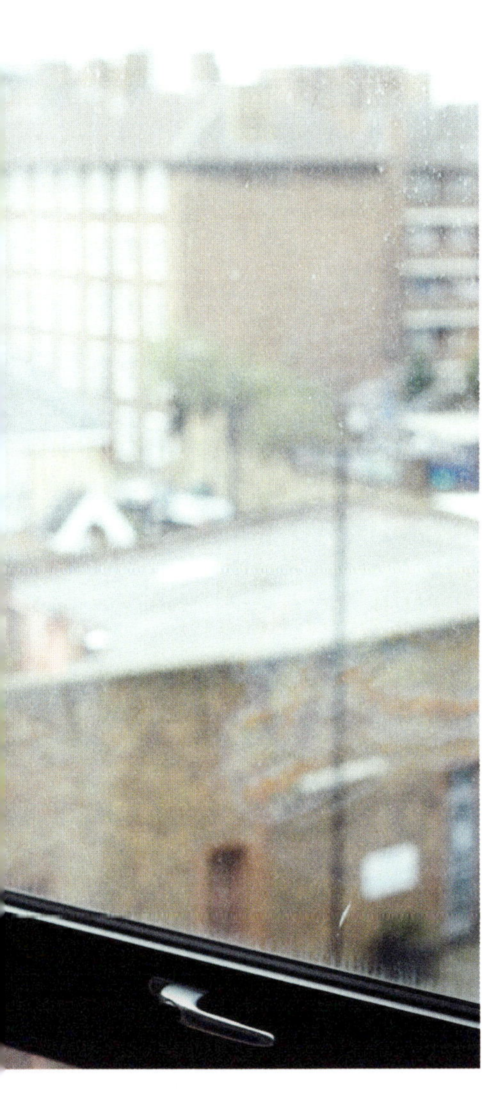

Theresa and Thomas

Nicola and Jemima

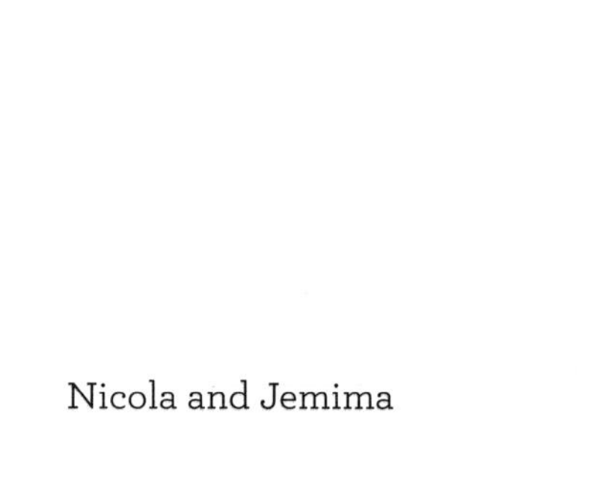

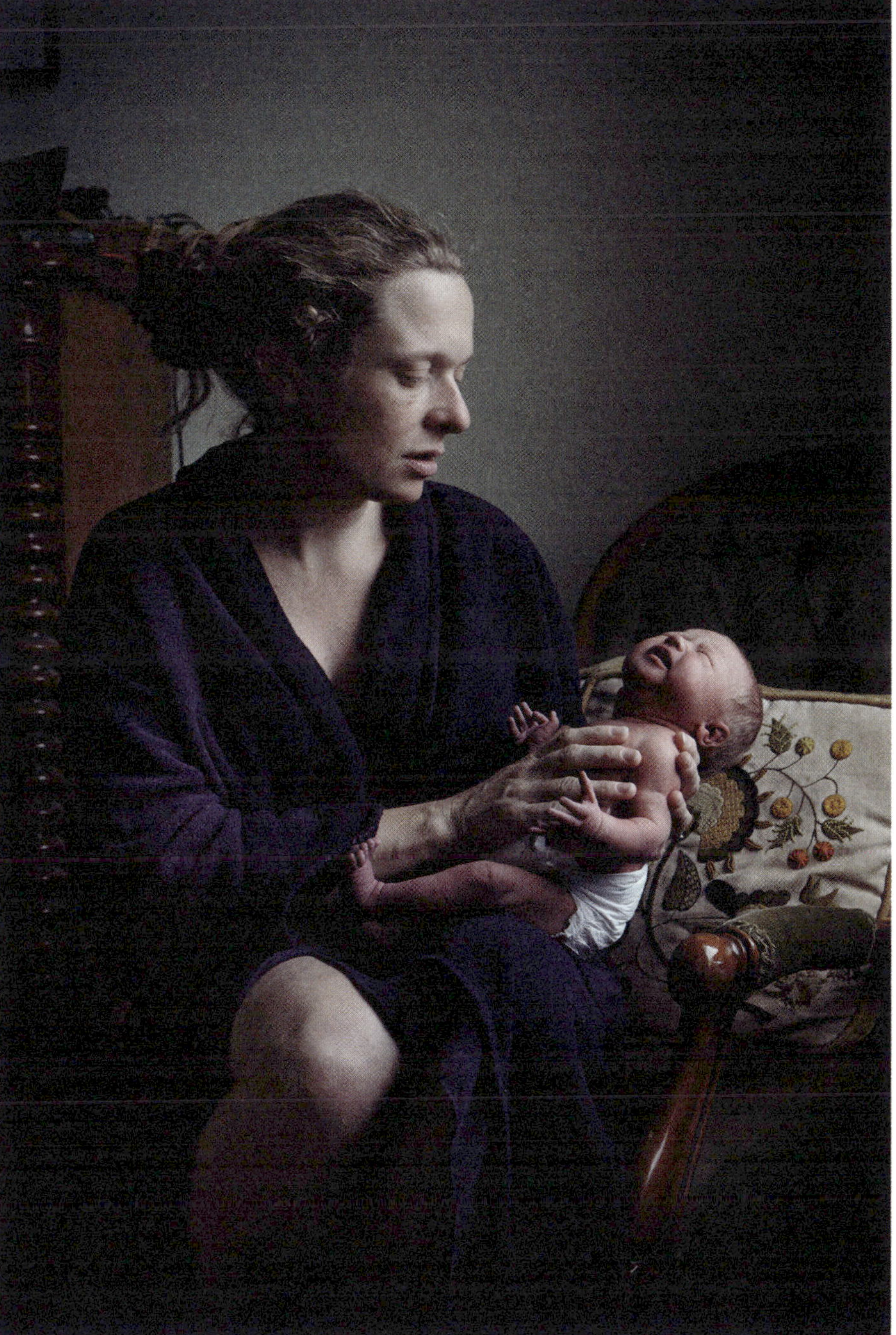

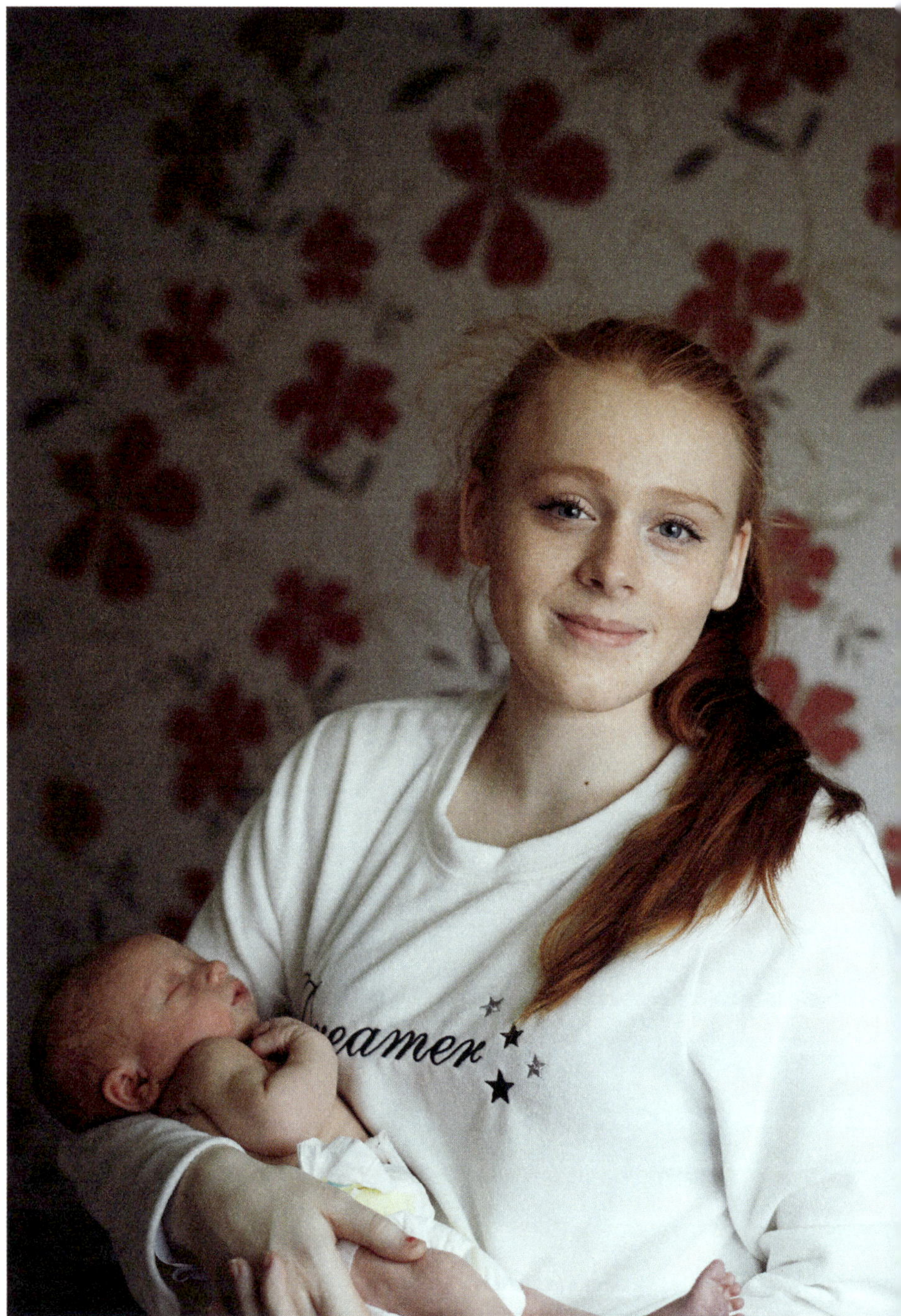

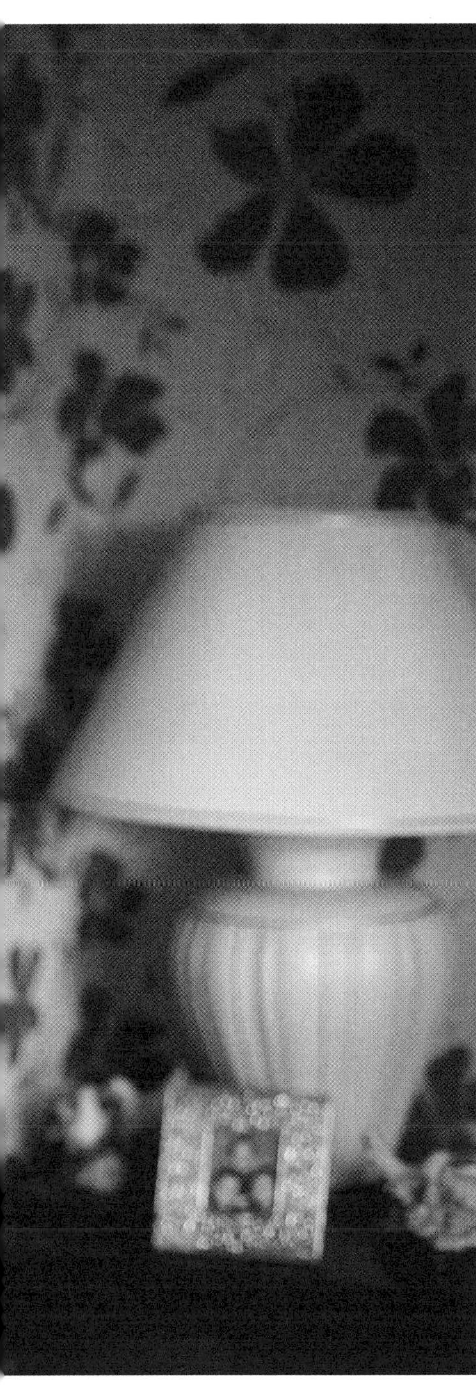

Xanthe and Louie

Trini and Carmen

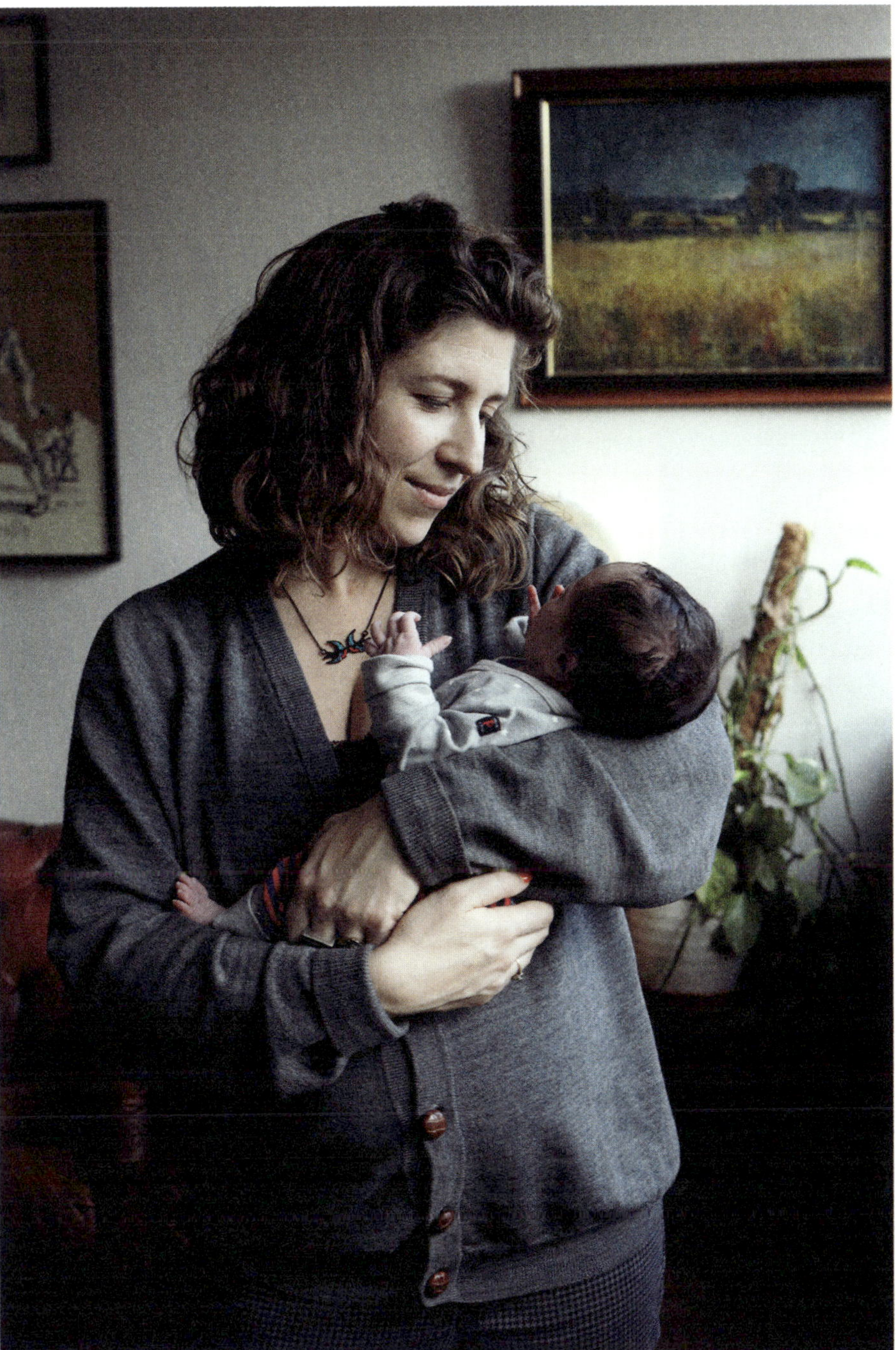

Cassie and Levi

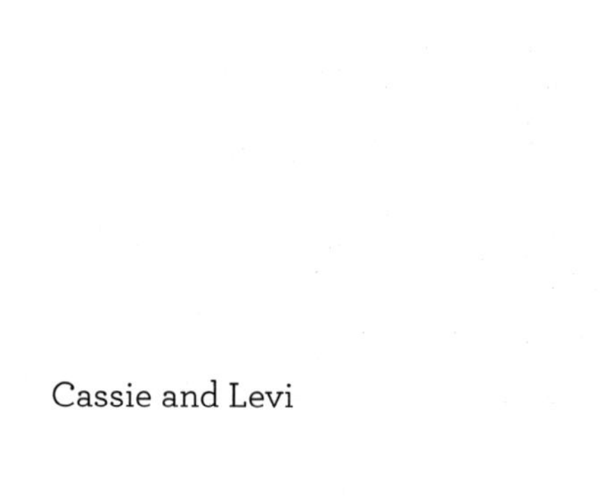

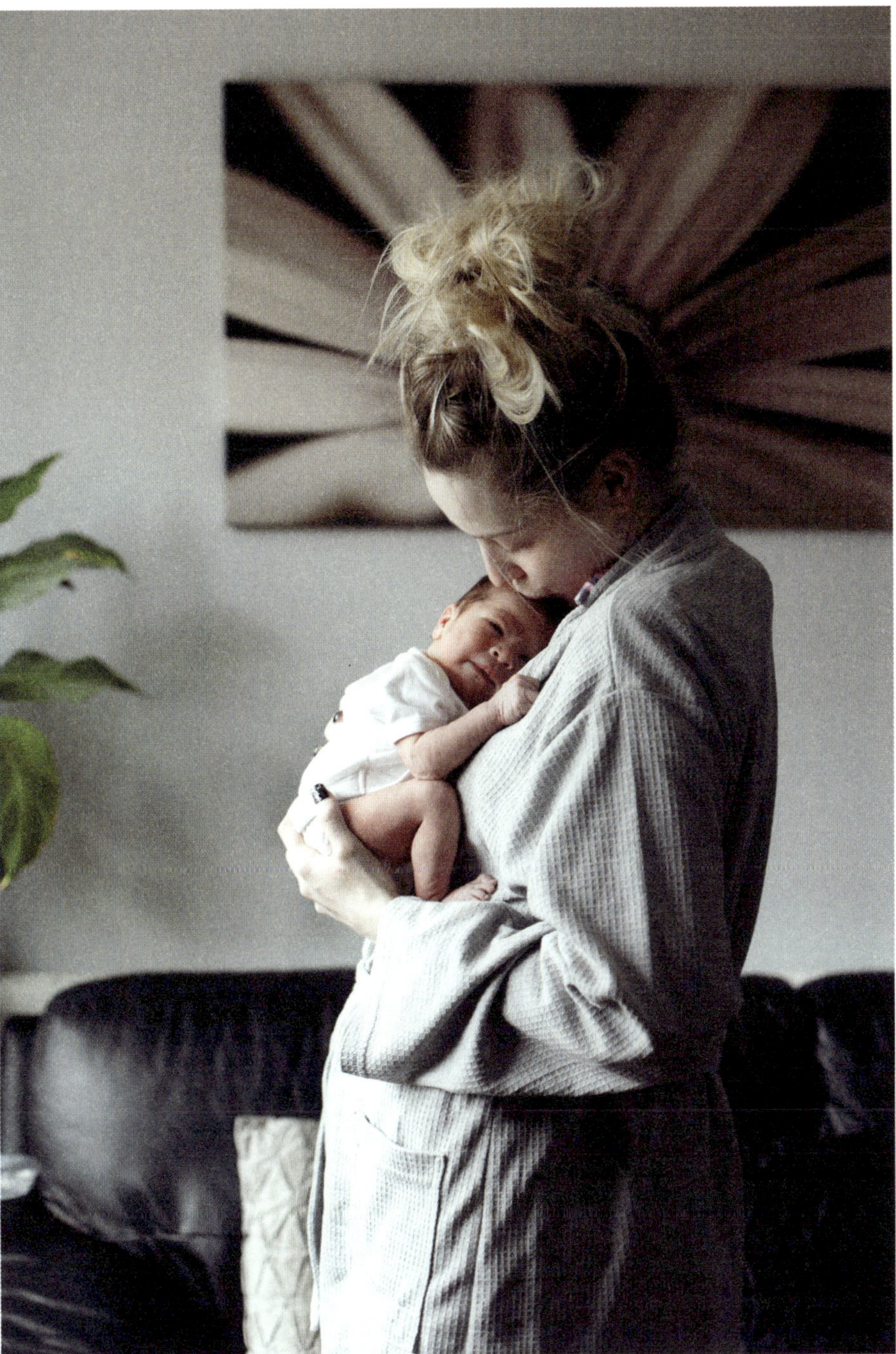

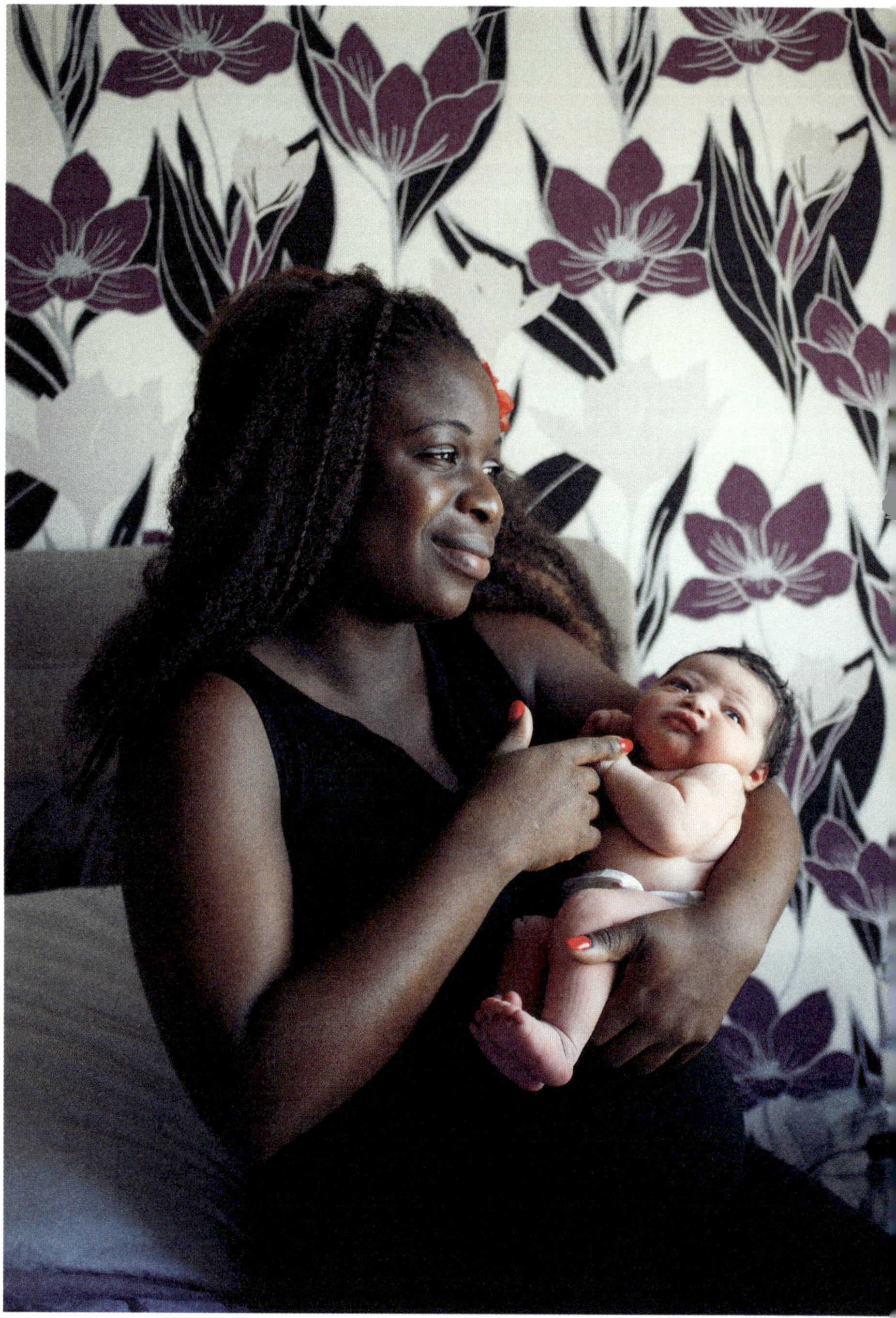

Shenelle and Arissa

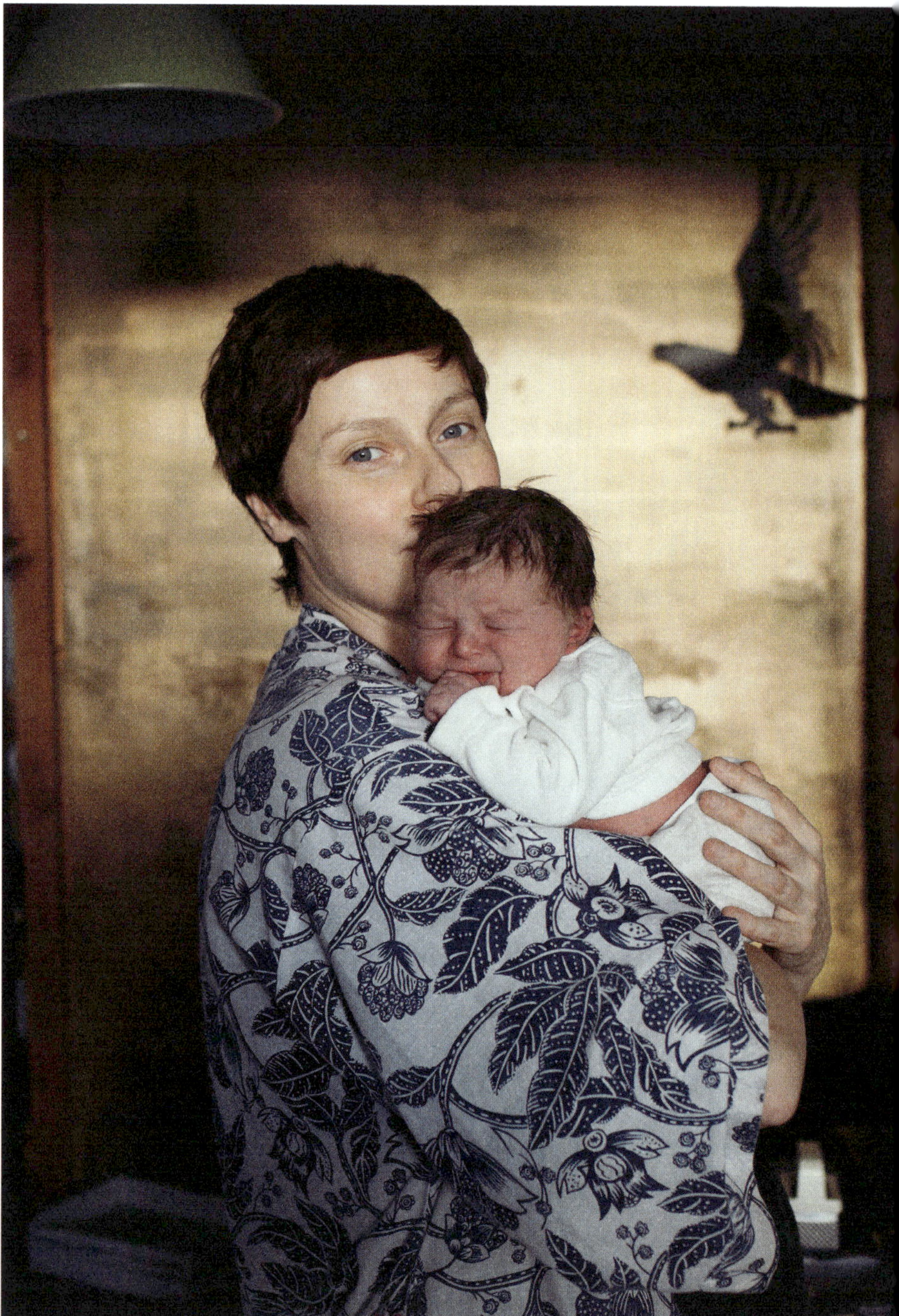

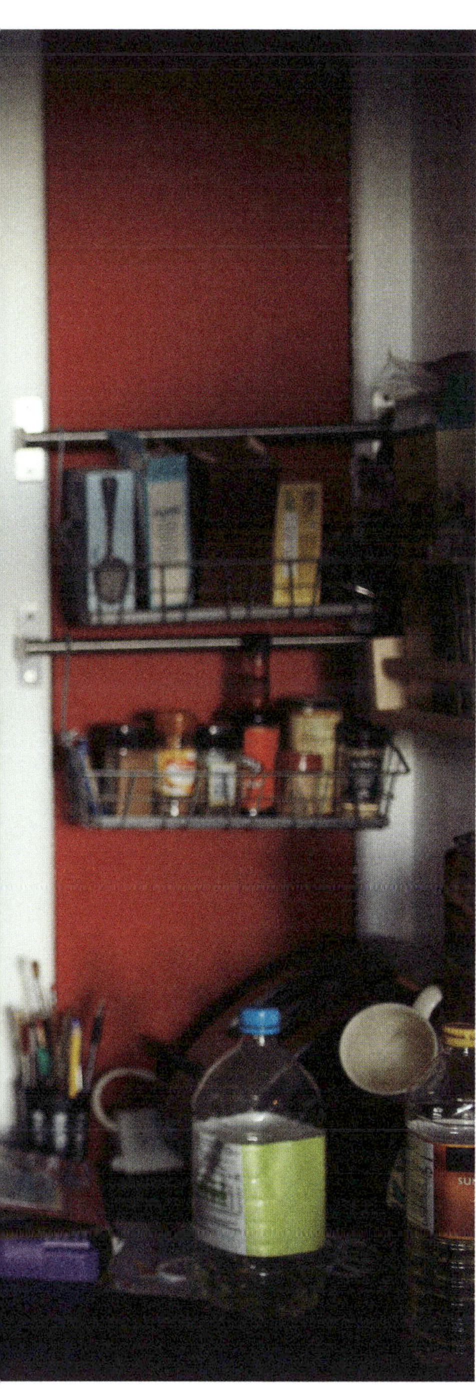

Mairead and Fia

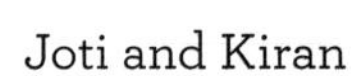

Joti and Kiran

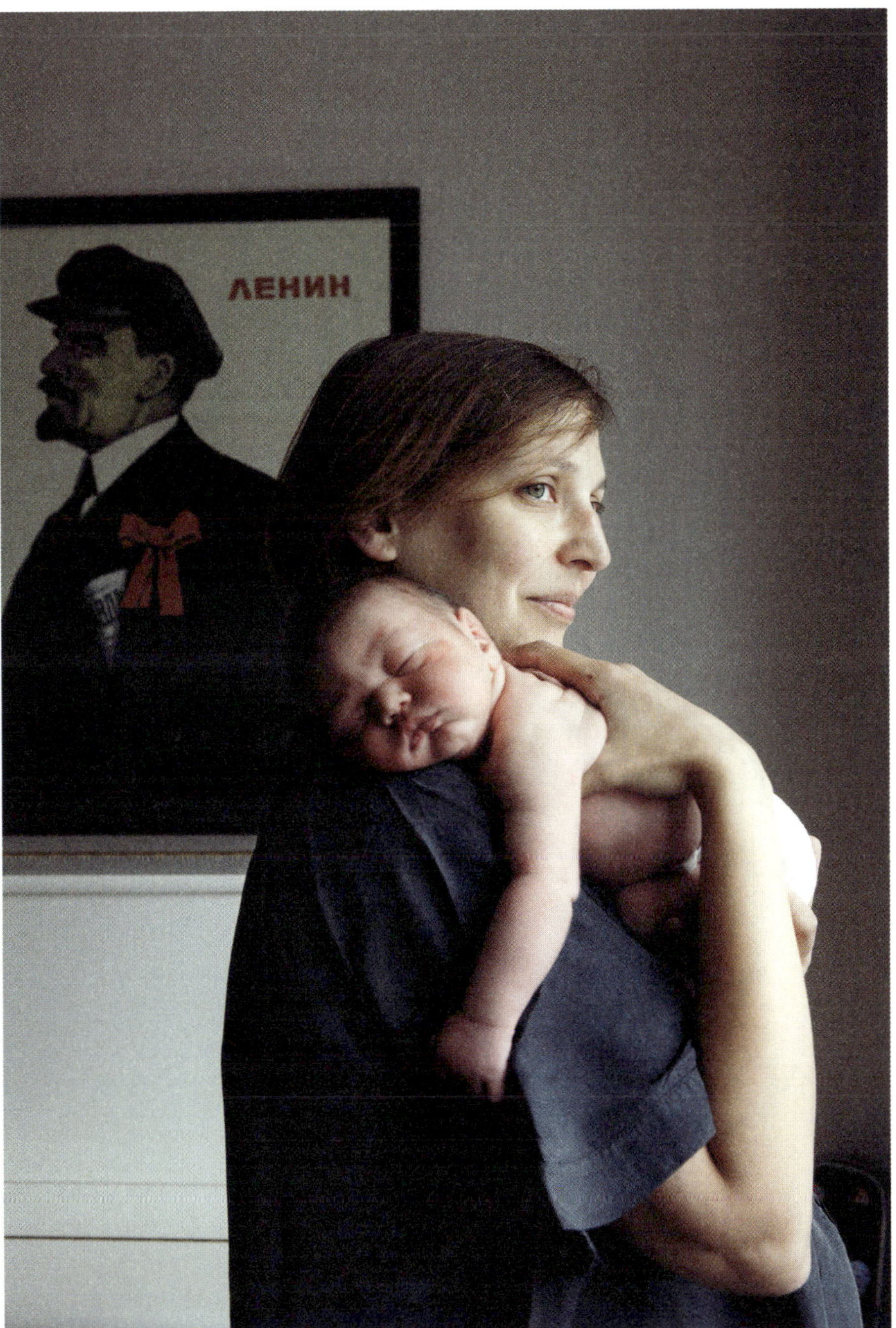

ЛЕНИН

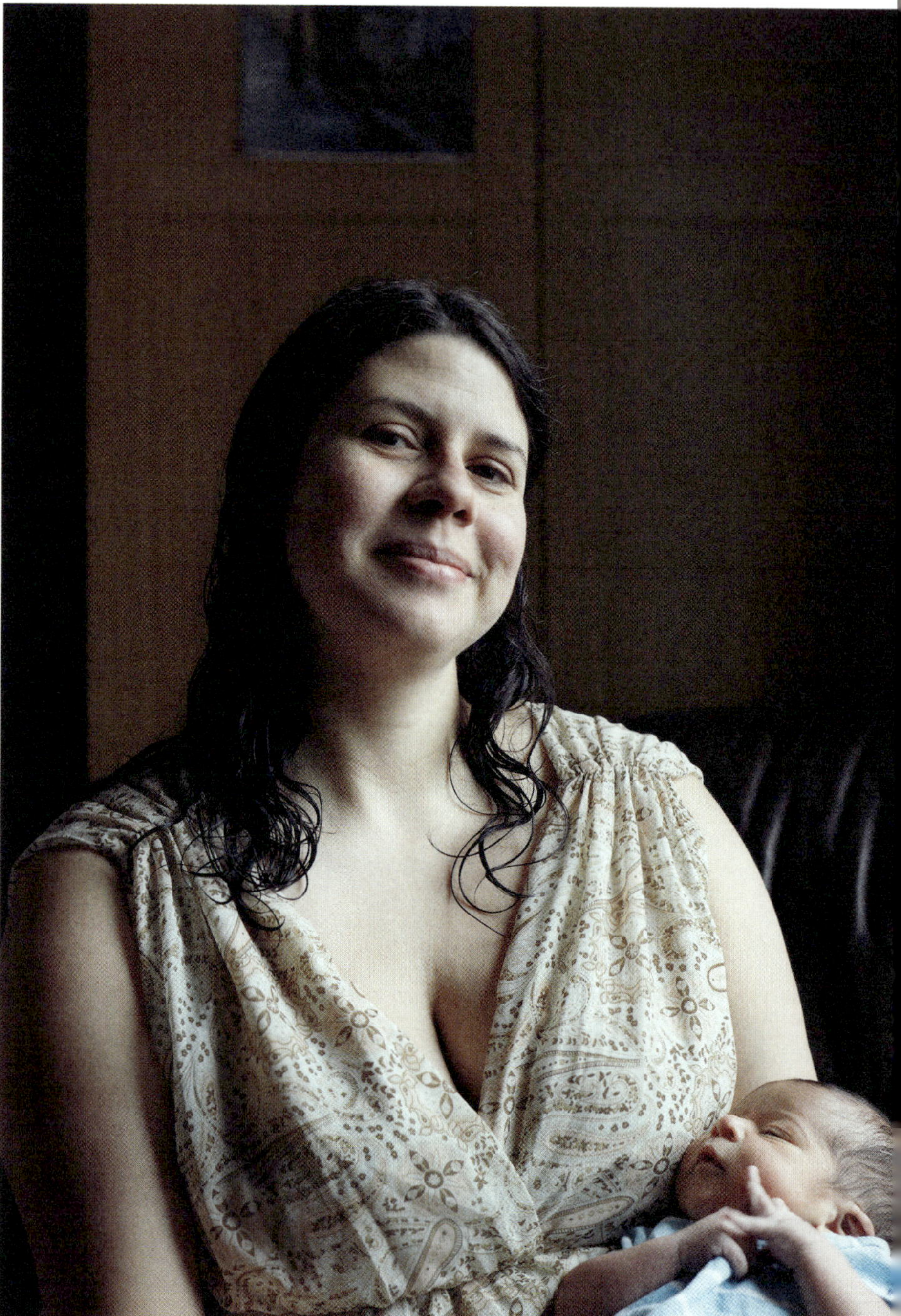

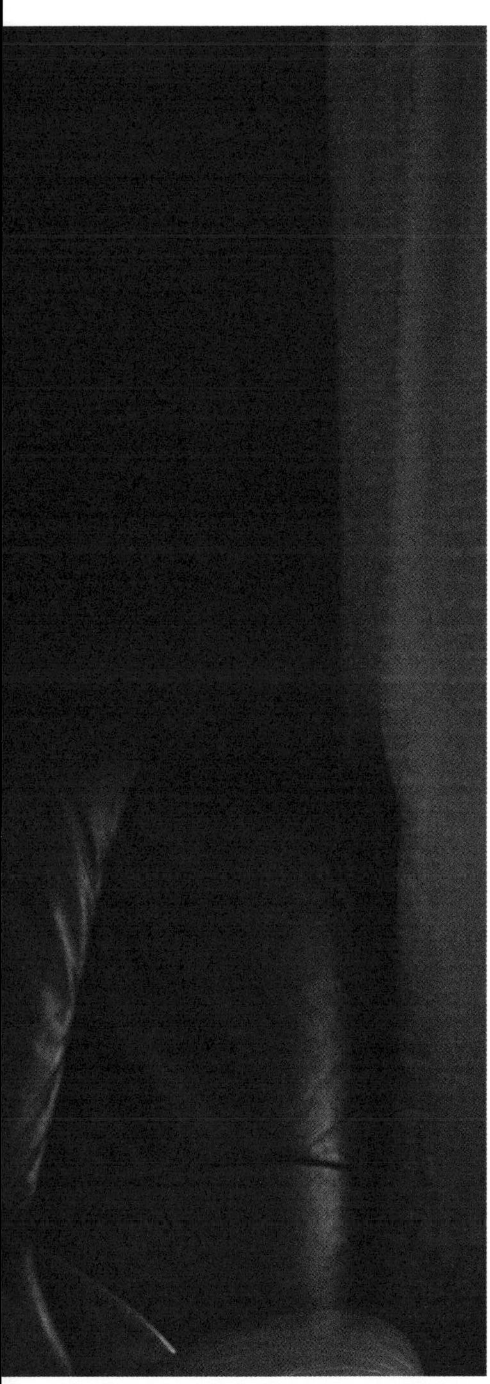

Rut and Jonian

ALONG THE HACKNEY CANAL

FREYA NAJADE

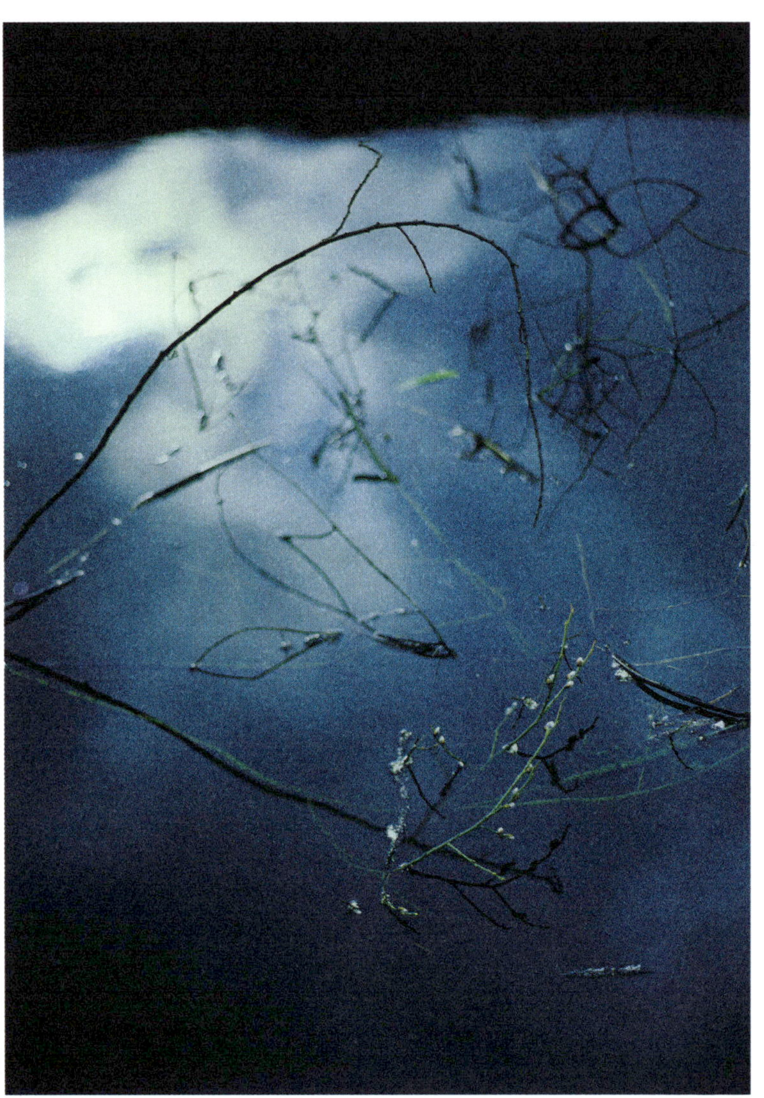

Moments of sublime natural beauty captured along East London's man-made waterways.

A shimmering web of waterways weave serenely through East London, mostly hidden from view. Seen on a map they look like lines on the palm of a hand and in a way that's what they are. Built in the 19th century to move goods, these liquid roads have many tales to tell. Parts of the canal were threatened by the advent of trains – a more efficient mode of transport – they narrowly avoided demolition and remain today, a tranquil escape from the wheezing, stinking traffic above.

When Freya Najade moved to East London from Germany in 2007, she found herself drawn to the canals and spent relaxing days wandering up and down there, taking in Limehouse, Mile End, Hackney Wick, Springfield Park, photographing whatever caught her eye. Every season offered something new – lush, verdant marshland, the sparse, spindly branches of trees just visible through the winter mist, buttercups bursting through the frost, blossoms in spring.

Though people barely feature, Najade, who does architectural photography alongside personal work, isn't coy about their presence. We see traces of human activity throughout – in the muddy carcass of an abandoned motorbike, in a plastic bag that floats gently in the water like a ghost. The canals are a fluid border between the wildness of nature and the wildness of city life.

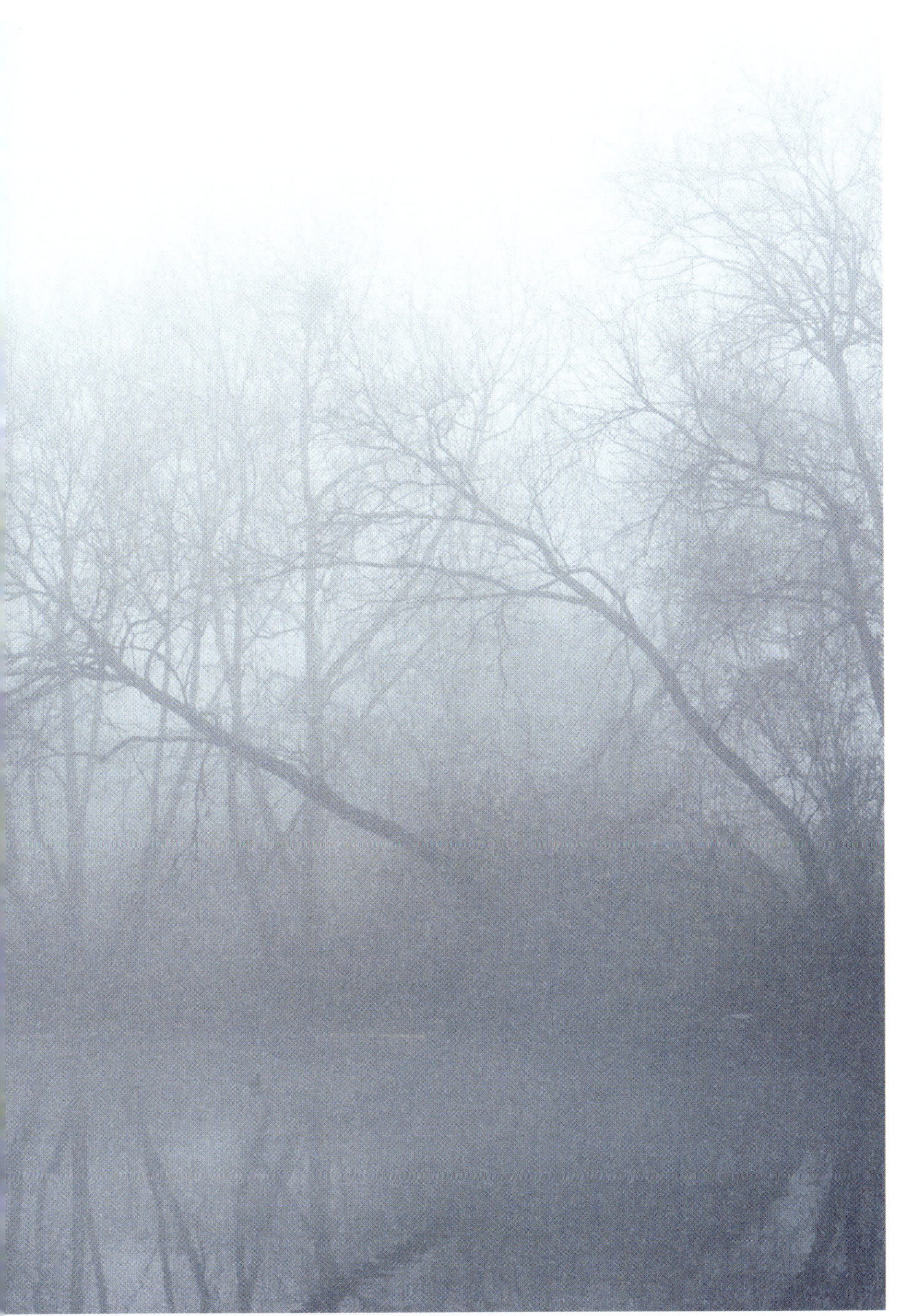

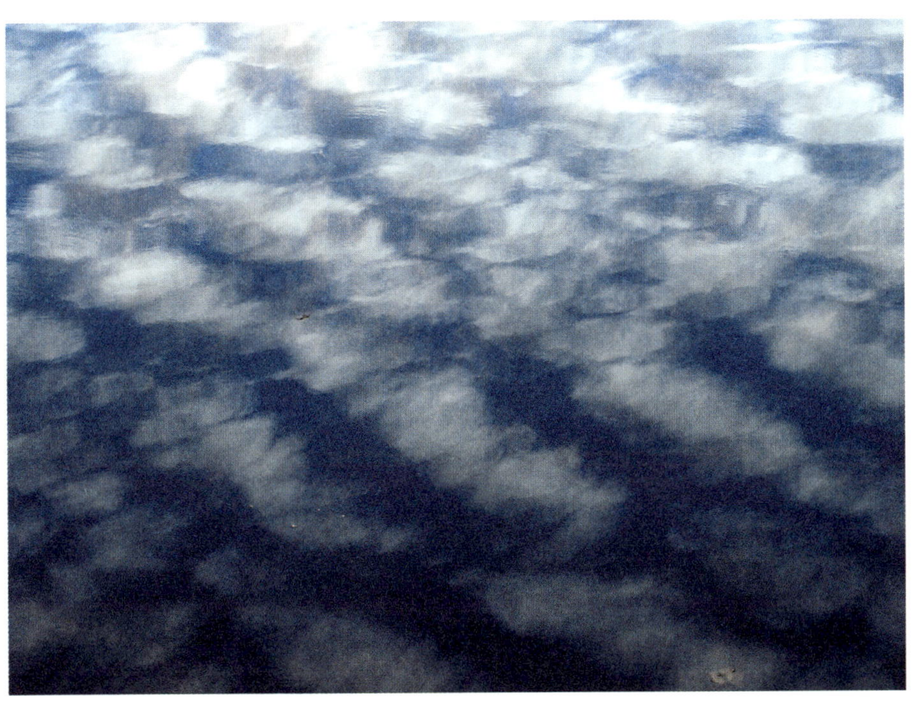

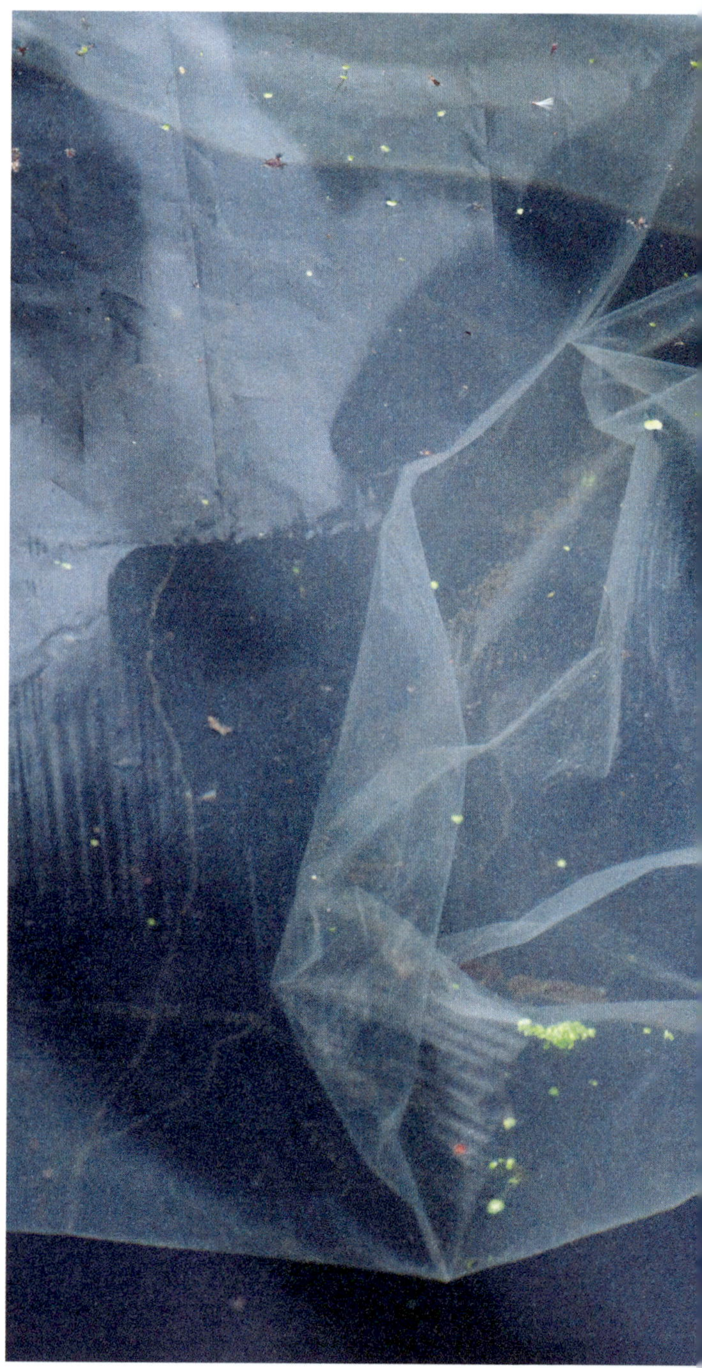

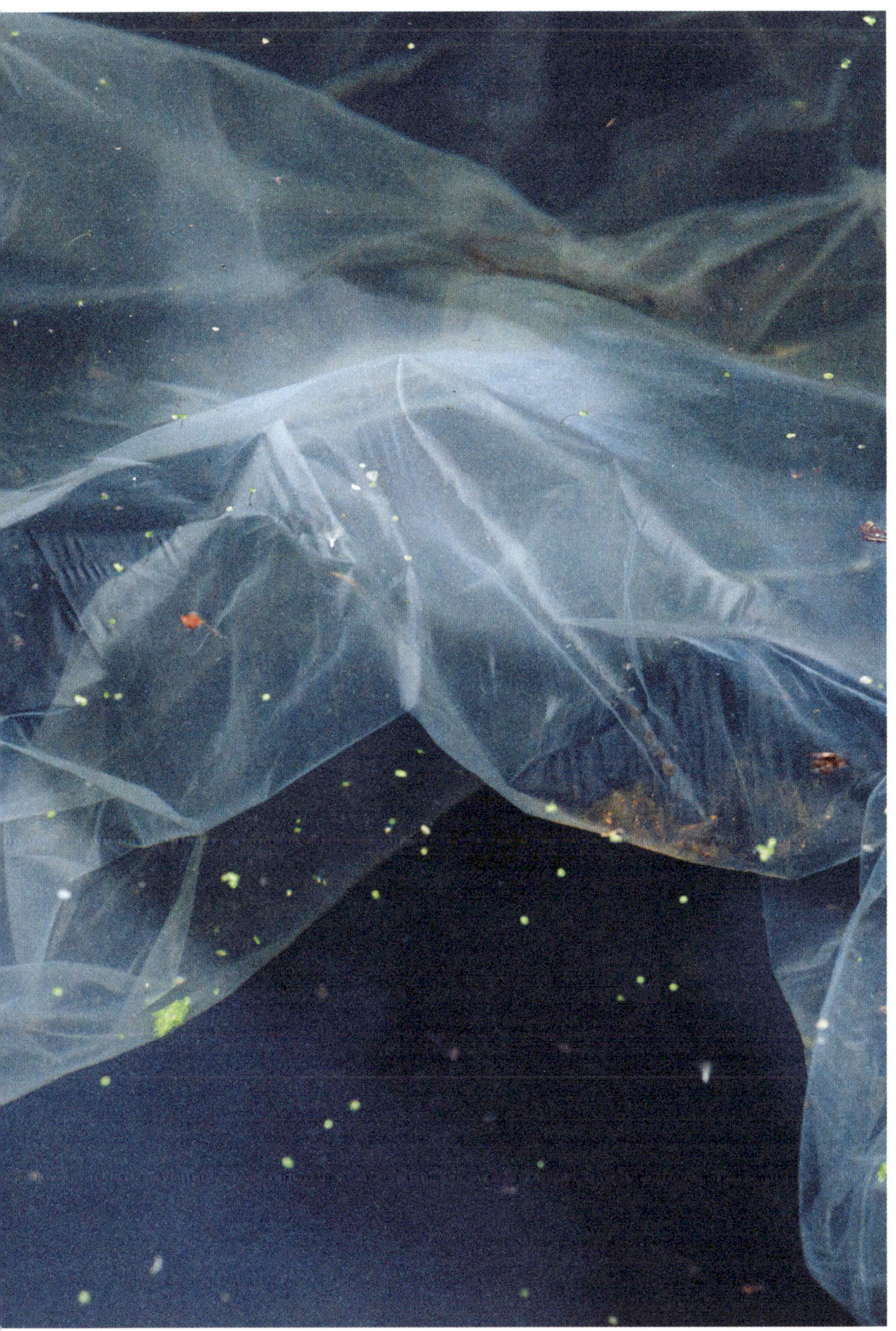

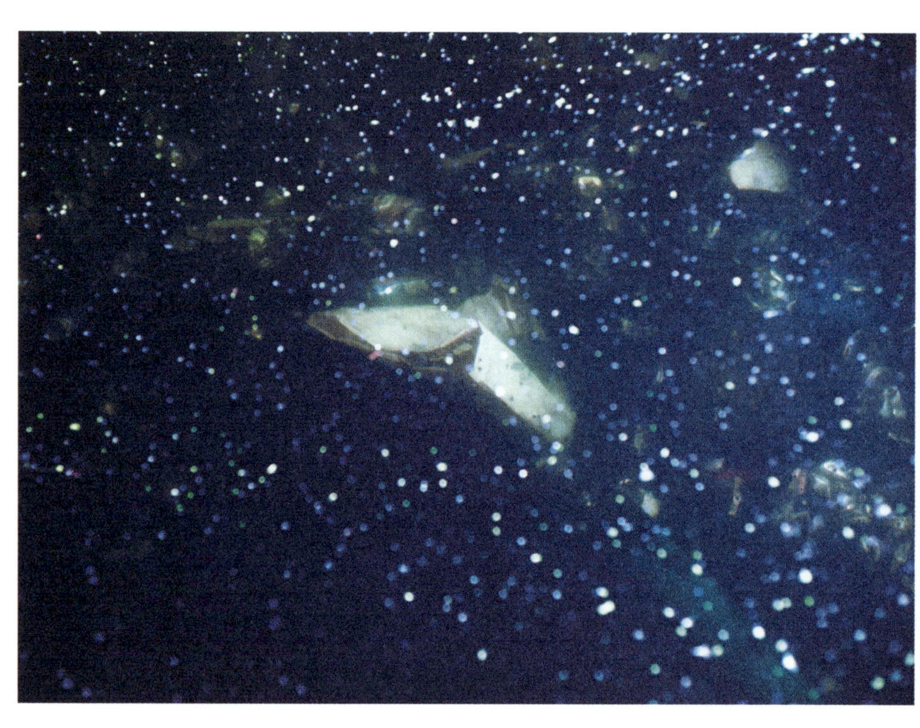

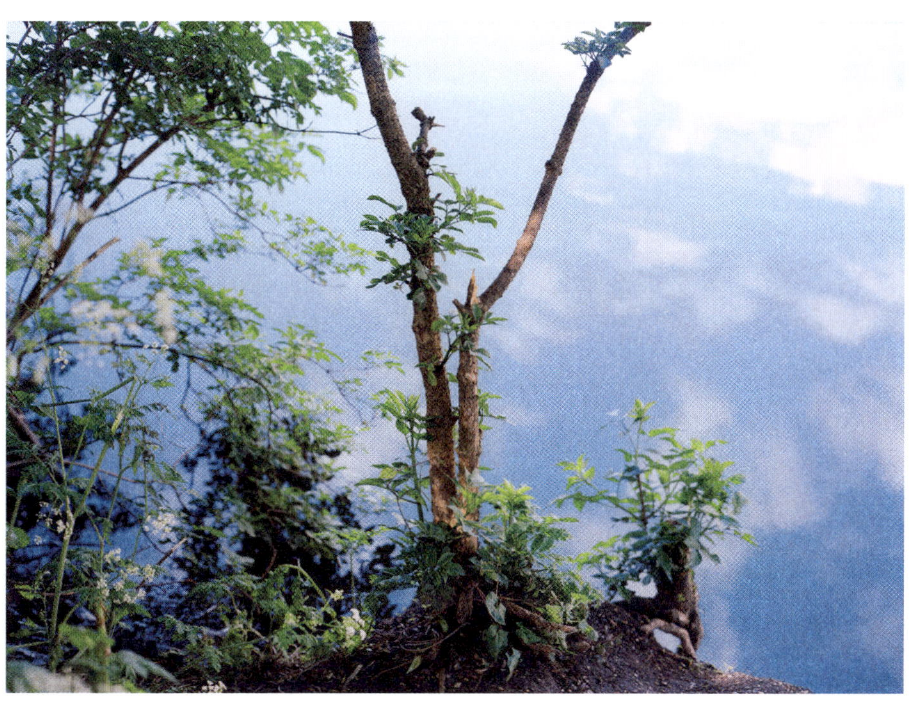

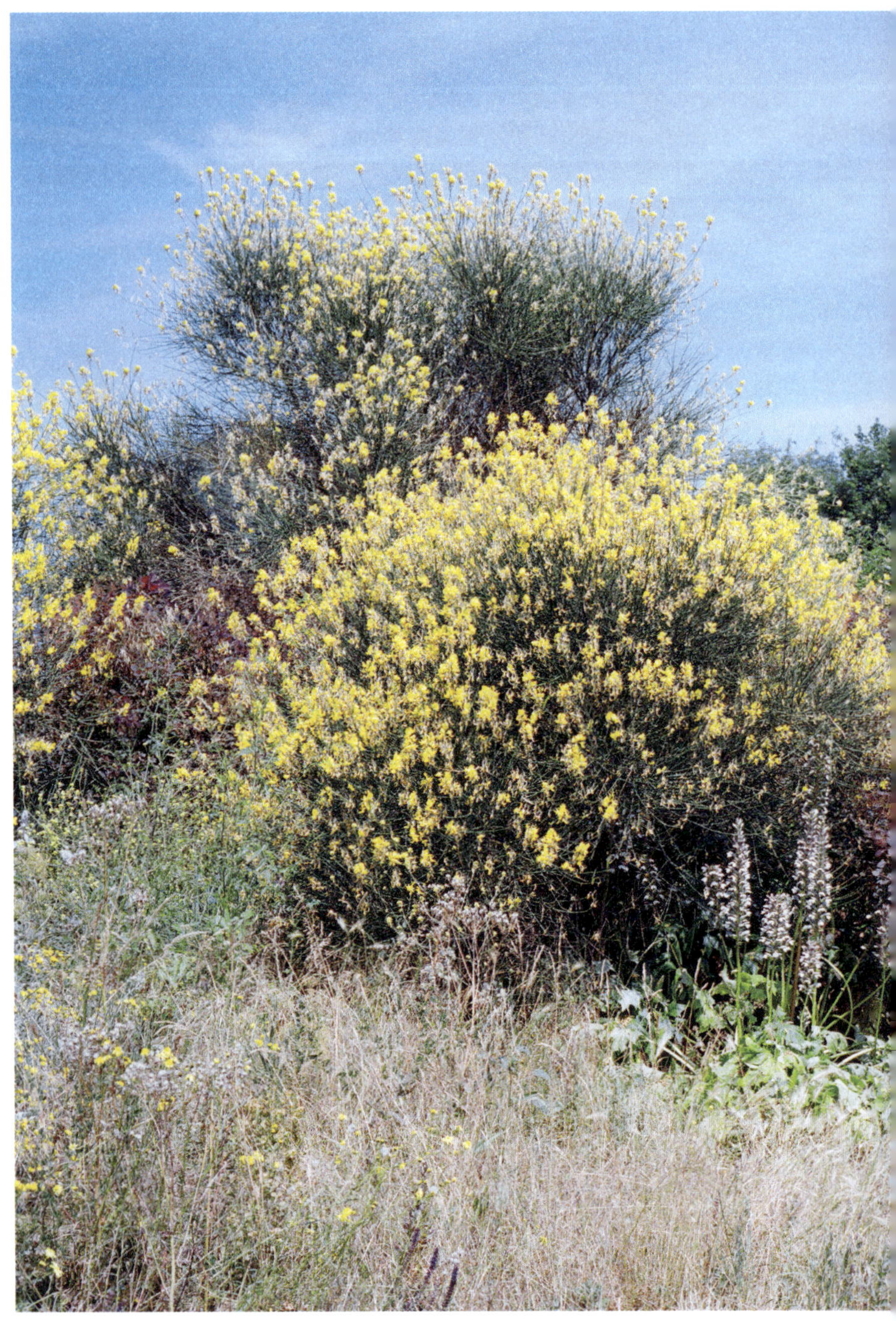

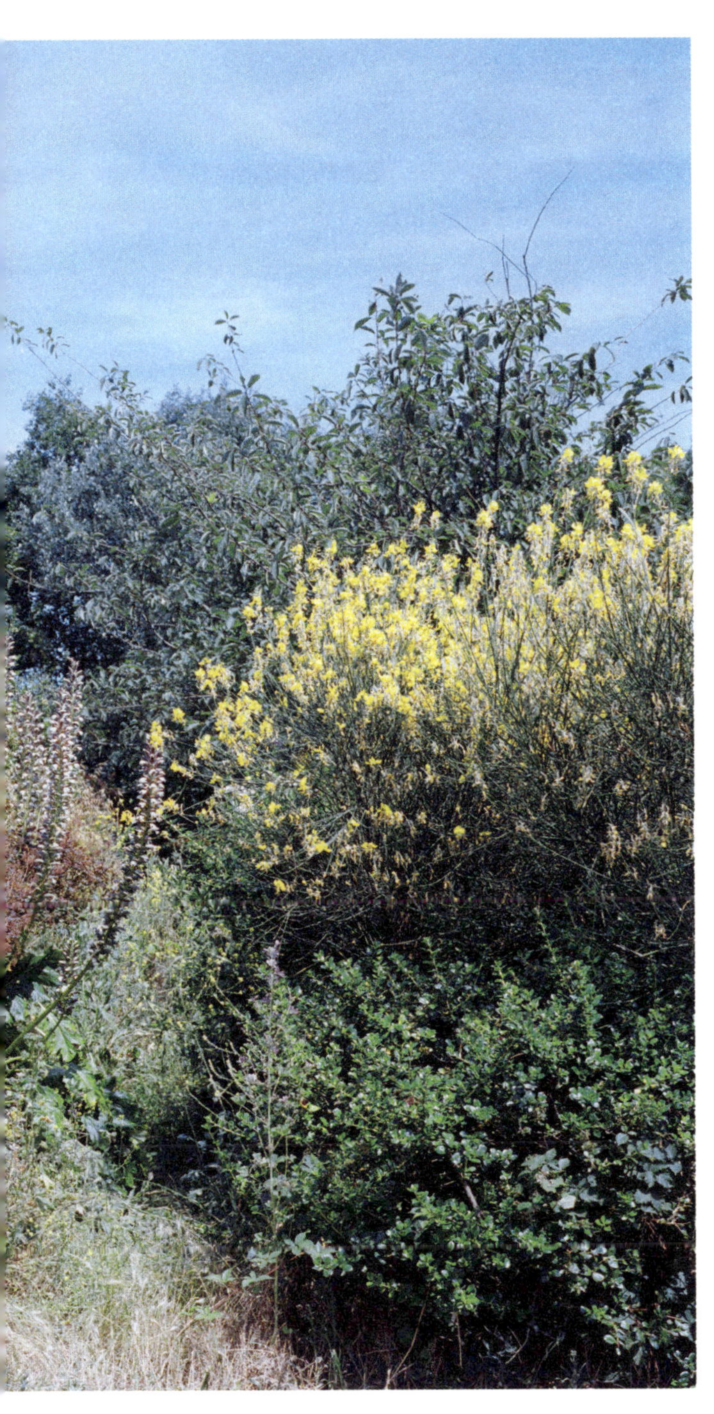

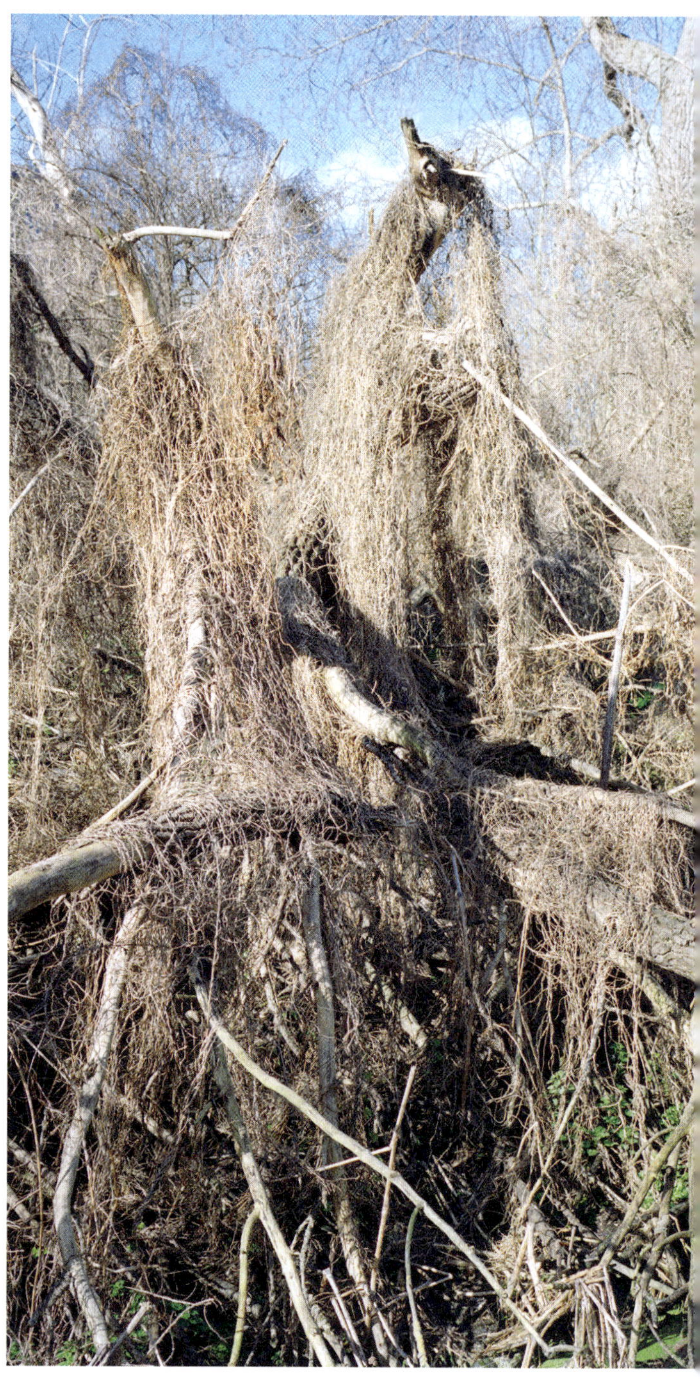

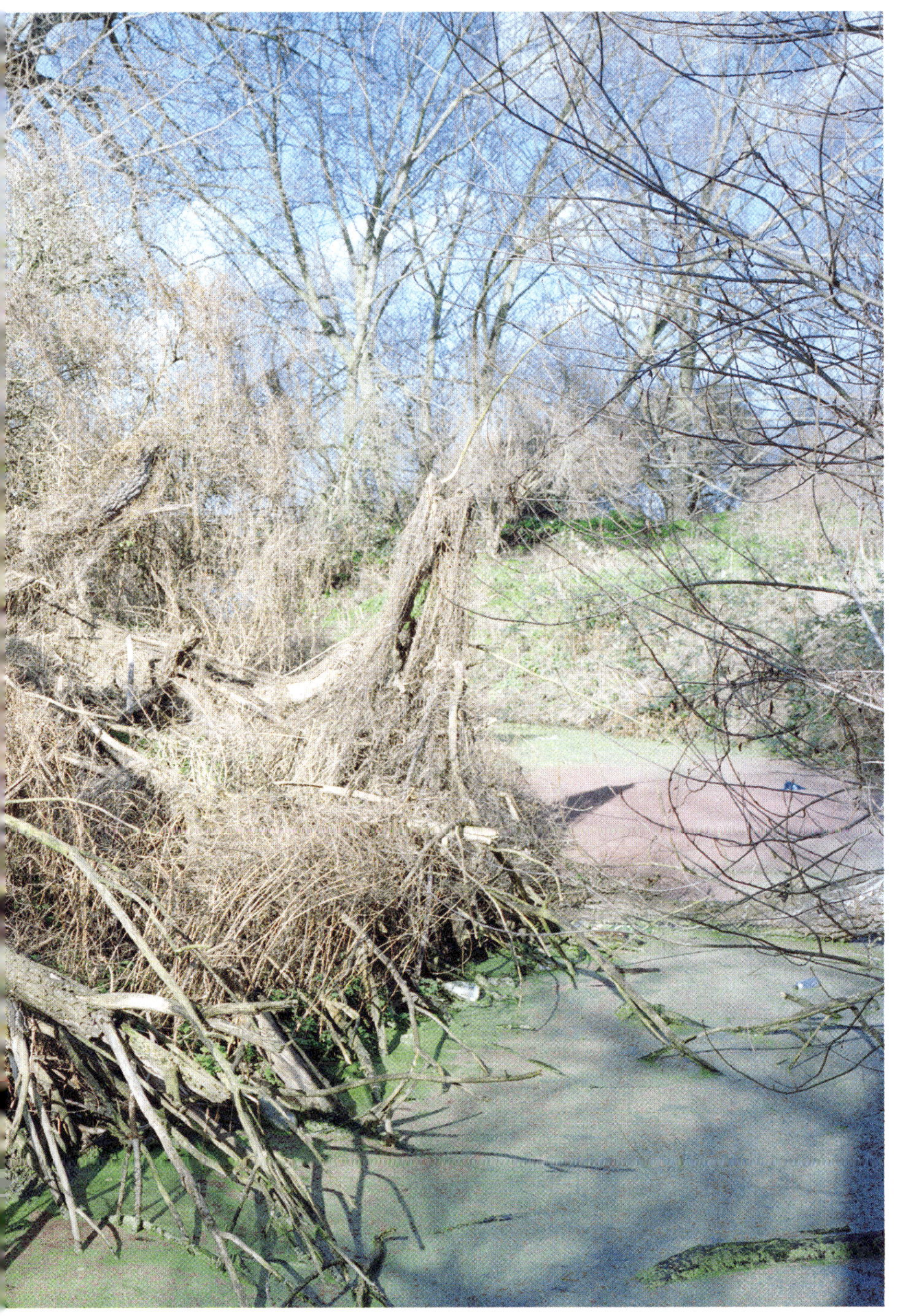

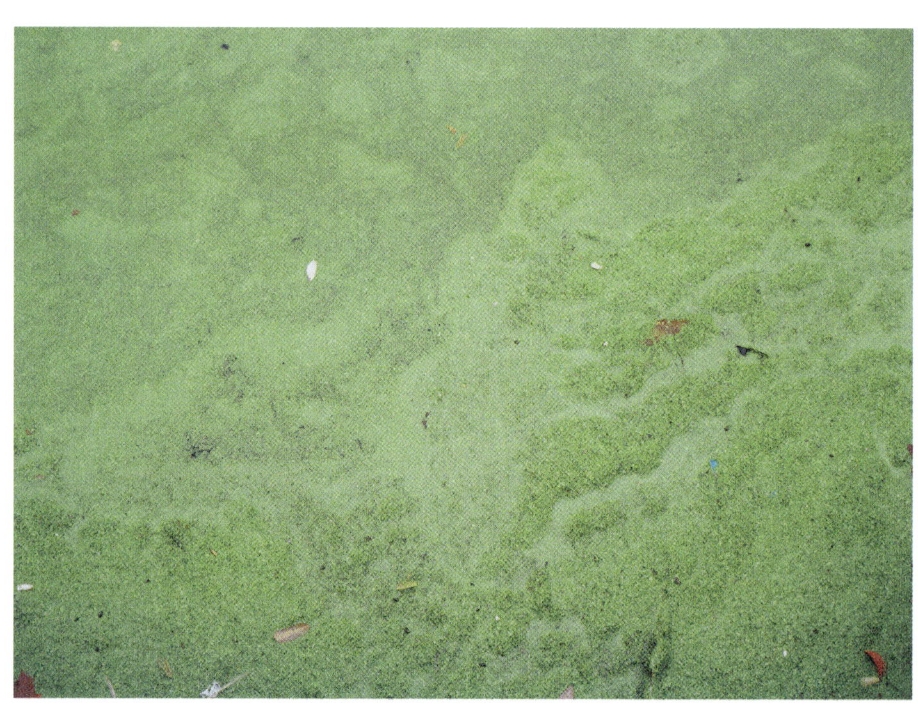

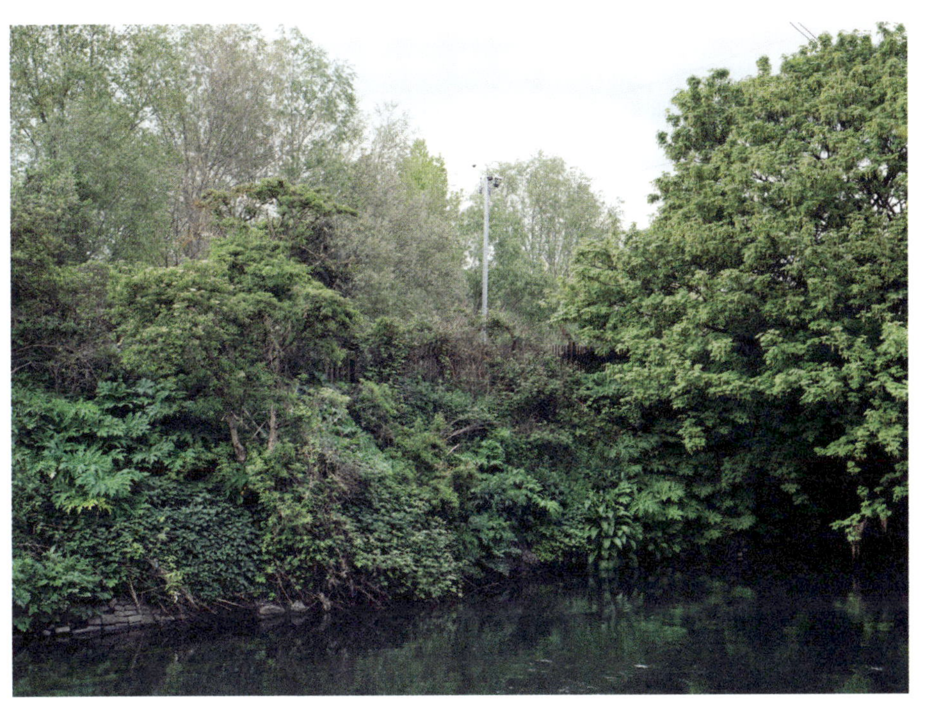

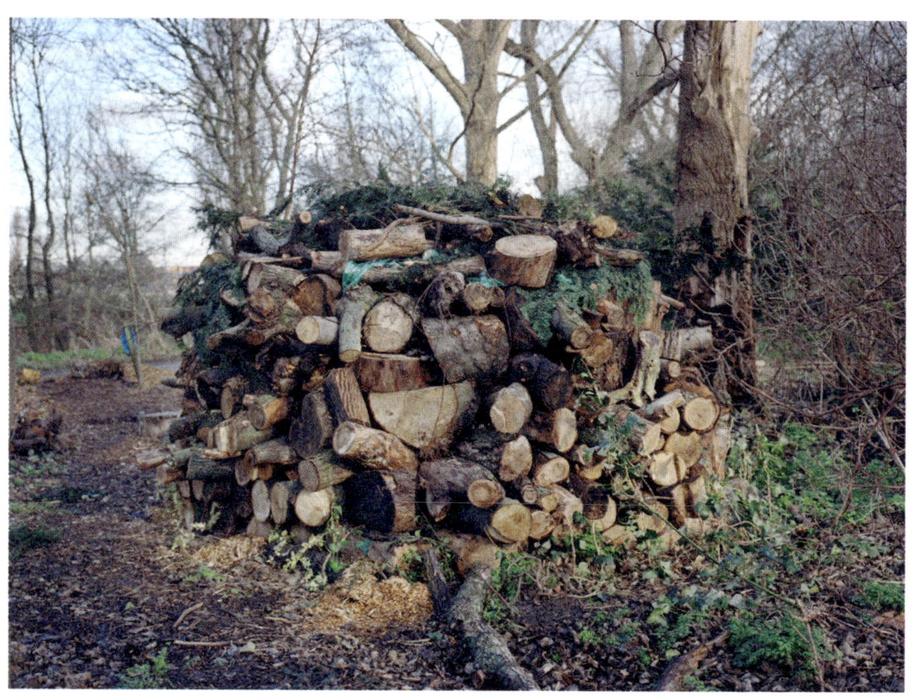

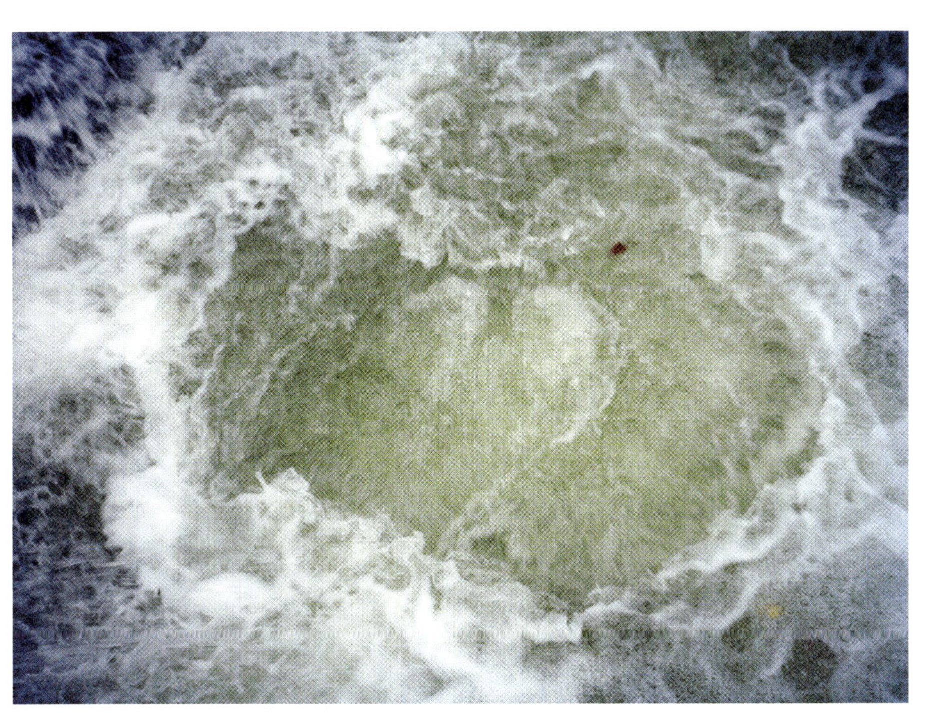

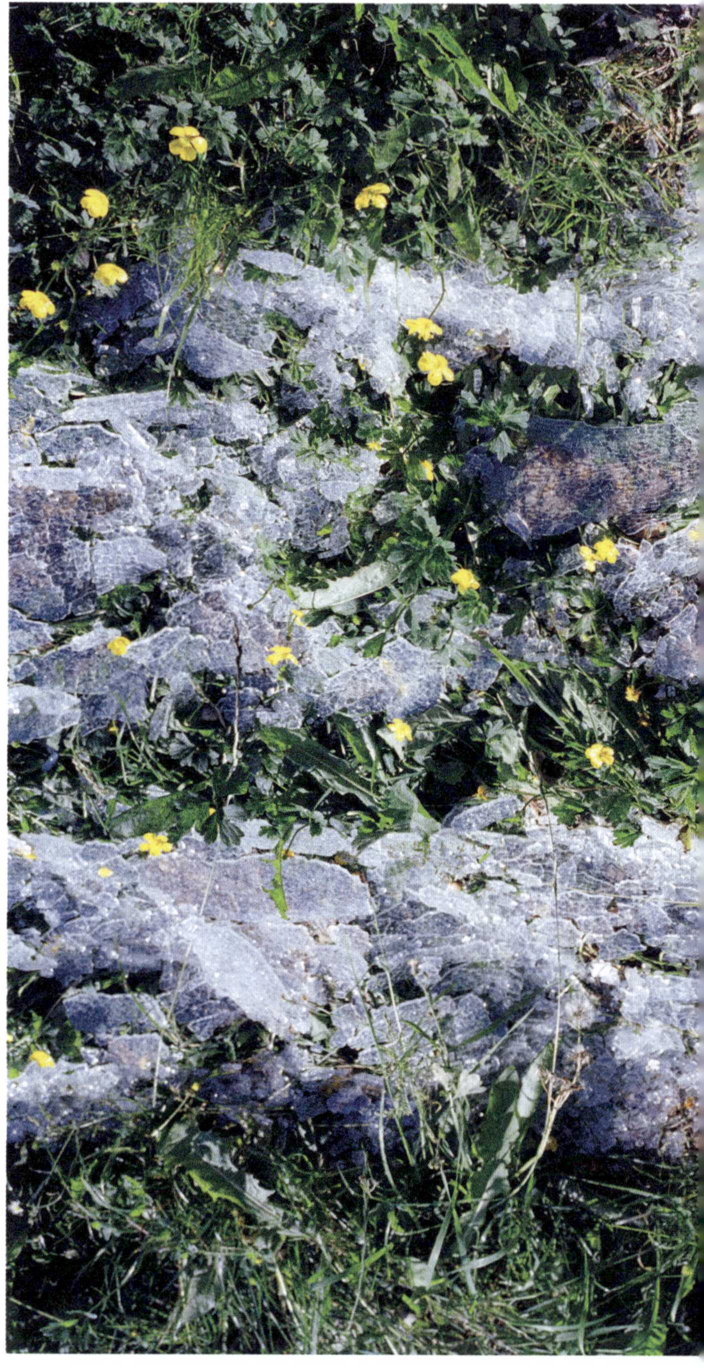

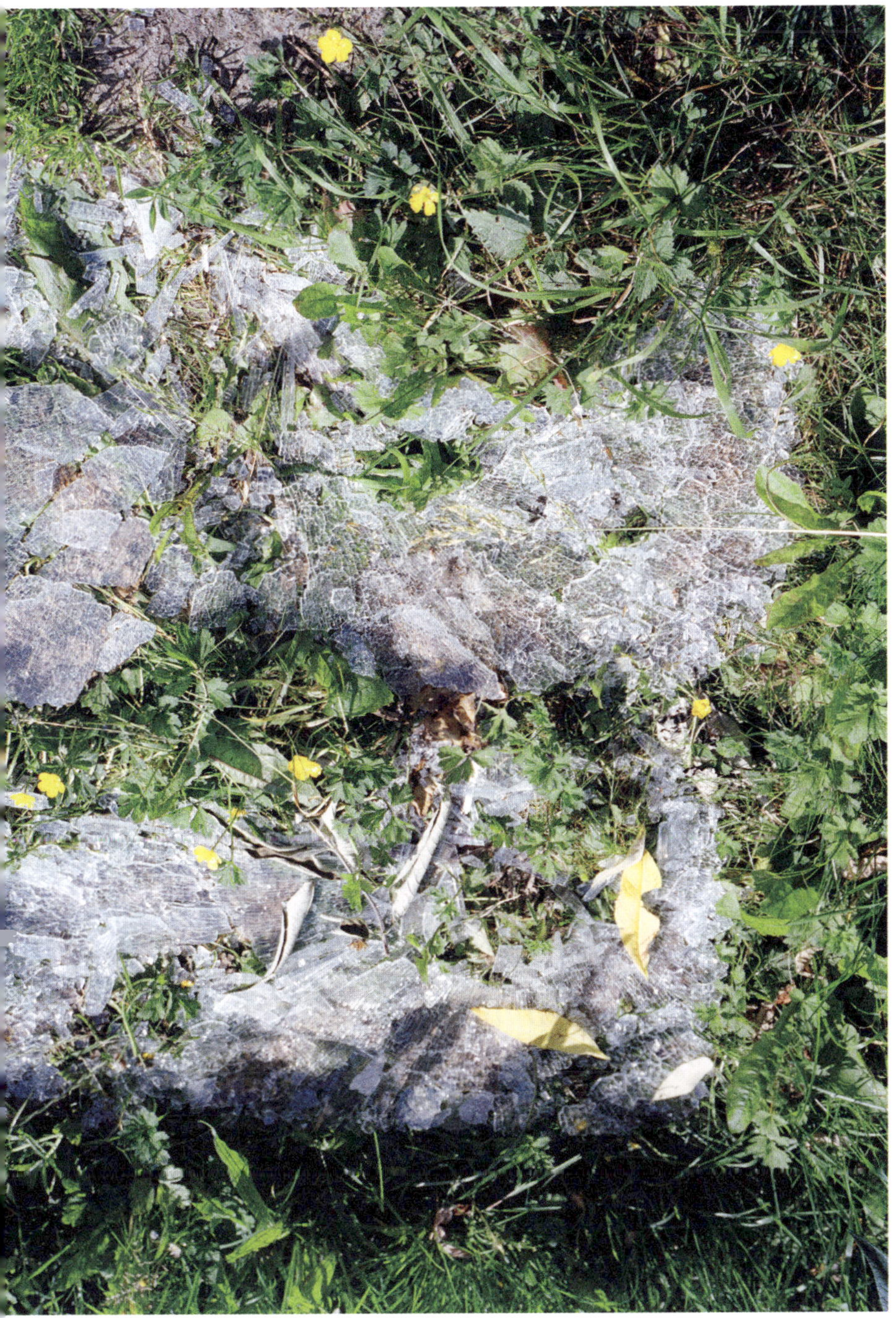

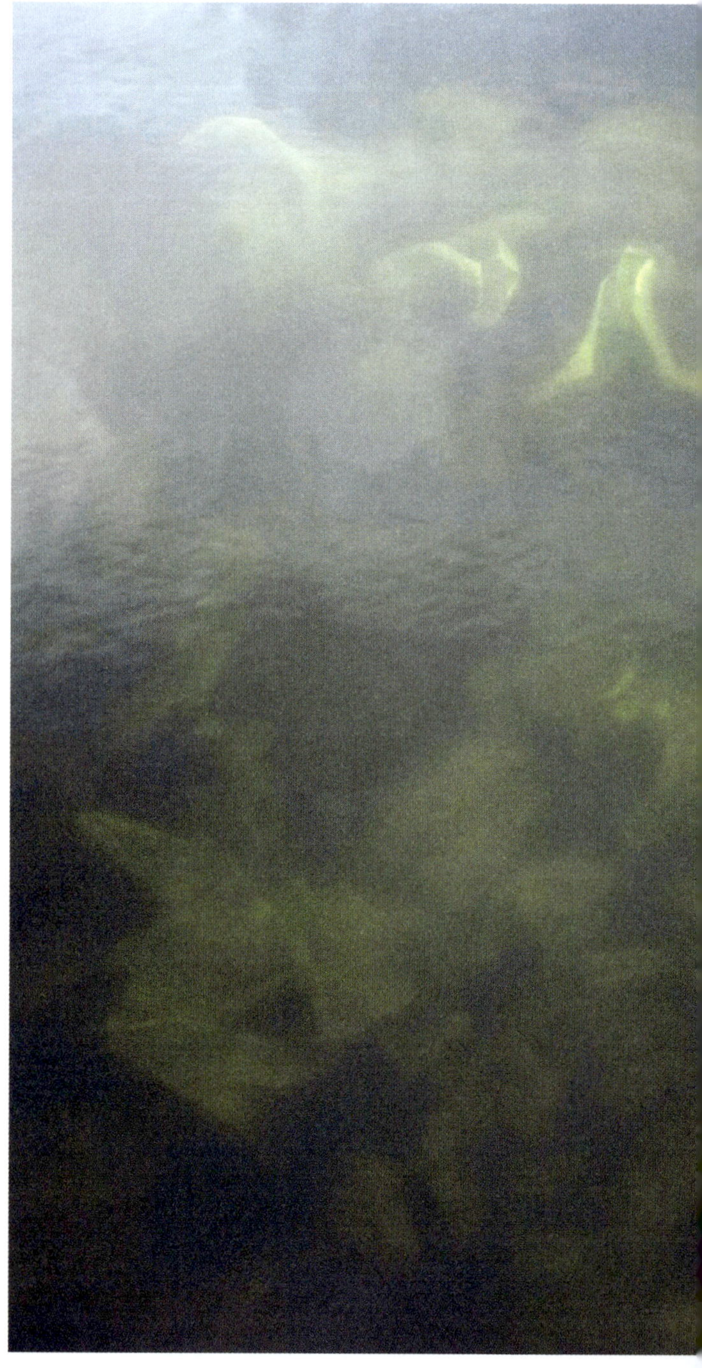

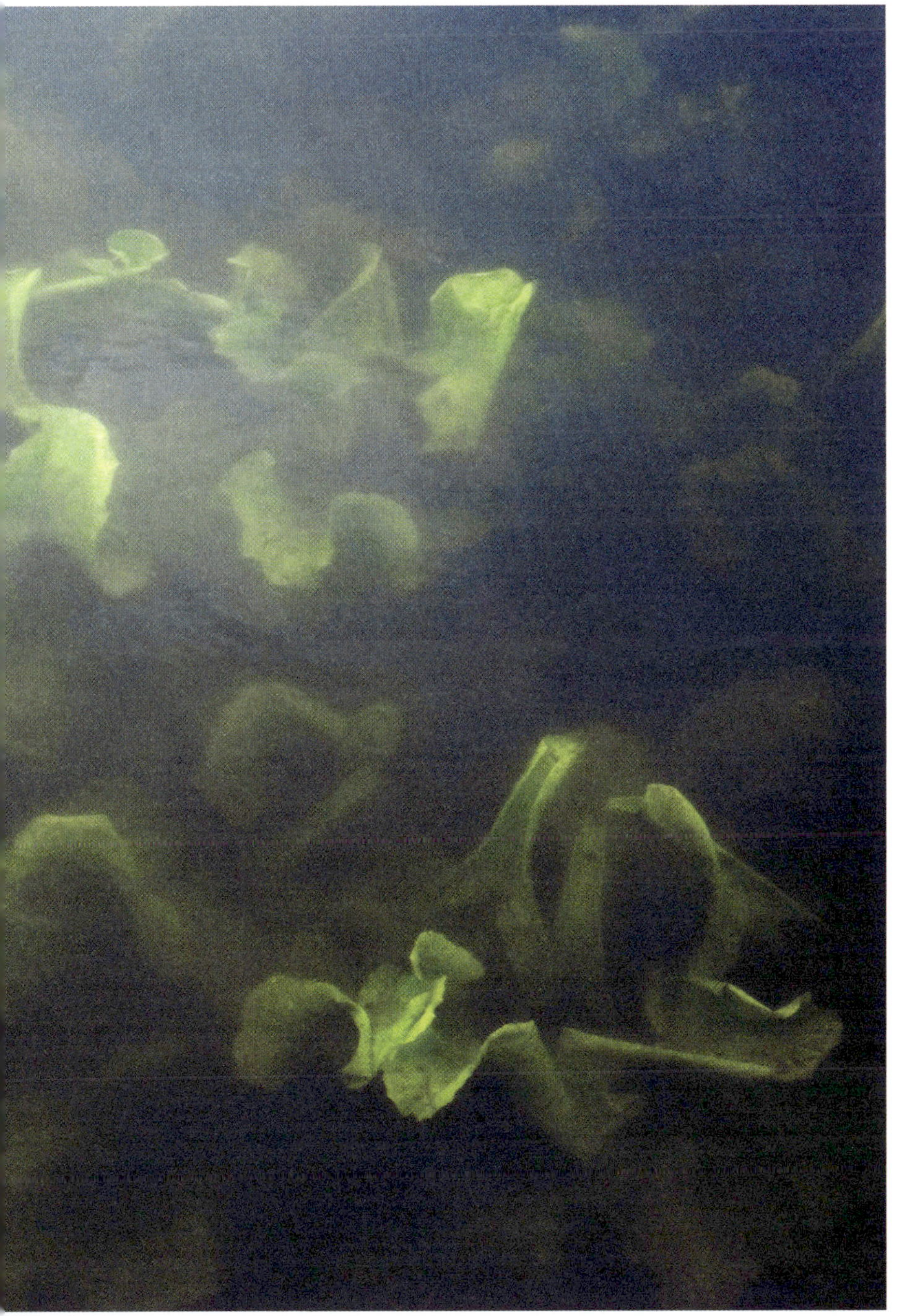

EAST LONDON SWIMMERS

MADELEINE WALLER

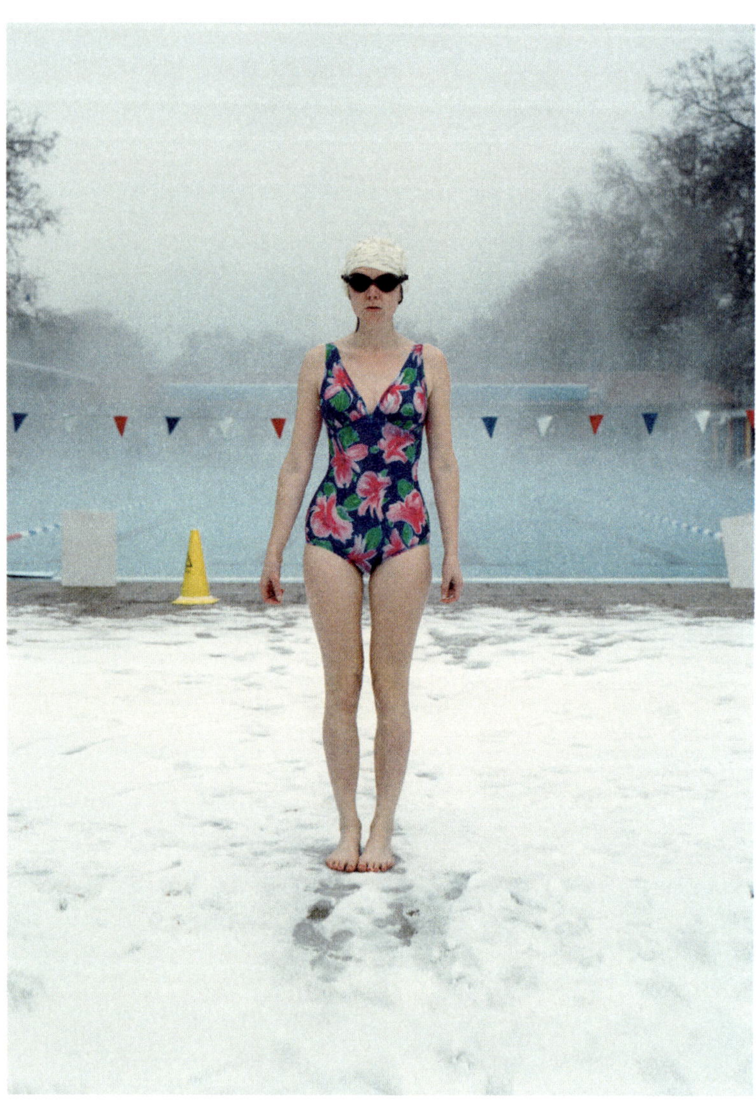

In a pool you are truly yourself. Mild minnows become ferocious sharks as soon as they put on a pair of goggles. Or
others whose bodies – through age, health or pregnancy – now
slow them down glide elegantly through the water, free again.
Photographer Madeleine Waller captures this dual identity in
her series on the swimmers braving an outdoor dip in London
Fields Lido.

Full-length portraits show the swimmers first clothed and
then in their swimming gear standing on the edge of the pool,
which reopened in 2006 after nearly two decades of neglect.
Artists, travel agents, filmmakers, bus drivers, property devel-
opers; they range in age from 11 to 65. They come for different
reasons. Some taught themselves to swim and do it now as a
panacea to traumatic past experiences, others learnt in
childhood and can't quite shake their competitive spirit.

For all, swimming is more than exercise – it's a ritual. In
interviews with Waller they describe the 'peace' and 'happiness' they find in the water, escaping the brutal pace of
London life. It's a way to feel alone in a city of nearly 9 million
people. Many compare the sensation to flying through the air.
As one swimmer says, 'It is the most accessible means of
being in another world.'

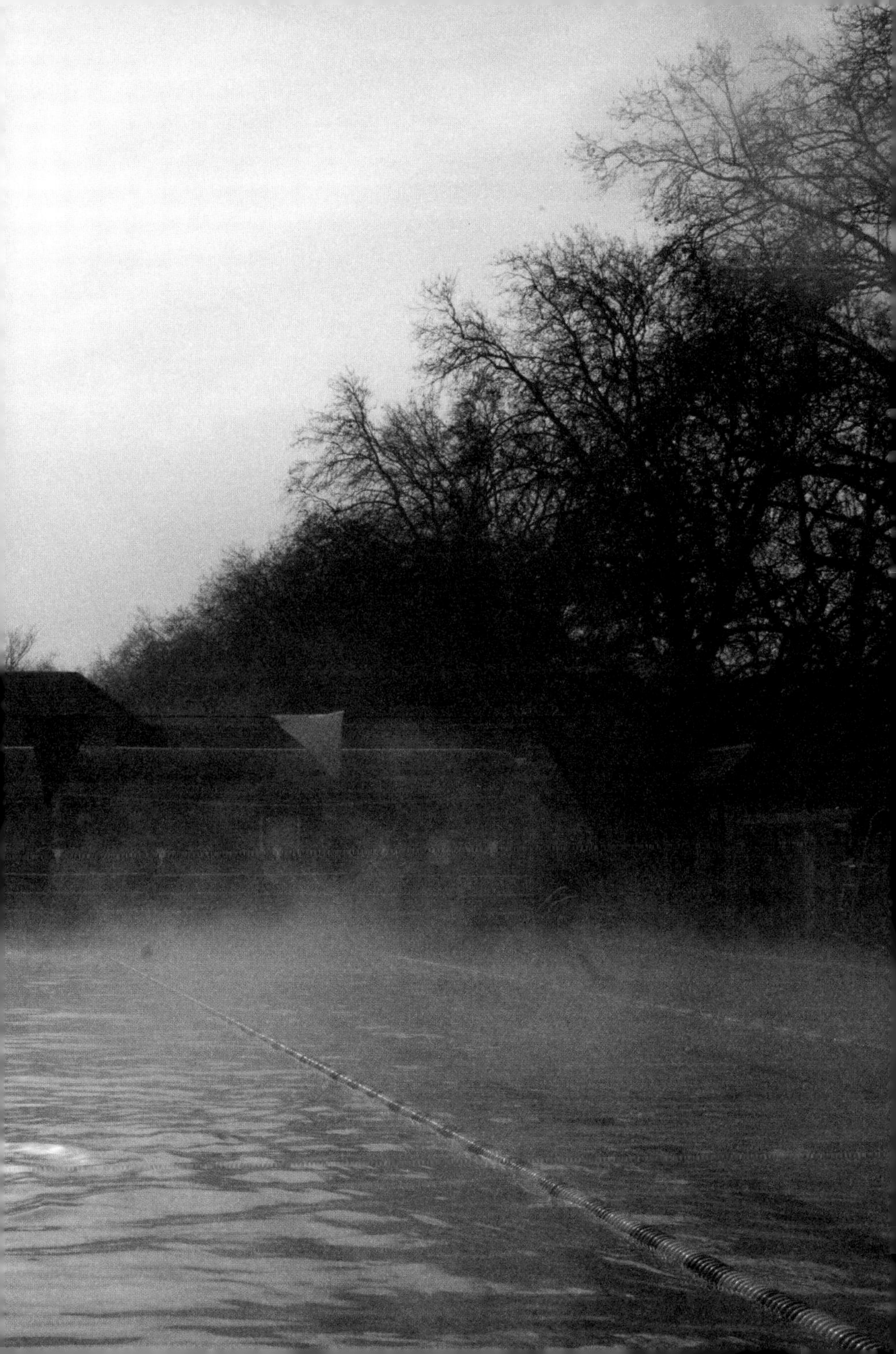

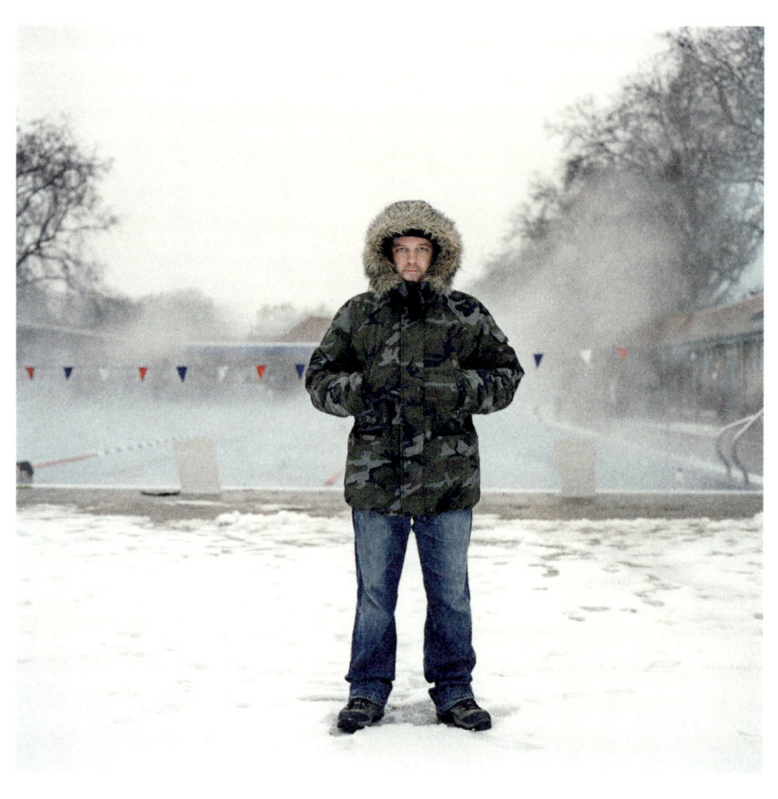

Name Stuart
Age 37
Occupation Travel advisor

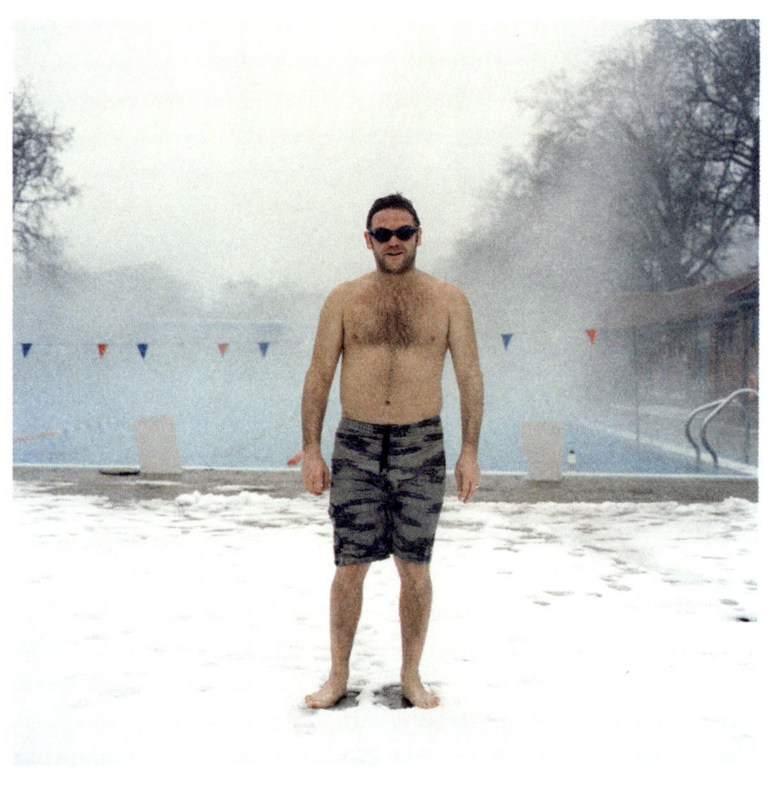

I have swum in outdoor pools all over the world –
in Australia, Singapore, Hong Kong and recently in Jamaica.
But the lido is like having your own private beach in the
centre of Hackney. It's known as 'Hoxton Beach'. Where else
can you get so many semi-naked people in London?

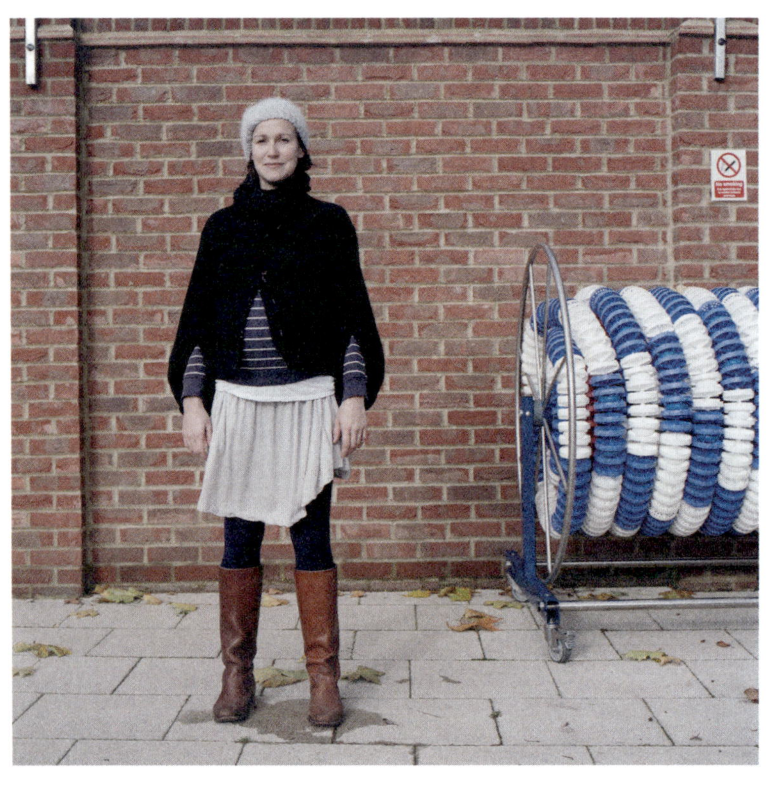

Name Lucy

Age 32

Occupation Filmmaker

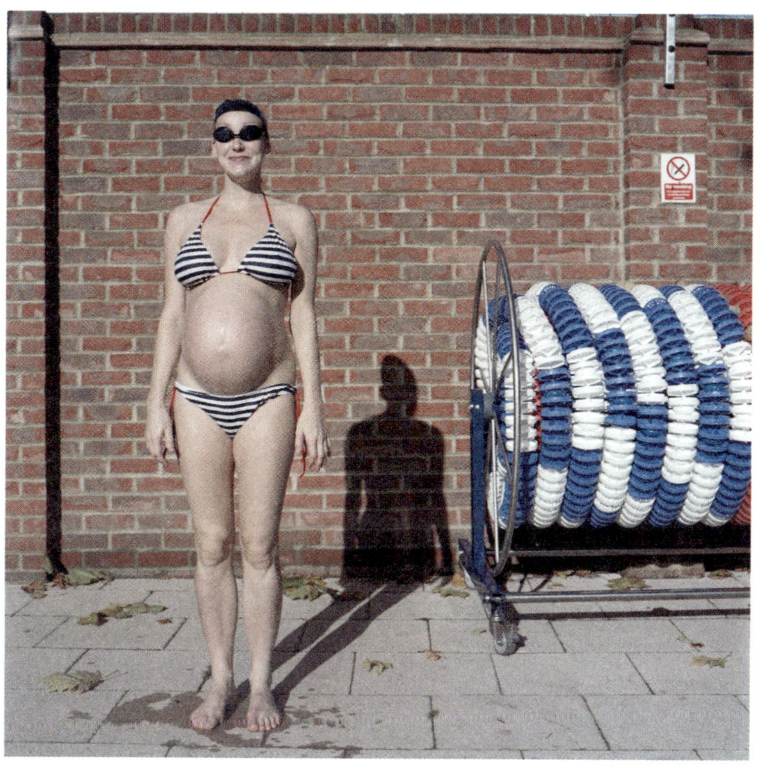

*I swam my way through pregnancy; it was a moment
alone with myself and the baby. I felt I was light
for once. When I was young I always wanted to be
a ballerina – now when I swim I can dance, I can make
different shapes in the water. It's a secret moment.*

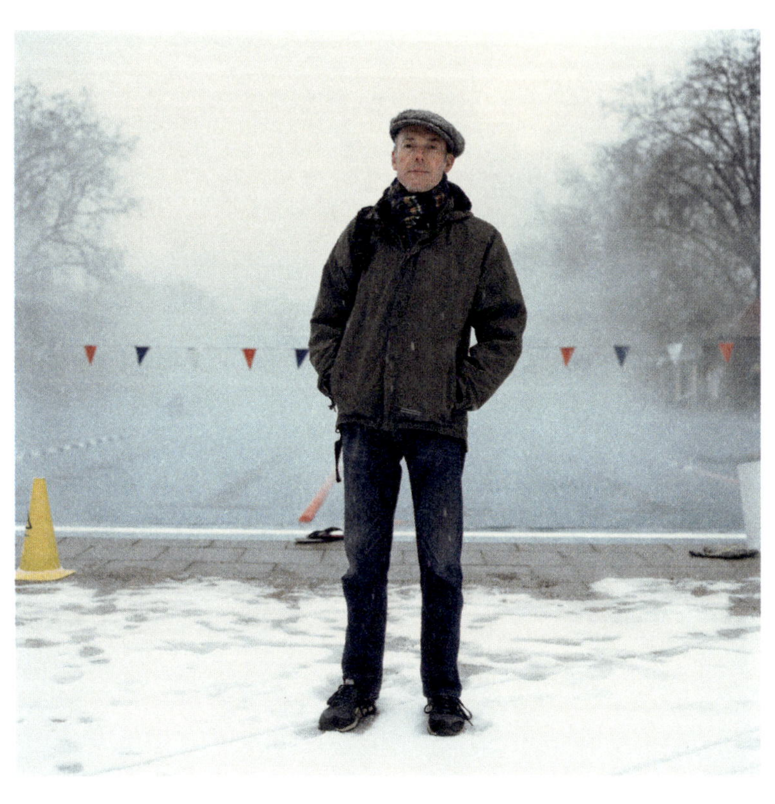

Name Mike

Age 65

Occupation Jazz musician

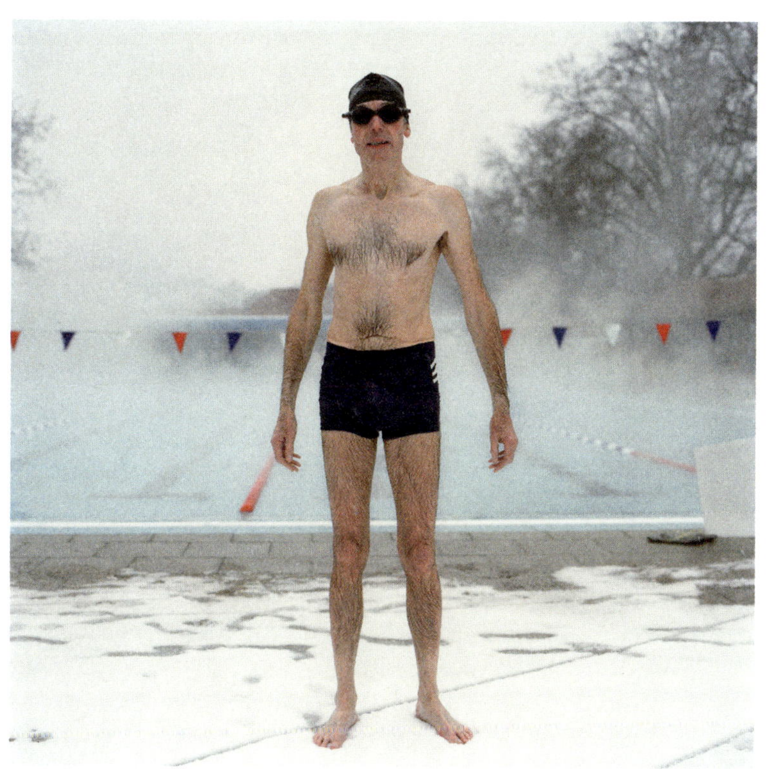

When I was 30 I nearly drowned in a garden swimming pool.
People watching thought I was having fun until a 12-year-old
saved me. I have always loved the water but I didn't learn
to swim until I was 44. It felt like I was learning to fly –
conquering a new element. That feeling never goes away.

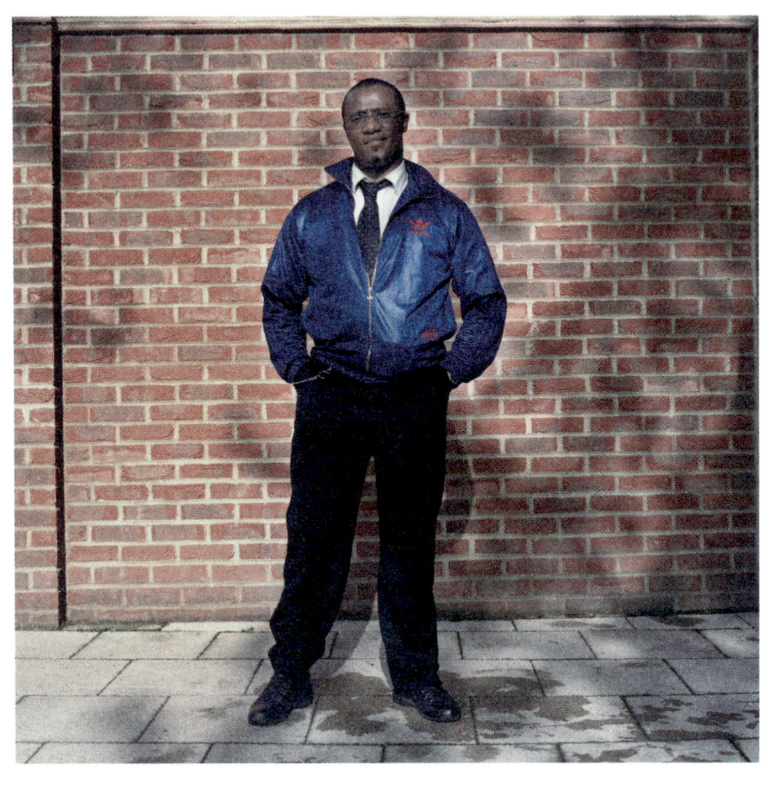

Name Paul

Age 44

Occupation Bus driver

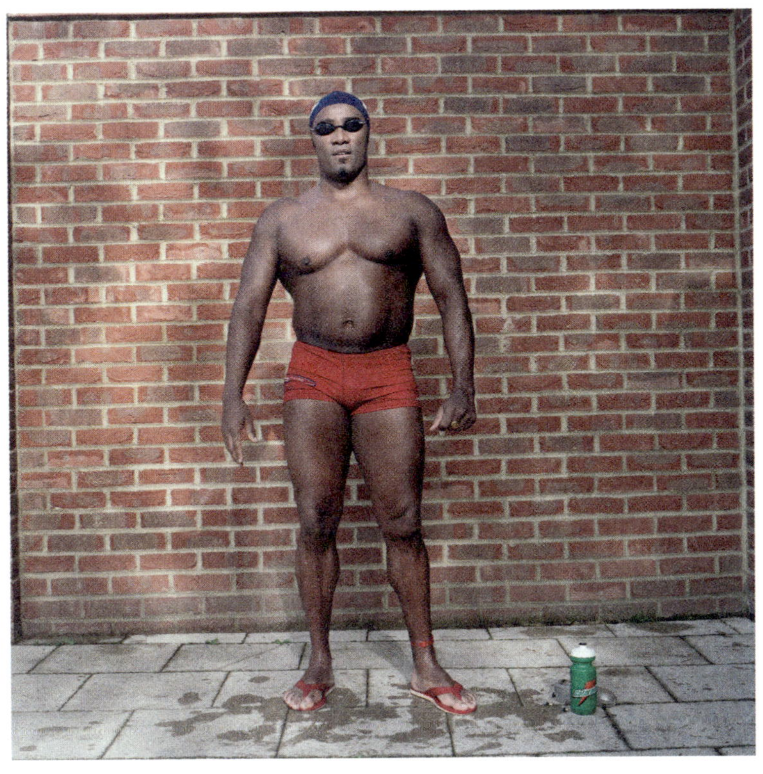

I have a few hours off between shifts of driving the bus and I find swimming helps me relax. The thing about driving in London is that no one seems to care. Swimming is about taking pride in yourself. You have to have discipline. If you are good at something then go for it. We aren't here forever.

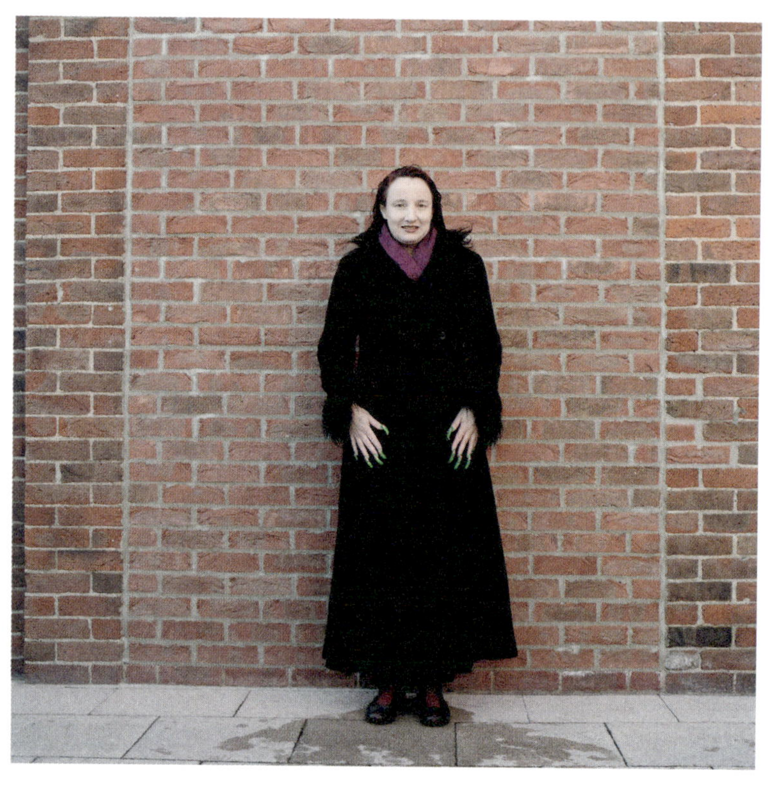

Name   Kathryn
Age   Mid-40s
Occupation   Office worker

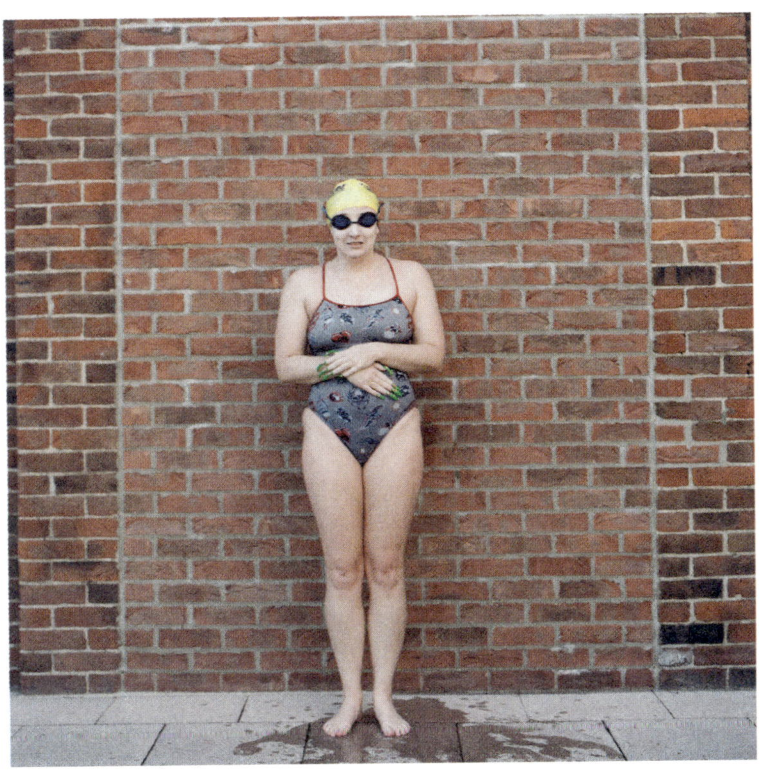

I used to go to a lot of alternative clubs. Now I feel I've got too old for that and I've taken to regular swimming. It becomes an addiction. When I first started, the endorphins kicked in after 16 laps. Today I feel good after 1½ kilometres. Sometimes when I'm dreaming, I'm dreaming of swimming. It's happiness.

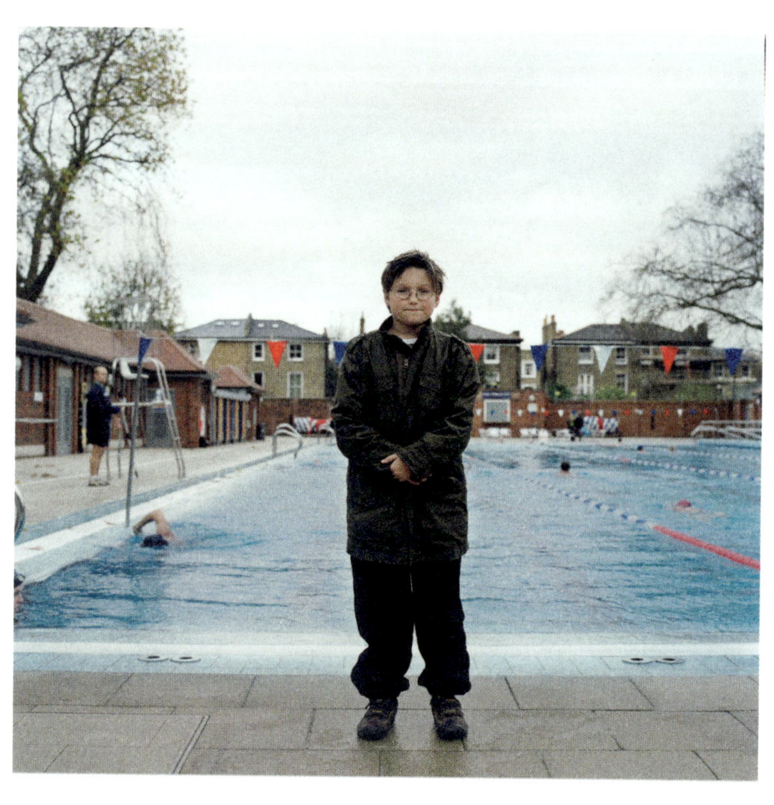

Name Sam

Age 11

Occupation Student

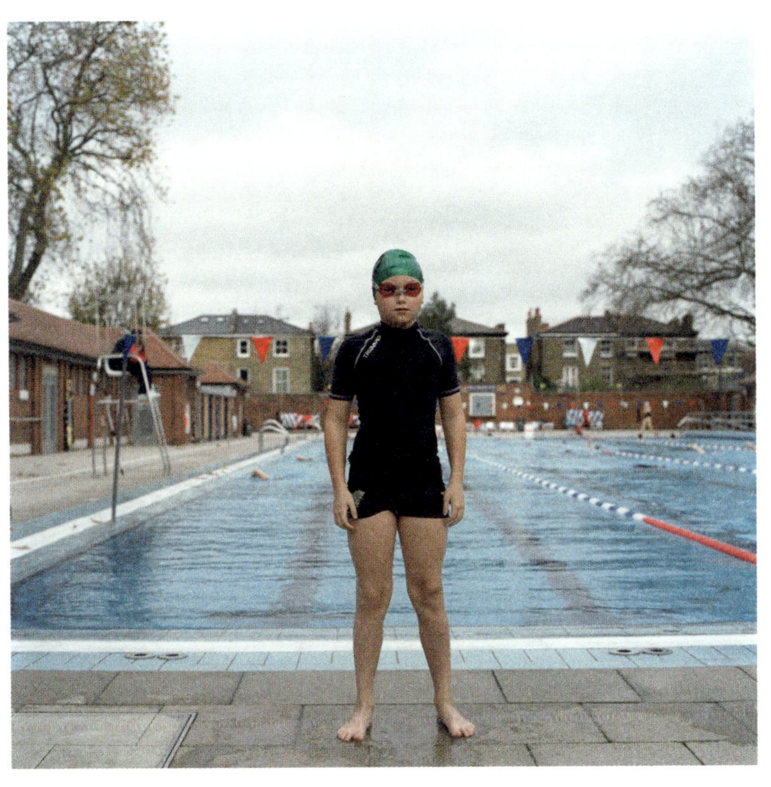

*When I swim I play songs in my head, inspirational songs,
to motivate myself. On the 25th or 26th lap I sometimes play
'Just Keep Swimming' from the film 'Finding Nemo'.
When I come out I feel proud of myself
for what I have achieved.*

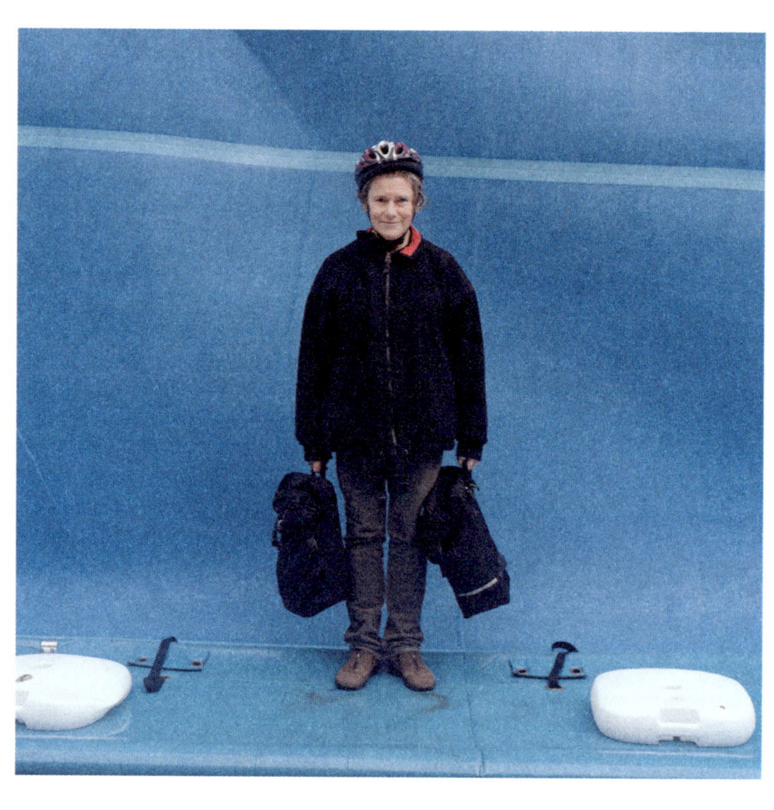

Name Amanda
Age 65
Occupation Artist

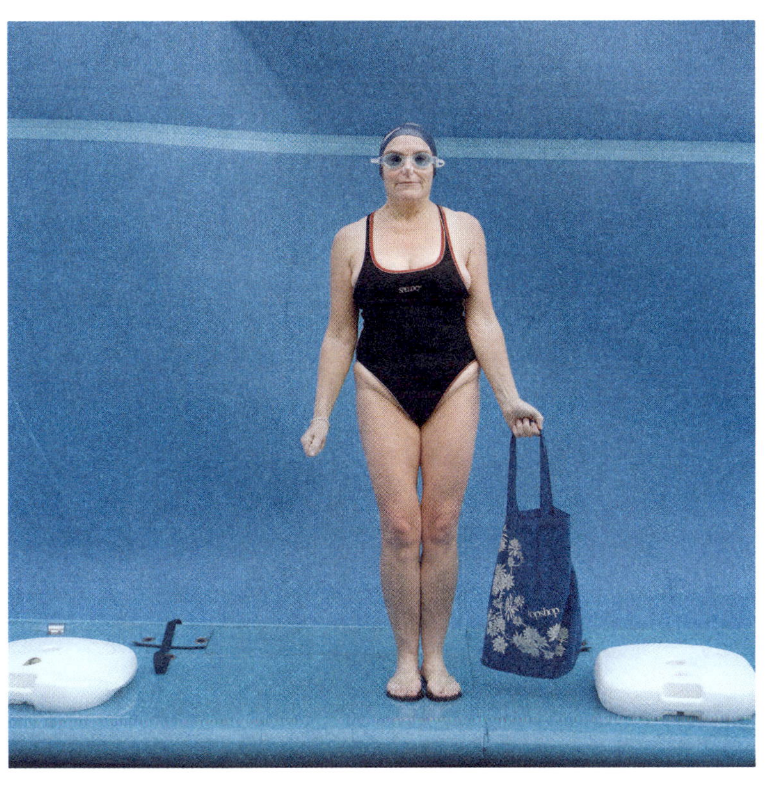

I take my grandchildren swimming. Once my four-year-old grand-daughter had overcome her fear of being underwater and taught herself to swim, she finally relaxed and floated spread-out like a star. It was as if she was saying 'I trust the world'. I felt the most immense happiness.

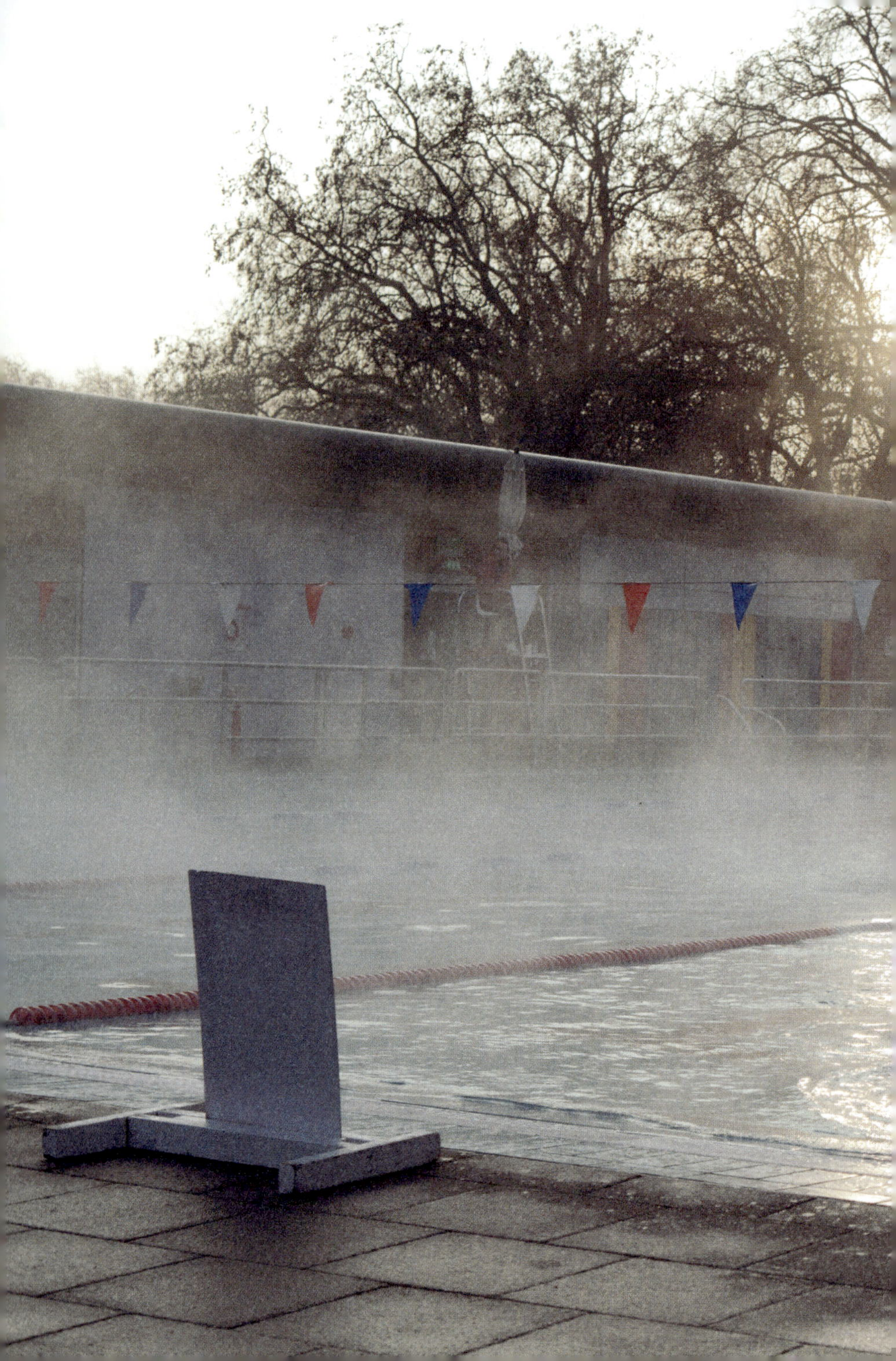

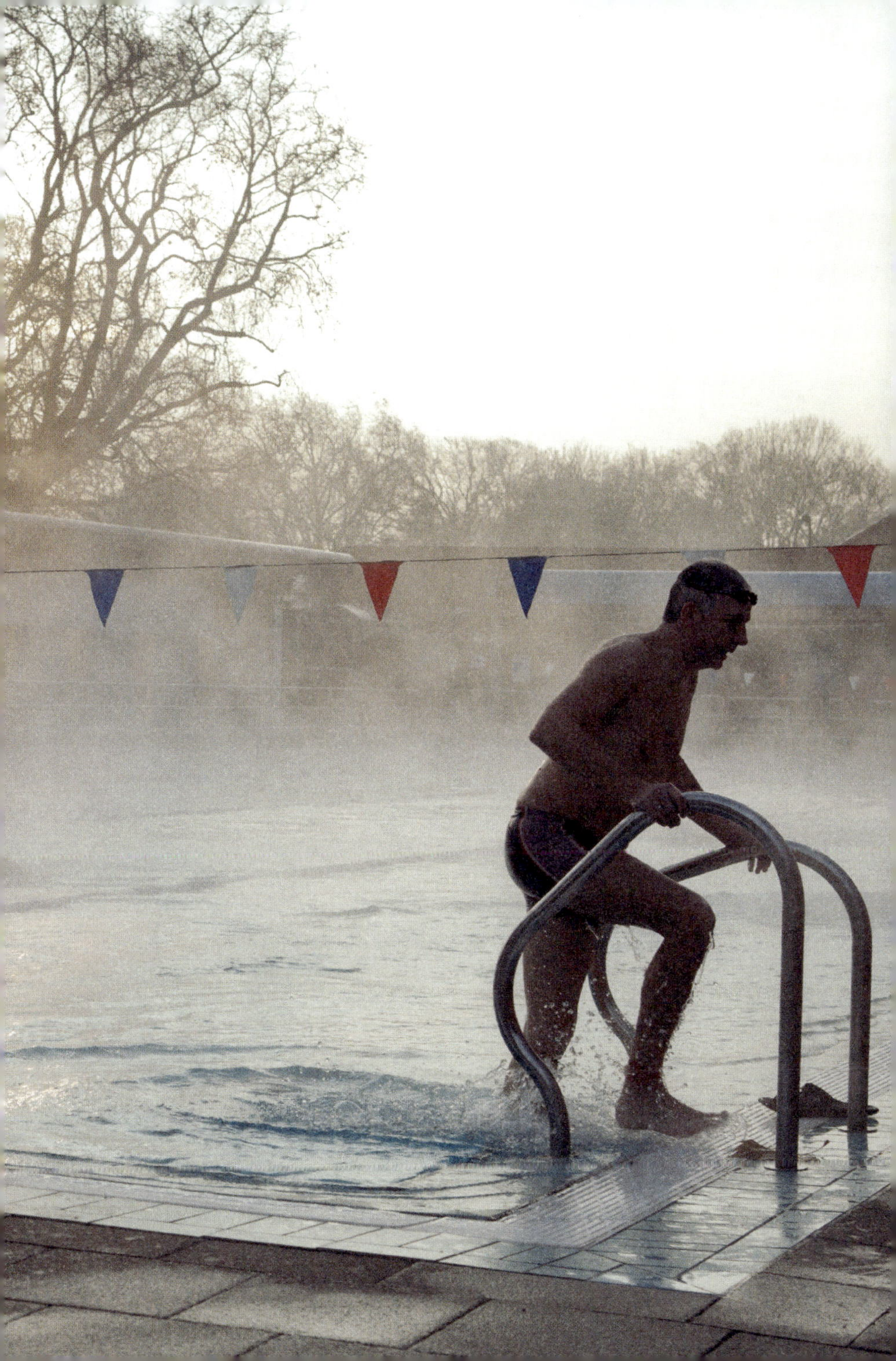

A PORTRAIT OF HACKNEY

ZED NELSON

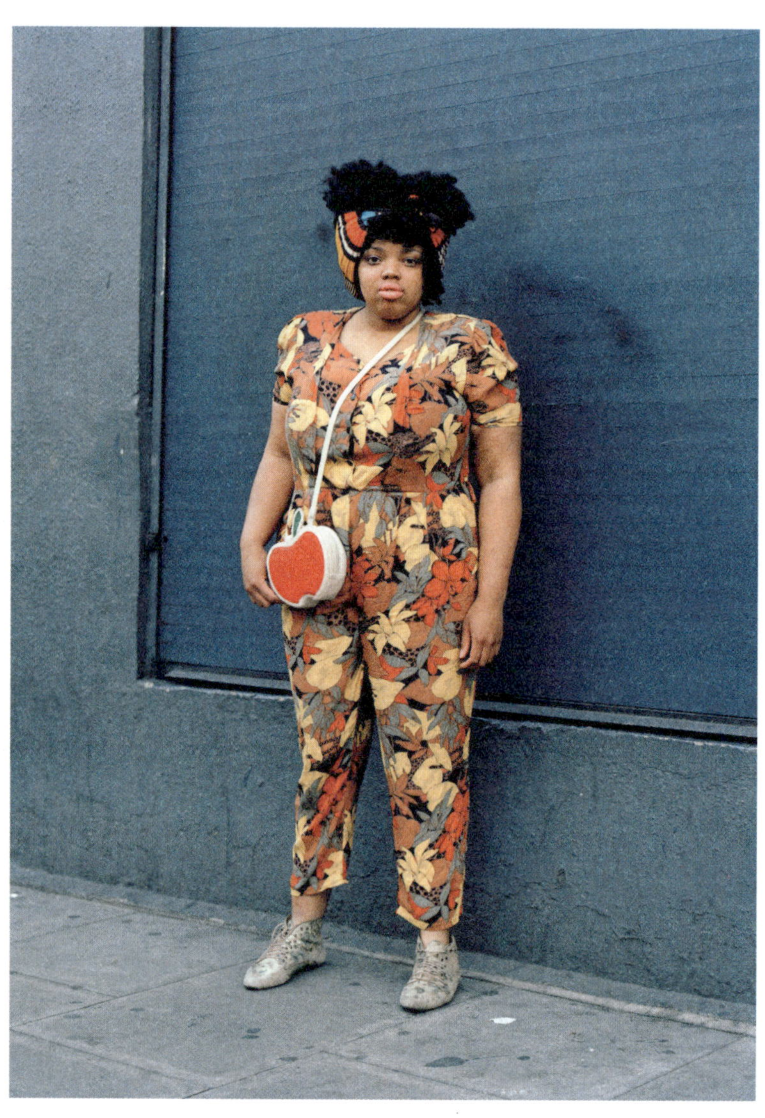

A photographer pays homage to the everchanging landscape of his home neighbourhood.

Two cities exist in parallel, sharing the same space at the same time, though rarely interacting. This is the idea behind sci-fi novel *The City and The City* by China Miéville but it could just as easily be a description of Hackney – a borough that has come to typify London gentrification where a teenager is gunned down in daylight, streets away from a swanky new gallery opening.

Photographer Zed Nelson was three when he moved to Hackney from East Africa and it's the place he's called home ever since, although he's spent much of his life abroad, covering stories throughout the world. He's best known for his work on gun culture in the US and the global beauty industry. Unlike those projects, this blend of portraits, documentary and street photography has a personal hue.

These are the streets where Nelson smoked spliffs and got arrested as a young punk, before discovering photography. He shows Hackney in all its variety and complexity. The deprivation, the hope, the melancholy and the humour. We see kids in hoods, crumbling walls, a couple canoodling on the canal, a nesting swan. It's a meditation, he writes, 'on the confusion of cultures, clash of identities and the beauty and ugliness' – a viewpoint into the city and the city.

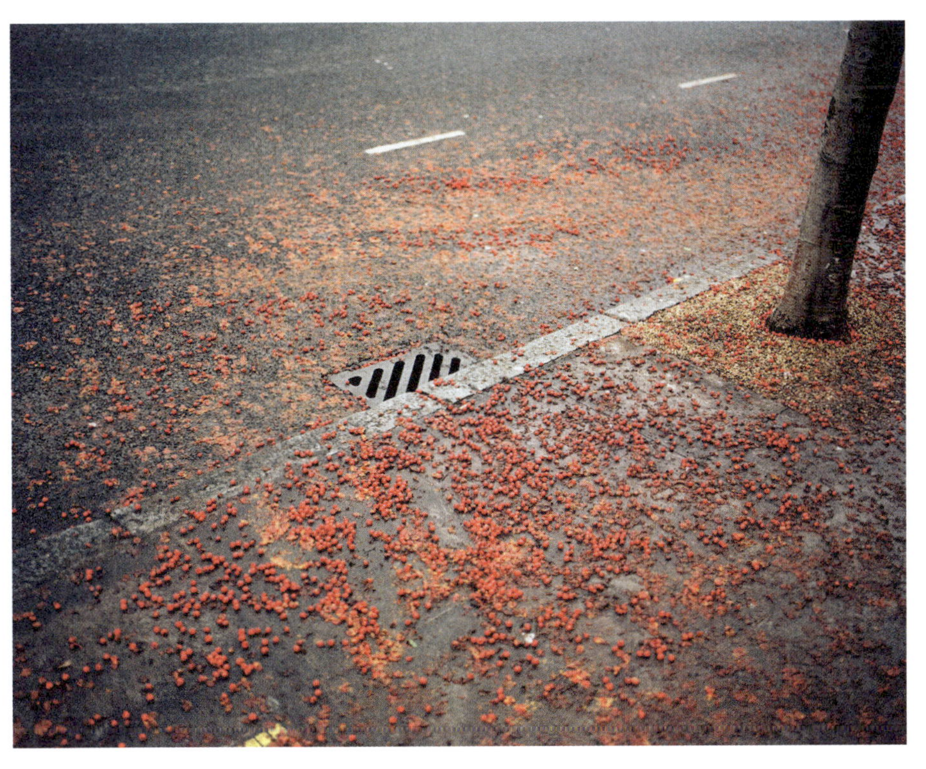

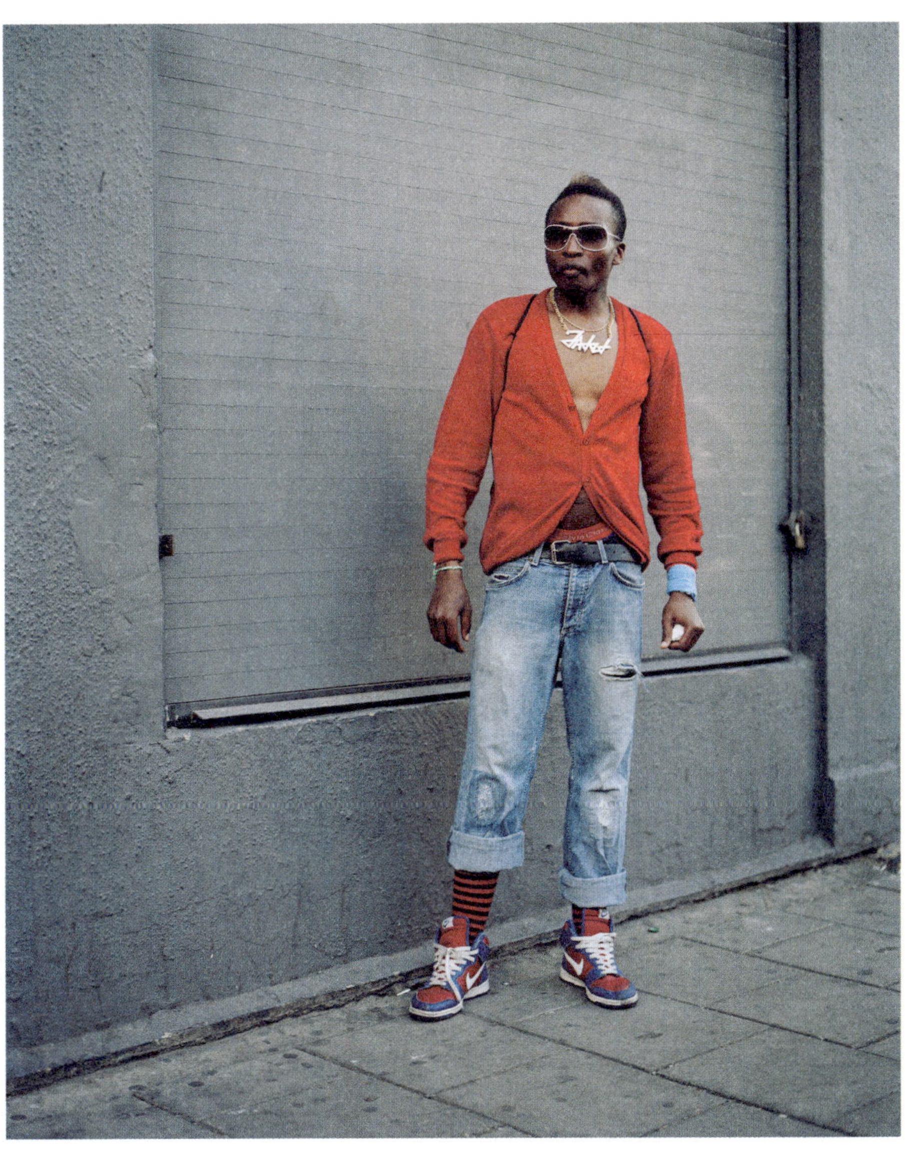

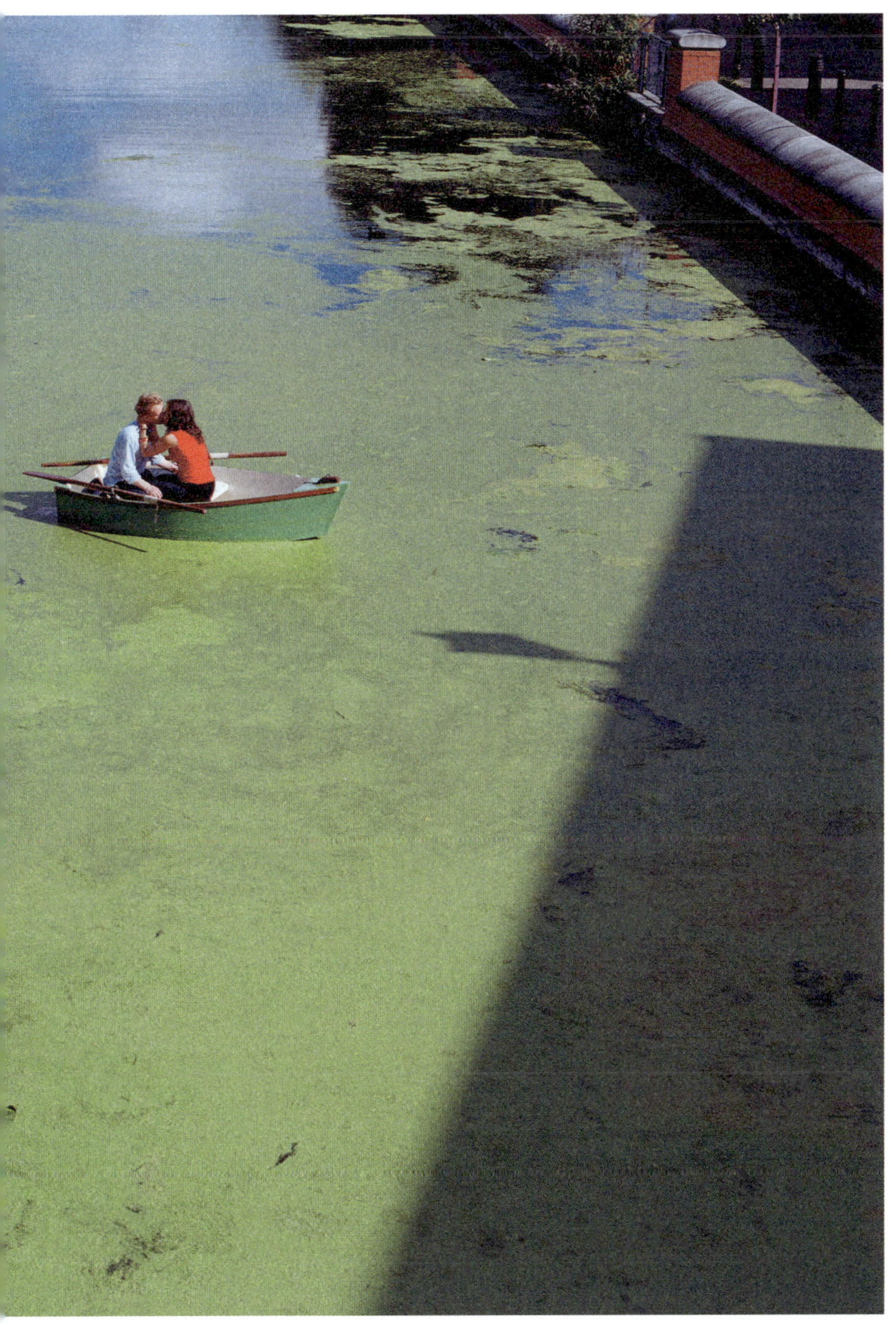

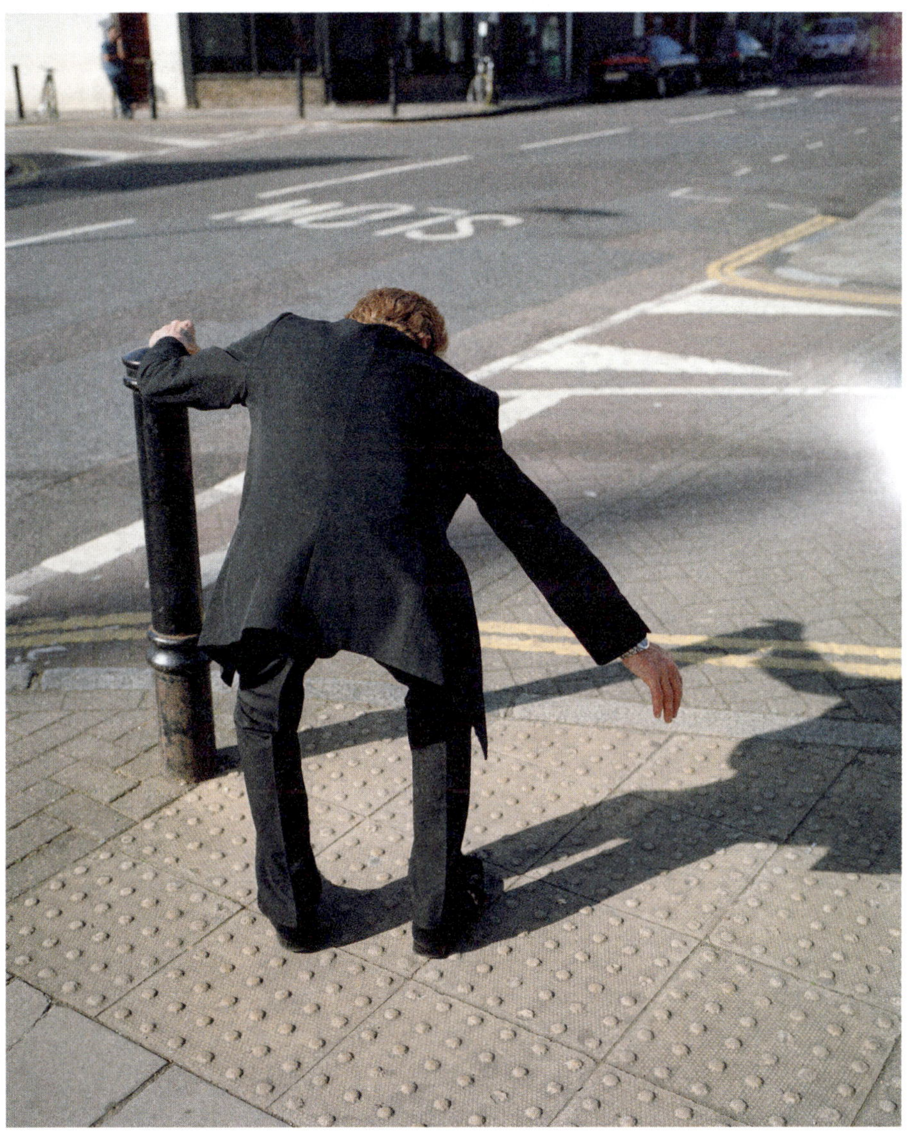

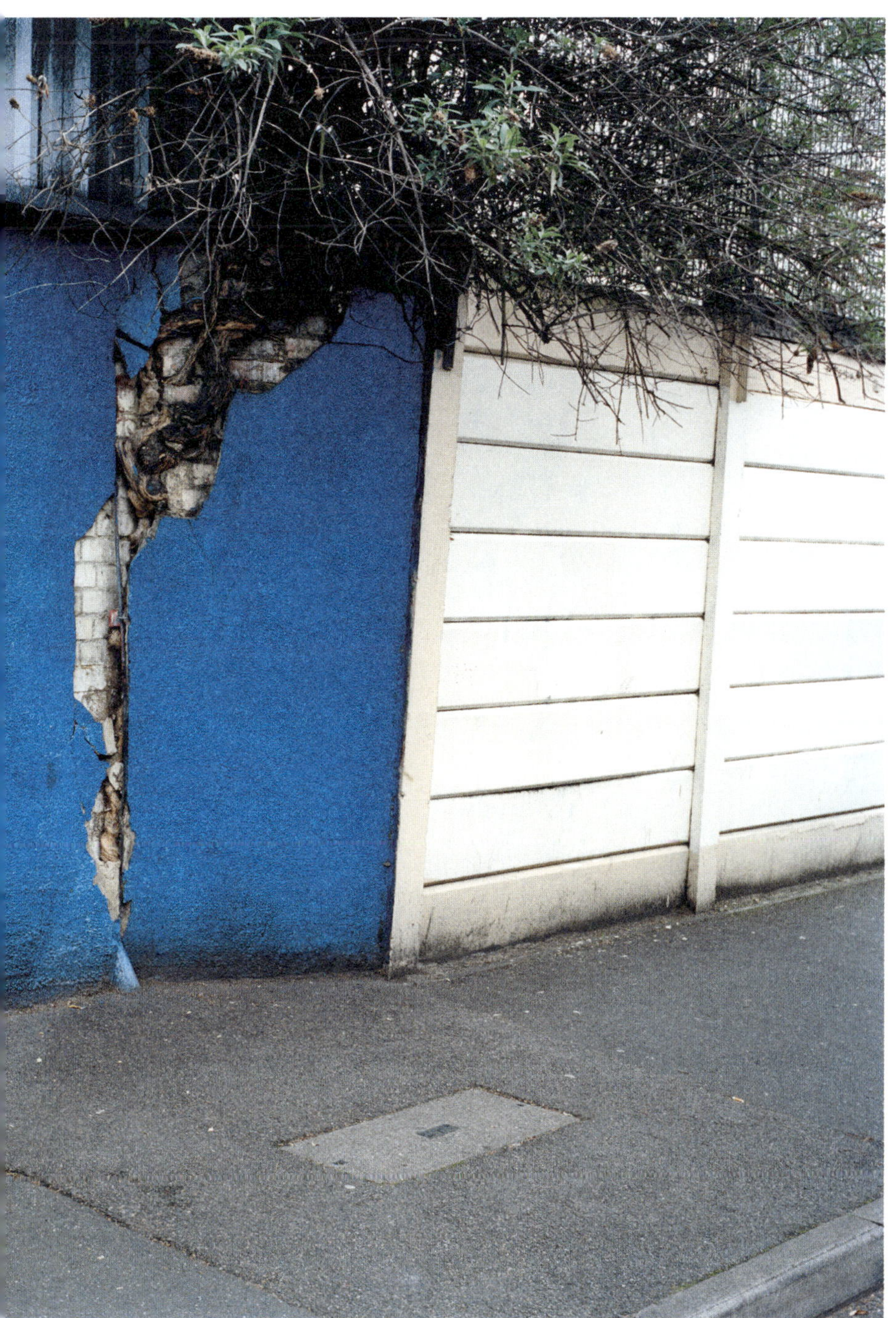

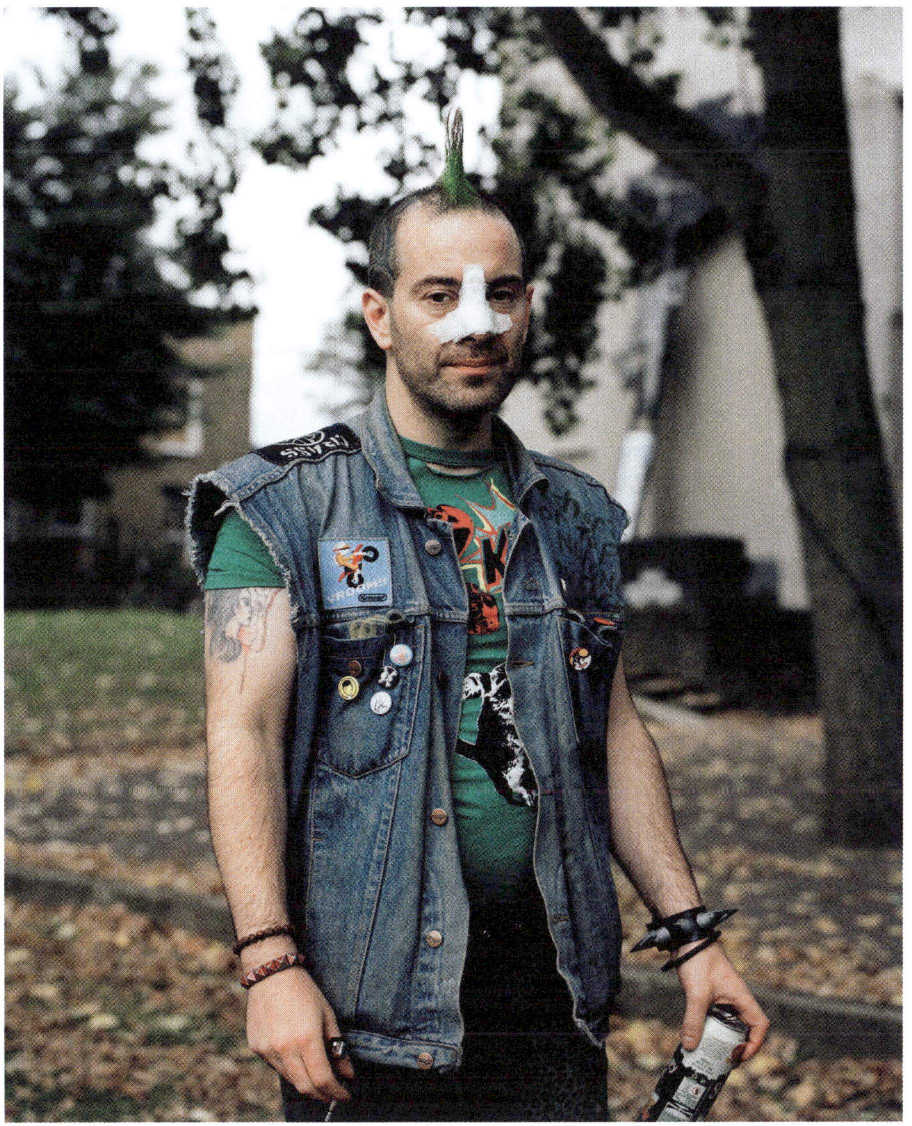

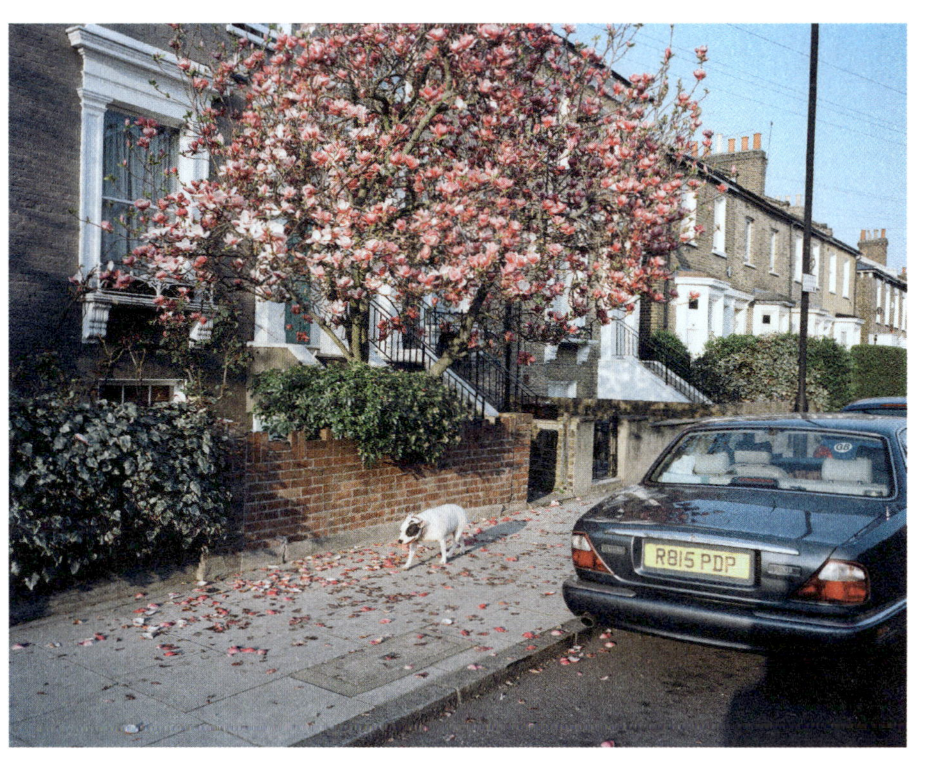

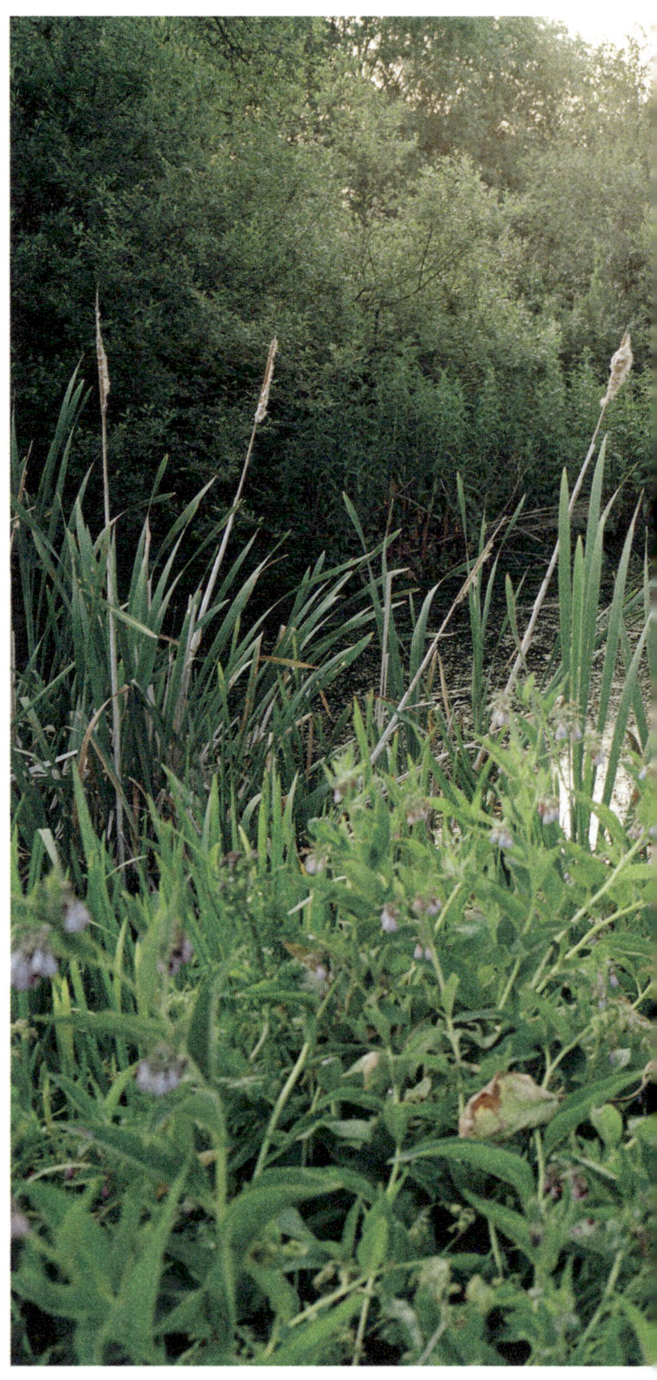

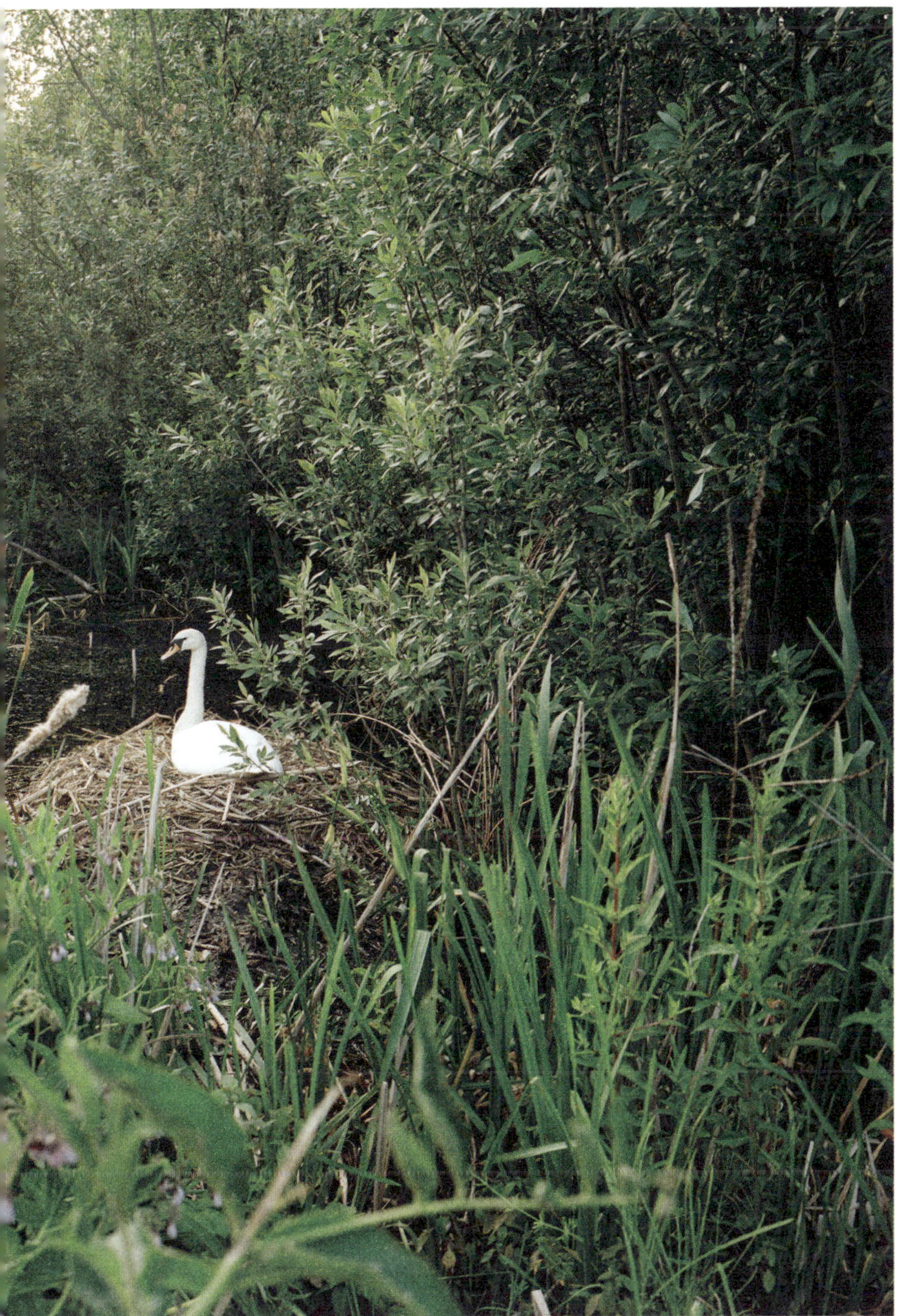

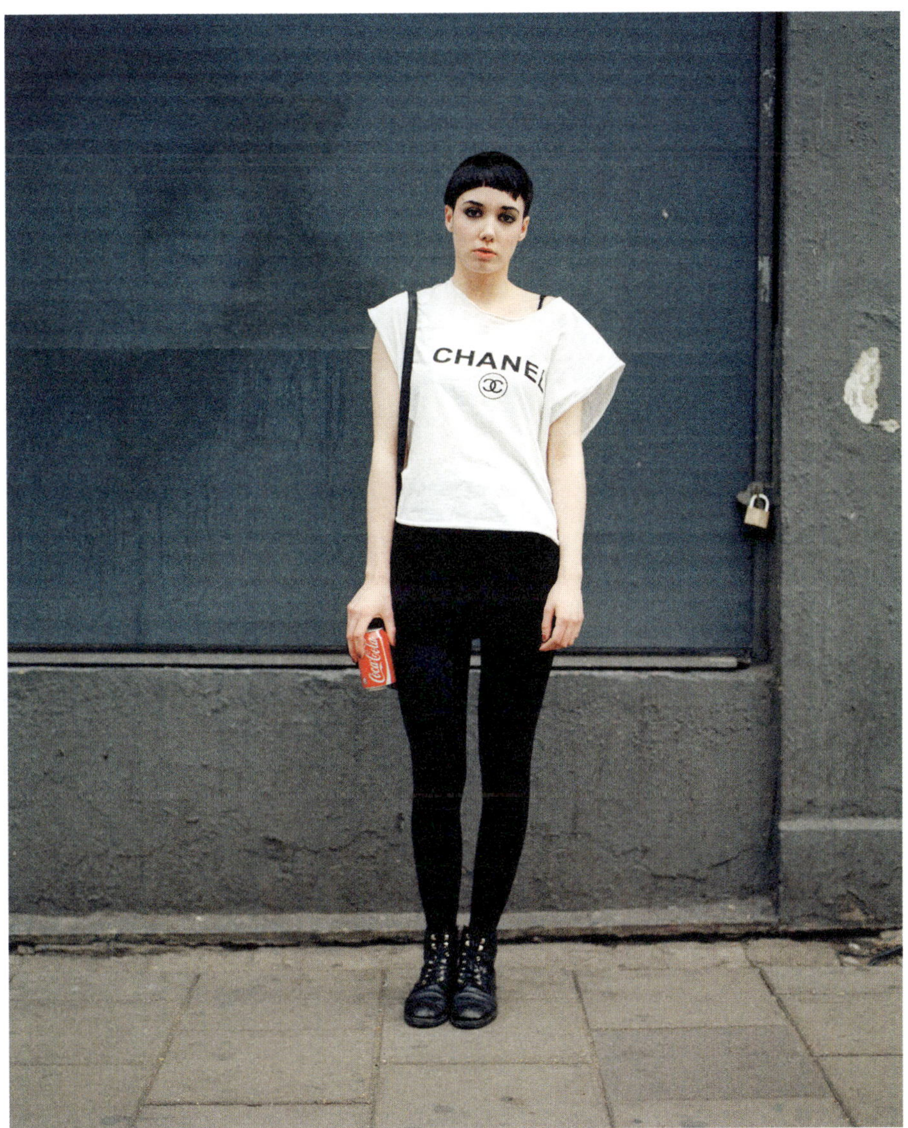
CHANEL
Coca-Cola

'It was the best of times, it was the worst of times, it was the age of wisdom, it was the age of foolishness, it was the epoch of belief, it was the epoch of incredulity, it was the season of Light, it was the season of Darkness, it was the spring of hope, it was the winter of despair, we had everything before us, we had nothing before us, we were all going direct to Heaven, we were all going direct the other way ...'

A Tale of Two Cities, Charles Dickens (1812–1870)

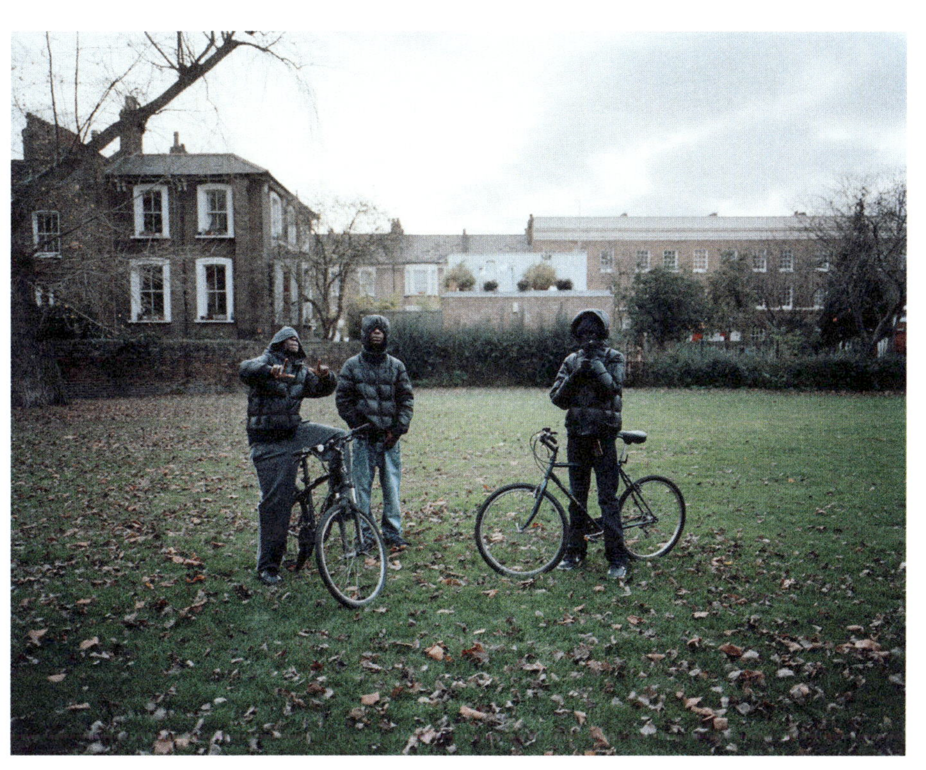

LOST IN THE CITY

NICHOLAS SACK

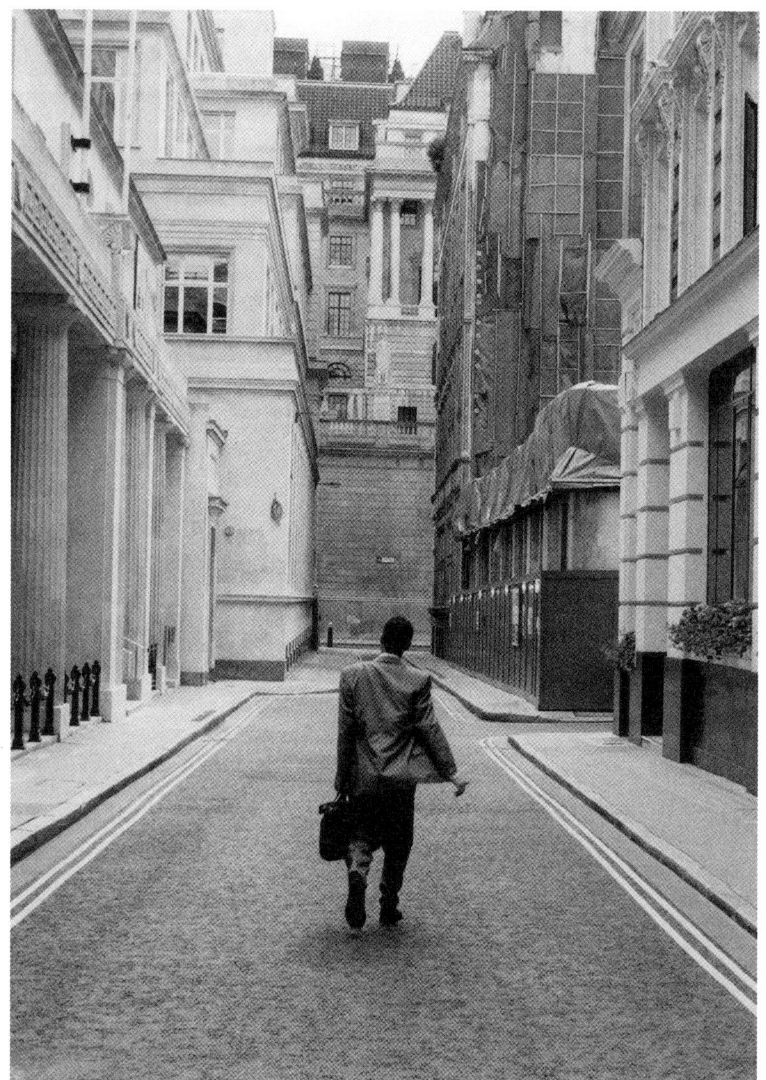

Venture down to the City on the weekend and you'll find a strange place. While the rest of East London heaves with visitors, the Square Mile falls silent. Dominated by austere-looking buildings, pretty much devoid of nature, it doesn't quite feel like a real place, more of an empty set. But Monday to Friday is showtime at the London Stock Exchange and Nicholas Sack has been quietly capturing street scenes round here, mostly during lunchtime, for some three decades.

Initially attracted by the financial district's unique architecture, the photographer's focus shifted over the years to the people and their relationship to the buildings – often one of alienation. But there's a rhythm in these neat geometric configurations. Sack seeks out patterns. He watches and waits until light and shadow, line and shape, concrete and flesh arrange themselves in his frame.

These anonymous figures – particularly the men, with their matching suits and briefcases – at times have a comic air. As they unconsciously fall into step with one another, Sack sees John Cleese and his Ministry of Silly Walks. But, through our post financial crisis lens, there's invariably an undertone of seriousness to these pictures, too. In the great crash of 2008, money, jobs and morals were lost in the City. Perhaps they will never be found.

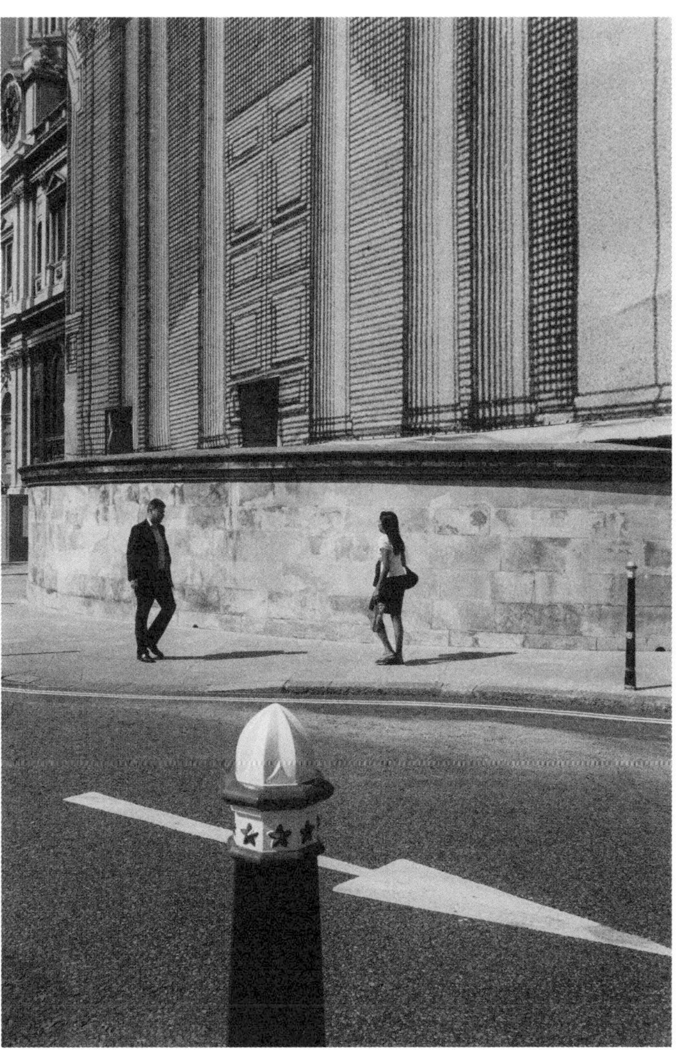

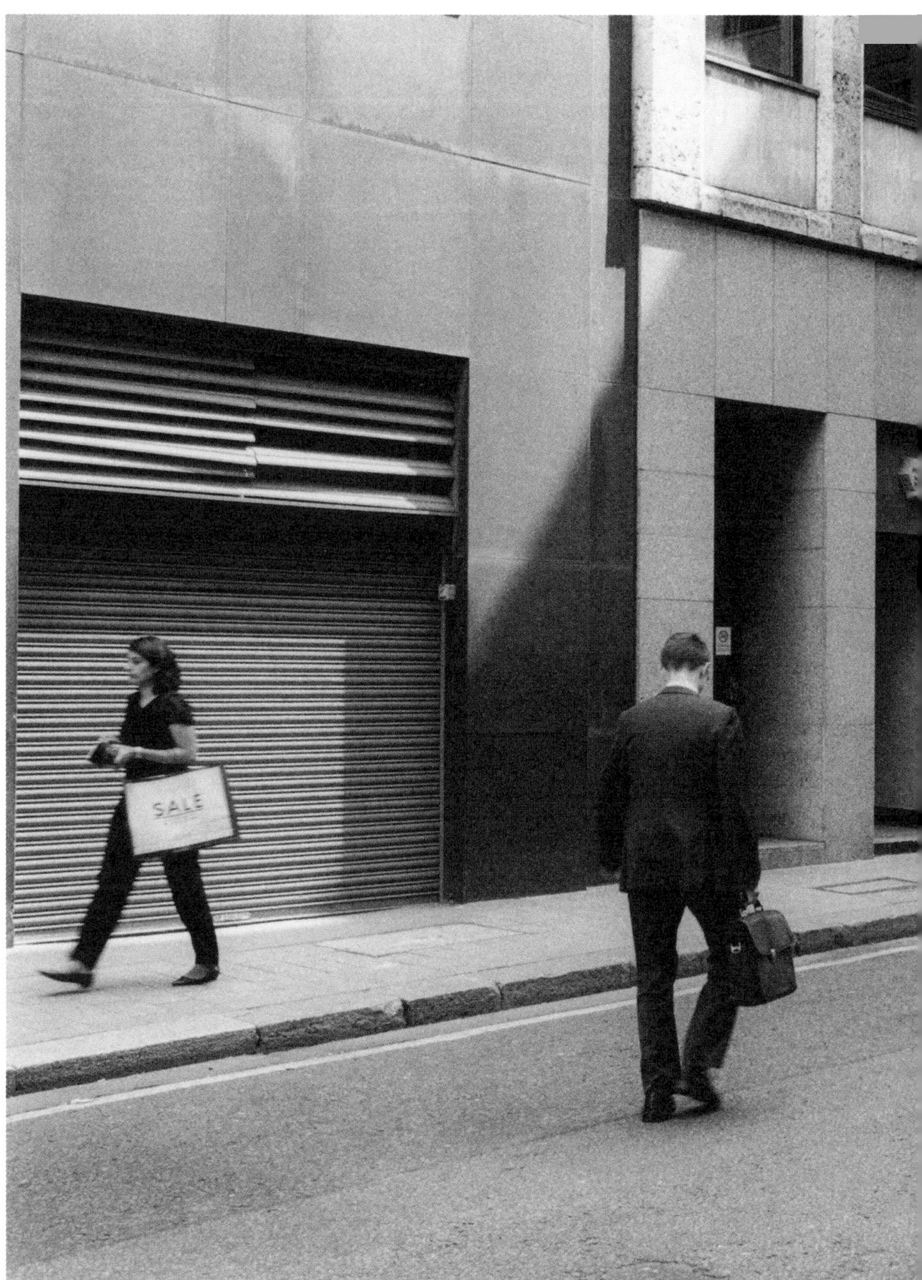
SALE

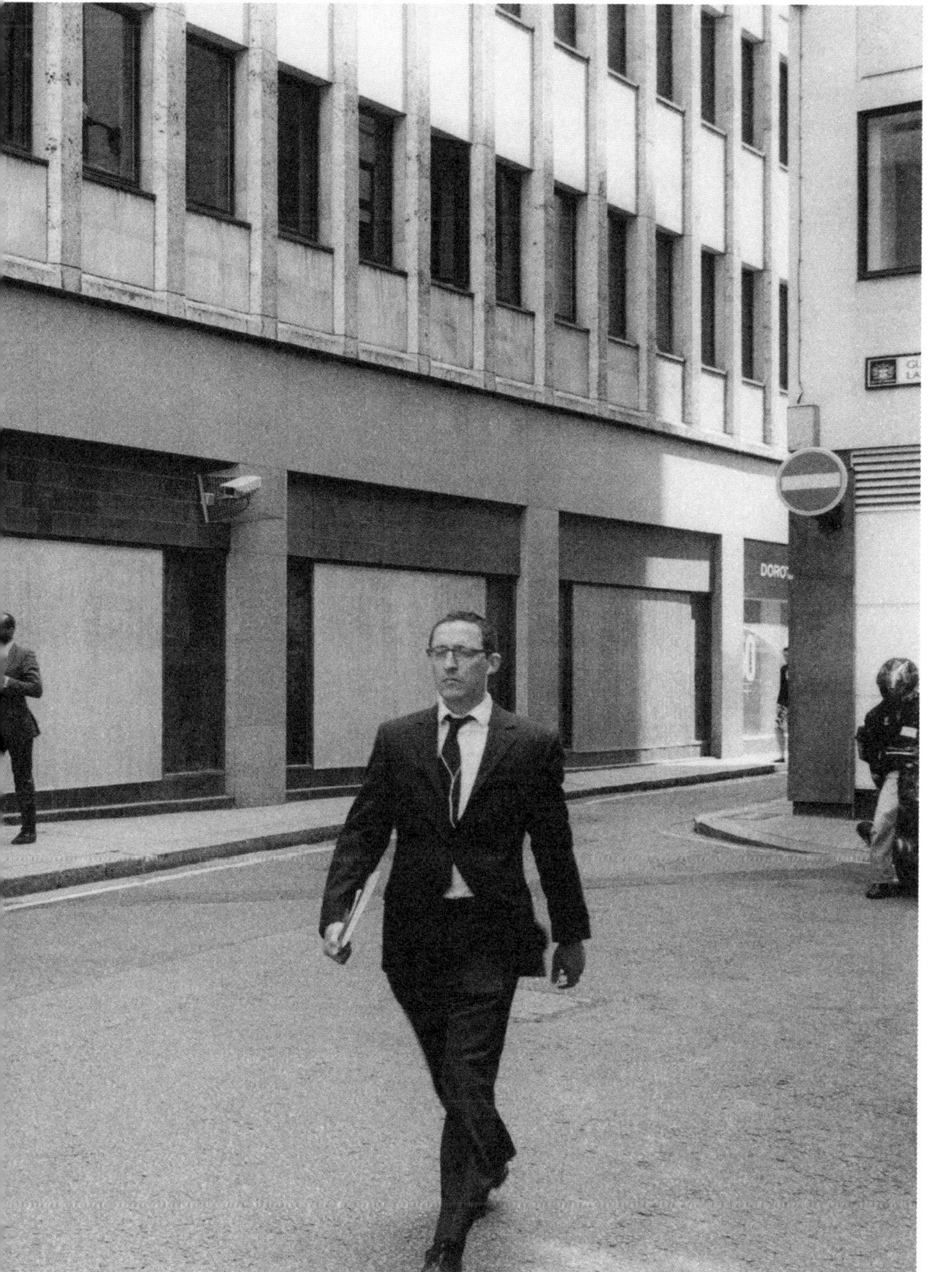

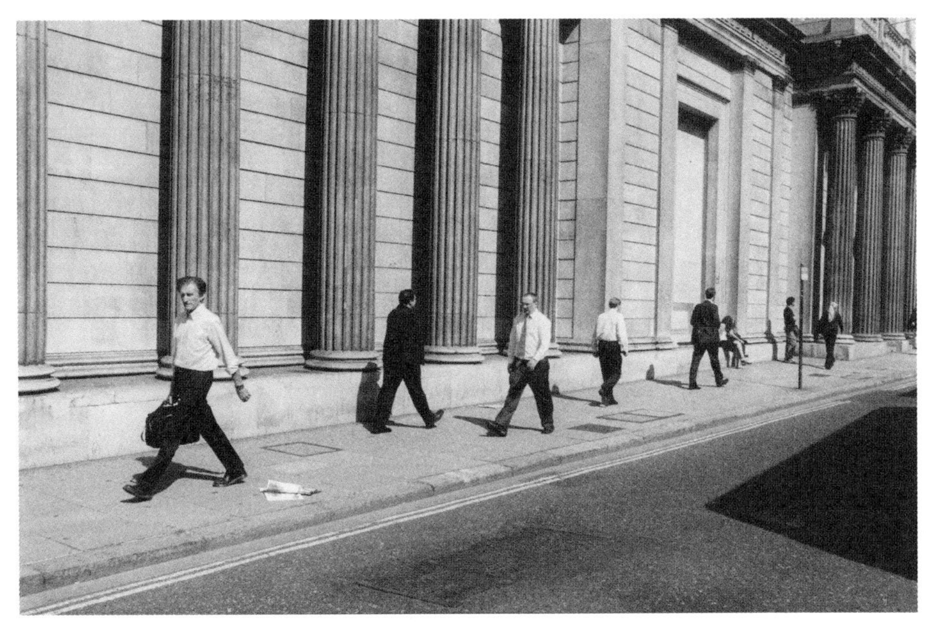

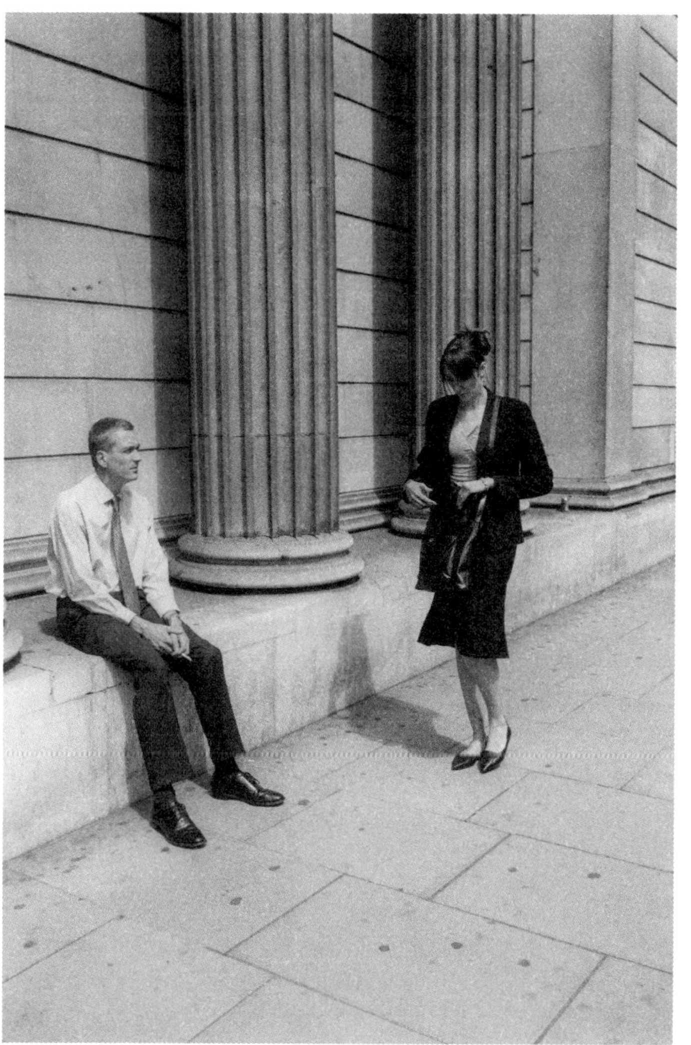

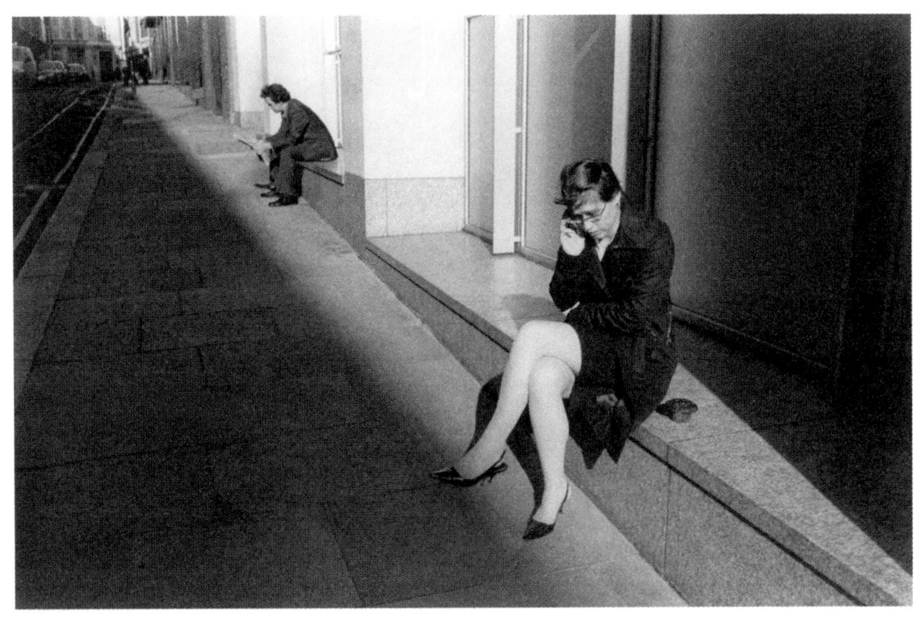

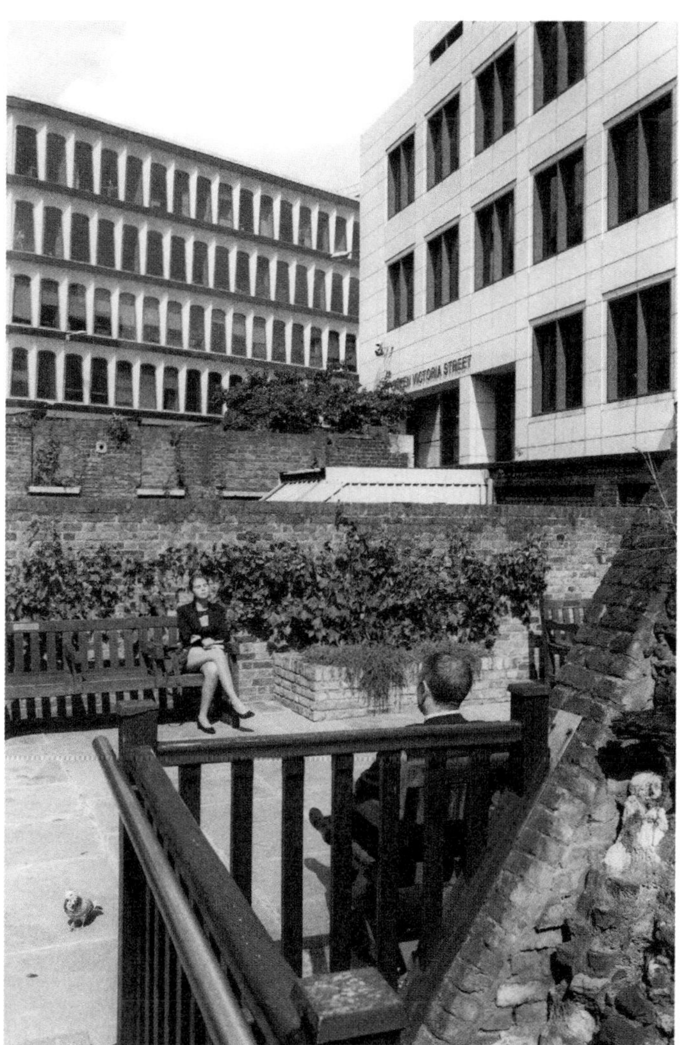
QUEEN VICTORIA STREET

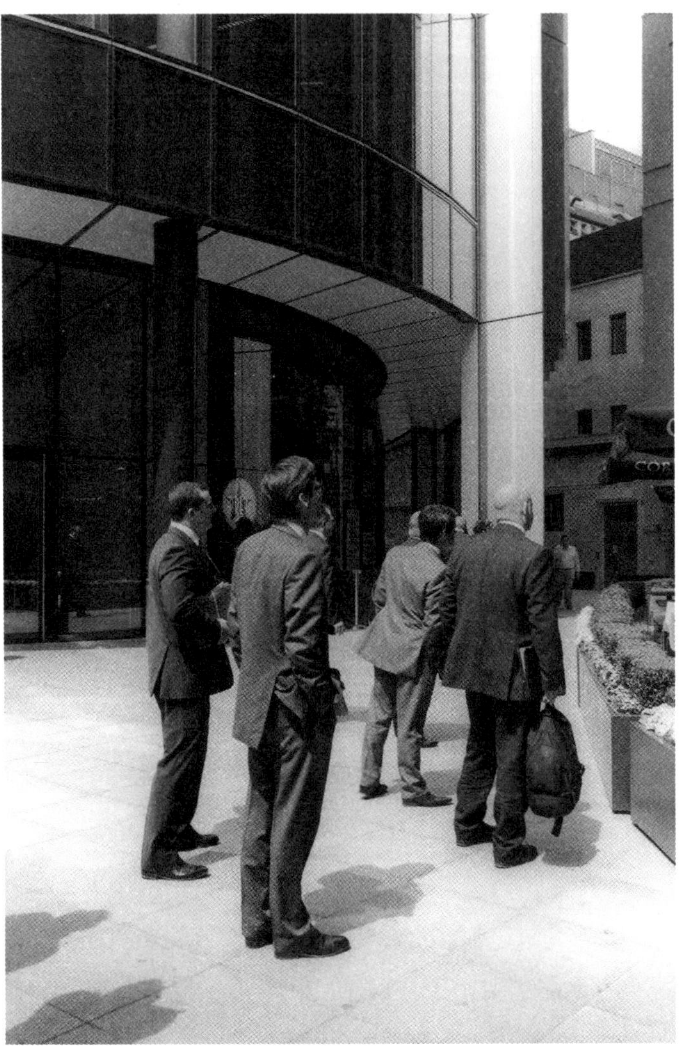

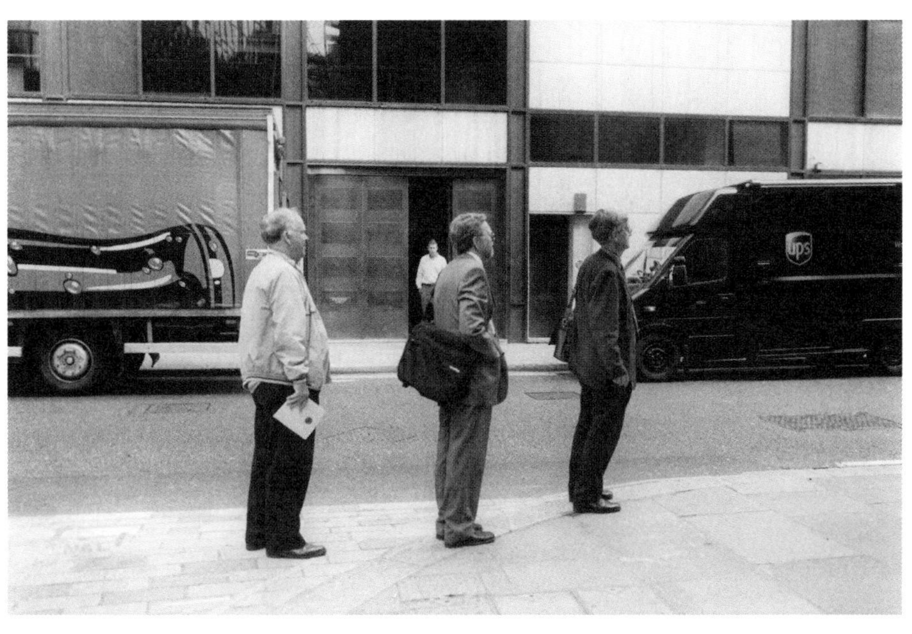

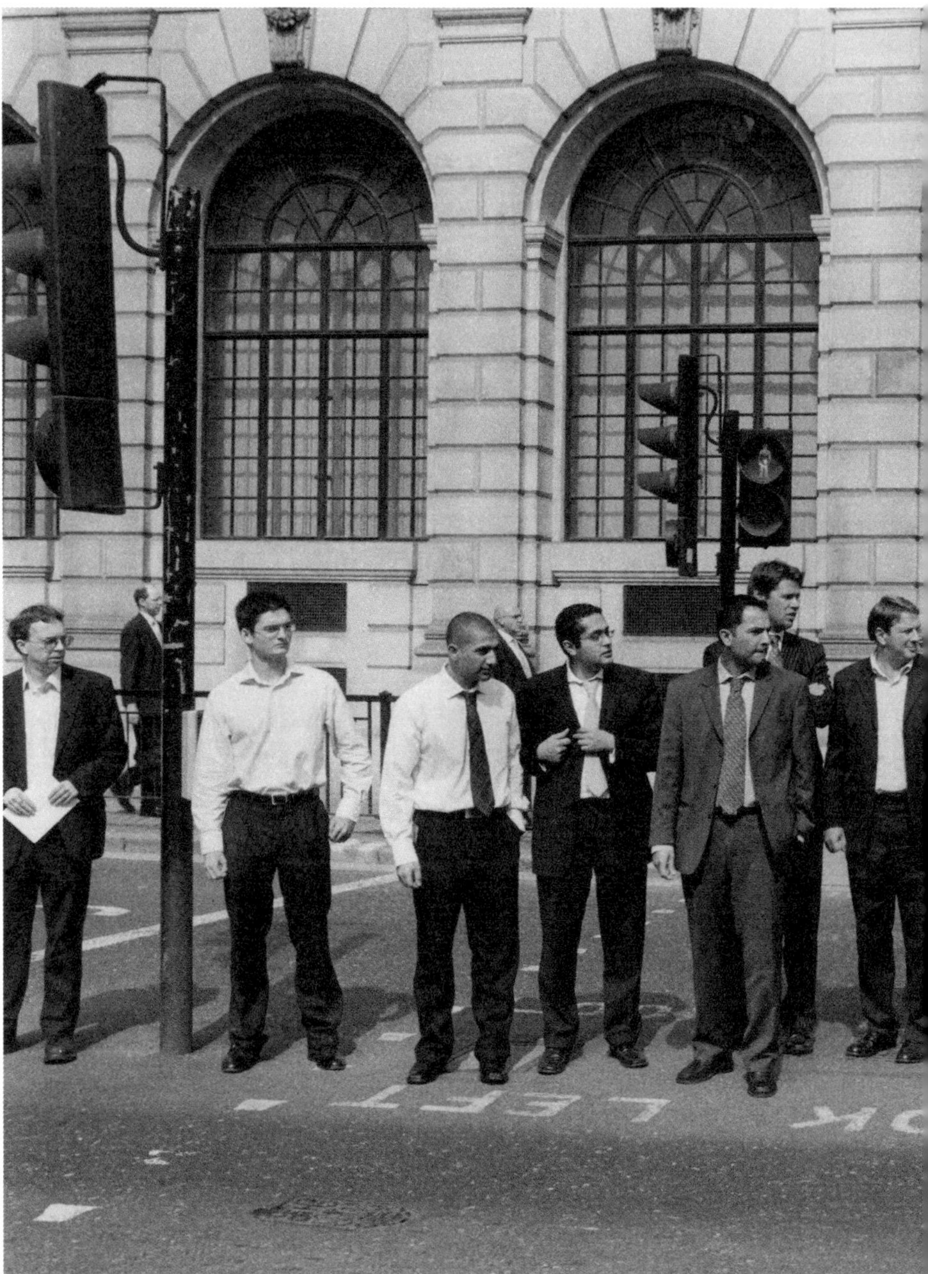

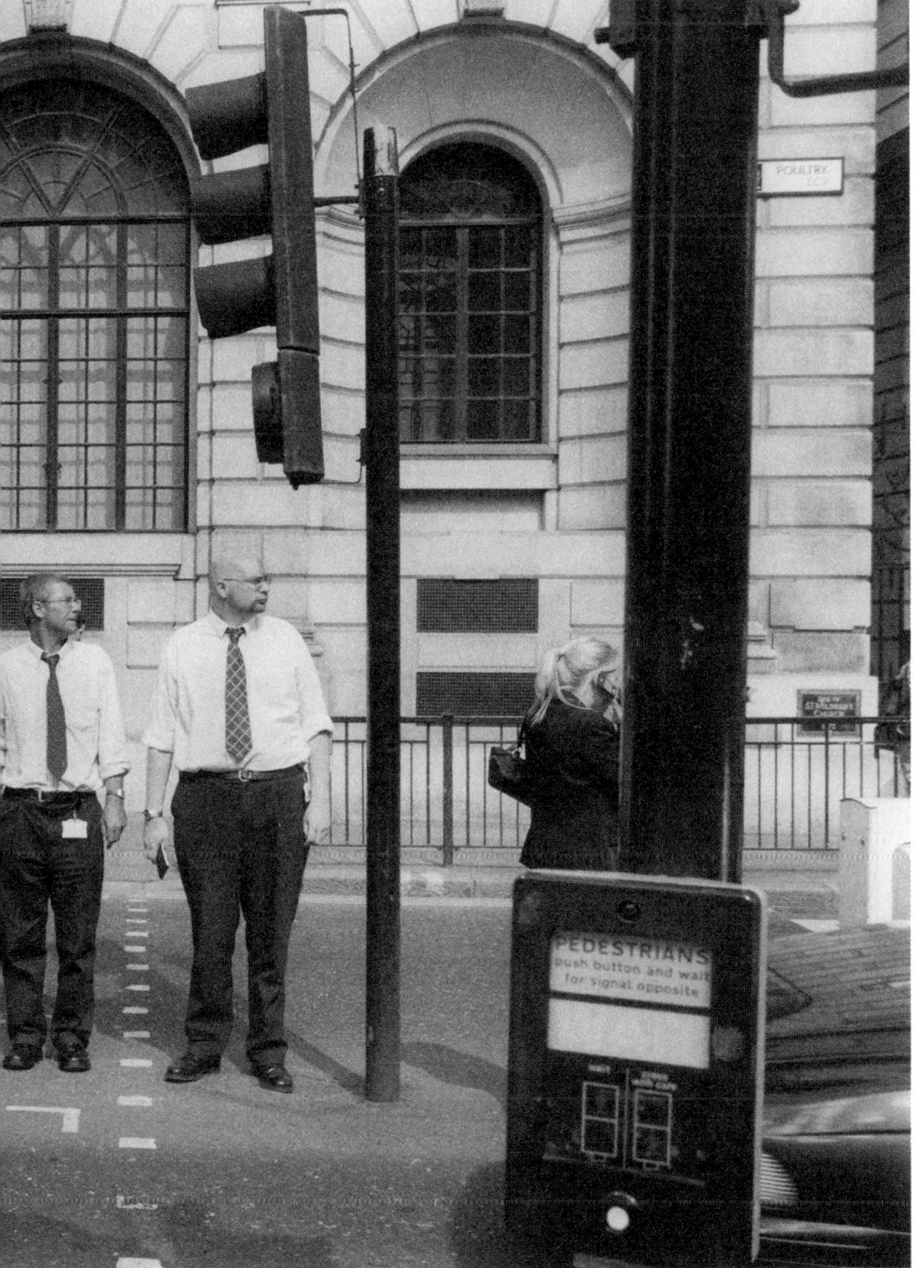
POULTRY
EC2
PEDESTRIANS
push button and wait
for signal opposite

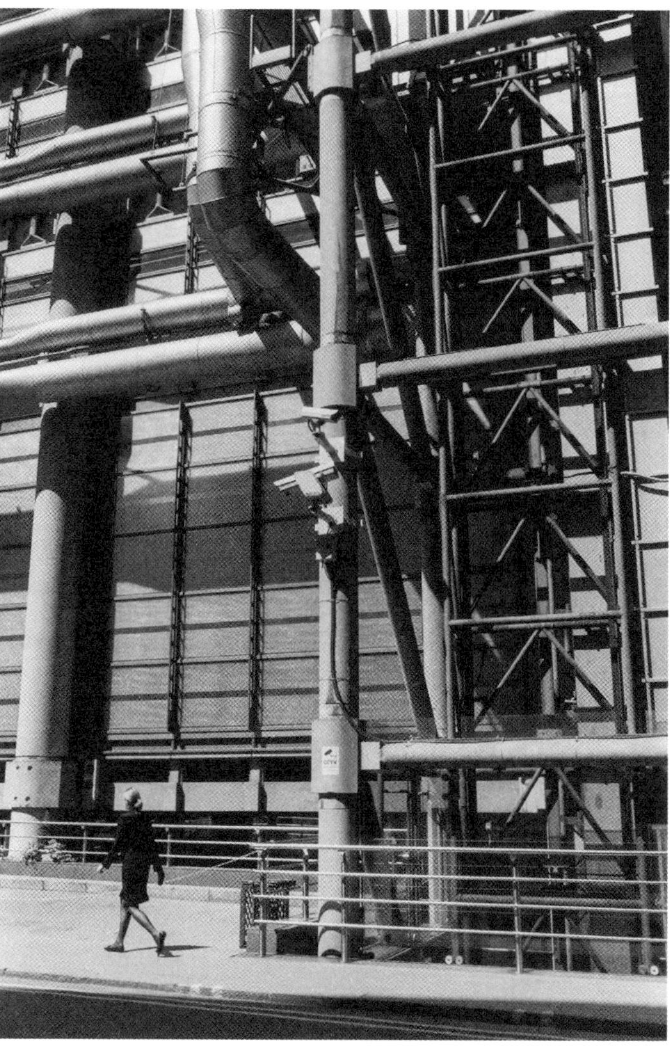

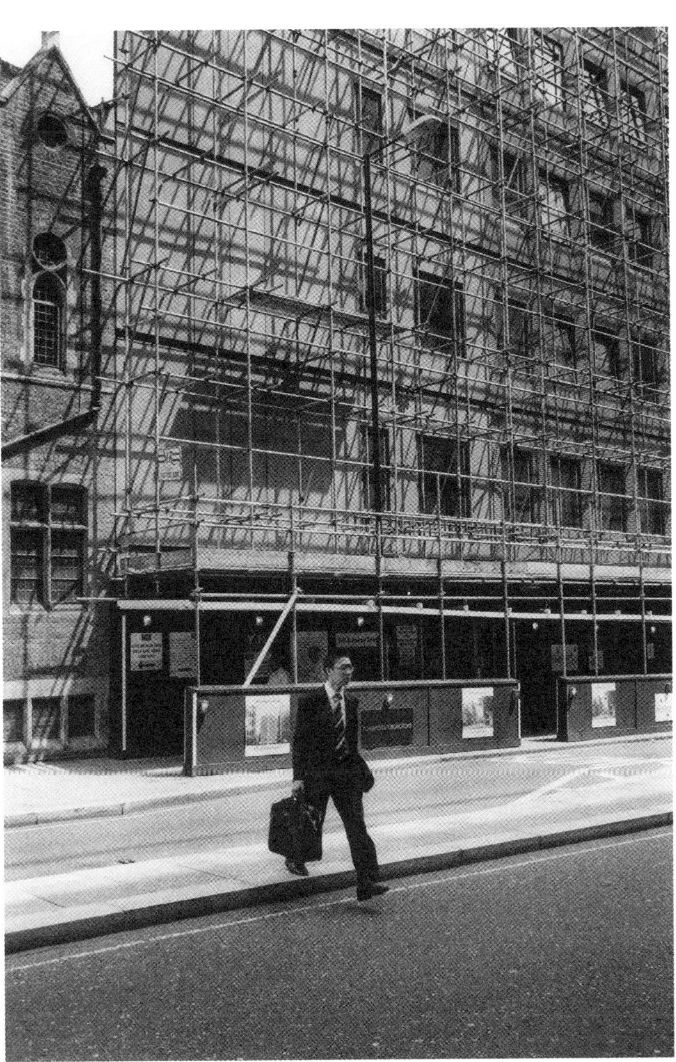

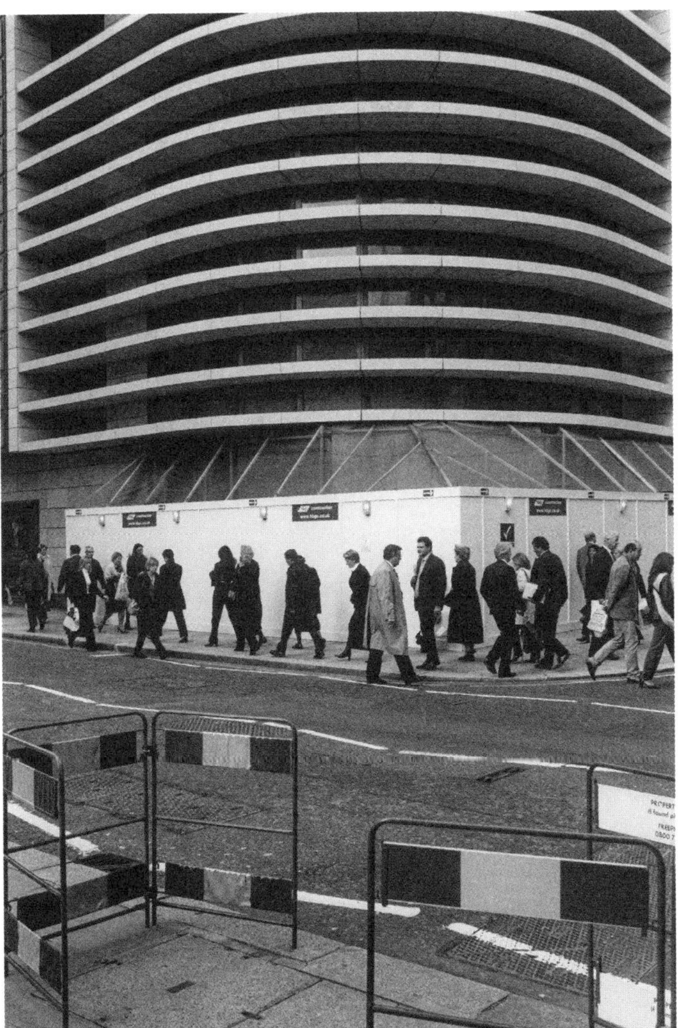

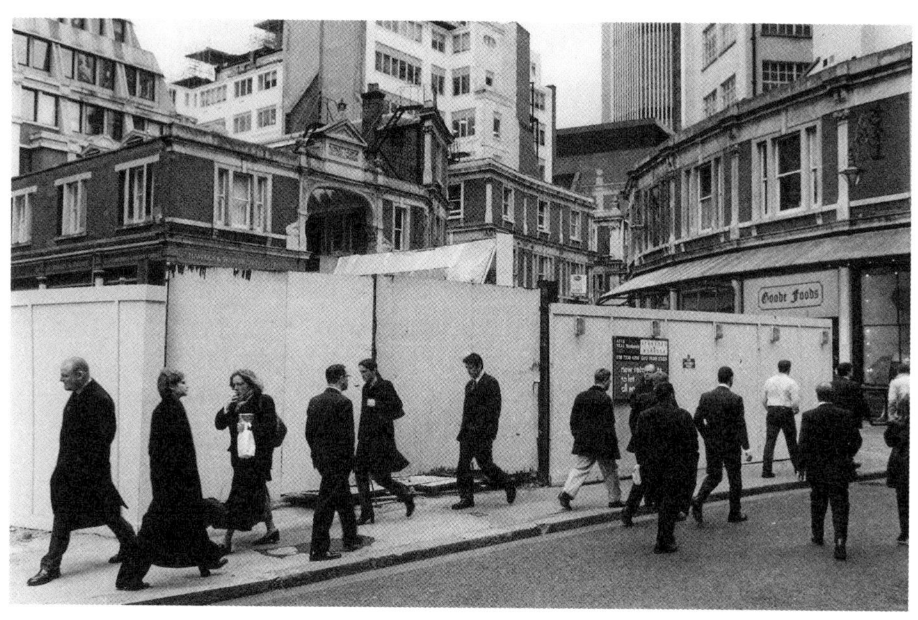

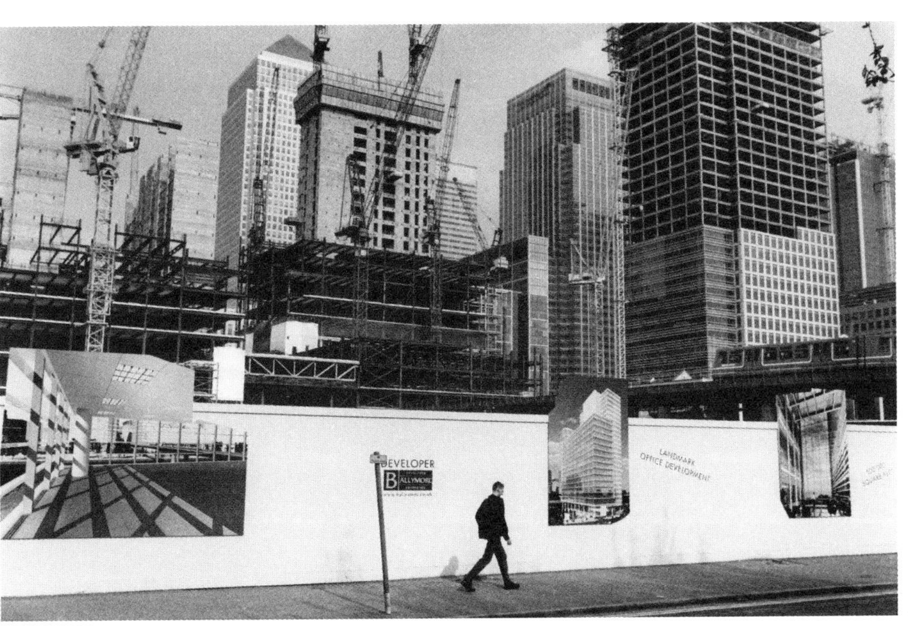
DEVELOPER
BALLYMORE
LANDMARK
OFFICE DEVELOPMENT

COLUMBIA ROAD

JOHANNA NEURATH

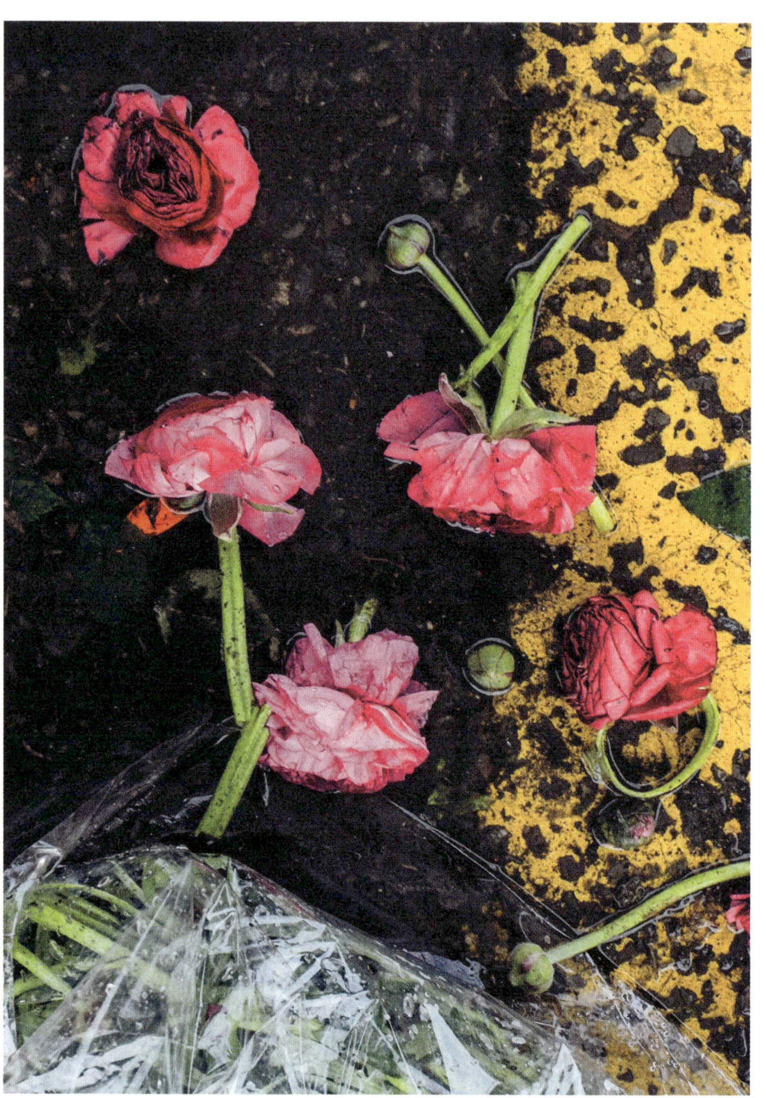

Still lifes of the end-of-day scraps on the pavements around East London's famous flower market.

East London's not short on markets but Columbia Road has got to be one of the most photogenic. For two decades Hackney local Johanna Neurath was there virtually every Sunday. A 'street photographer on high days and holidays' and a design director in illustrated publishing Monday to Friday, she was drawn to the colourful market as a source of inspiration for book covers.

Unlike a typical street photographer, she didn't just shoot what was happening around her – the sea of scarlet tulips, hot pink ranunculus, yellow freesias, snapped up by fashionistas sipping flat whites – she pointed her camera straight down at the rubbish-strewn street itself. What she found there was surprisingly beautiful. Crushed petals and shreds of plastic of every hue floating in shimmering puddles, glinting in the late afternoon sun to form almost abstract canvases.

These are a world away from the artfully arranged, neatly stacked bundles of flora that usually feature in photographs of Columbia Road. But Neurath's no less intentional framing creates a new aesthetic. Her work tells us two things. That, cut flowers, no matter how gorgeous right now, are going to end up rotting in the bin (or hopefully the compost) before too long. And that even in obvious places, timeless pictures can lurk just out of view.

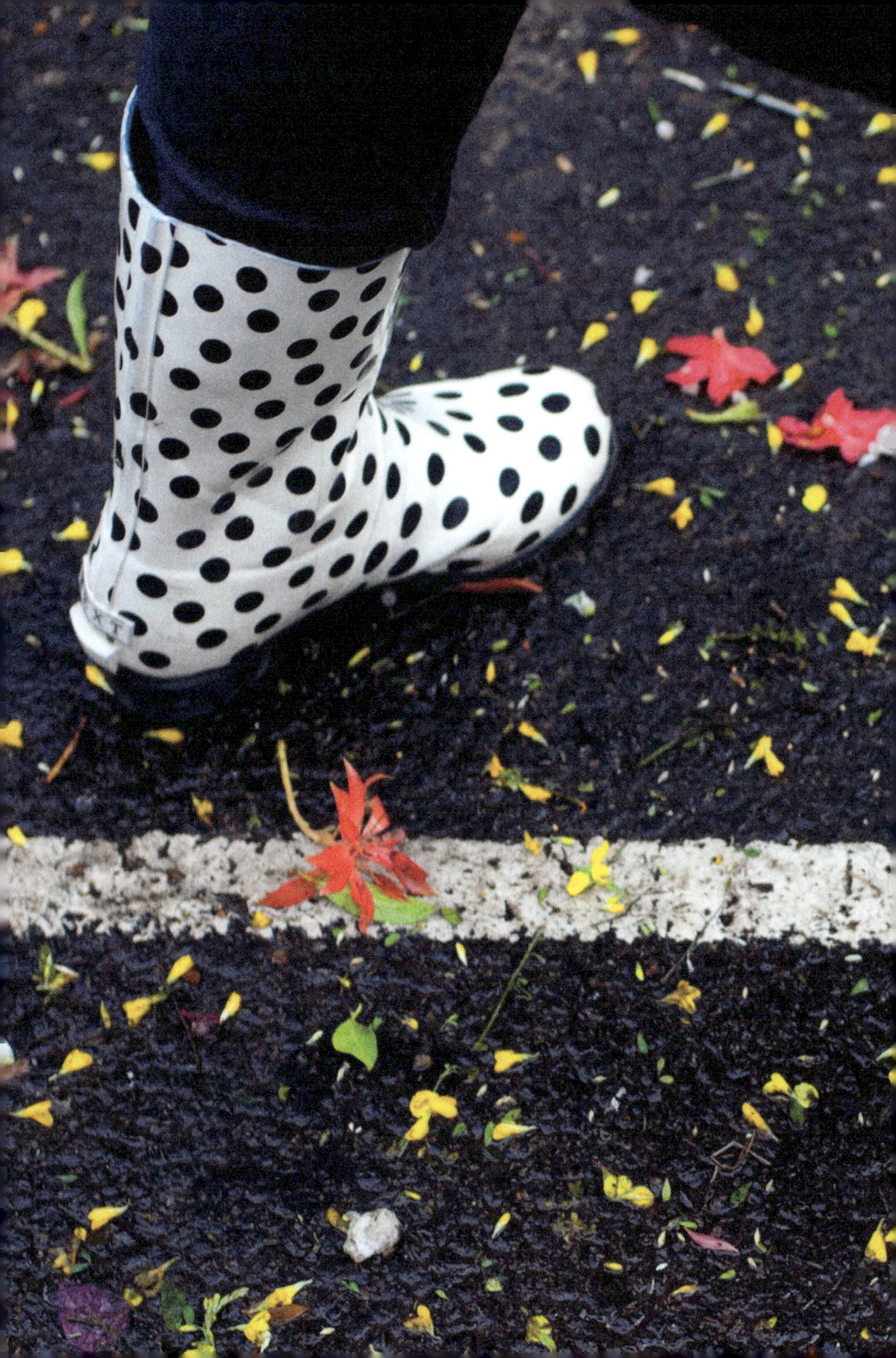

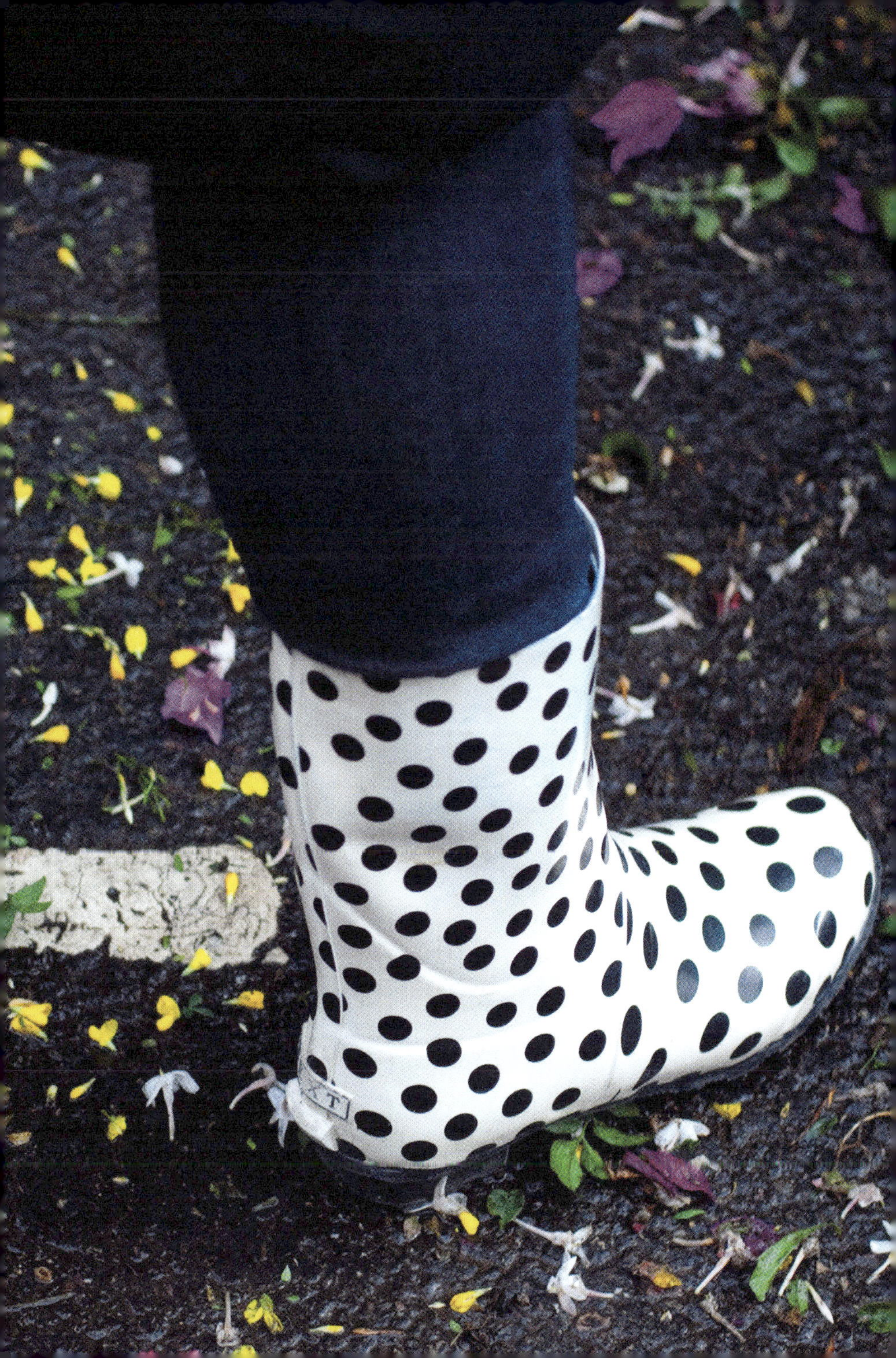

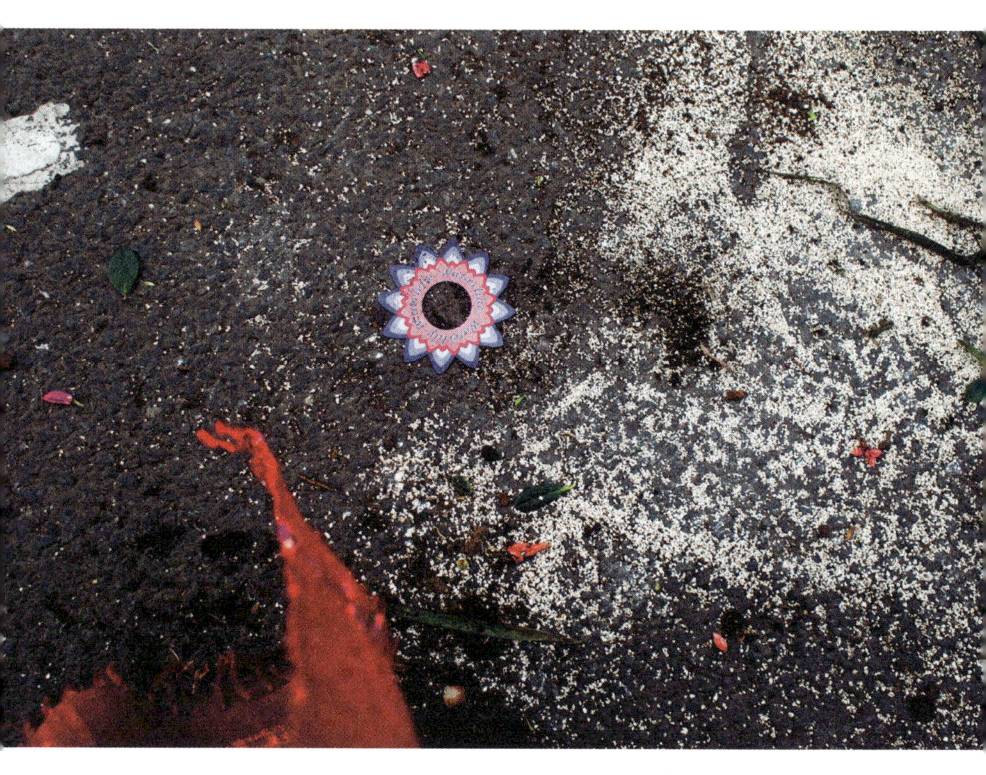

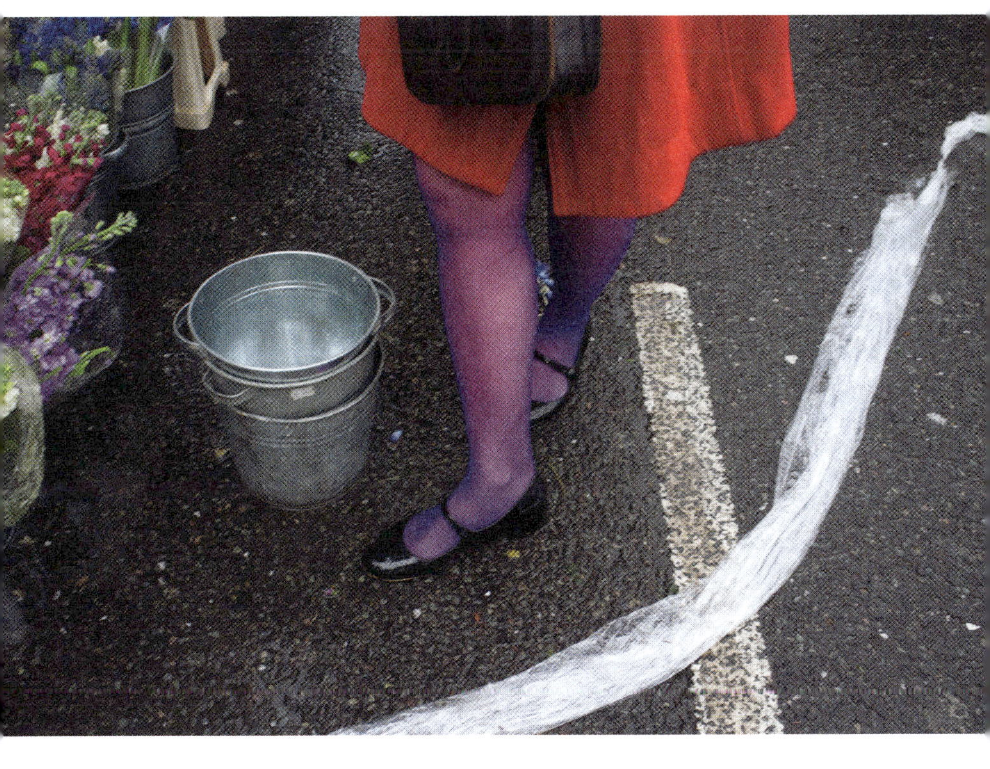

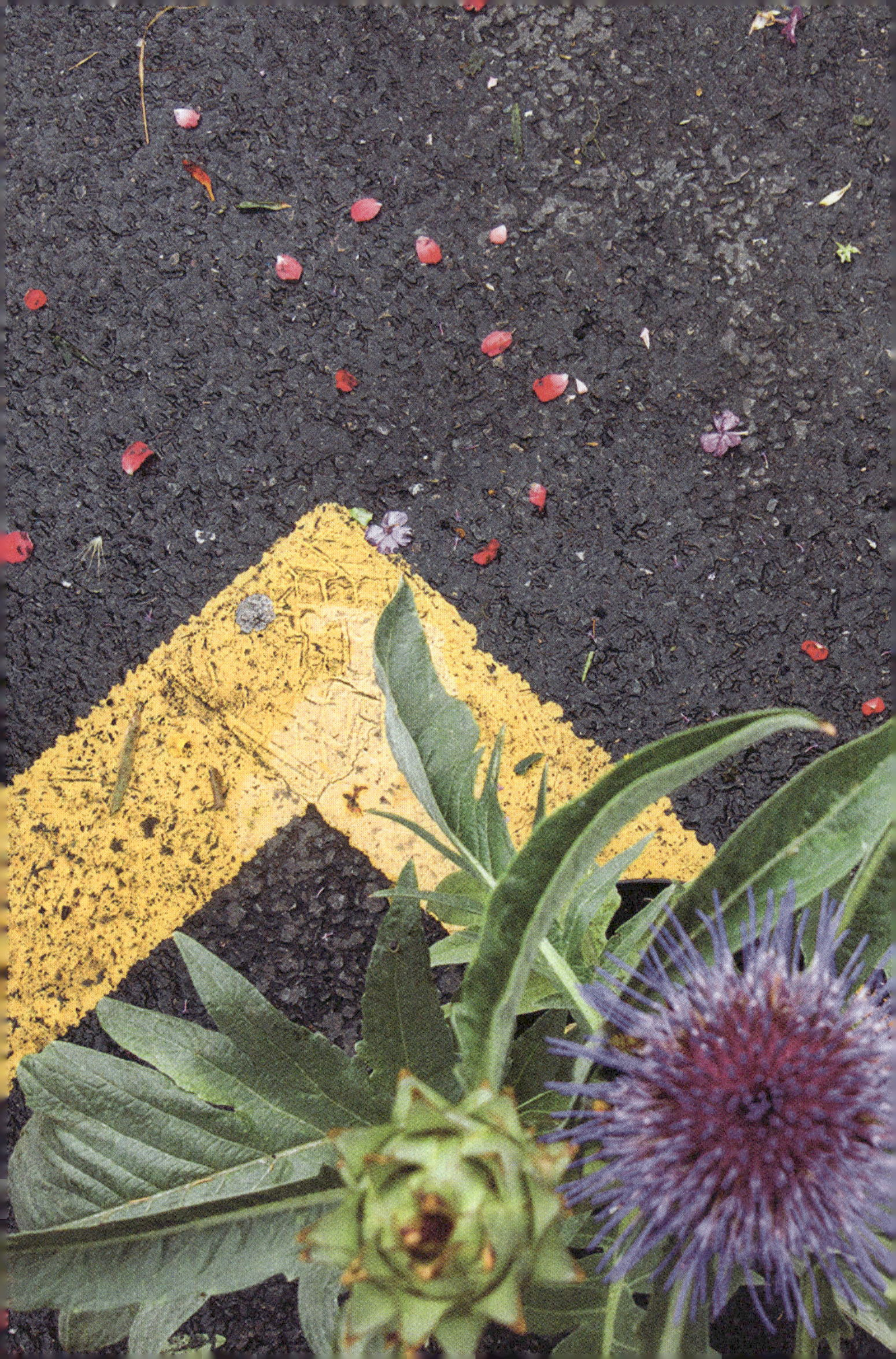

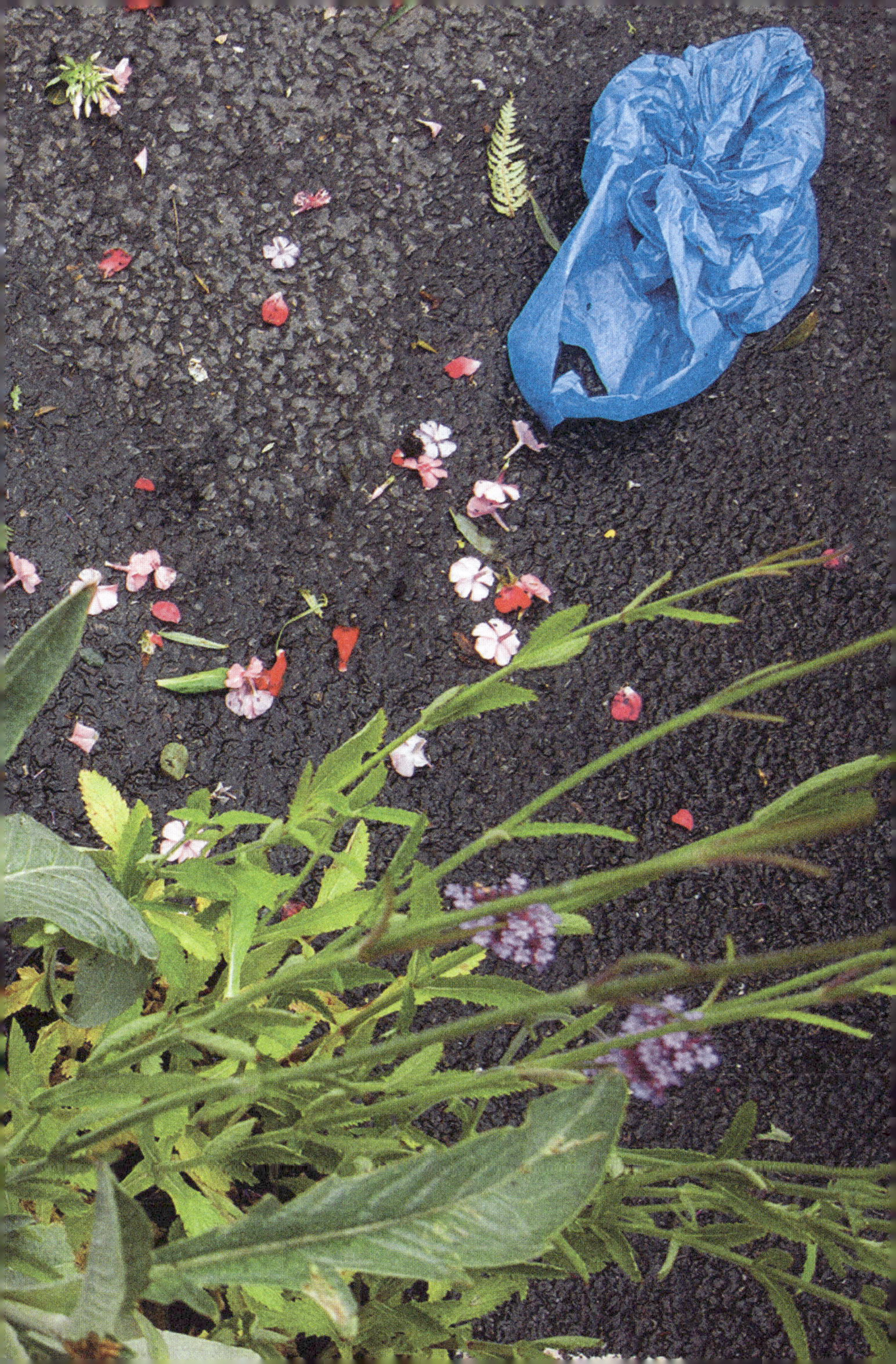

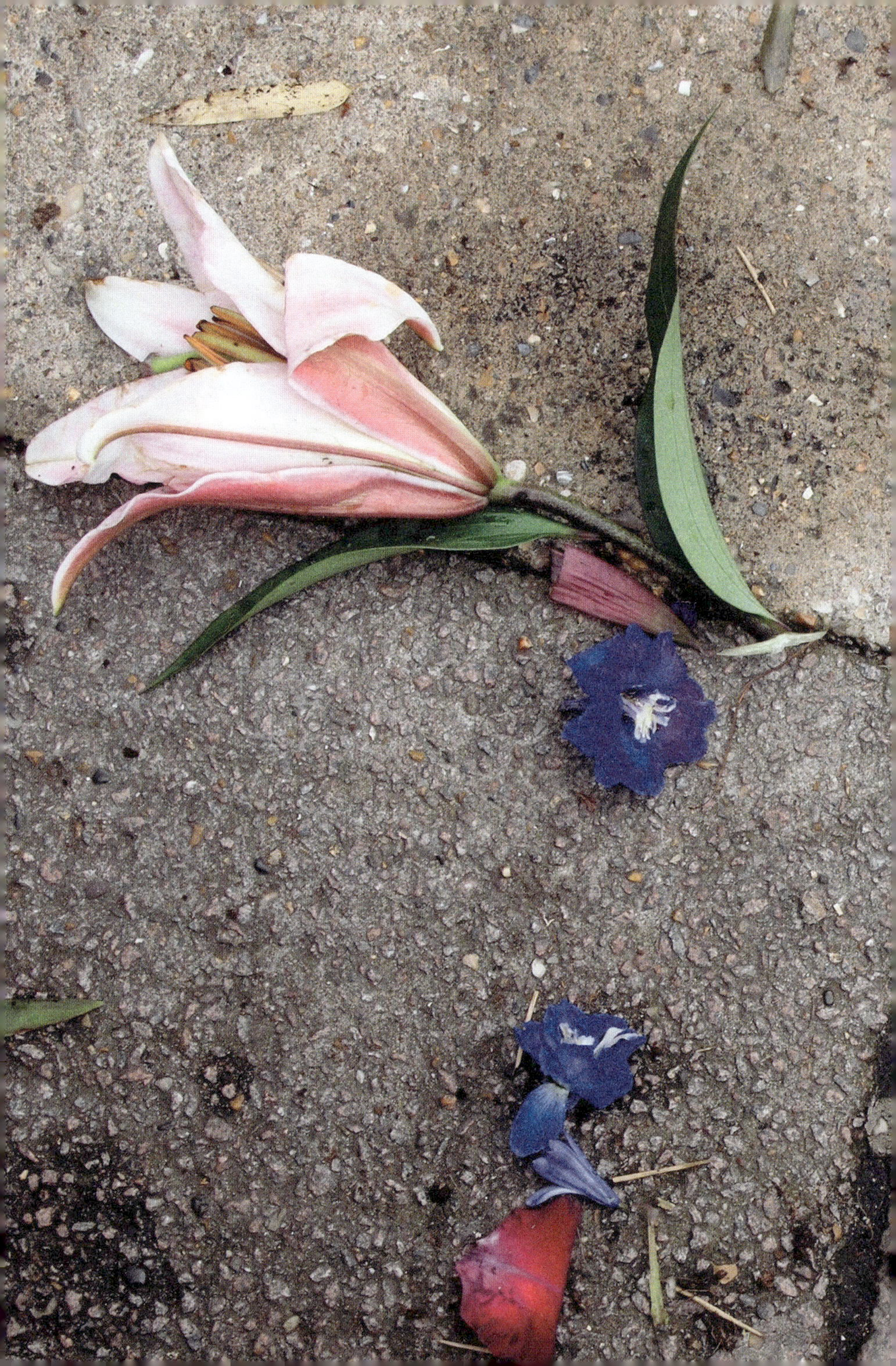

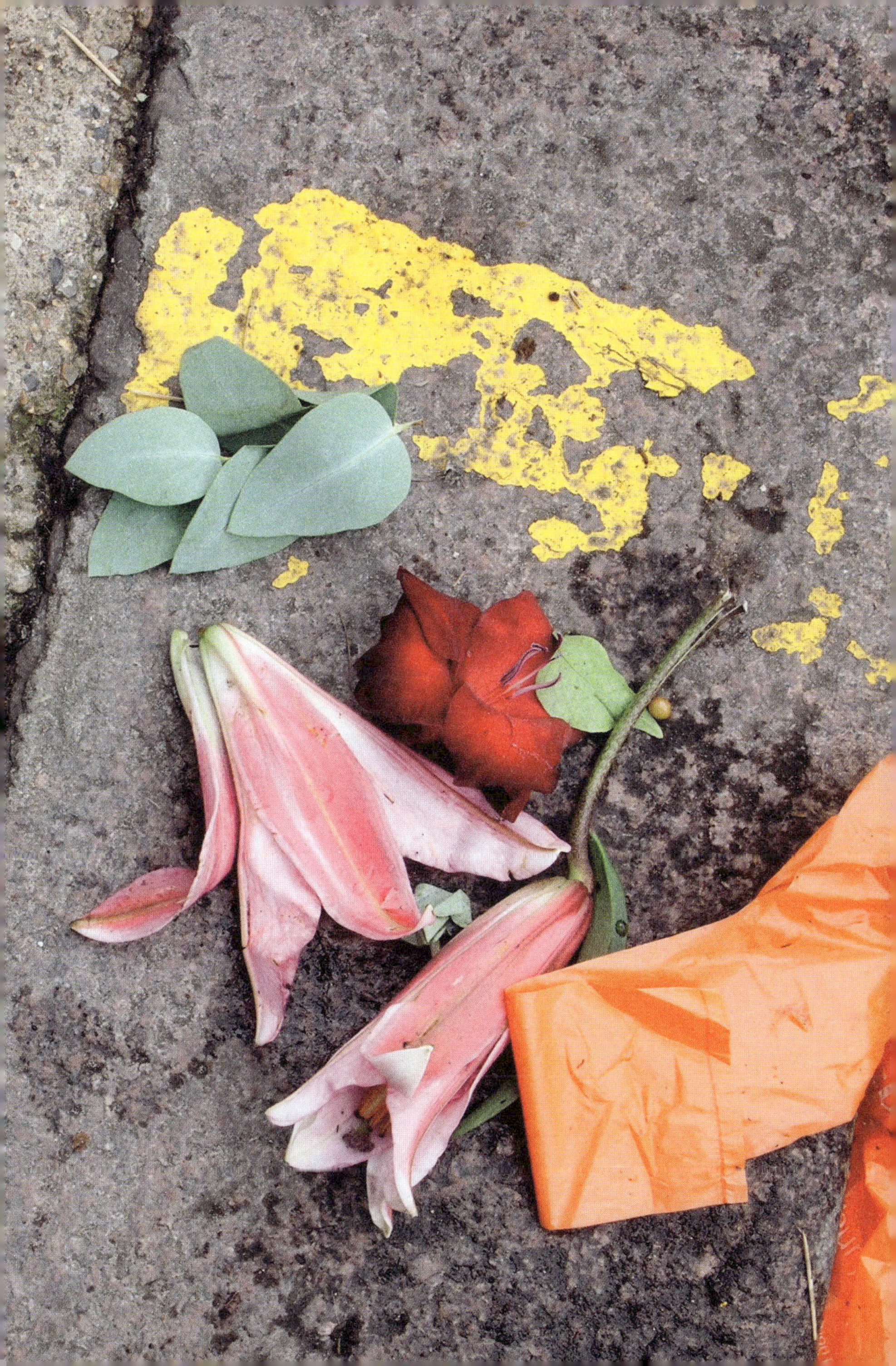

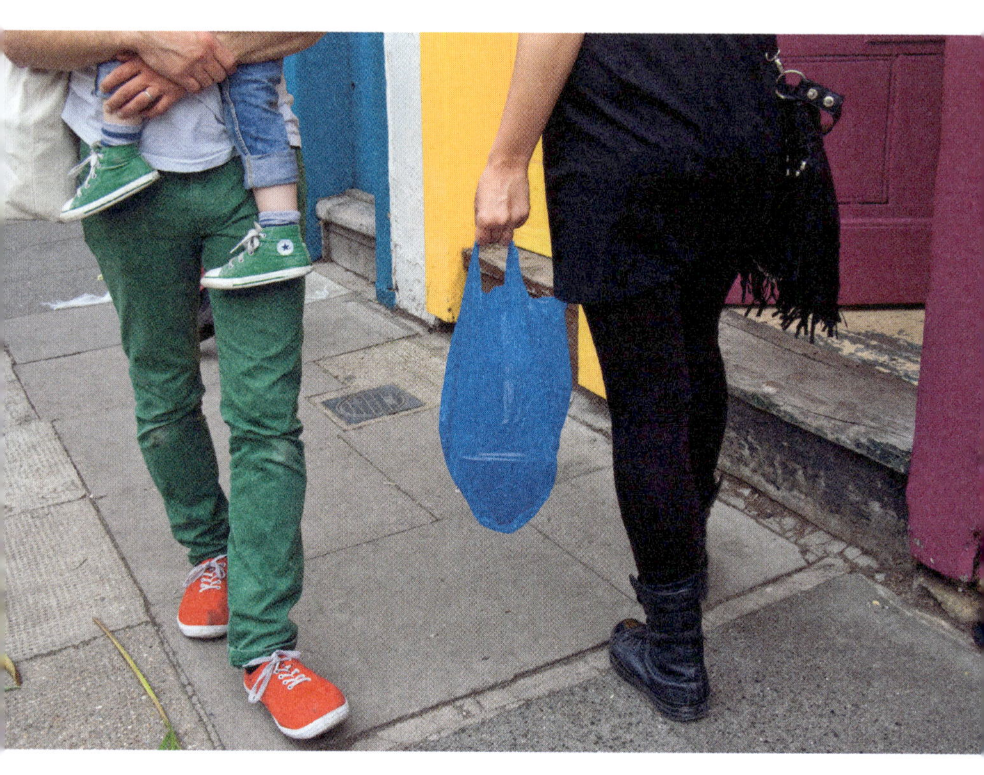

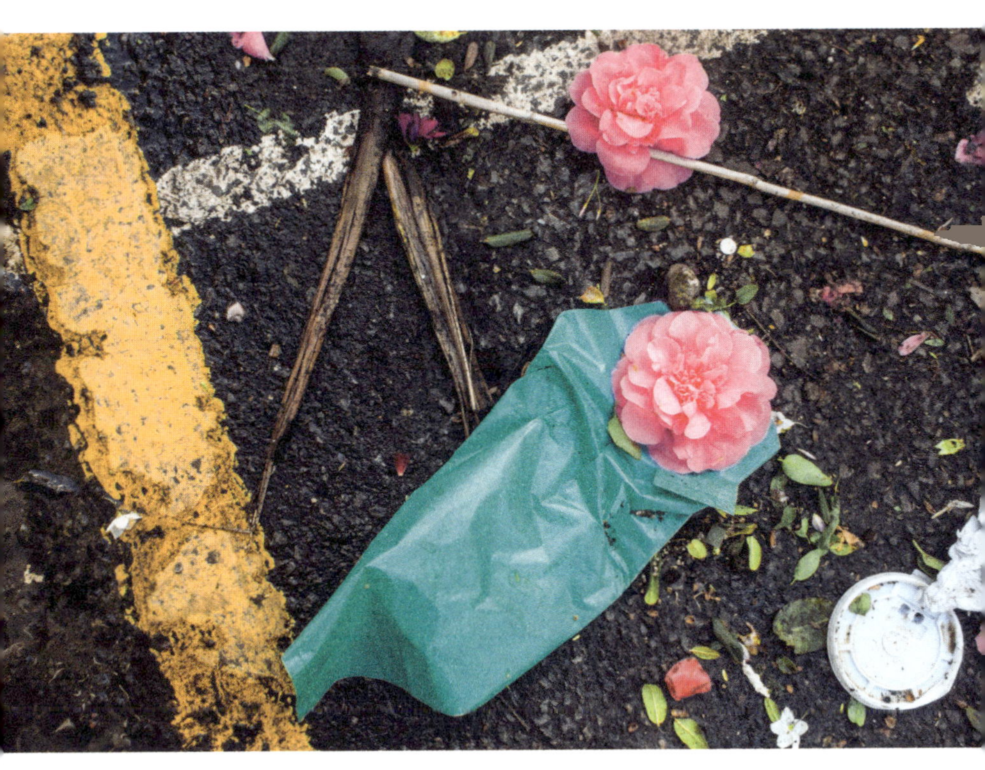

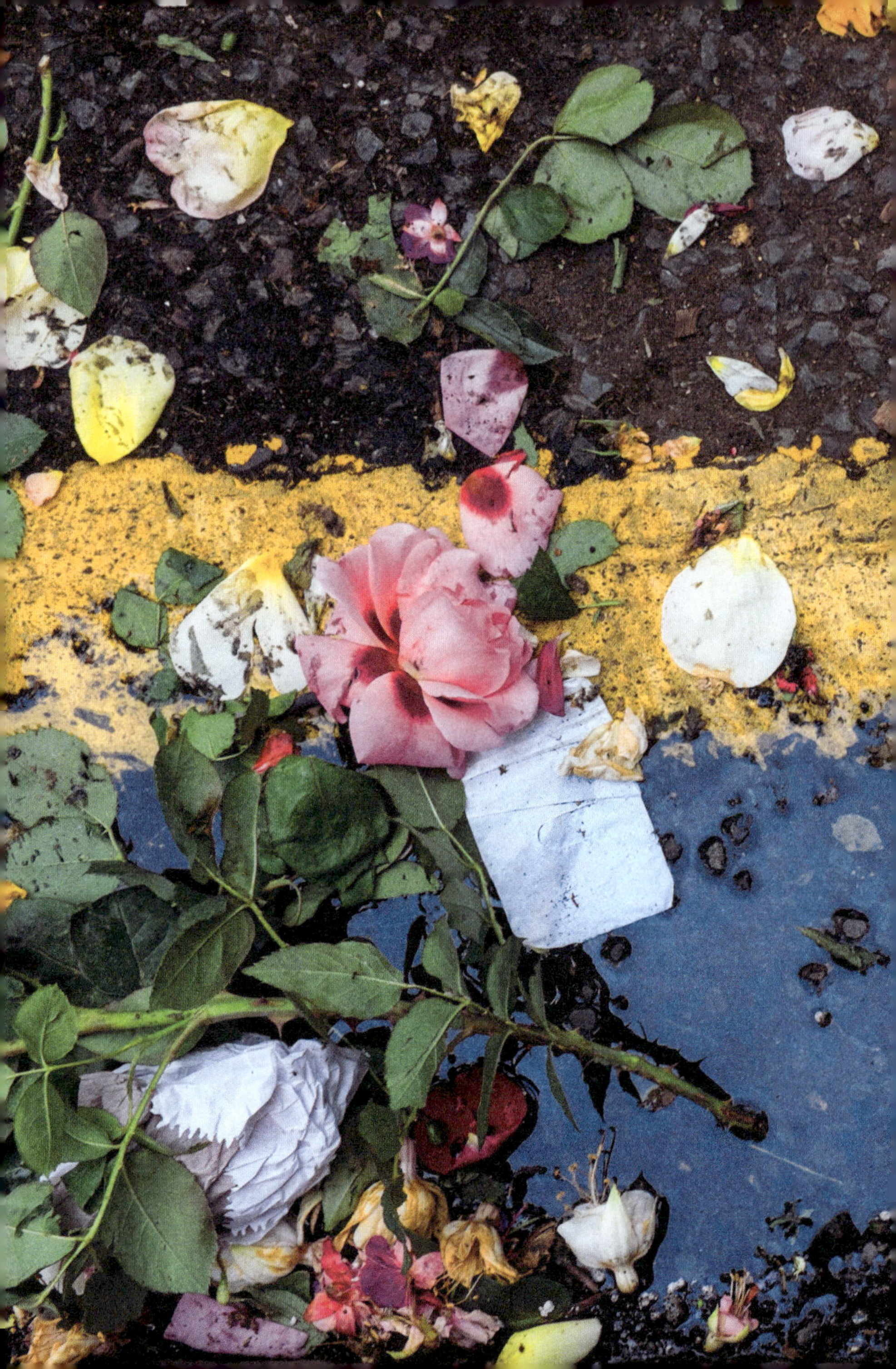

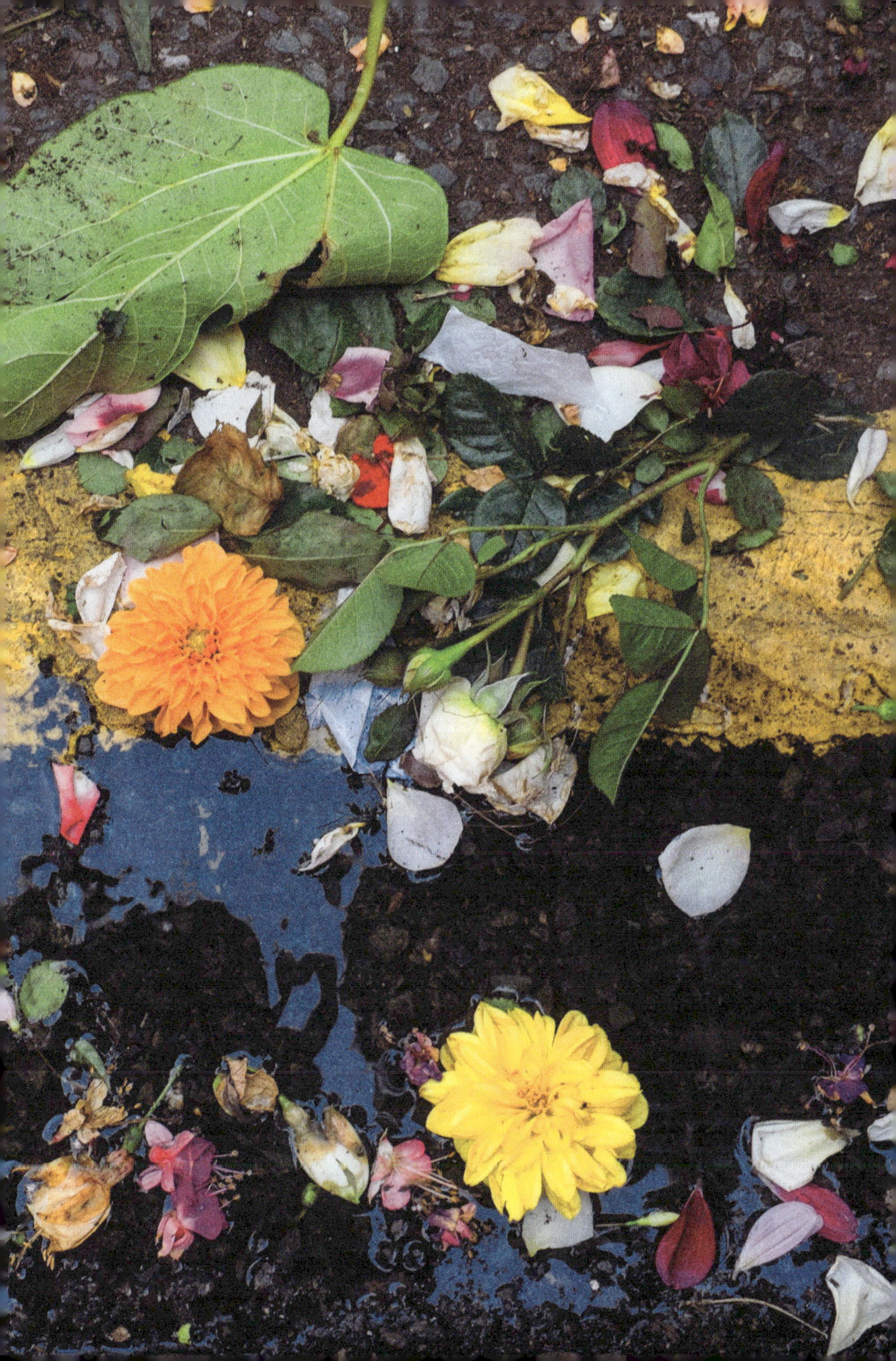

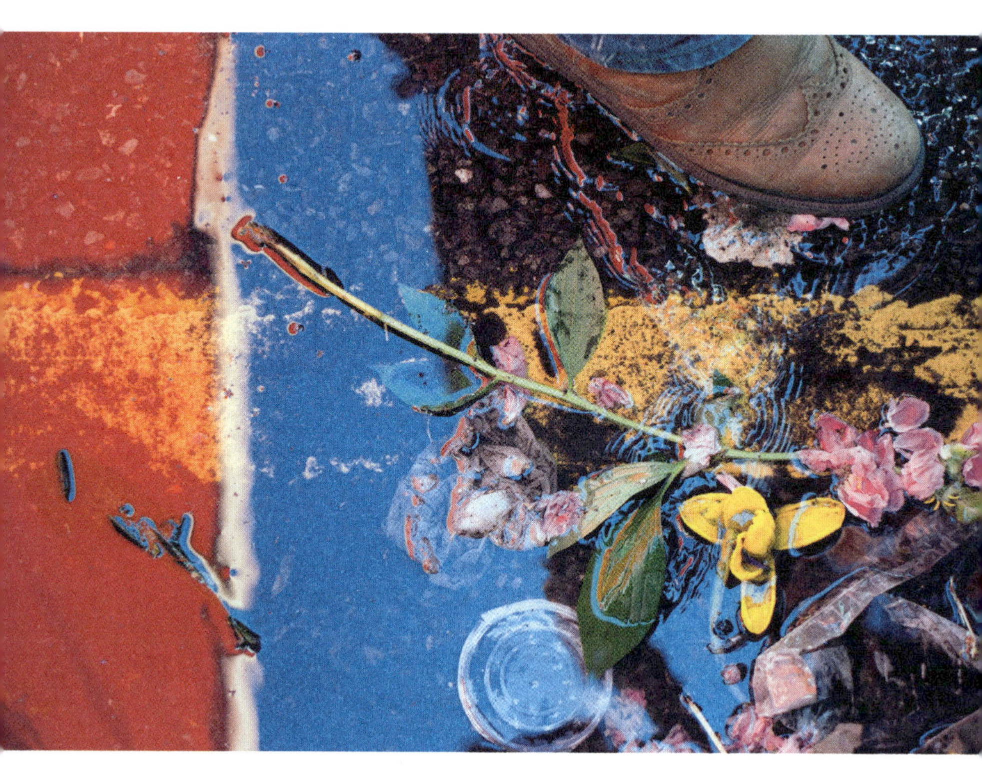

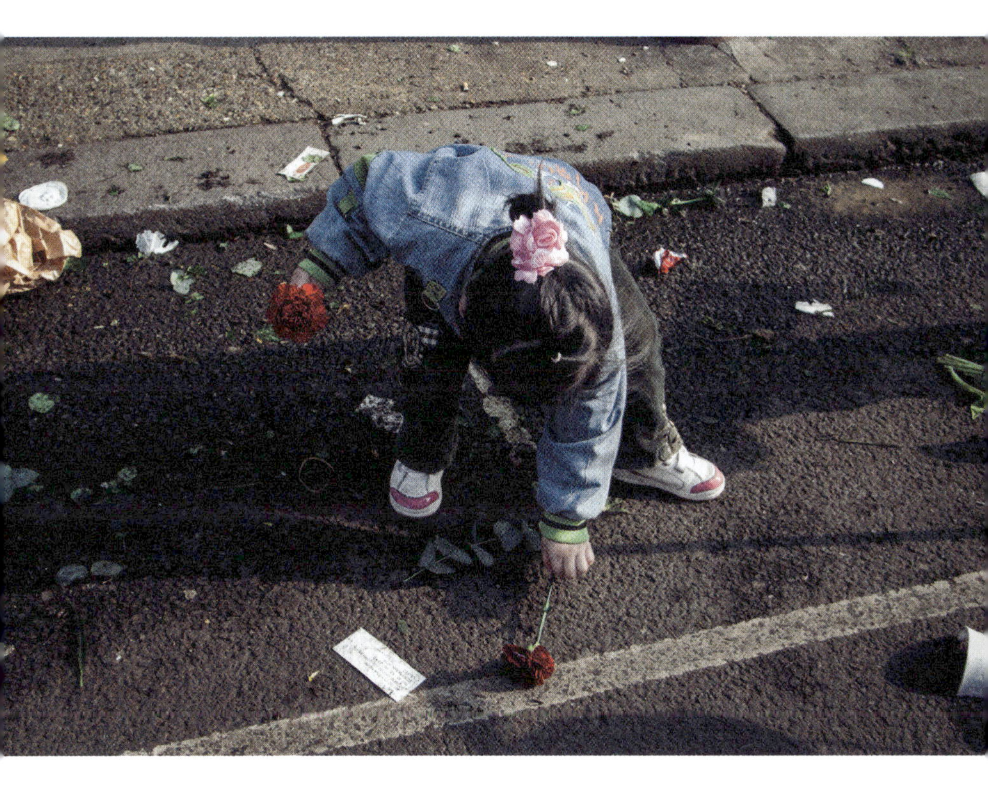

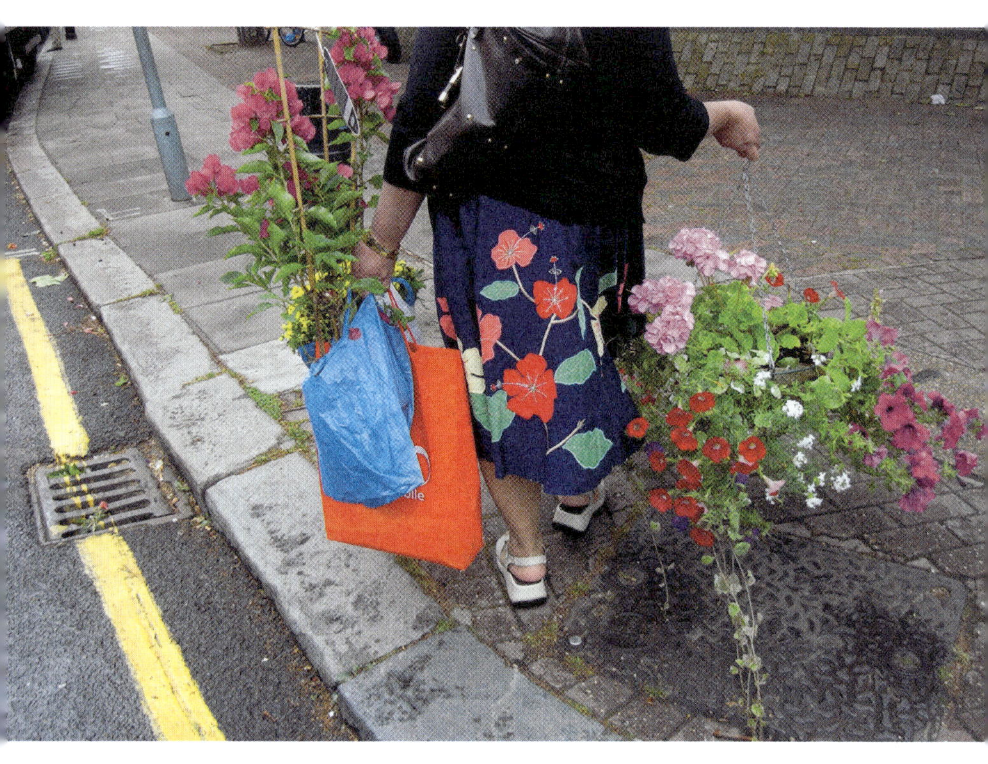

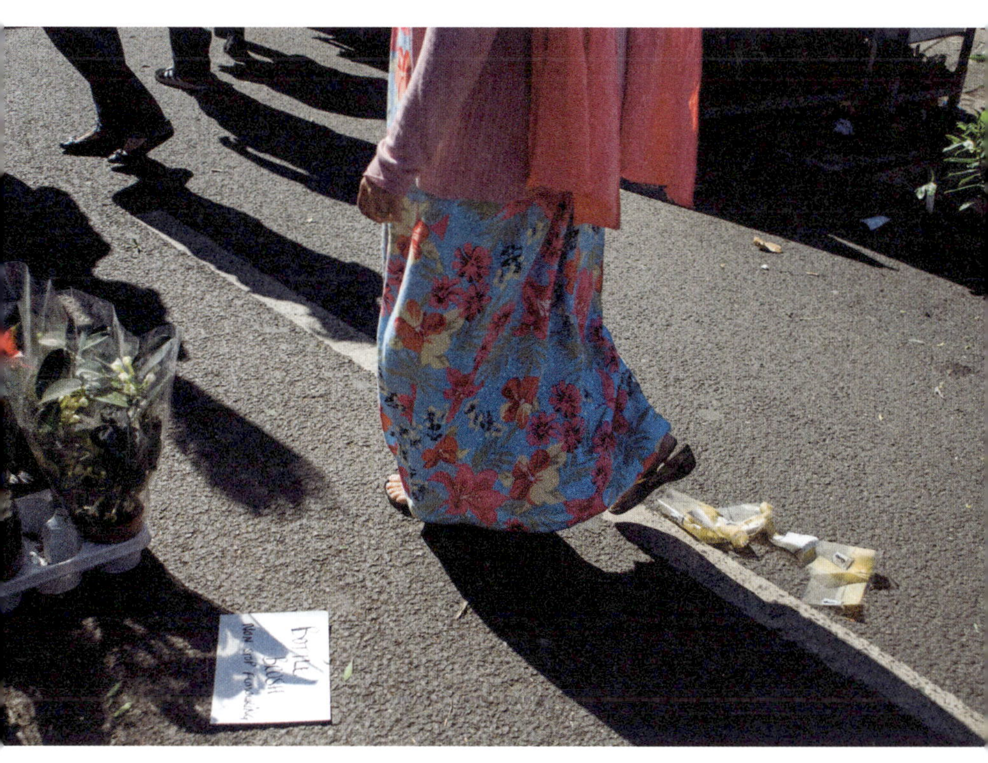
Butter
Bush
Non stop flowering

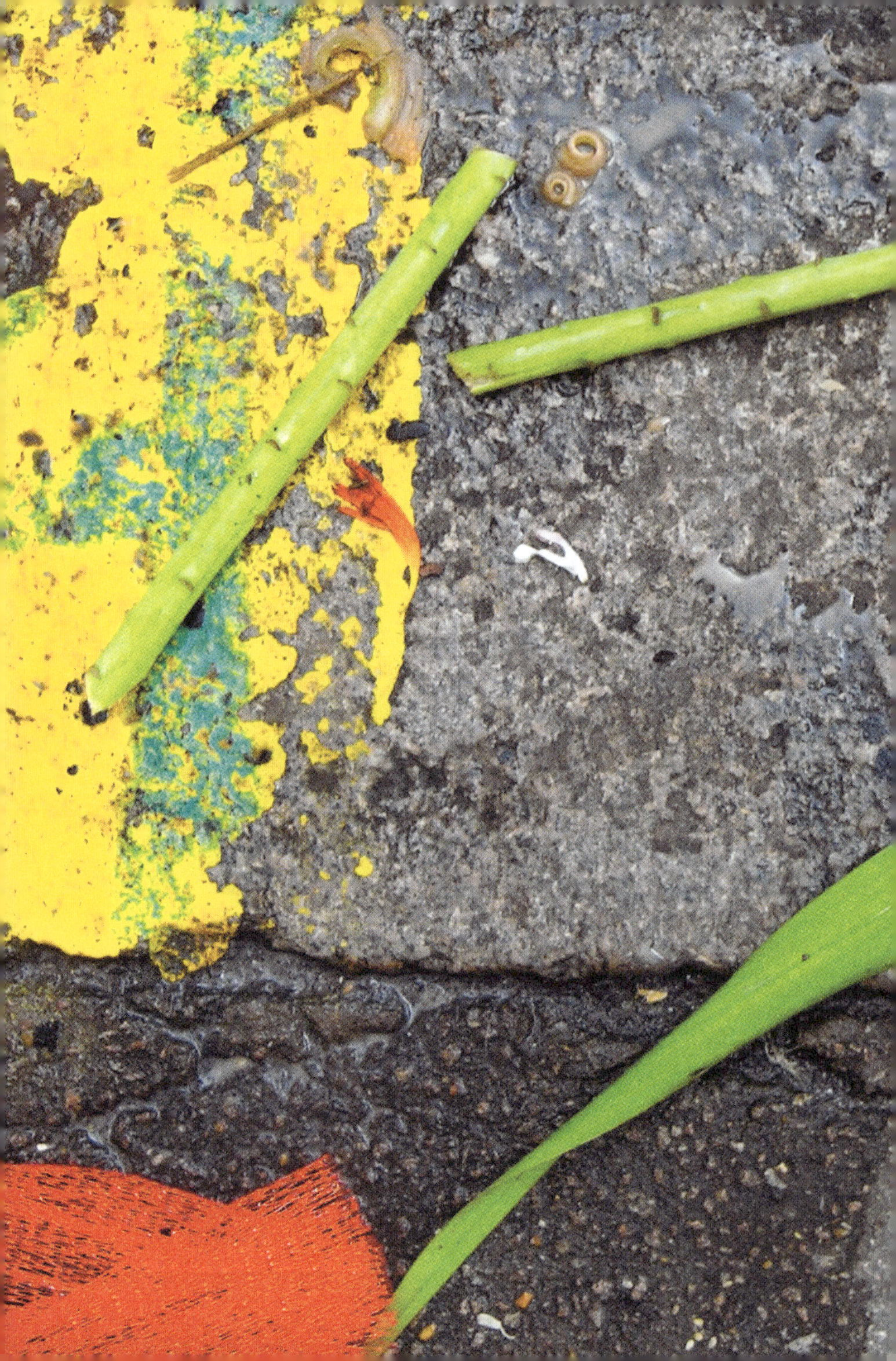

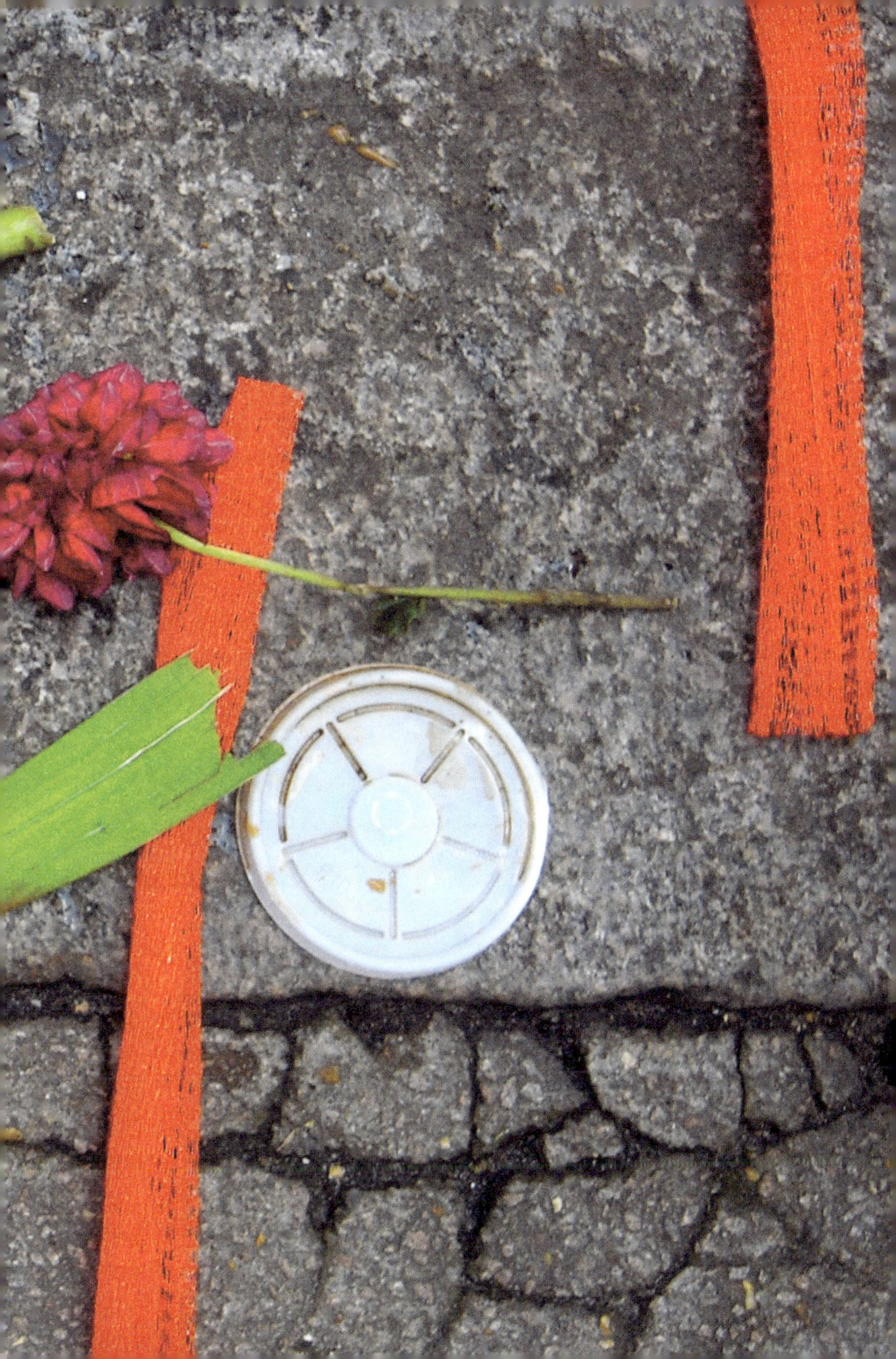

DRIVERS IN THE 1980s

CHRIS DORLEY-BROWN

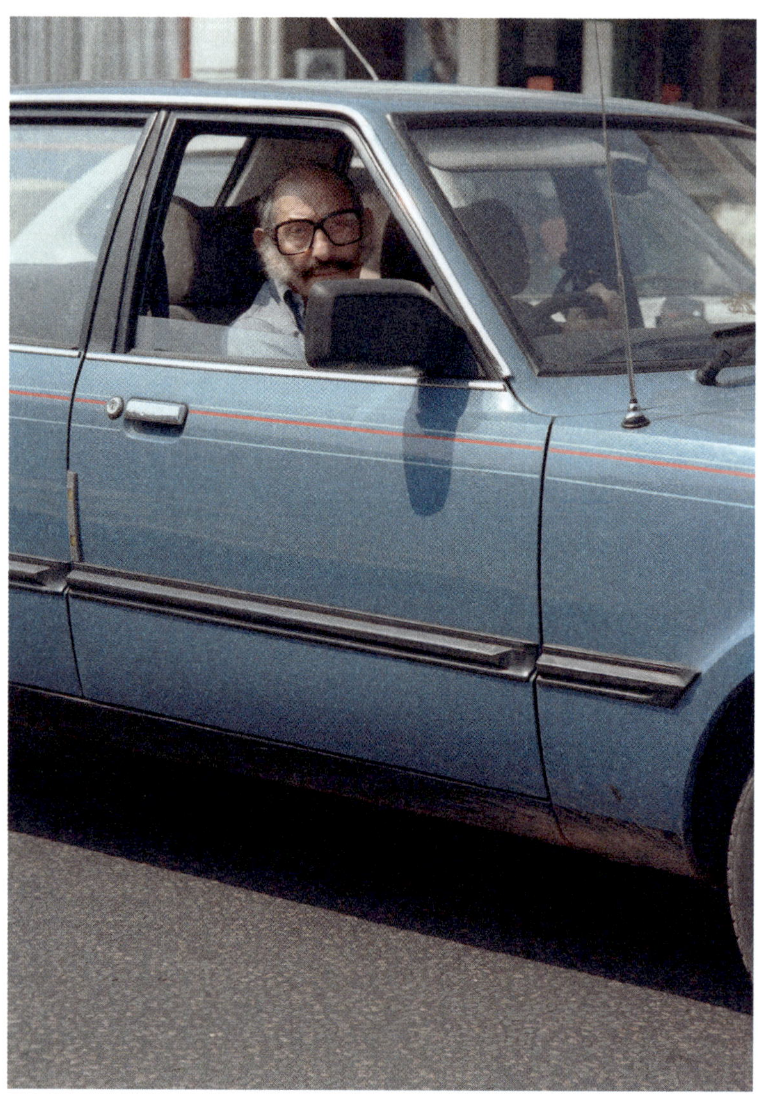

*Thatcher's Britain revealed through the windows
of cars stuck in East London traffic jams.*

One May morning in 1987, a young photographer called Chris
Dorley-Brown picked up his Rolleiflex and hit the streets of
Hackney. He was en route to the City, planning to document
the privatisation of Rolls-Royce – one of scores of state companies, including Jaguar, British Airways and British Gas,
that were put up for sale by Margaret Thatcher's government.

Dorley-Brown, whose East London lineage dates back two
centuries, had just started exploring colour film and the idling,
gridlocked traffic offered plenty of opportunity. Stuck in their
cars, these drivers and passengers exist in a world that's not
quite inside or outside. Bored, frustrated, restless, they have
an unguarded appeal that lends itself to portraiture. But for
years most of these 'prisoners of glass, metal and capitalist
reverie', as Dorley-Brown calls them, sat in his archive.

Seen today they give us a glimpse into another time.
There's nostalgic pleasure to be had in those 80s signifiers –
the battered Datsun 120y, the blue Cortina Mk5 Crusader
(opposite, on Mare Street, E8), oversized gold rings, and moustaches, so many moustaches. But while the sell-off policies
that peaked in the 80s were hugely influential, they were also
hugely divisive. What we're looking at here is a new beginning
or it's the beginning of the end. It depends who you ask.

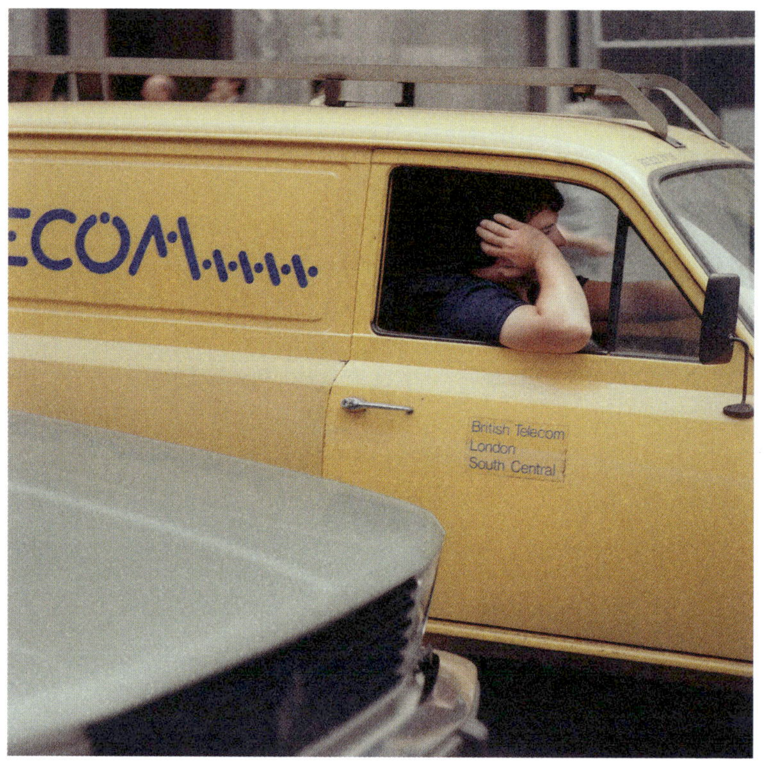

Vehicle unknown, location unknown

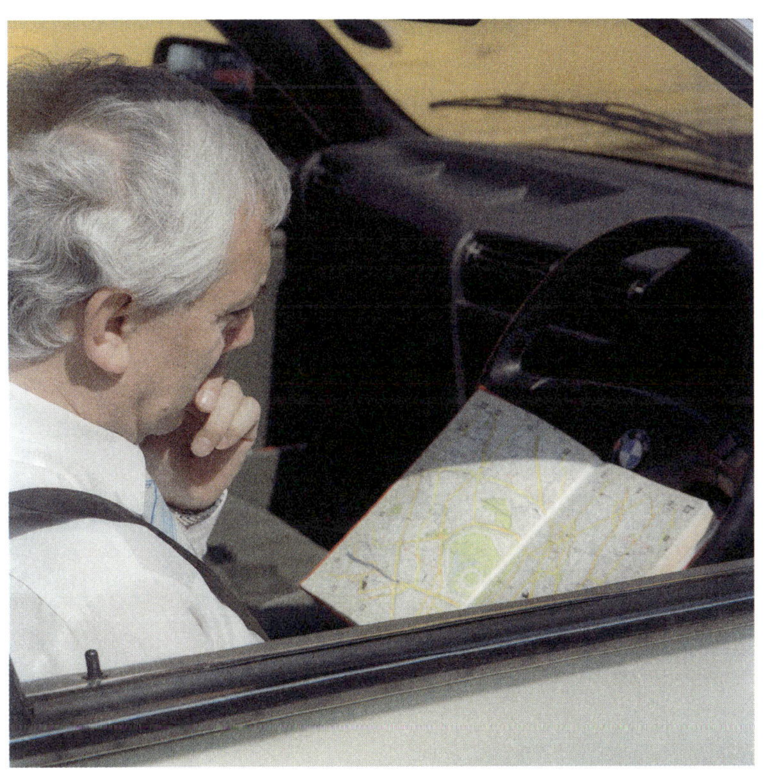

BMW 3 series, Old Street, EC1

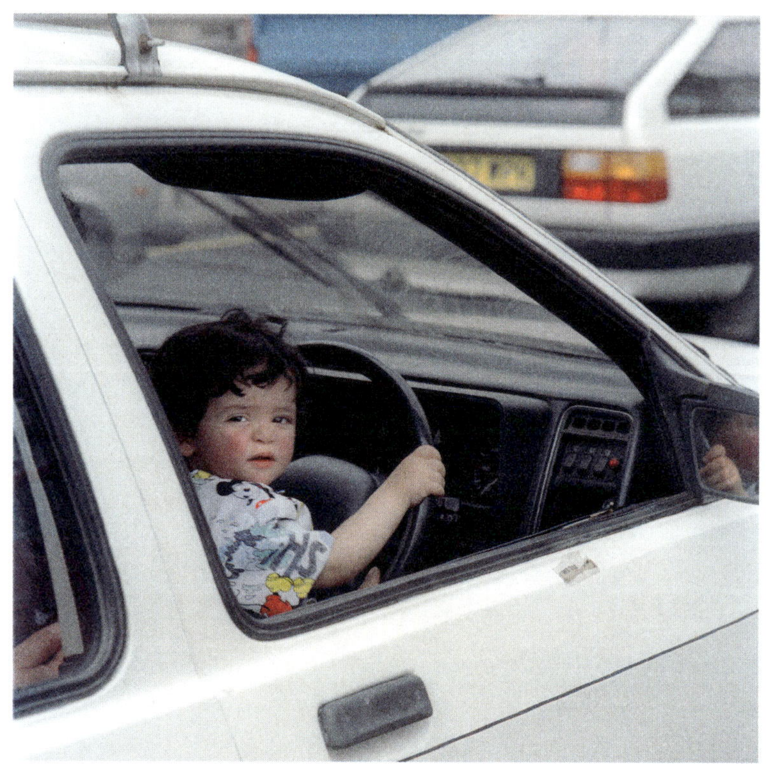

Ford Sierra, London Bridge, EC4

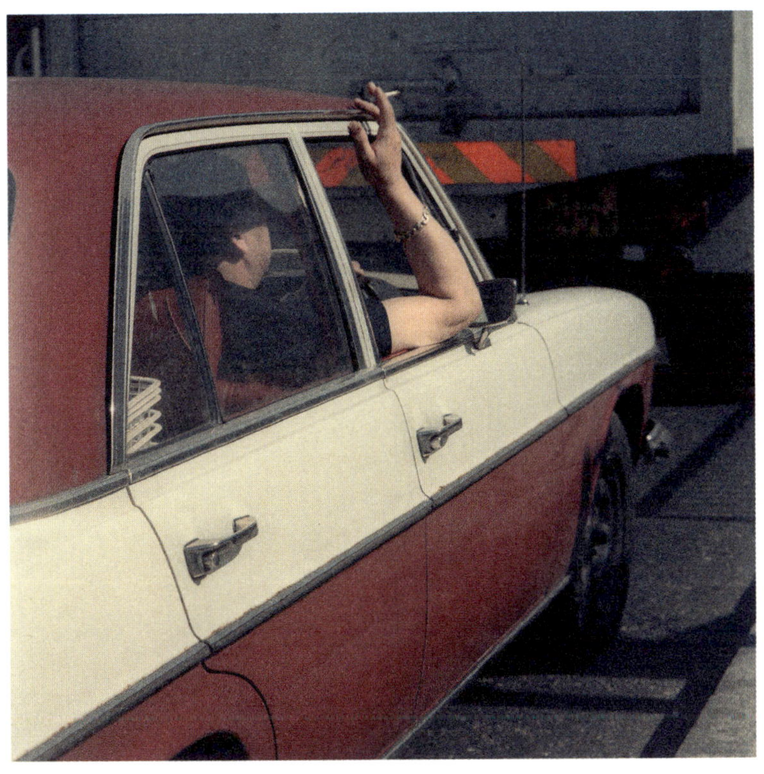

Mercedes-Benz W115 Series, London Bridge, EC4

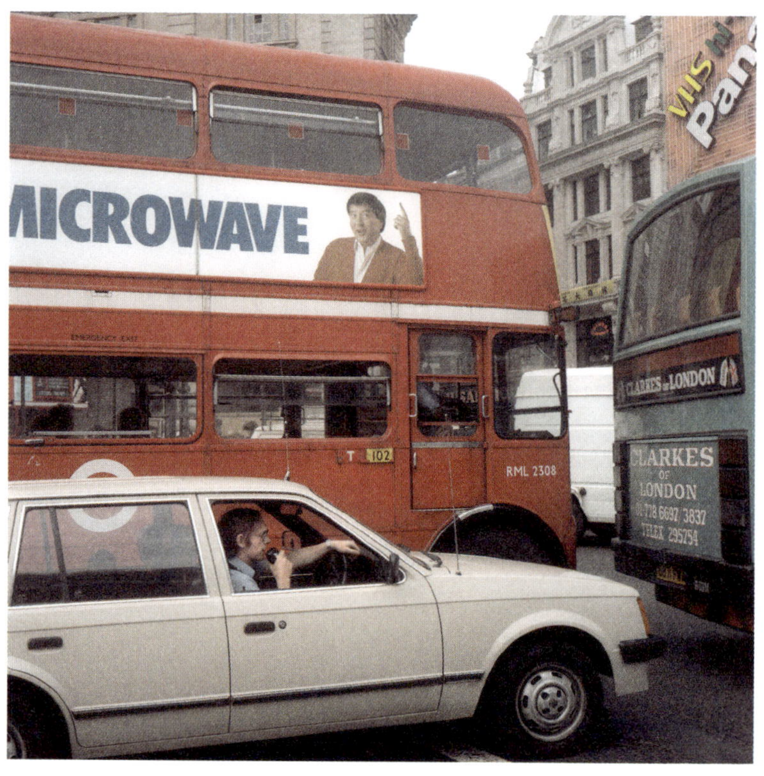

Vauxhall Astra Mk1, Piccadilly, W1

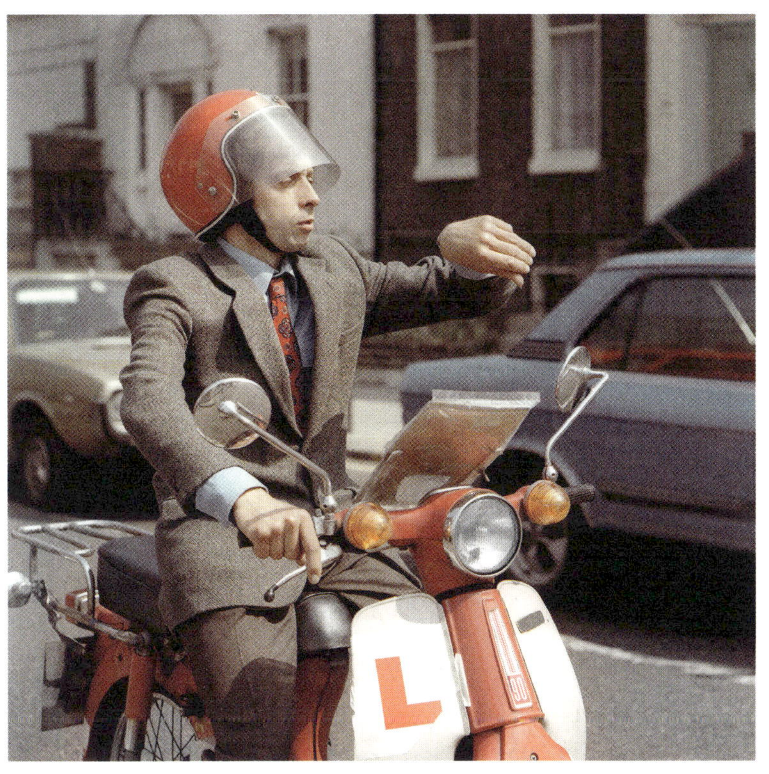

Honda 90 Moped, Mare Street, E8

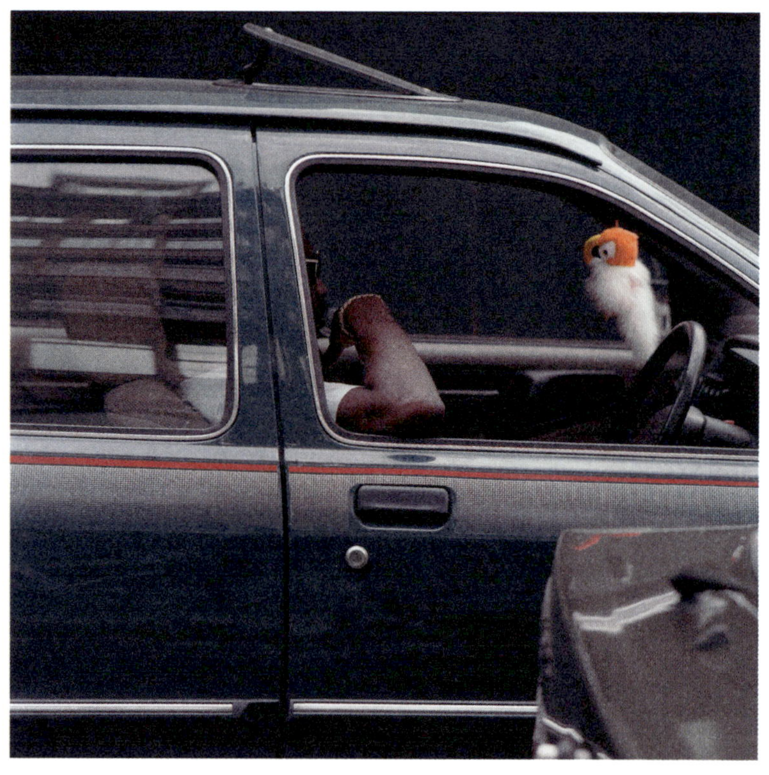

Ford Sierra XR4i, Bishopsgate, EC2

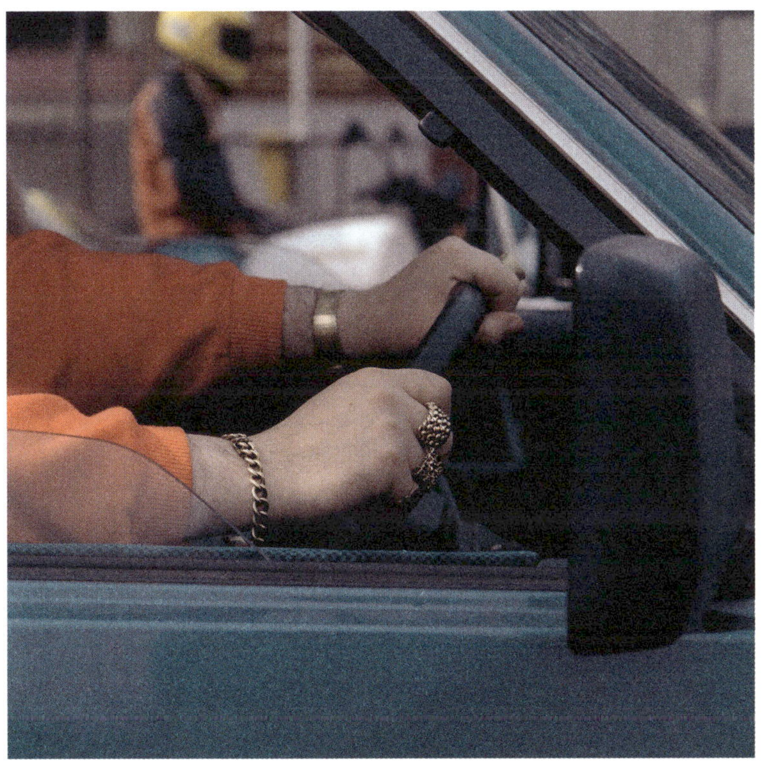

Vehicle unknown, location unknown

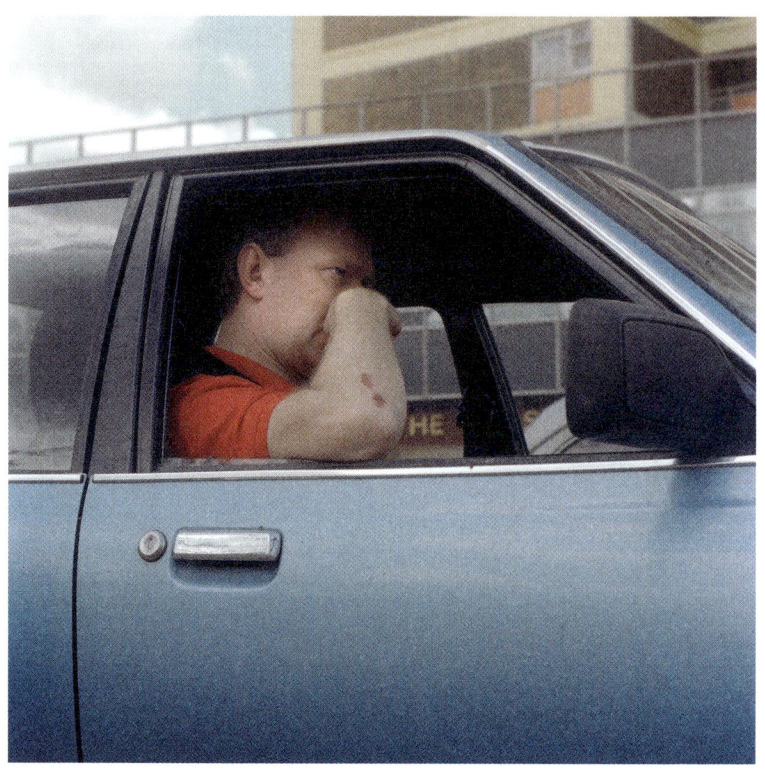

Cortina Mk4, Old Street, EC2

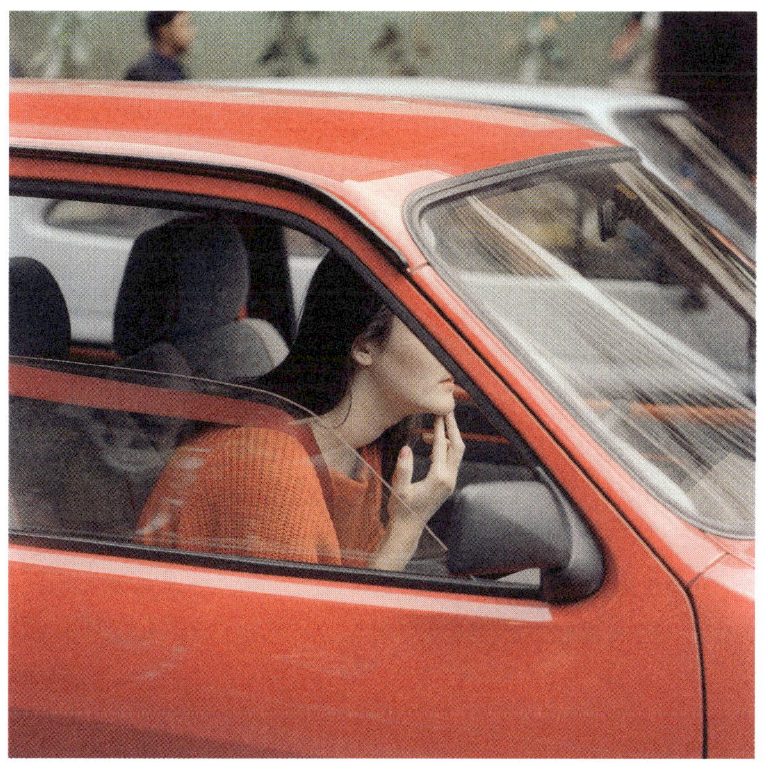

MG Metro, Norton Folgate, EC2

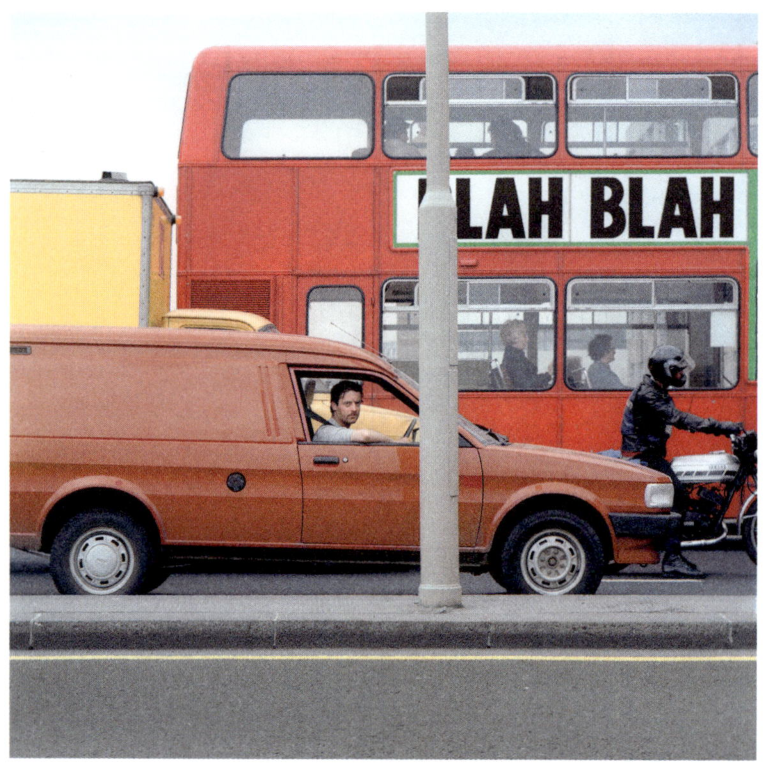

Austin Maestro City Van, London Bridge, EC4

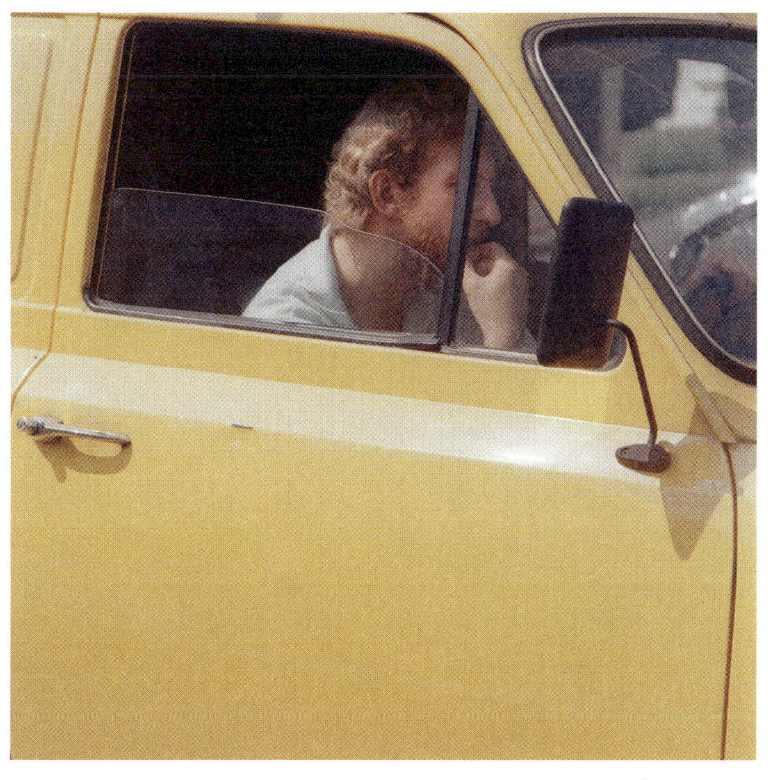

Bedford HA Van, Hackney Road, E2

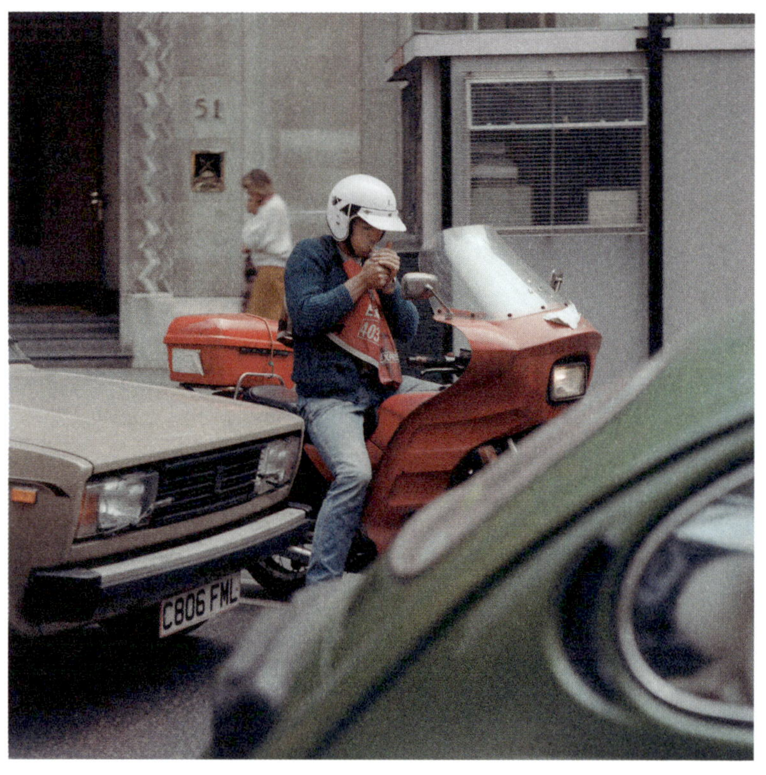

Vehicle unknown, Gracechurch Street, EC3

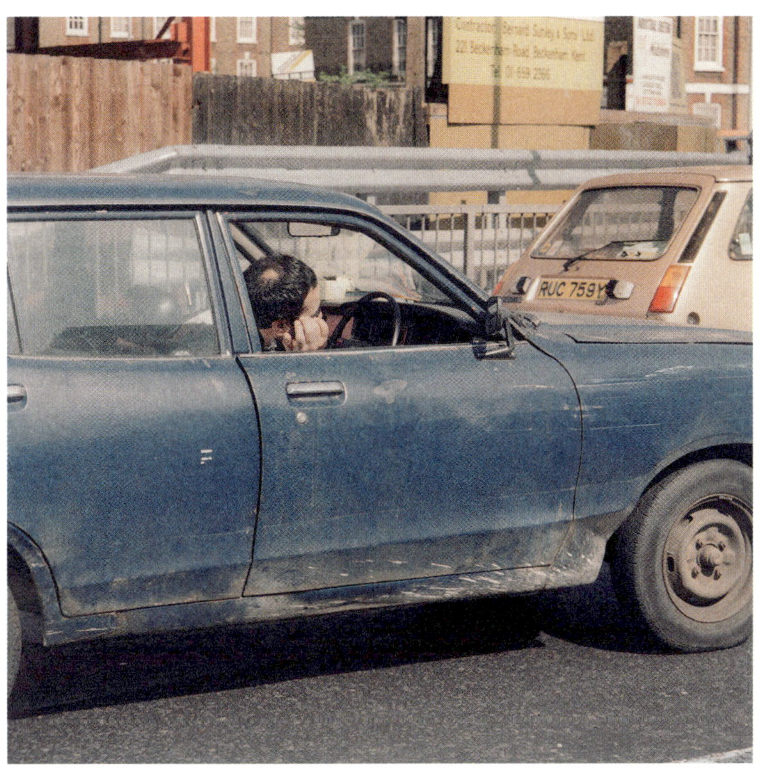

Datsun 120Y, Old Street, EC2

DALSTON IN THE 80s

ANDREW HOLLIGAN

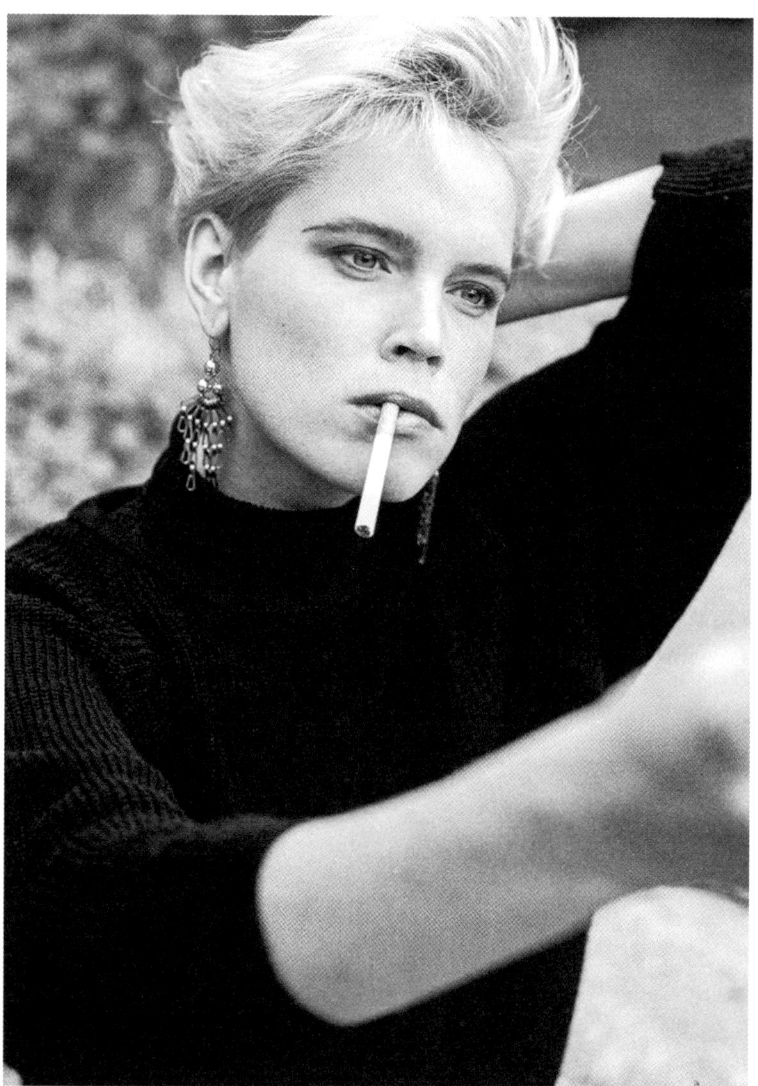

1984. British fashion photographer Andrew Holligan had just moved to Dalston from glamorous New York where he'd been working for the past three years. In those days, Dalston wasn't the hip hangout it is now. It was rundown, cheap and off the beaten track. His then wife, a model, wasn't impressed and at first Holligan spent his time moping around at home, hoping for work calls.

Everything changed when he began to venture out and document the residents of his adopted manor with a 1950s Rolleiflex camera. The 80s were a remarkable time. Rather like now, people were struggling, they were divided but there was also a real creative flourish and political engagement. That sense of history is a constant presence, clear in the posters for anti-apartheid demos, billboards about Greater London Council (scrapped in 1986) and graffiti extolling the BNP.

But there's also ordinary people getting on with their lives – a young man doing his paper-round, grannies on the hunt for a bargain at Ridley Road market, a mysterious man fixing a Mini. By 1986 Holligan was off again – this time to Australia – but he returned to East London a year later, living locally until he moved to the countryside in 2001. Dalston will always remain the place where he found 'mankind in all its forms'.

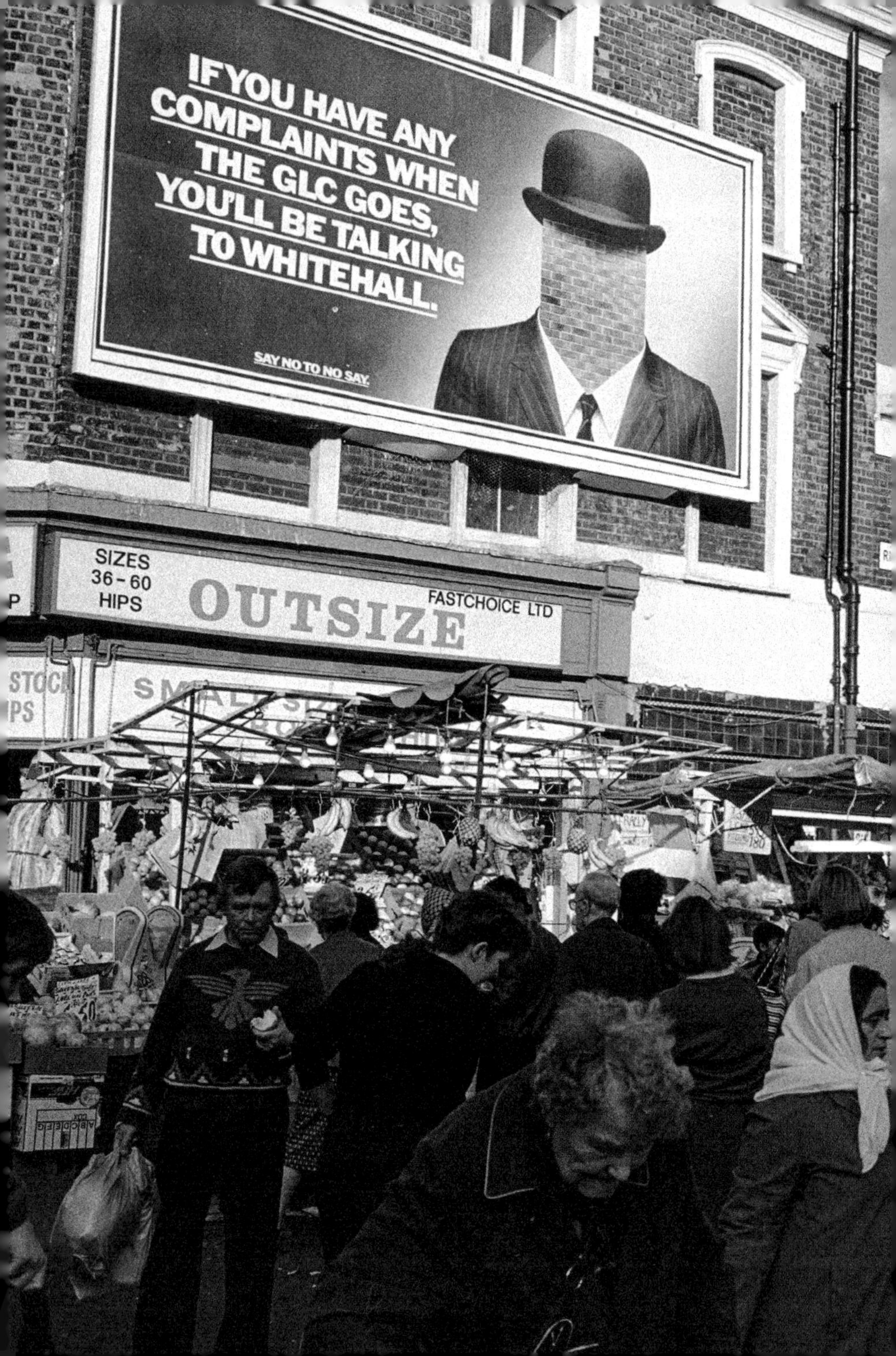

IF YOU HAVE ANY
COMPLAINTS WHEN
THE GLC GOES,
YOU'LL BE TALKING
TO WHITEHALL.
SAY NO TO NO SAY.
SIZES
36-60
HIPS
OUTSIZE
FASTCHOICE LTD

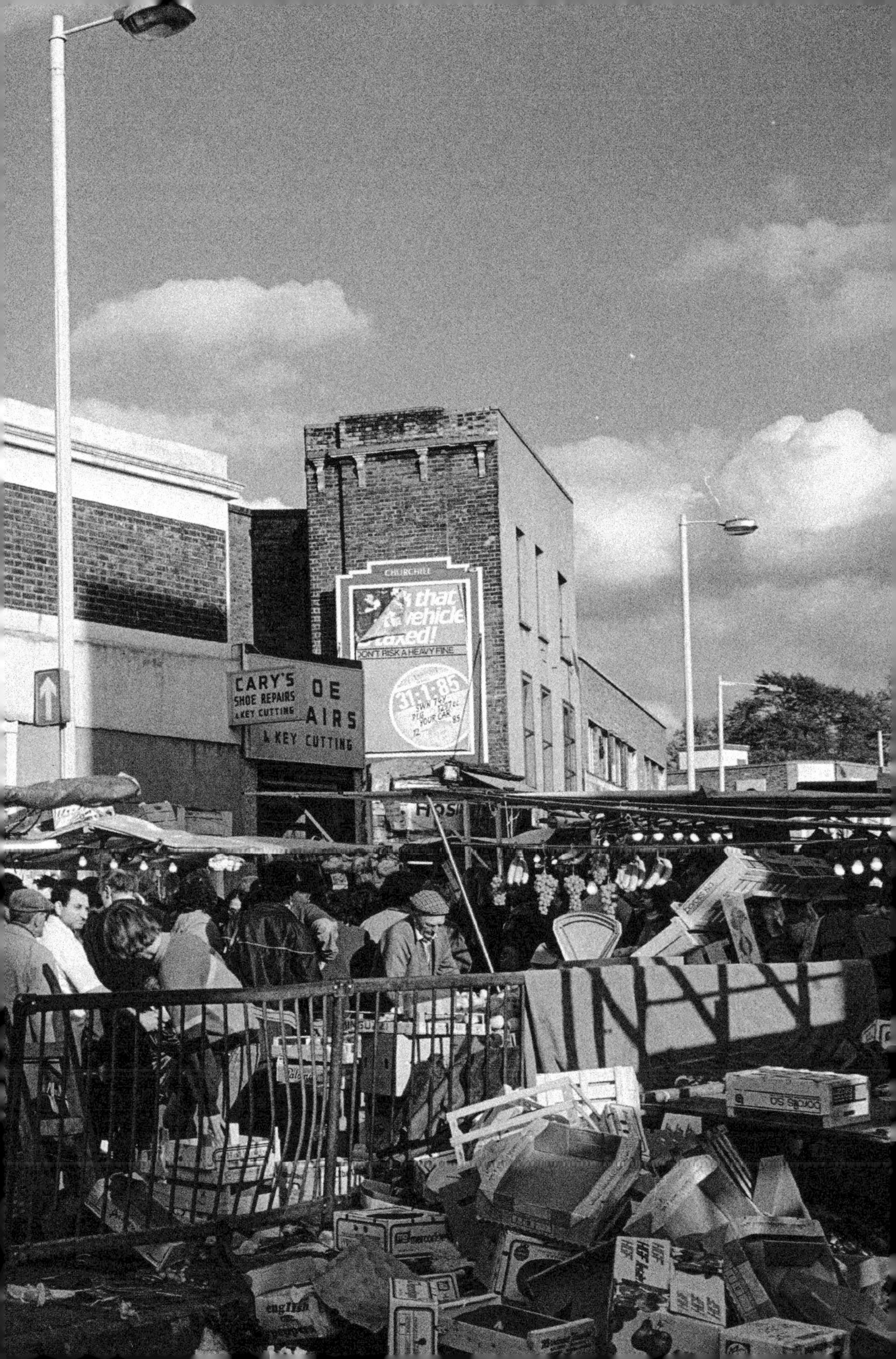

CARY'S
SHOE REPAIRS
& KEY CUTTING
OE
AIRS
& KEY CUTTING
CHURCHILL
that
vehicle
taxed!
DON'T RISK A HEAVY FINE
31·1·85

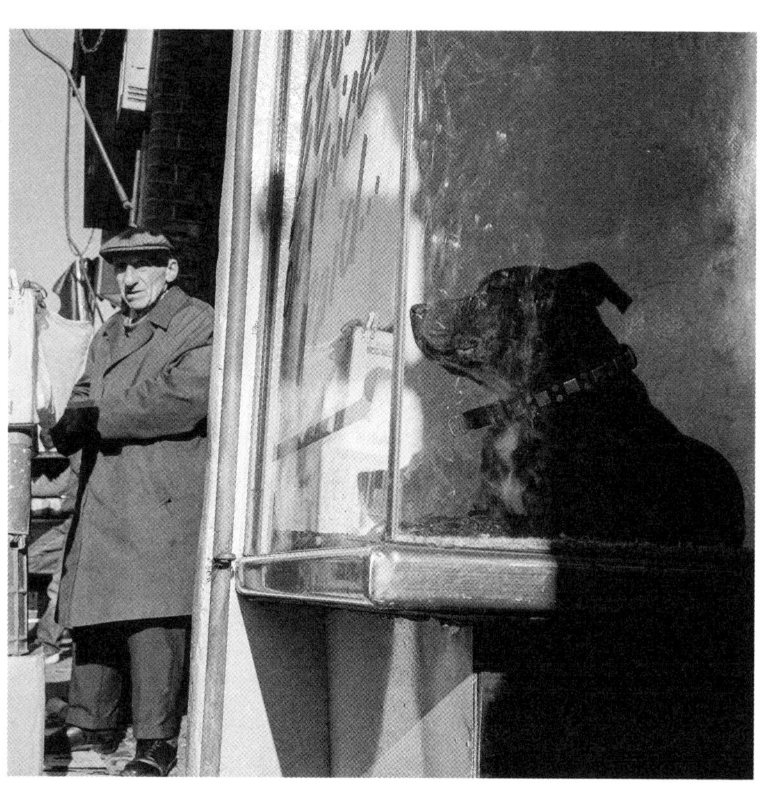

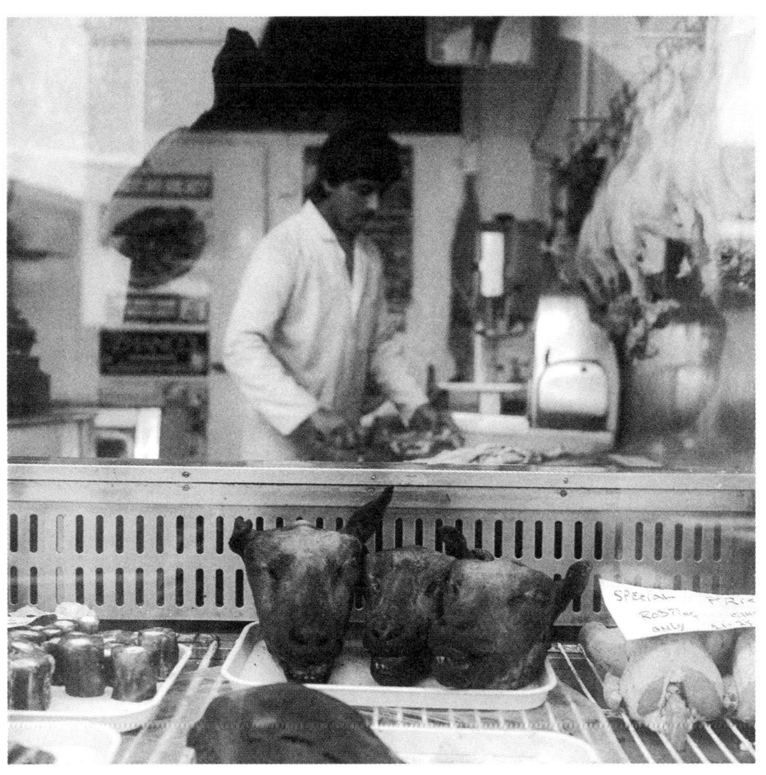

SPECIAL   PRIX
ROSTING
only

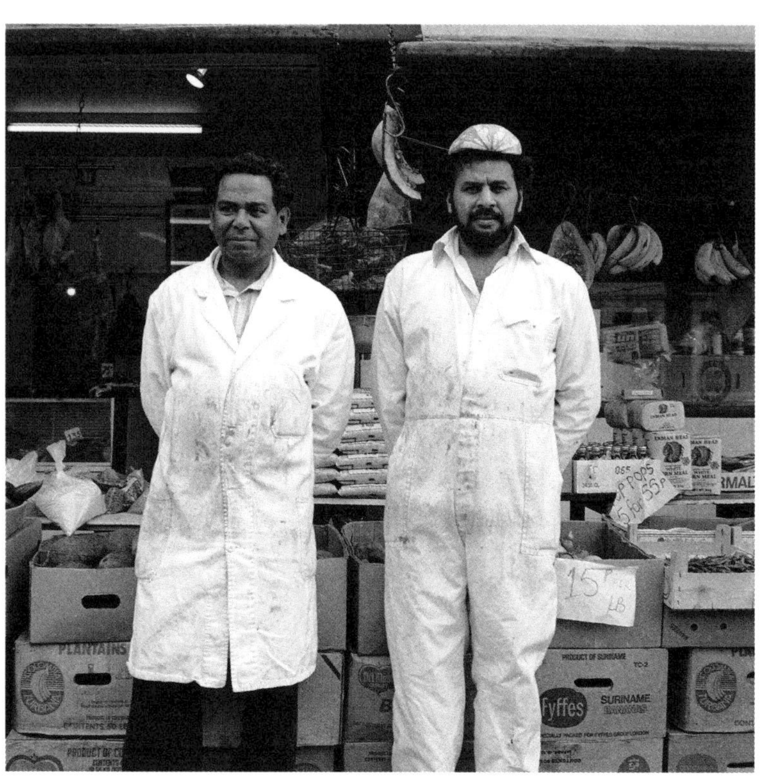

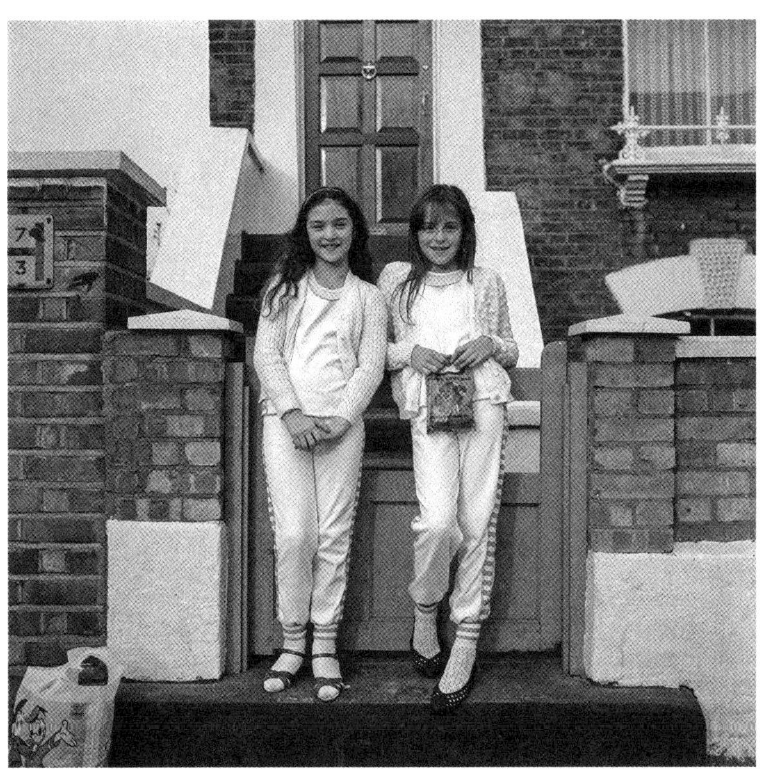

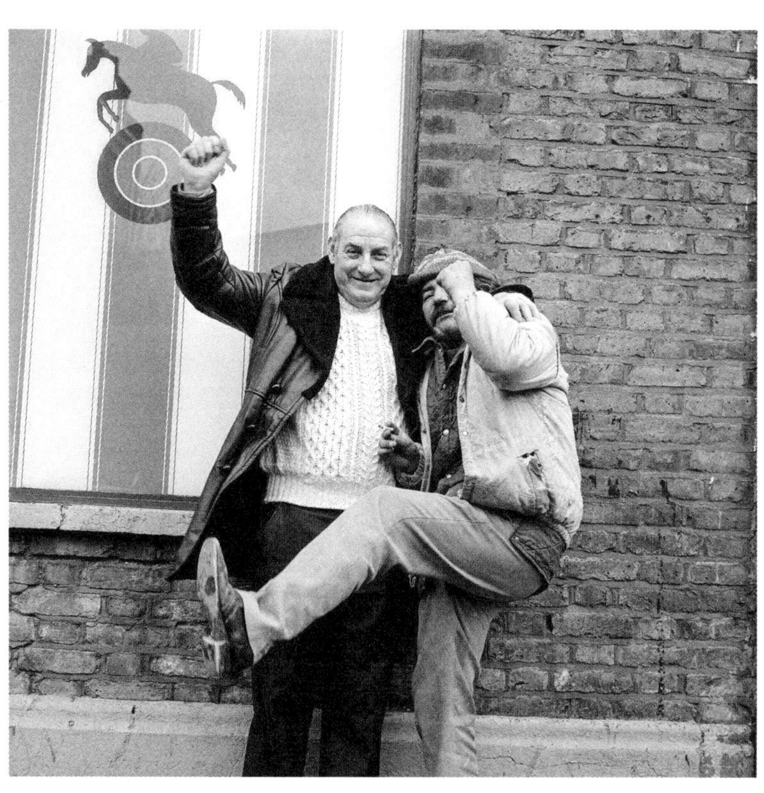

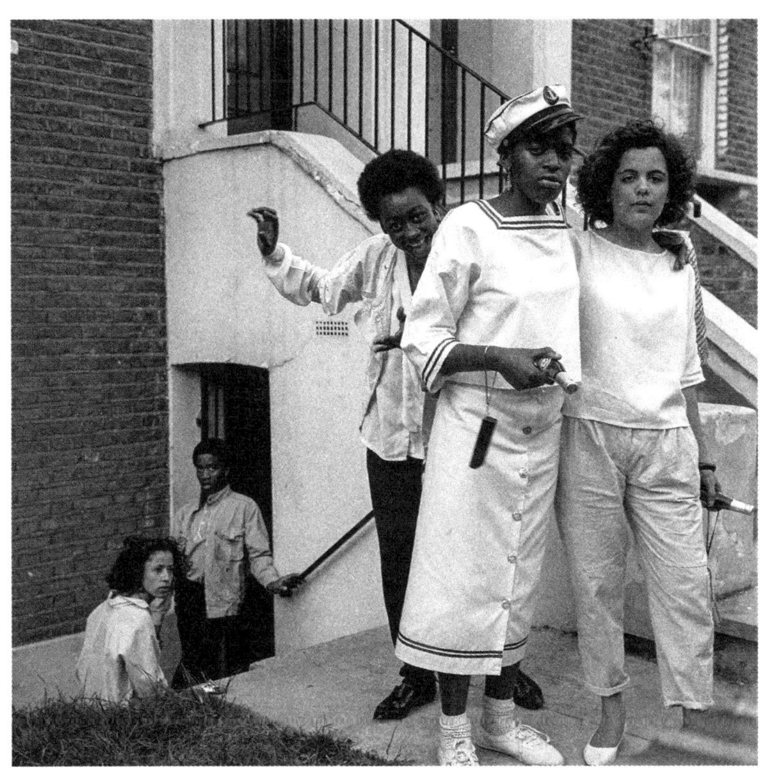

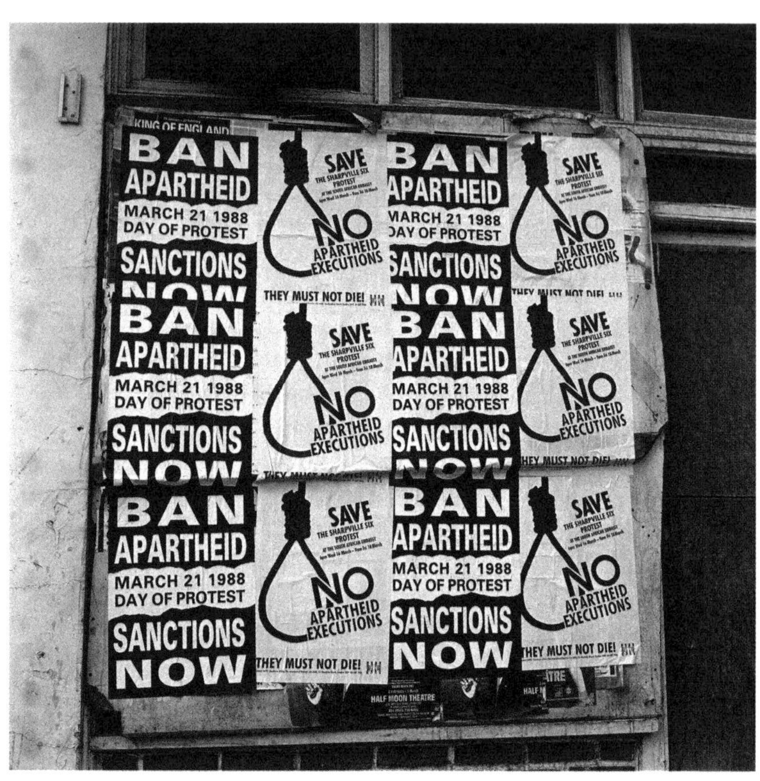
KING OF ENGLAND
BAN
APARTHEID
MARCH 21 1988
DAY OF PROTEST
SANCTIONS
NOW
BAN
APARTHEID
MARCH 21 1988
DAY OF PROTEST
SANCTIONS
NOW
BAN
APARTHEID
MARCH 21 1988
DAY OF PROTEST
SANCTIONS
NOW
SAVE
THE SHARPVILLE SIX
PROTEST
NO
APARTHEID
EXECUTIONS
THEY MUST NOT DIE!
HALF MOON THEATRE

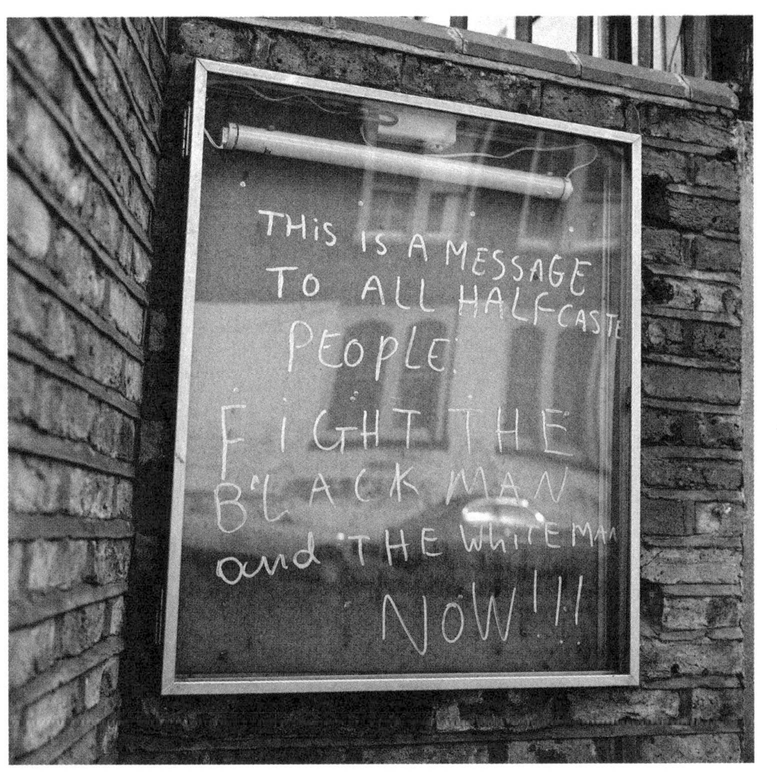

THIS IS A MESSAGE
TO ALL HALF-CASTE
PEOPLE.
FIGHT THE
BLACK MAN
and THE WHITE MAN
NOW!!!

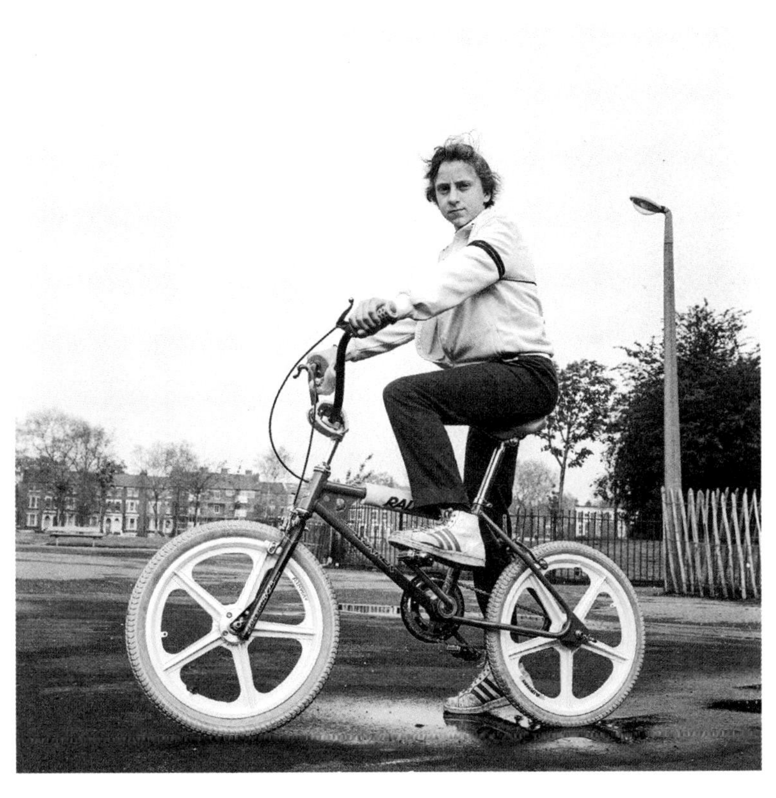

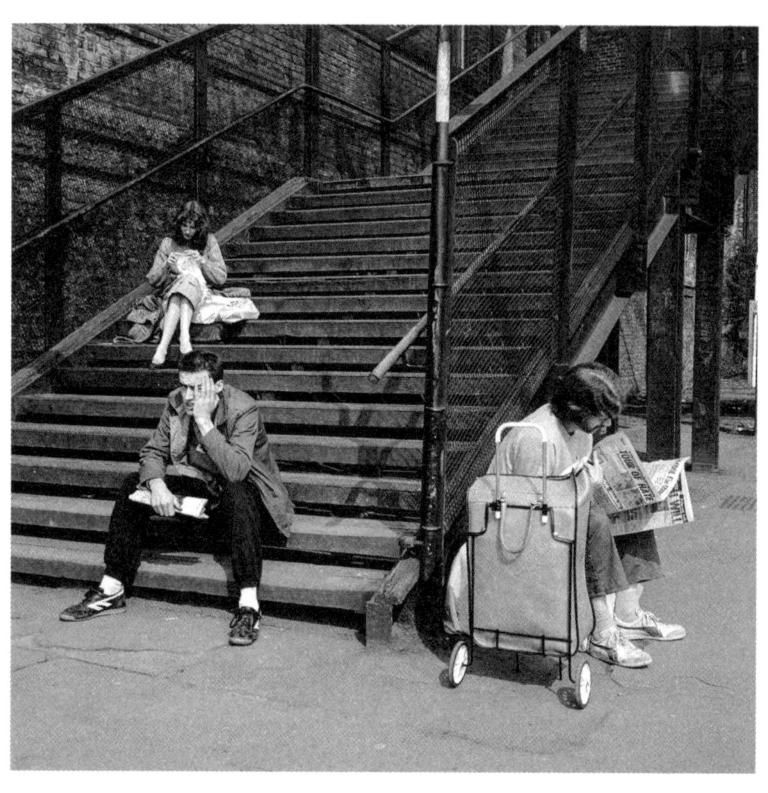

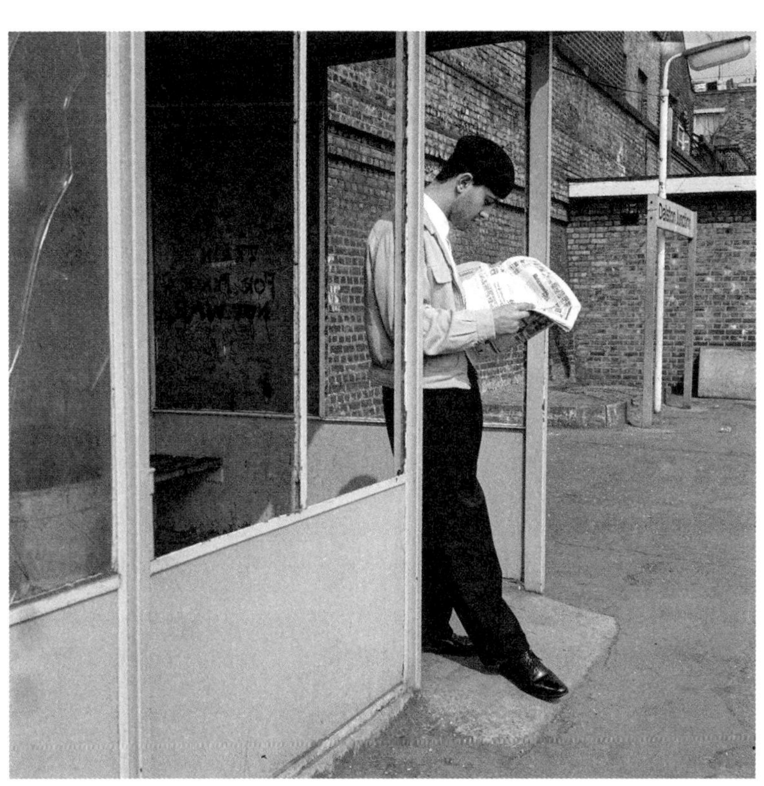

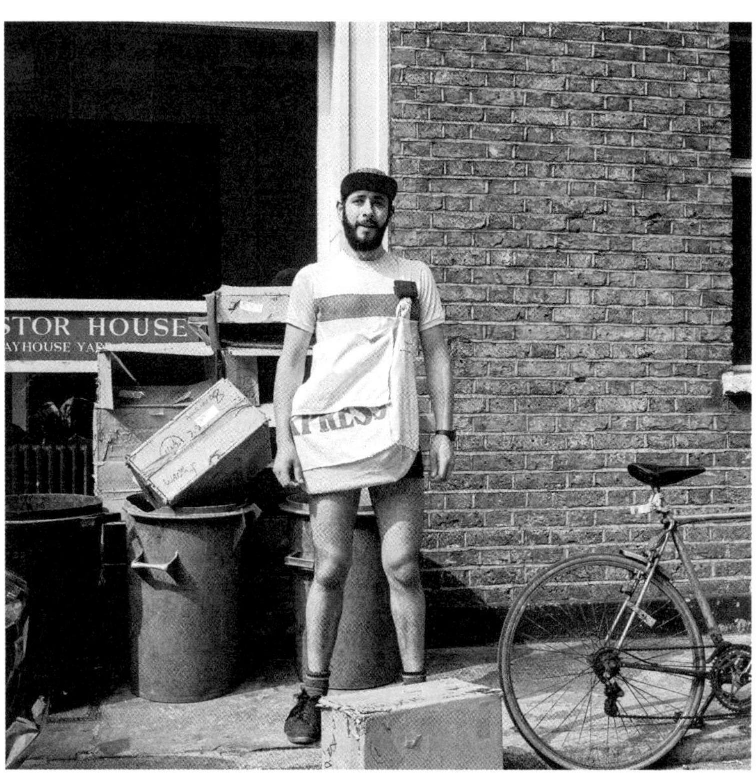
STOR HOUSE
AYHOUSE YAR
XPRESS

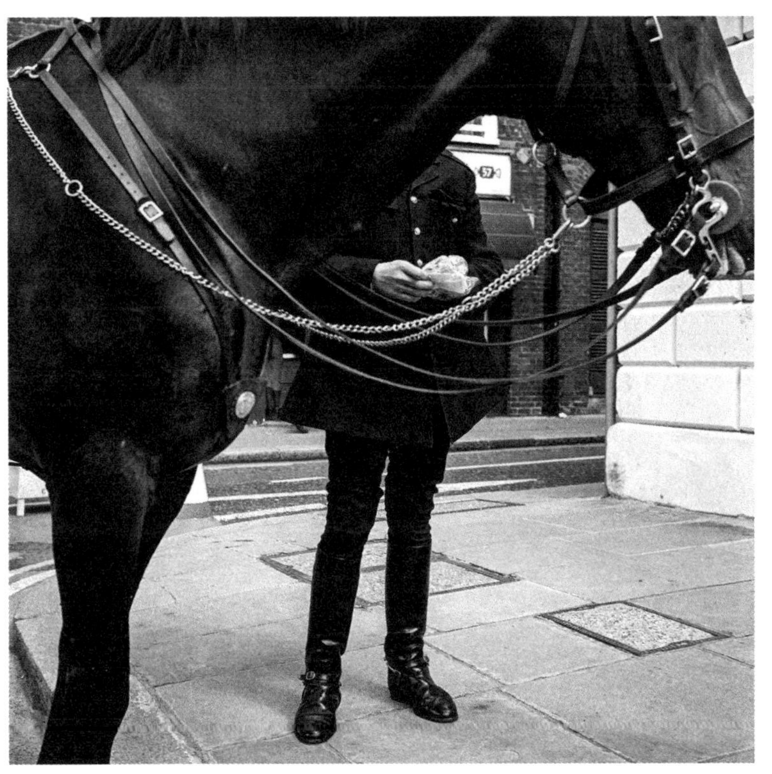

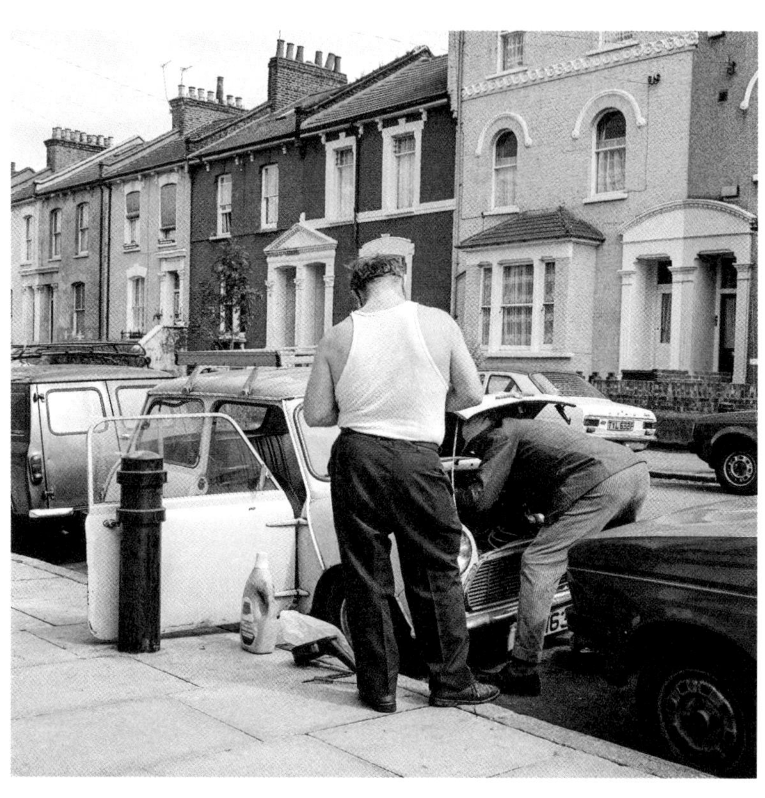

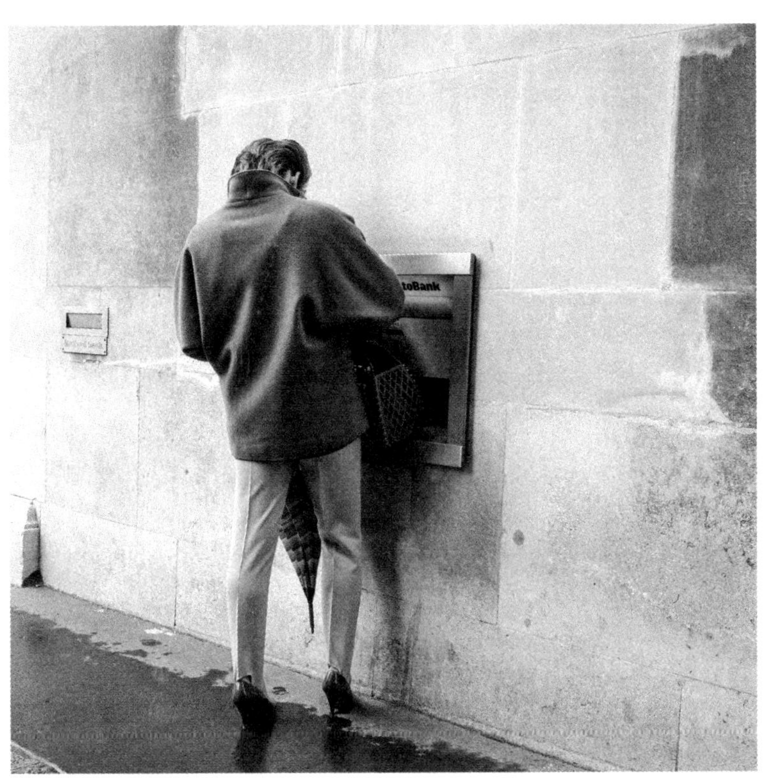

toBank

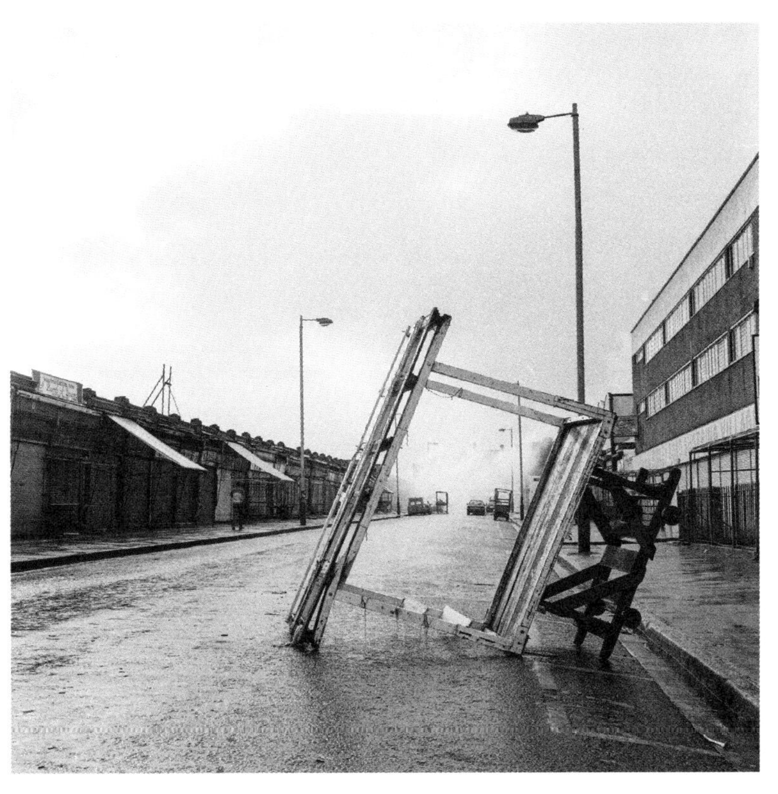

ADVENTURES IN THE LEA VALLEY

POLLY BRADEN & DAVID CAMPANY

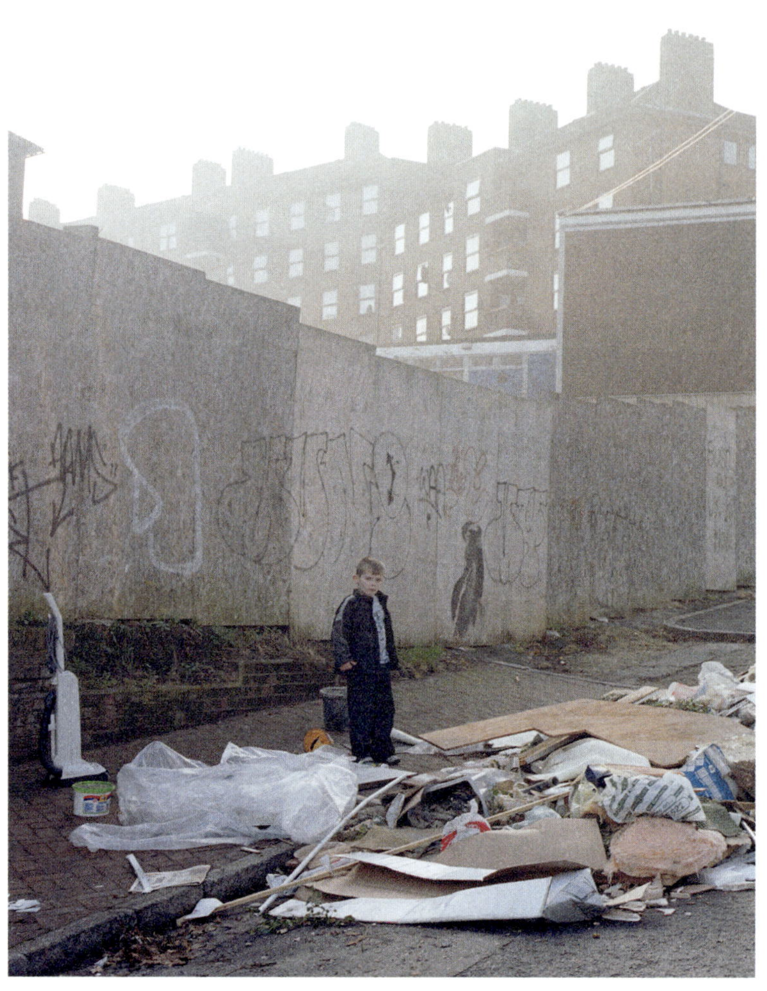

Tracing the route along the River Lea in the years before the 2012 Olympics changed it forever.

'There are Londoners who are drawn to its enigmatic allure, and Londoners who don't even know it is there.' David Campany is describing the Lea Valley, a stretch of land that runs 26 miles through London, Essex and Hertfordshire. Over the years the valley has served a variety of purposes – a railway route, a site for industry, for food growing, a water source, a nature reserve. In the 60s, derelict swathes of valley were redeveloped to create Lee Valley Regional Park.

Campany definitely falls in the first category of Londoner. Together with photographer Polly Braden, the curator and writer began exploring the valley by bike in 2004. The pair would weave along, one camera between them, capturing the constantly shifting array of sights they encountered along the way – kids dangling bare feet into the water, urban dirt bikers, dog walkers, ice cream sellers, swans, scrap yards.

This is a tribute and it's a record. Most obvious in the 'Fuck Seb Coe' graffiti, the impending 2012 Olympics looms. Now the Games have been and gone, leaving a transformation that has tamed many of these wild spots. These photographs preserve the valley as Campany remembers it, a 'strange, exciting, ugly, beautiful and unaccountably mysterious place'.

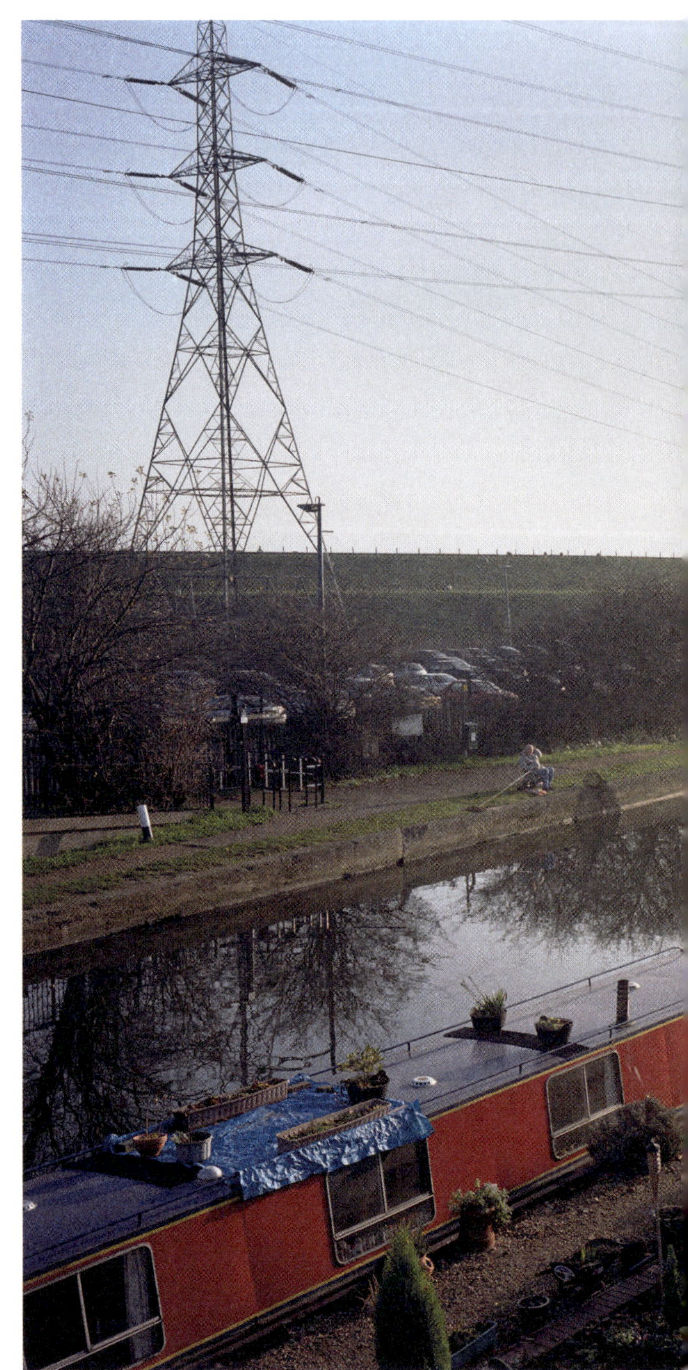

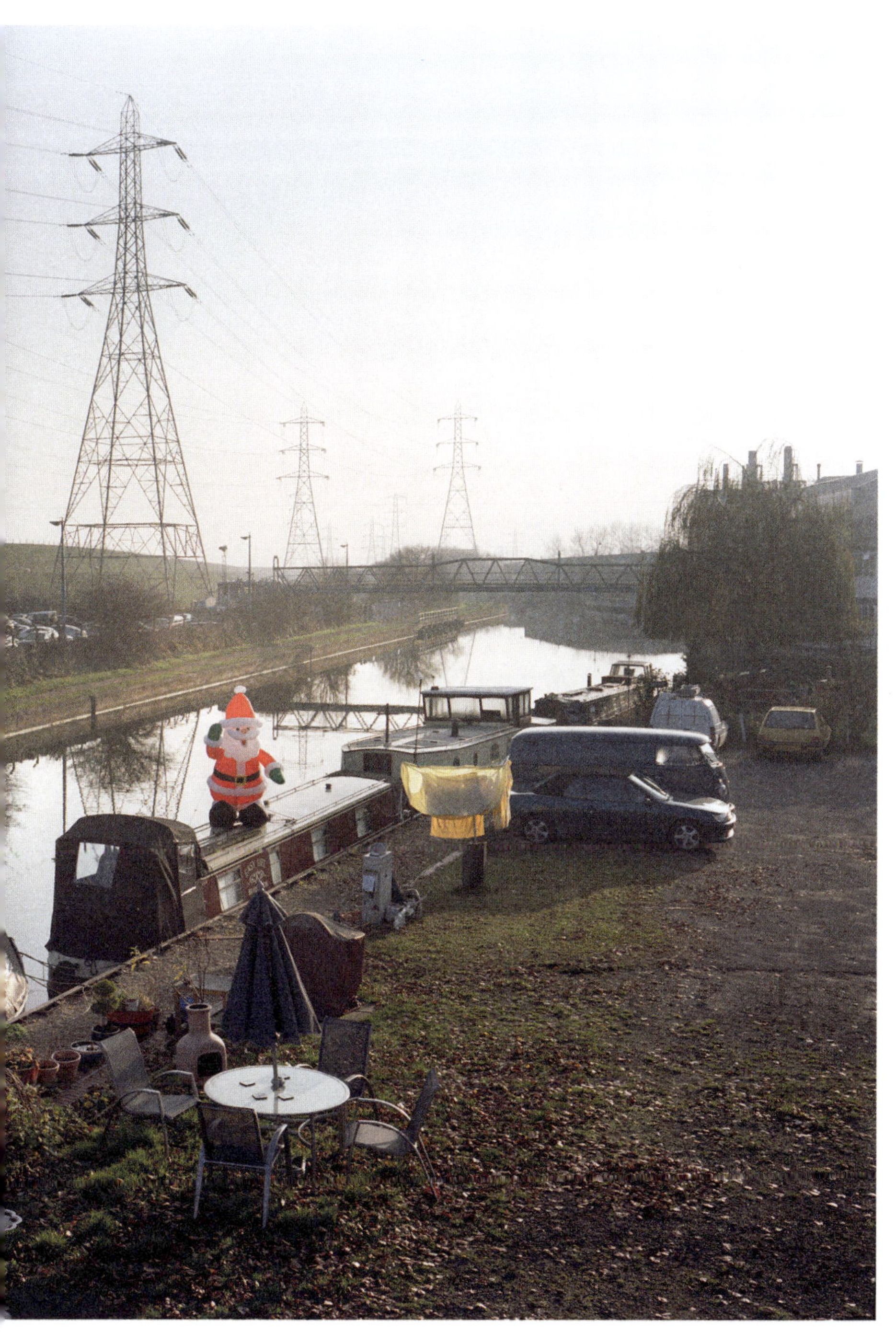

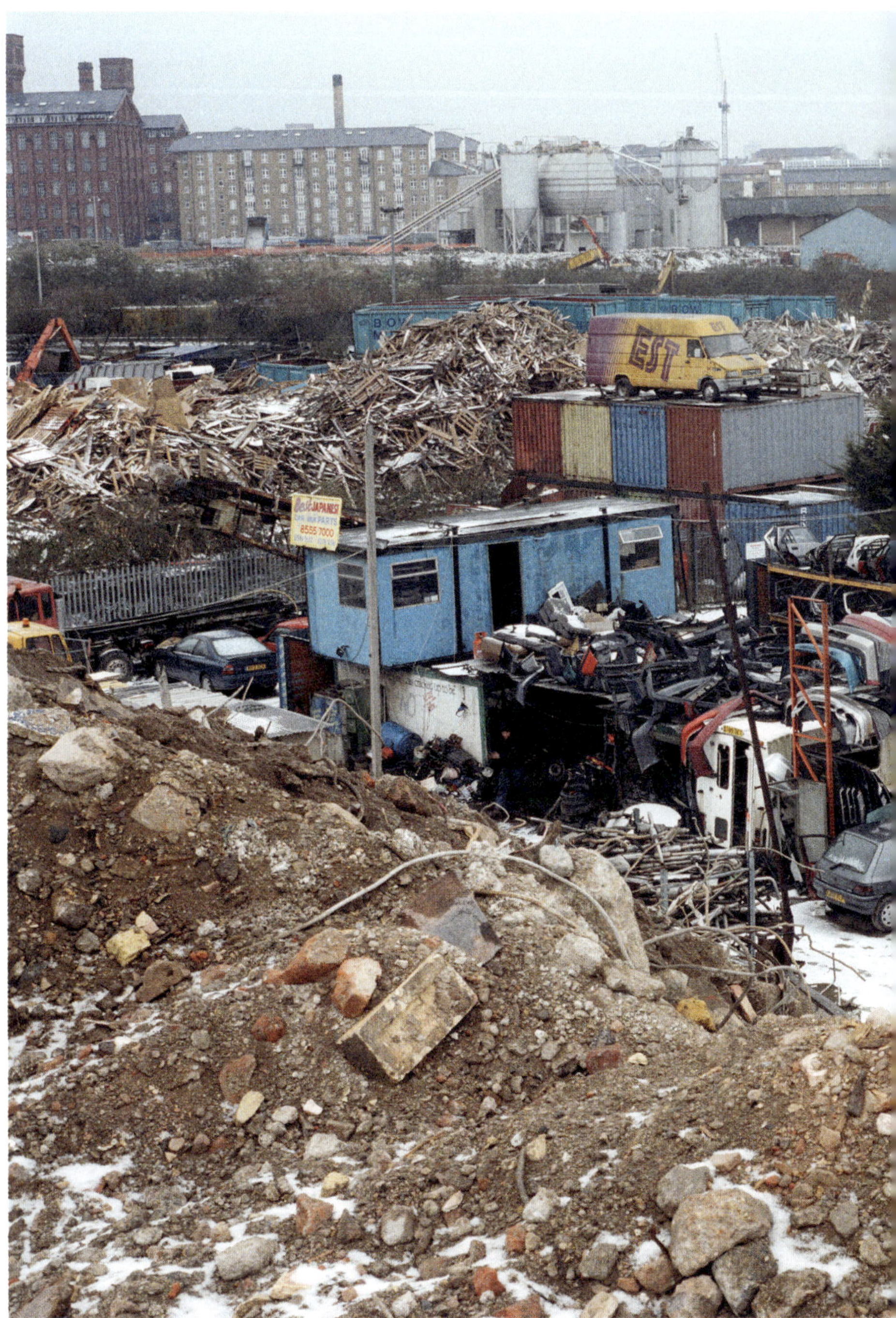

EST
Best JAPANESE
CAR VAN PARTS
8555 7000

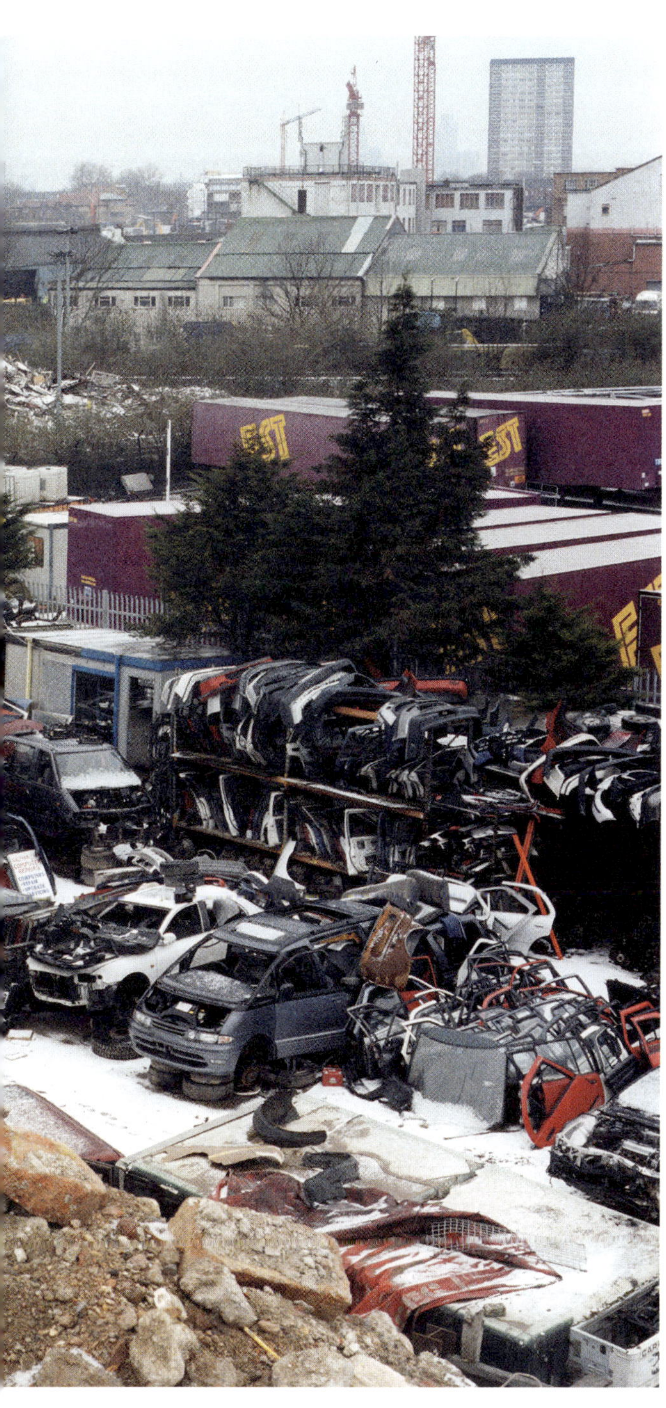

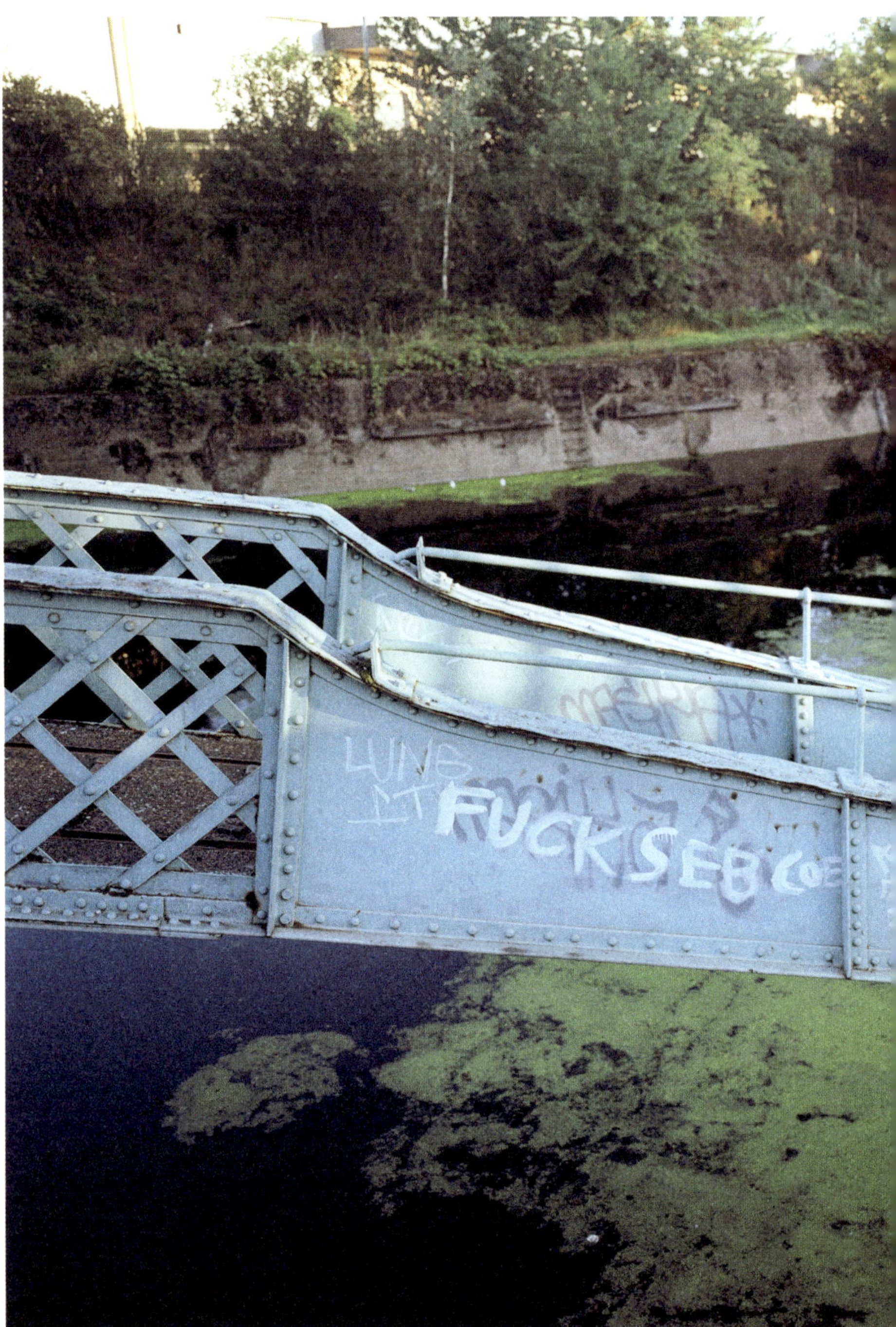

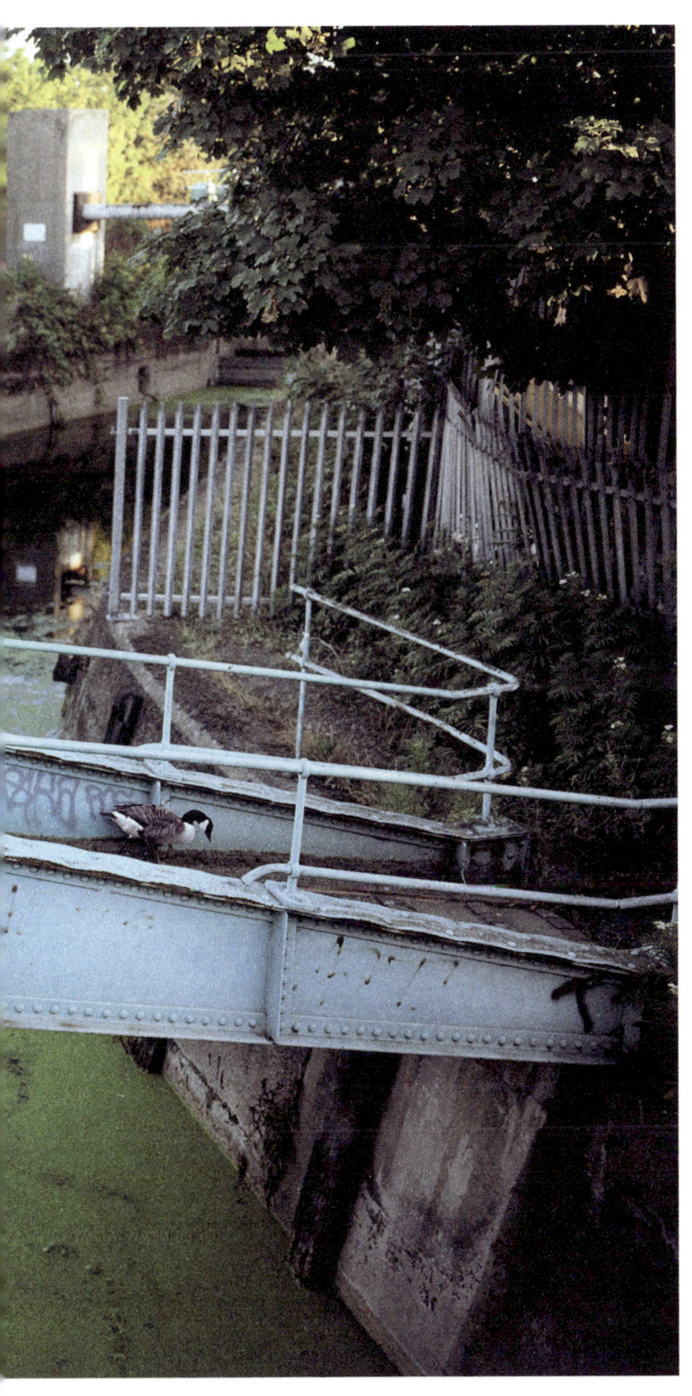

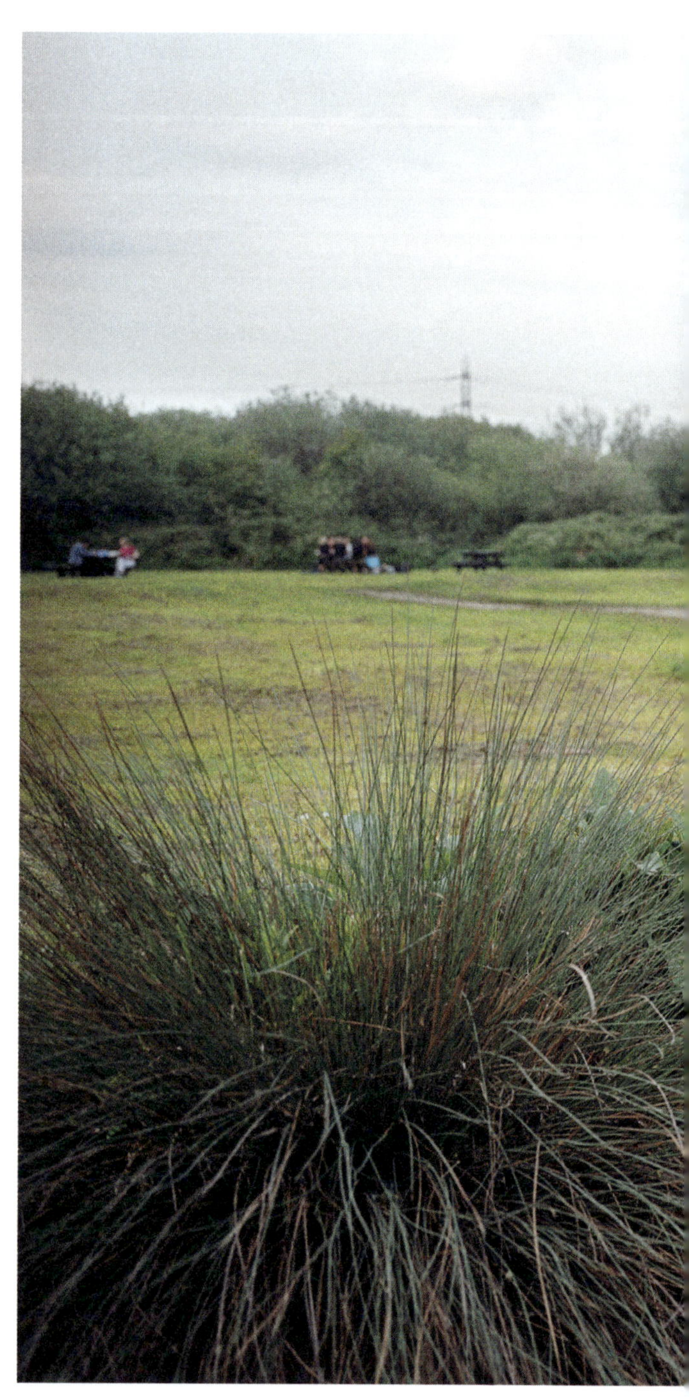

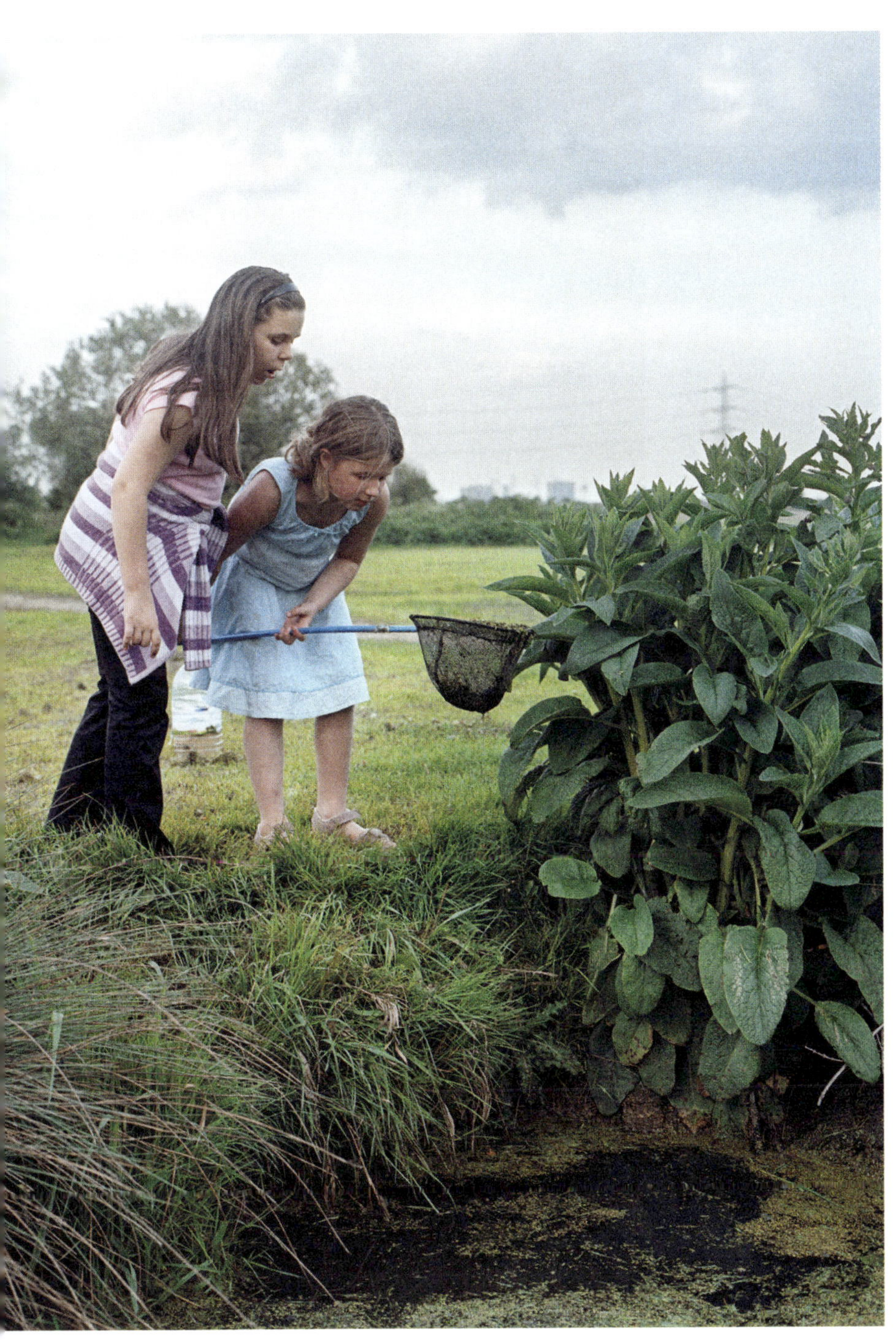

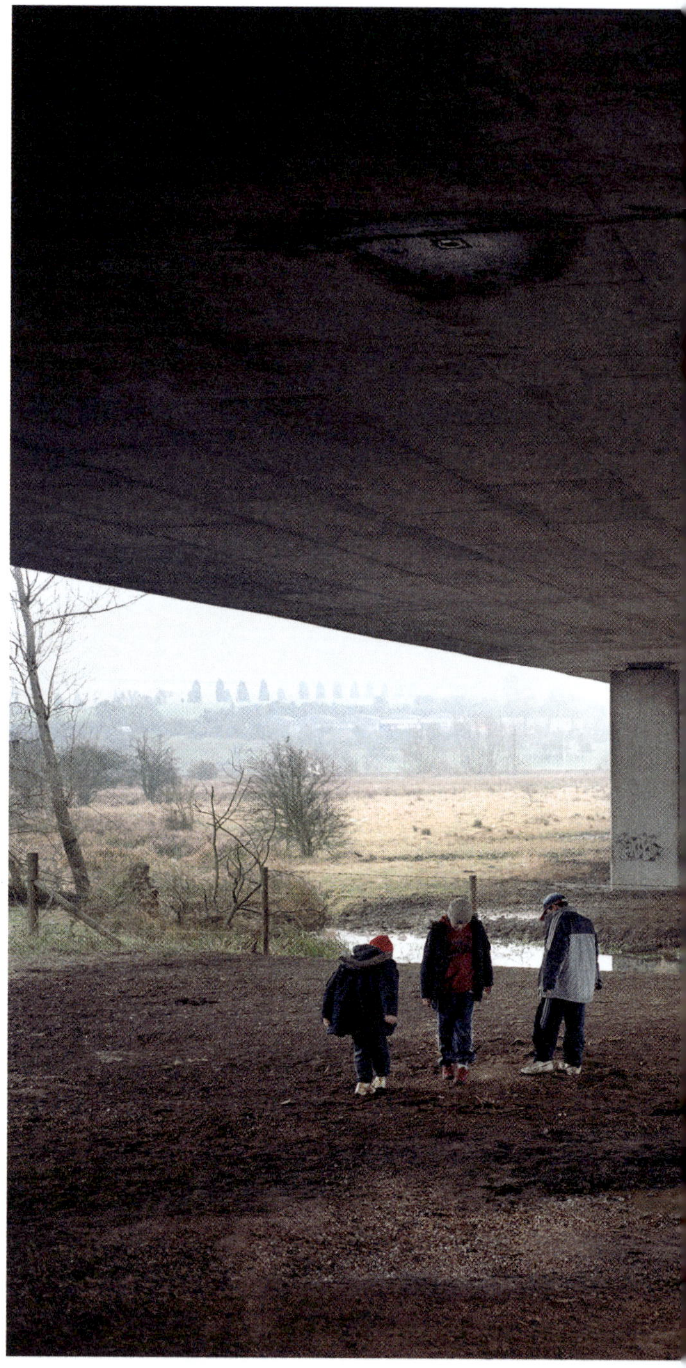

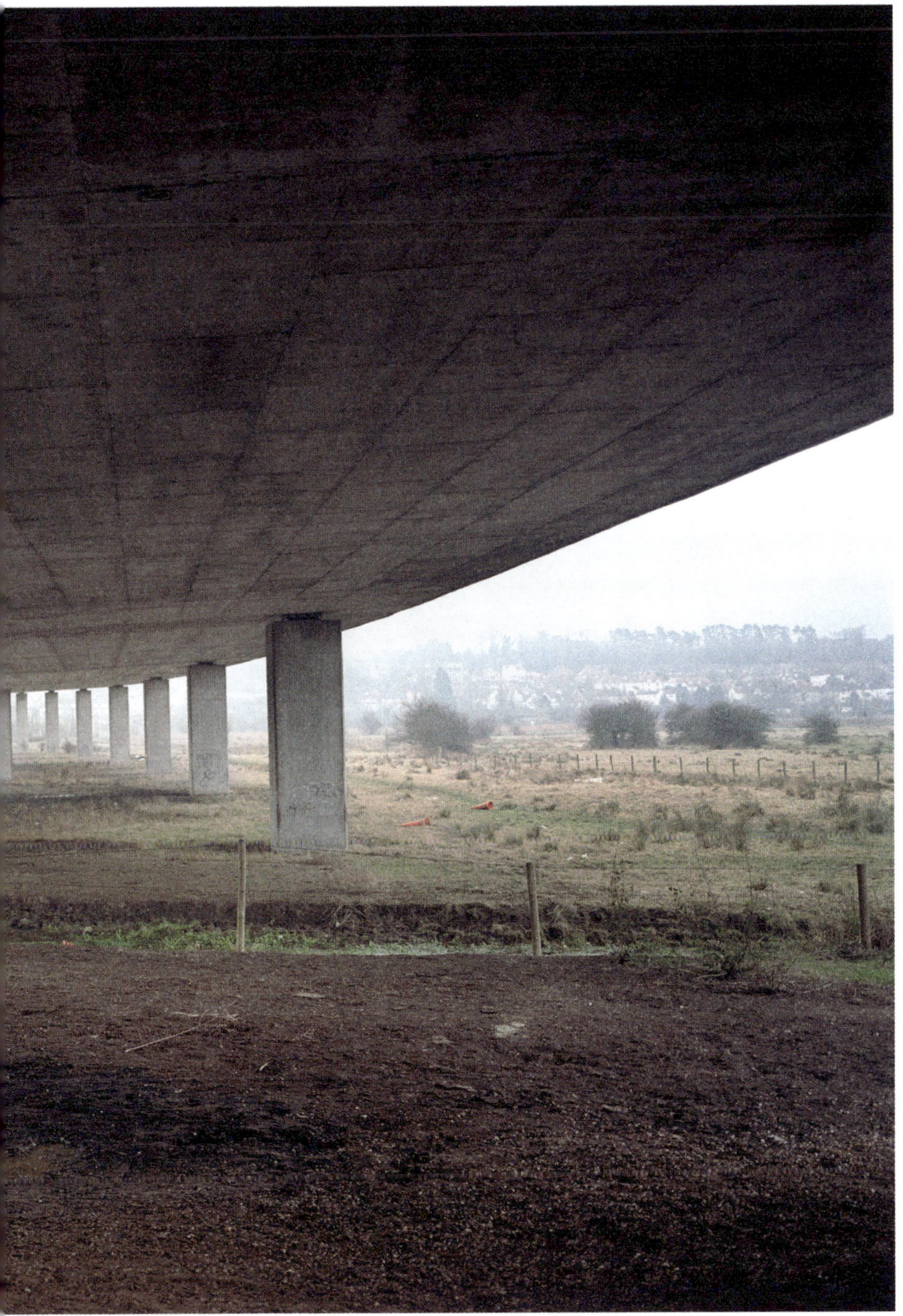

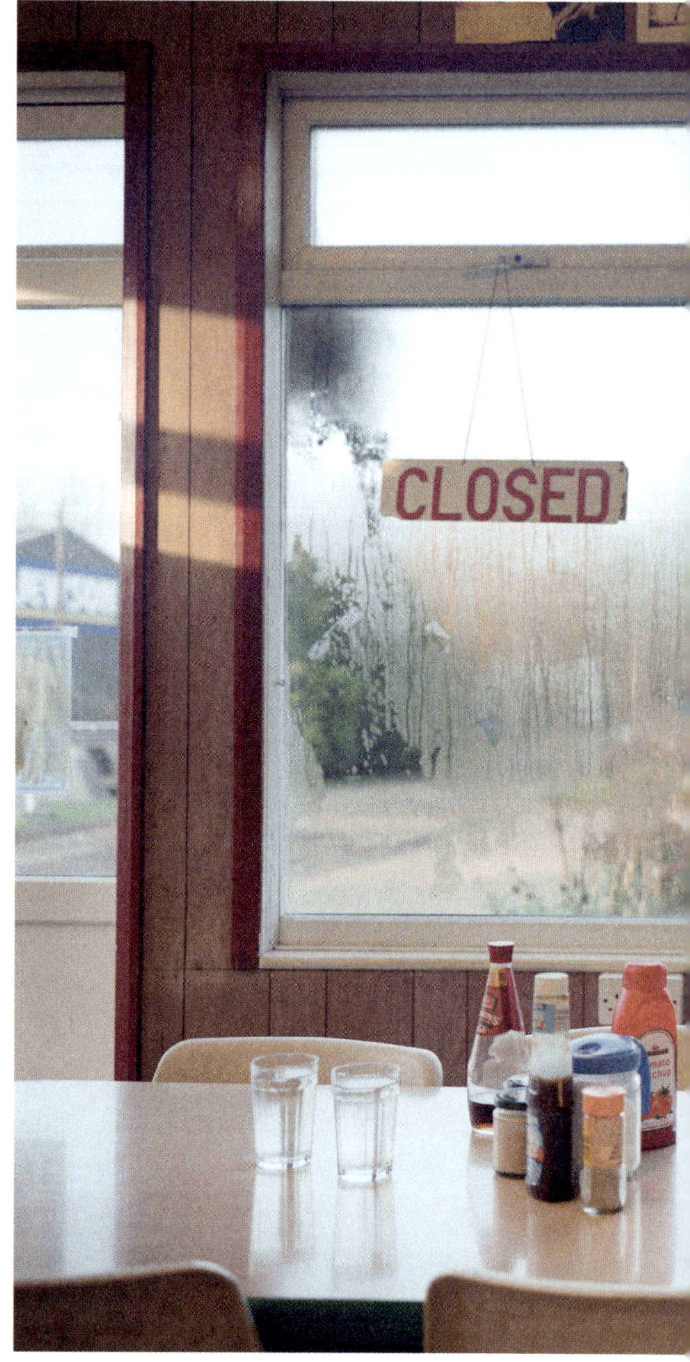
CLOSED

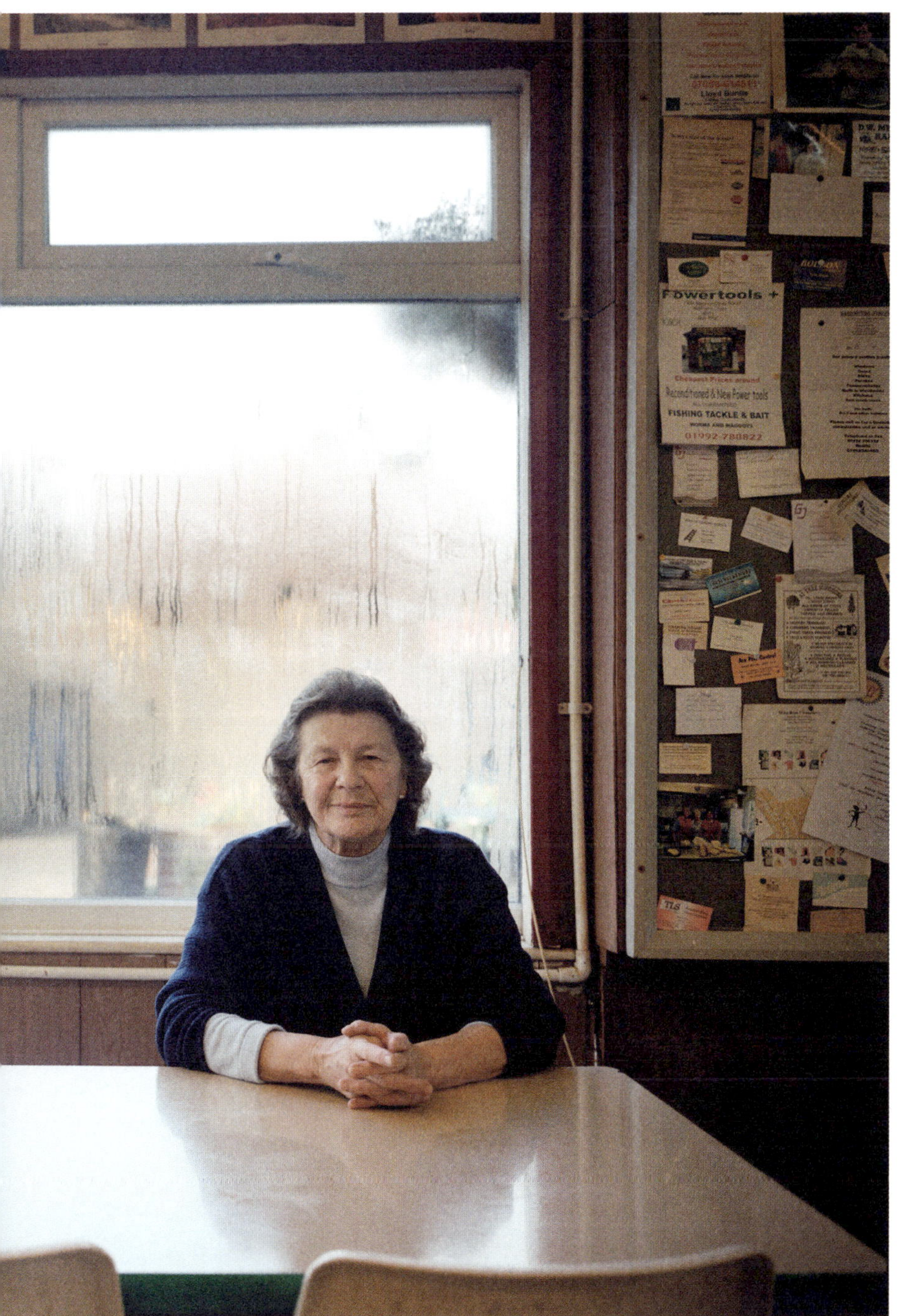

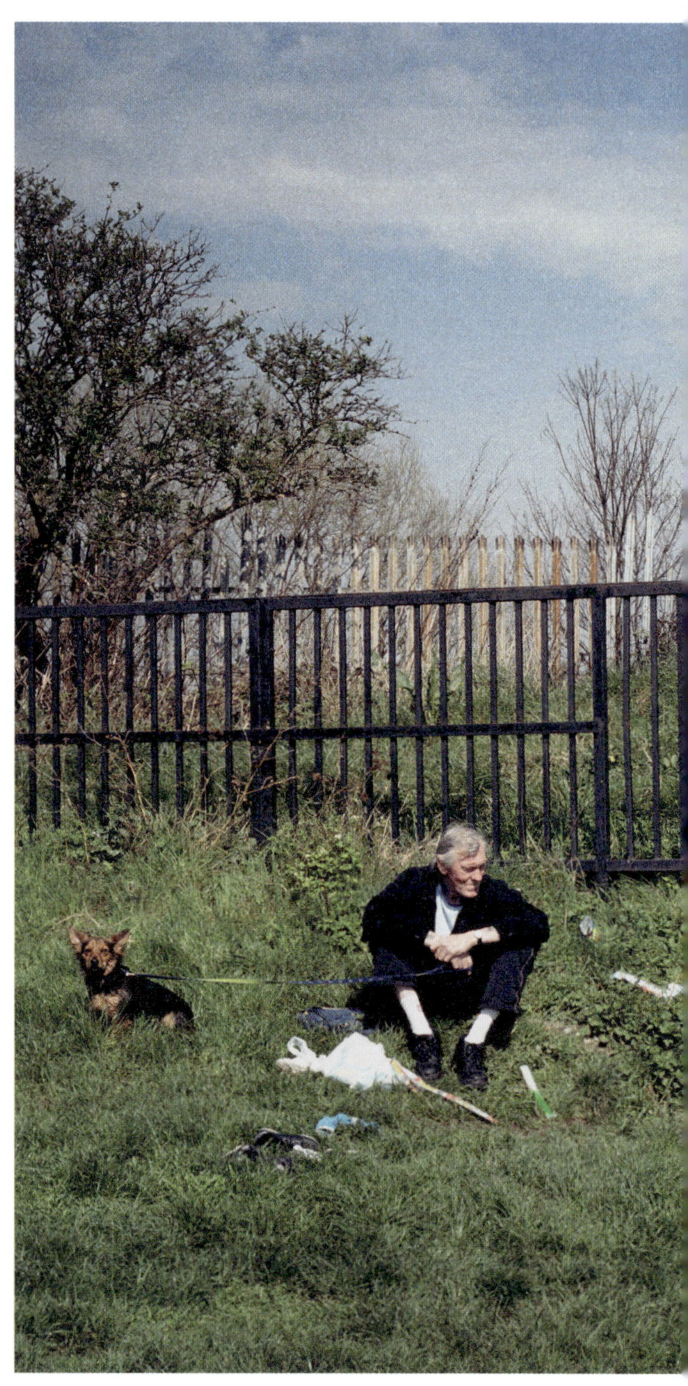

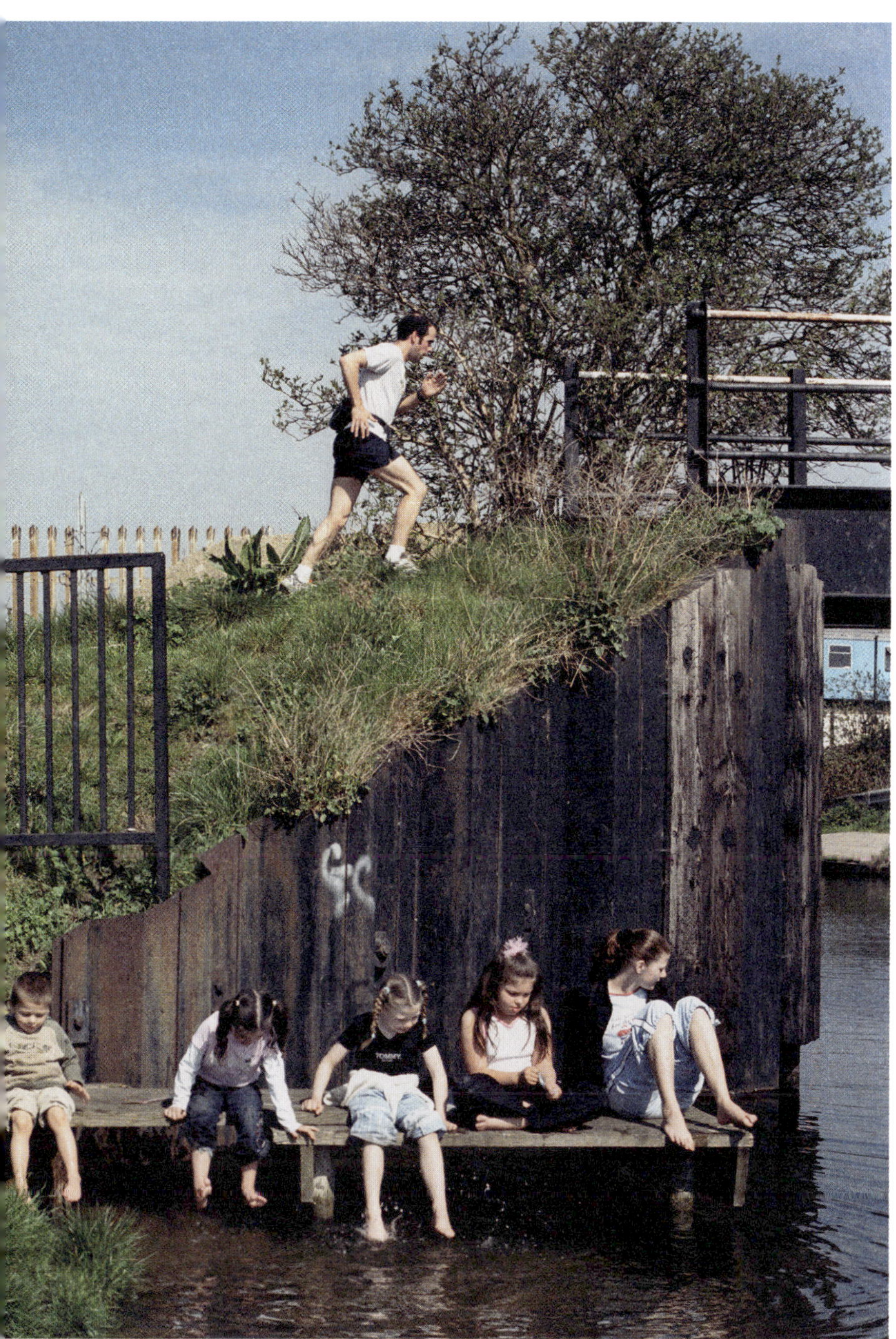

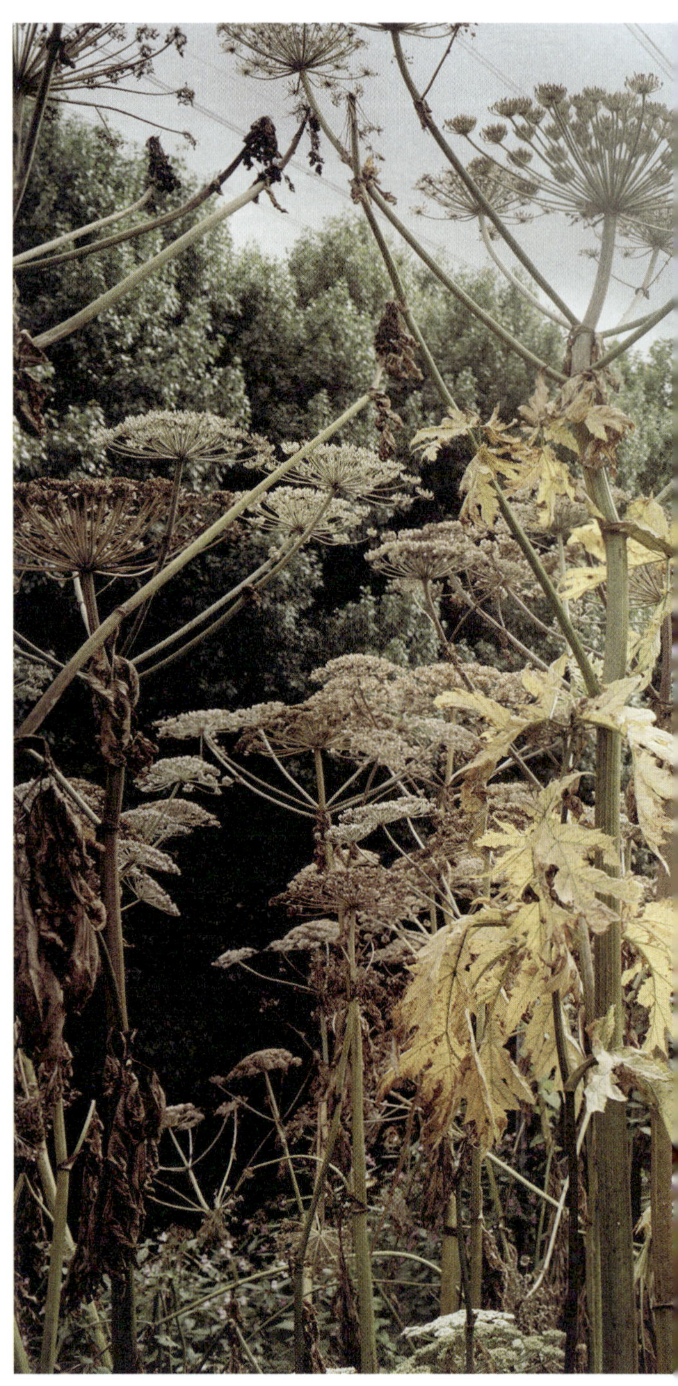

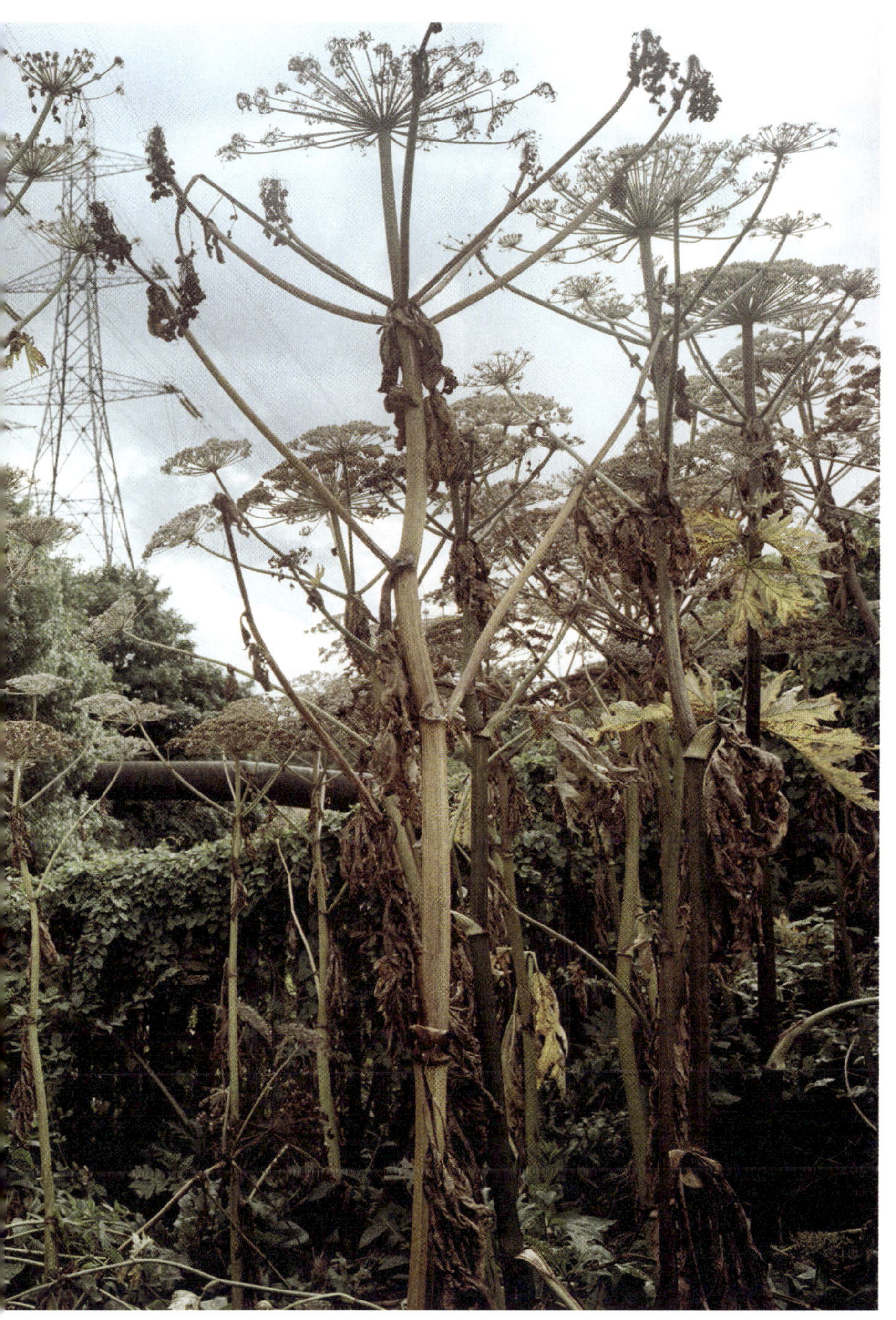

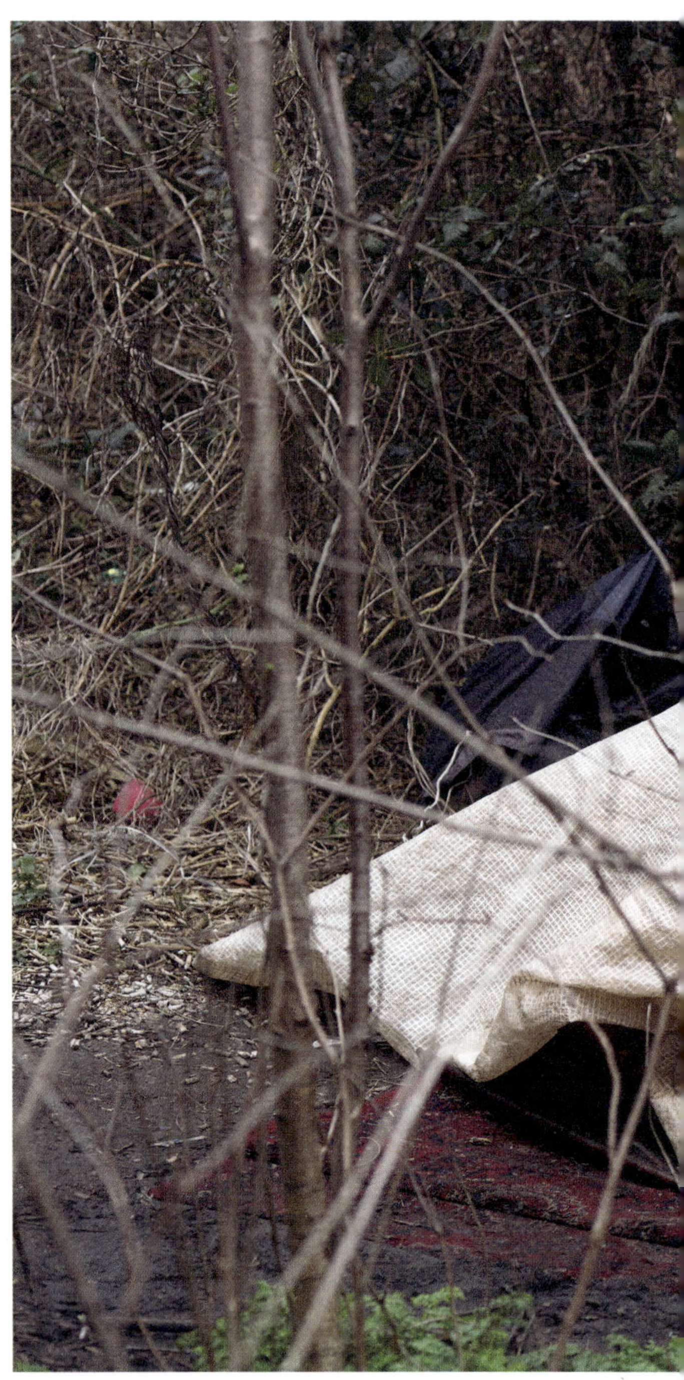

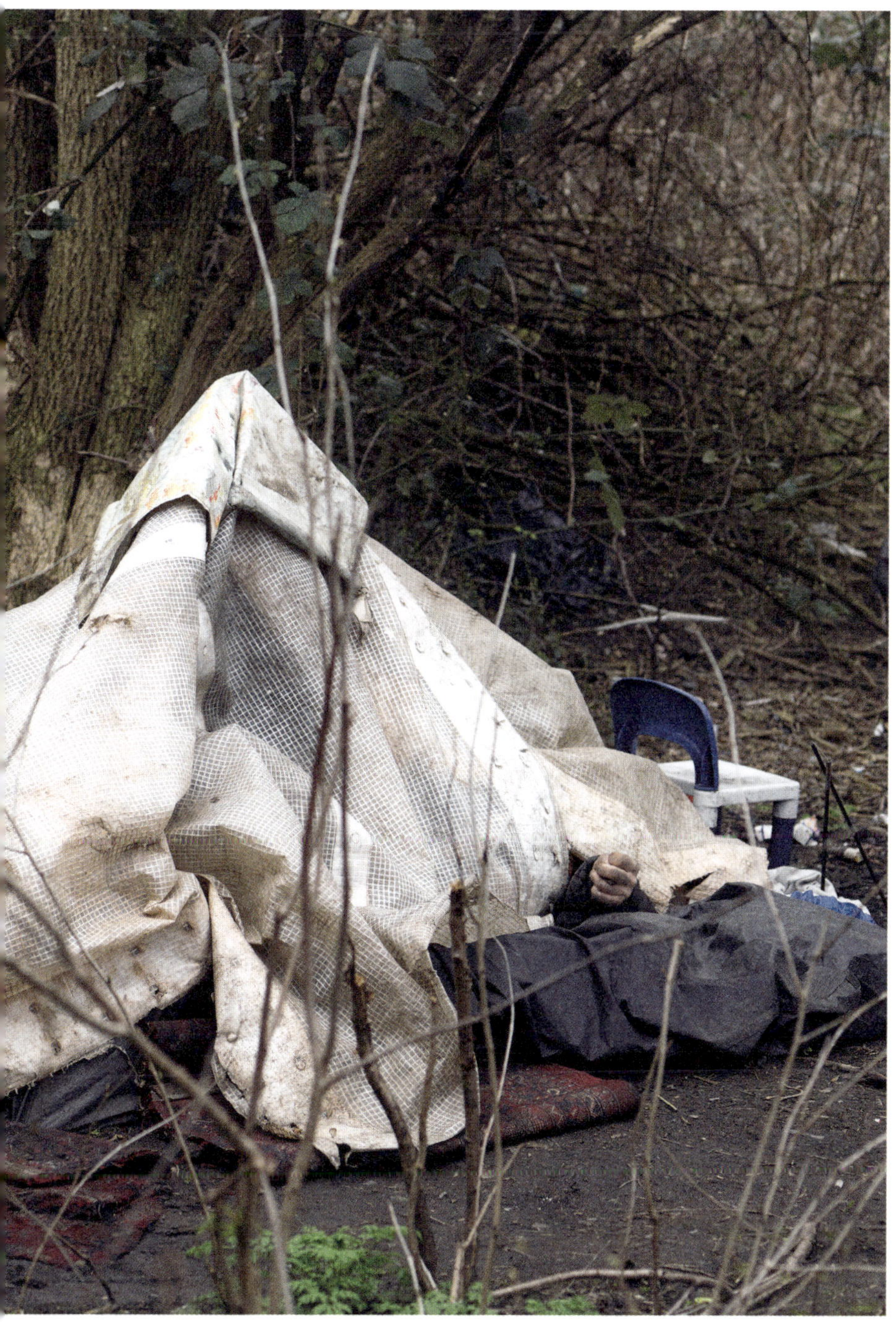

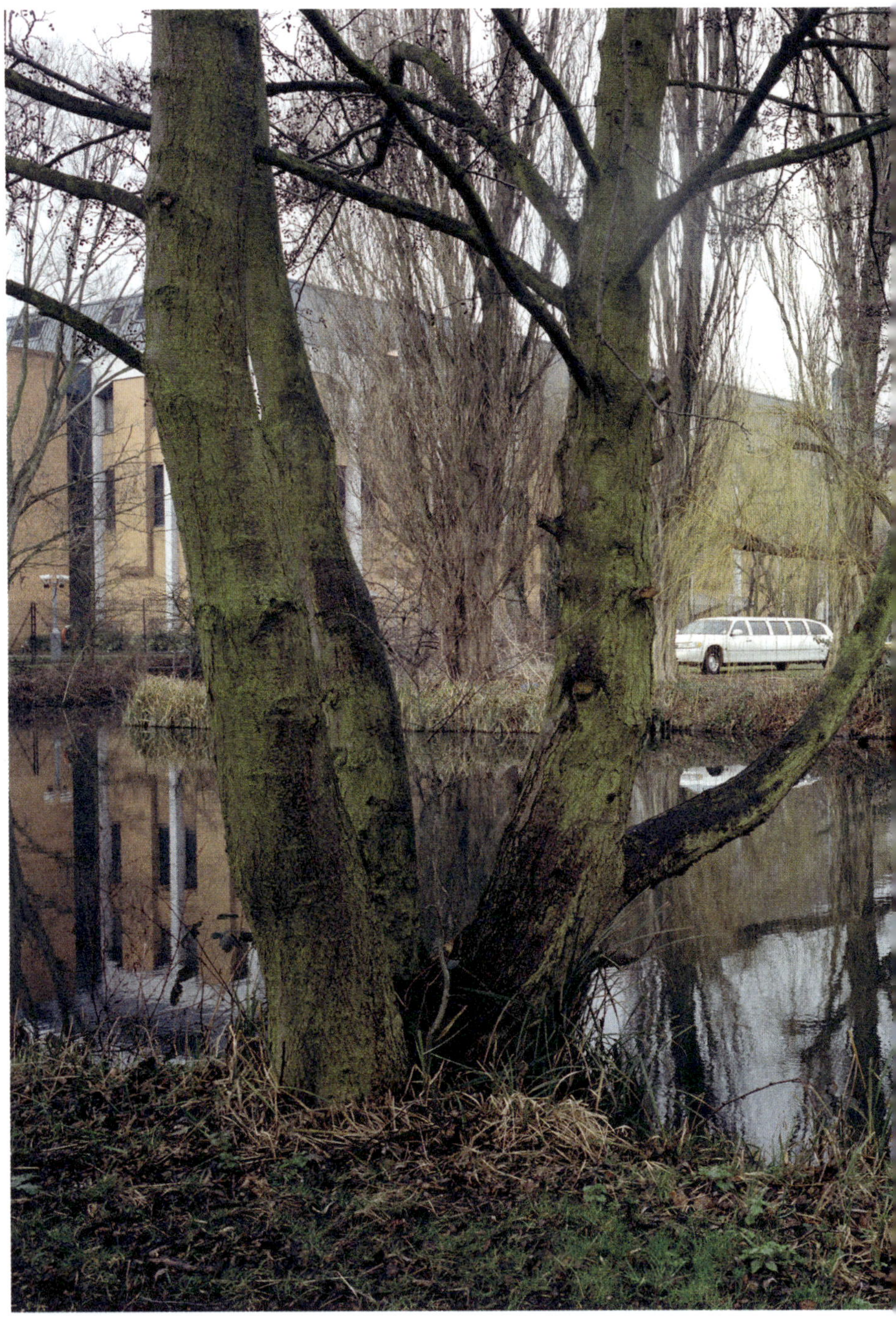

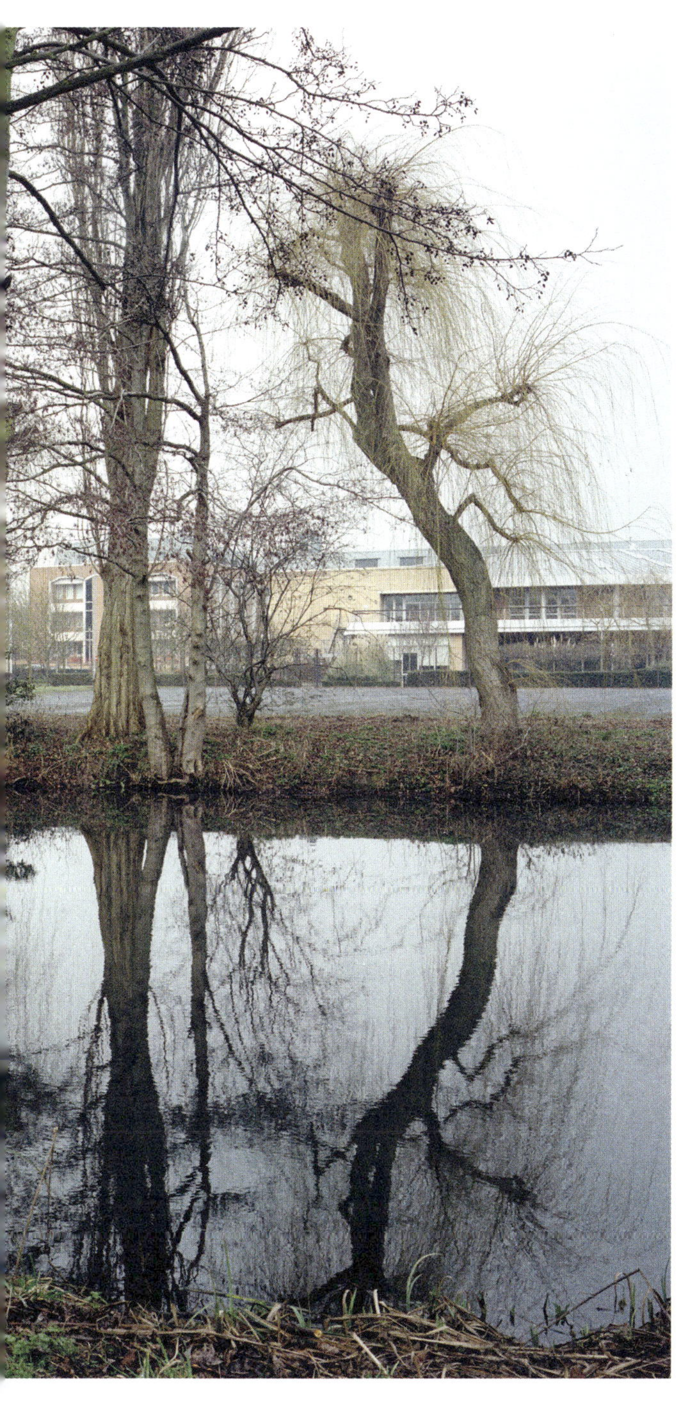

SUNDAY FOOTBALL

CHRIS BAKER

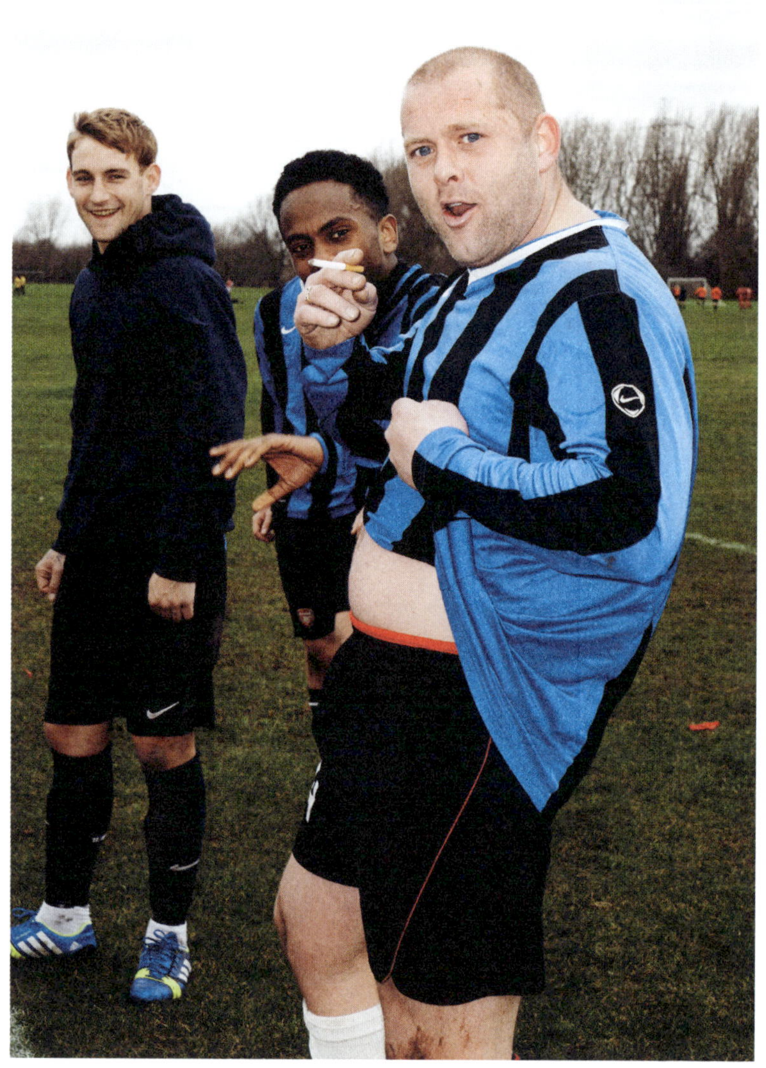

Welcome to Hackney Marshes. It was on these muddy fields that Leytonstone-born David Beckham's glittering football career kicked off. When Chris Baker decided to shoot a project on the Sunday League teams here, he wasn't hunting down future Beckhams, though. This is his 'ode to those players that turn up late, hungover and discussing last night's conquest'. A foul-mouthed, rambunctious tribe, prone to fights, sometimes out-of-shape, but fiercely devoted to their team.

And he's captured that scene in all its scruffy, joyful glory. Instead of shooting the goals, the dramatic action you'd normally expect of sports photography, he highlights the humorous details and the characters that make amateur football unique. We see discarded banana skins, spliffs surreptitiously rolled on the sidelines. We see water fights and waterlogged pitches. We see groups of men who – whatever their job, their age, their history – for those 90 minutes are united.

As a footie-crazed teenager, Baker did professional trials but it wasn't to be. Years later, he rediscovered his love for the game through Sunday League. 'Football was back to being playground football: hanging out with mates, having a laugh', he remembers. With *Sunday Football* he reminds us that sport isn't always about winning or losing. It's about playing.

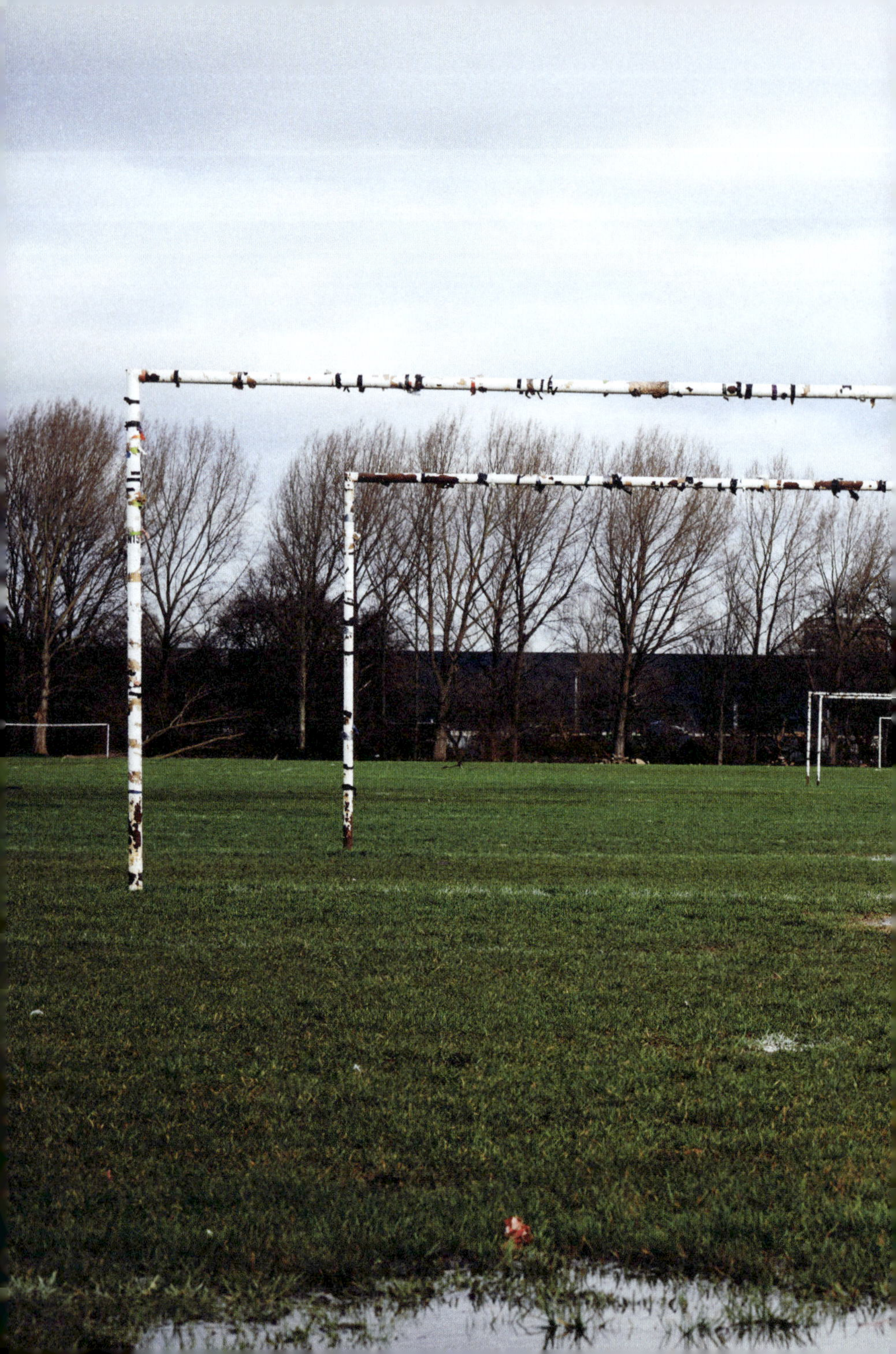

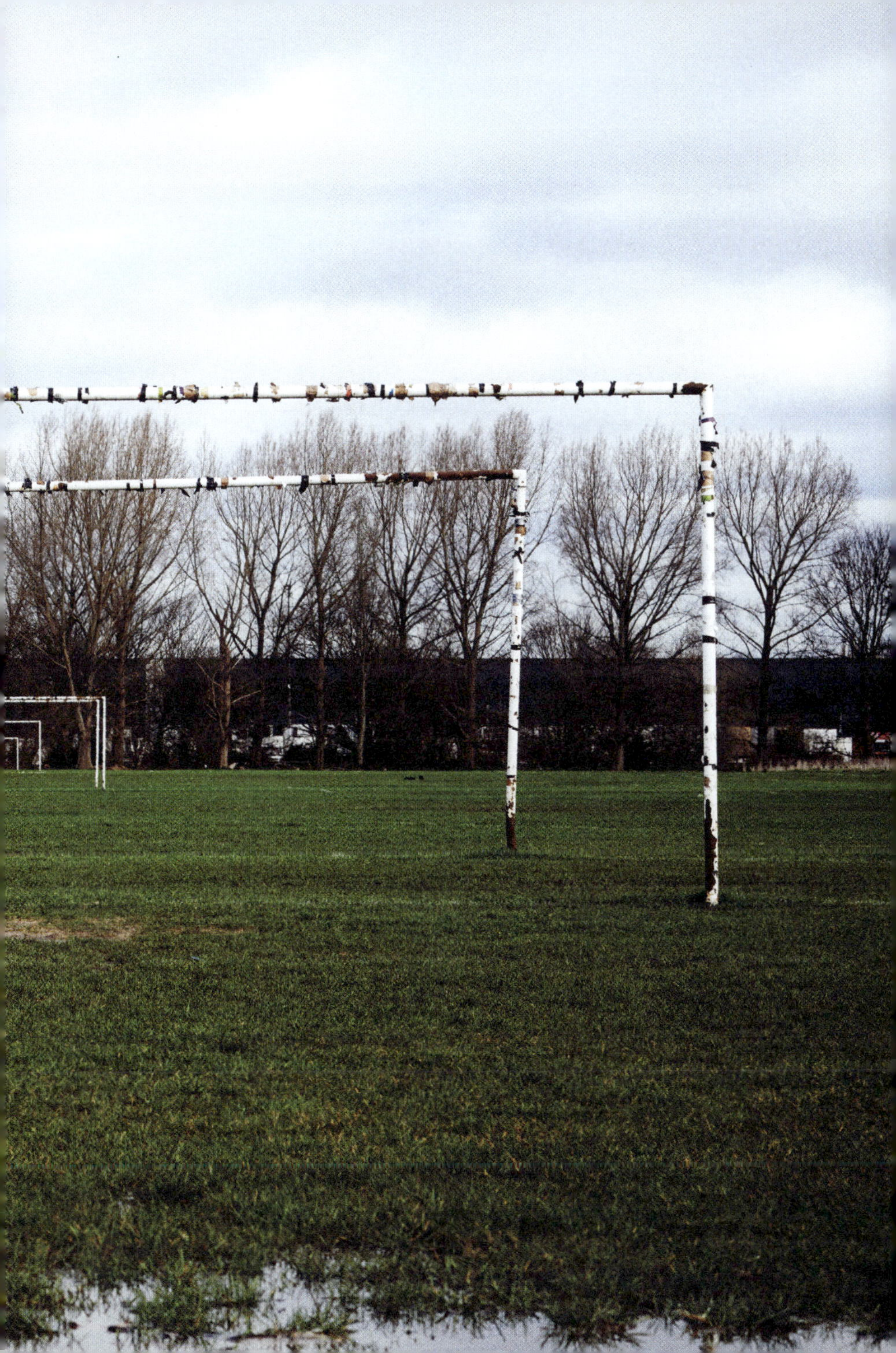

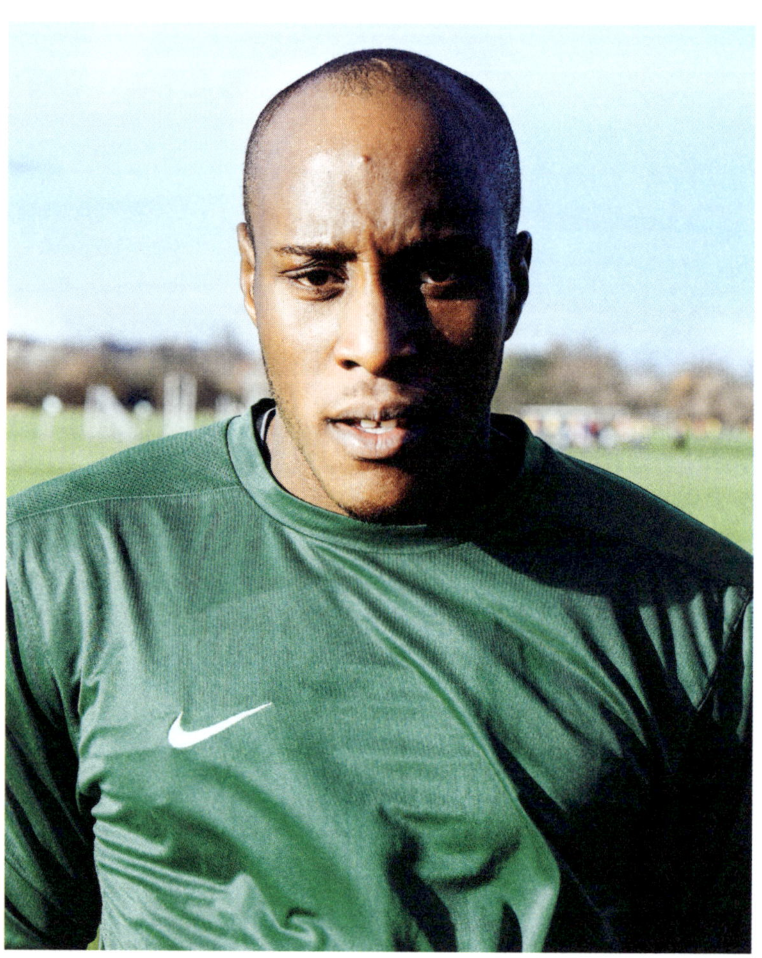

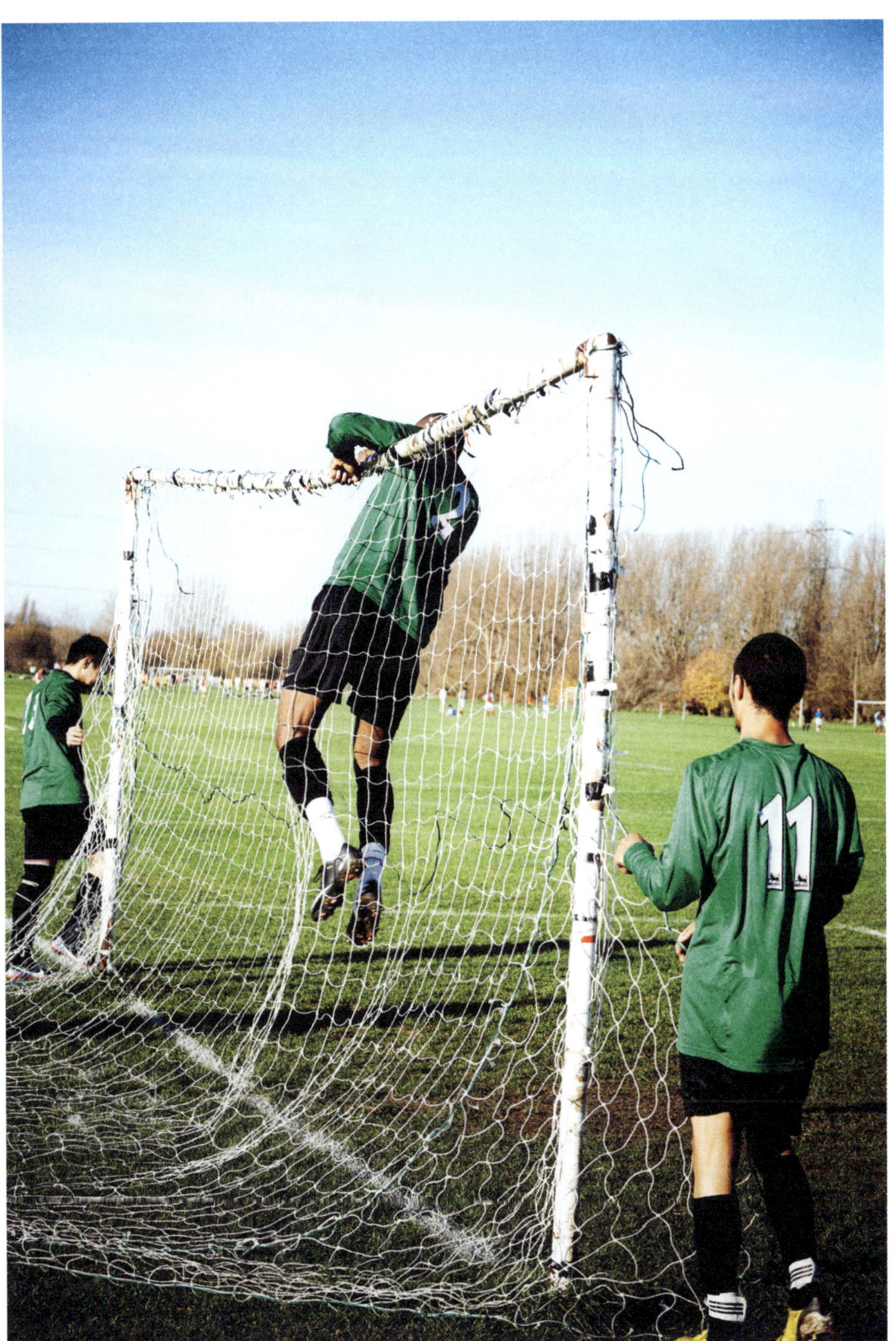

*'No one wants to pull out due to being hungover – such things
usually lead to being dropped for a couple of weeks.
Players' excuses include a car breakdown, an ill relative and,
my personal favourite, which was pretending I was stuck
in a lift. I even got out of bed and into my lift to add
authenticity to the phone call.'*

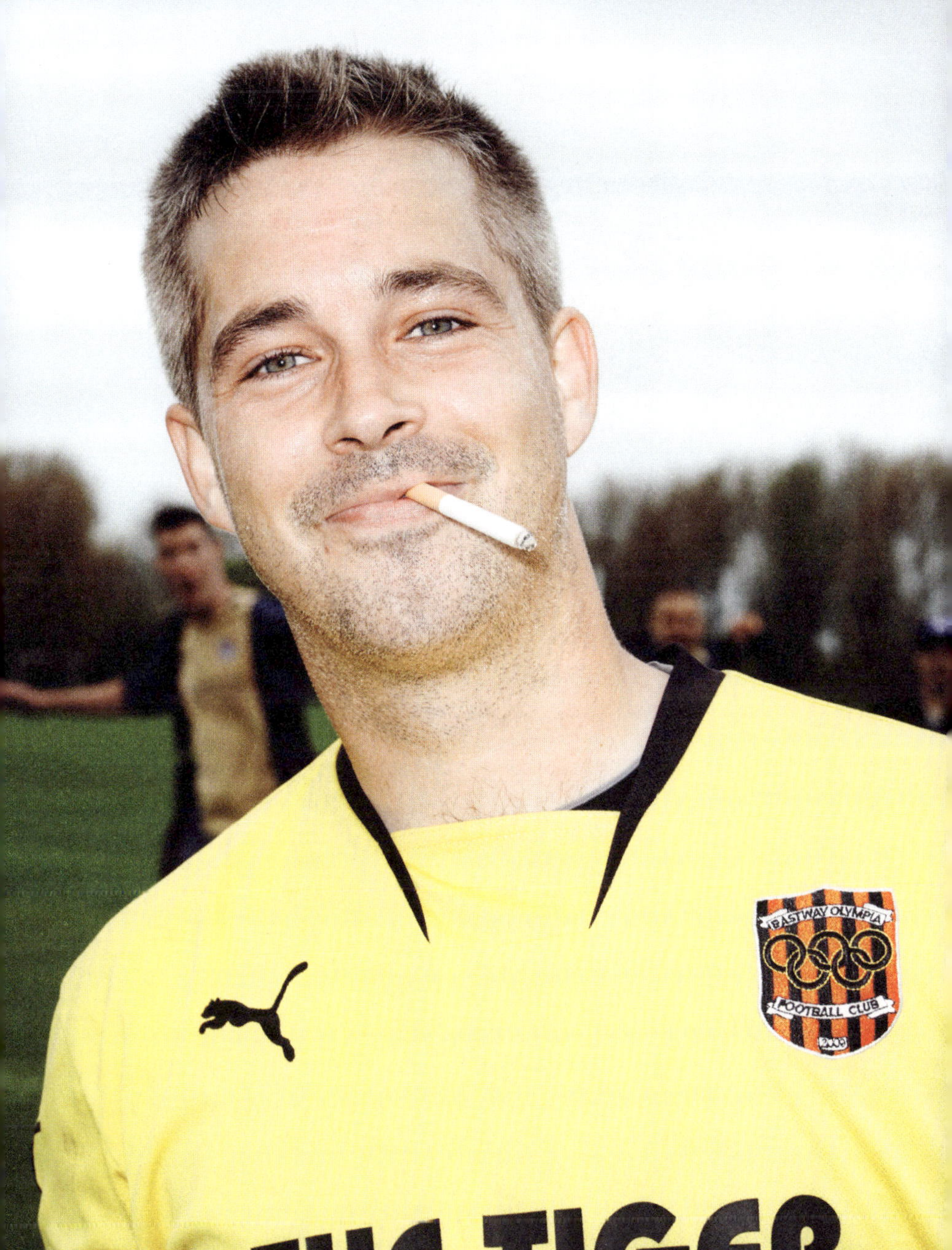

EASTWAY OLYMPIA
FOOTBALL CLUB
THE TIGER

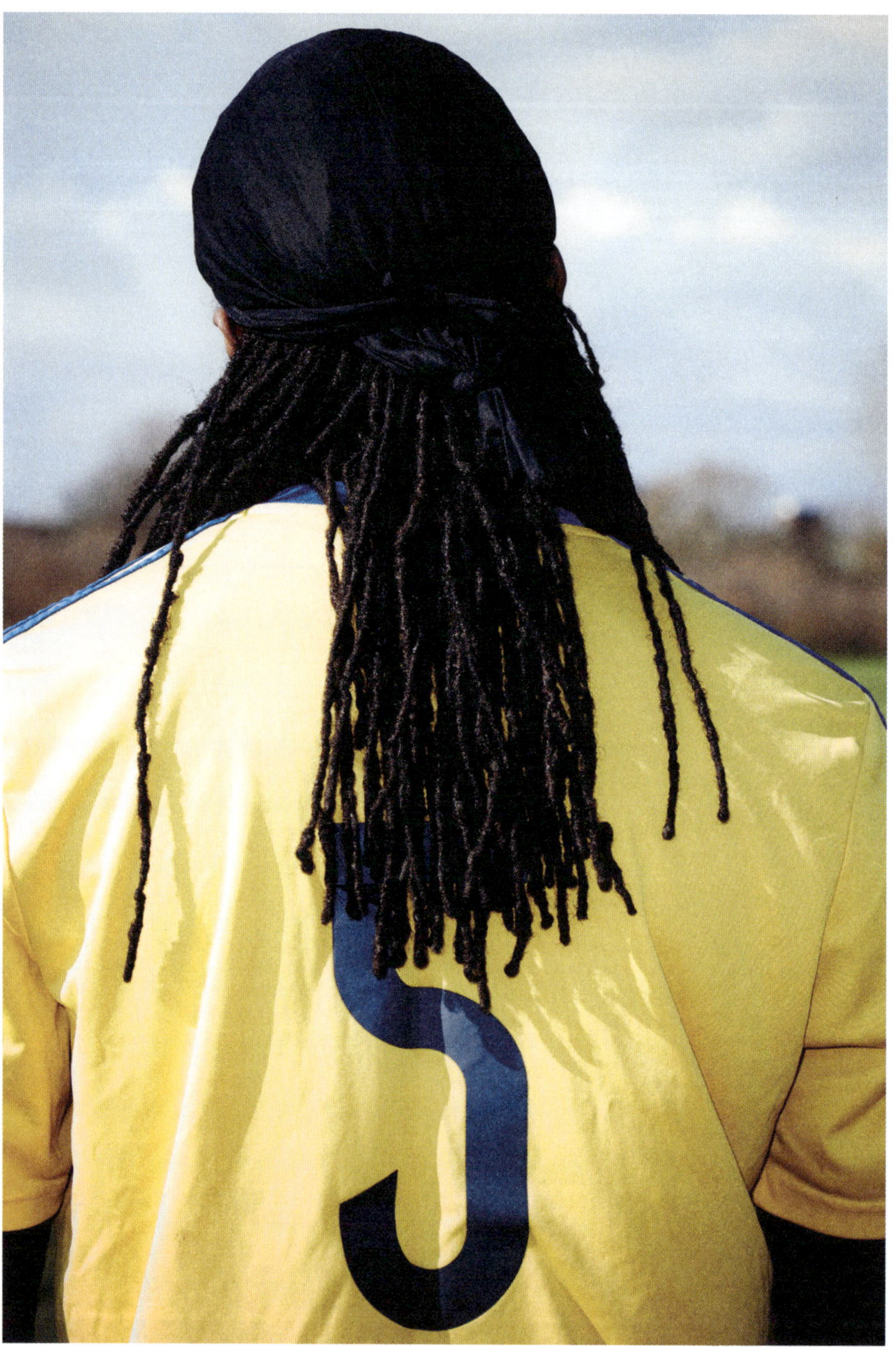

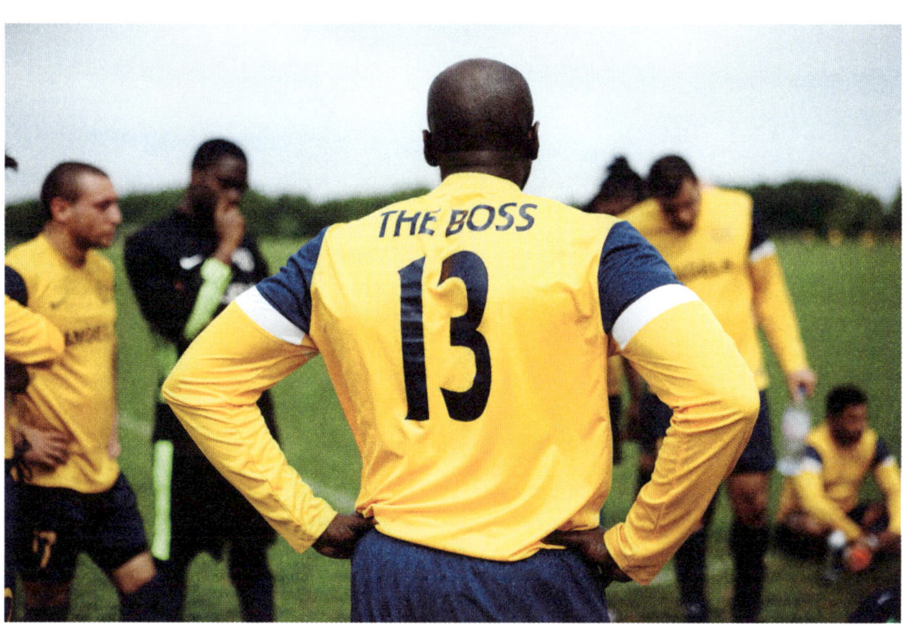
THE BOSS
13

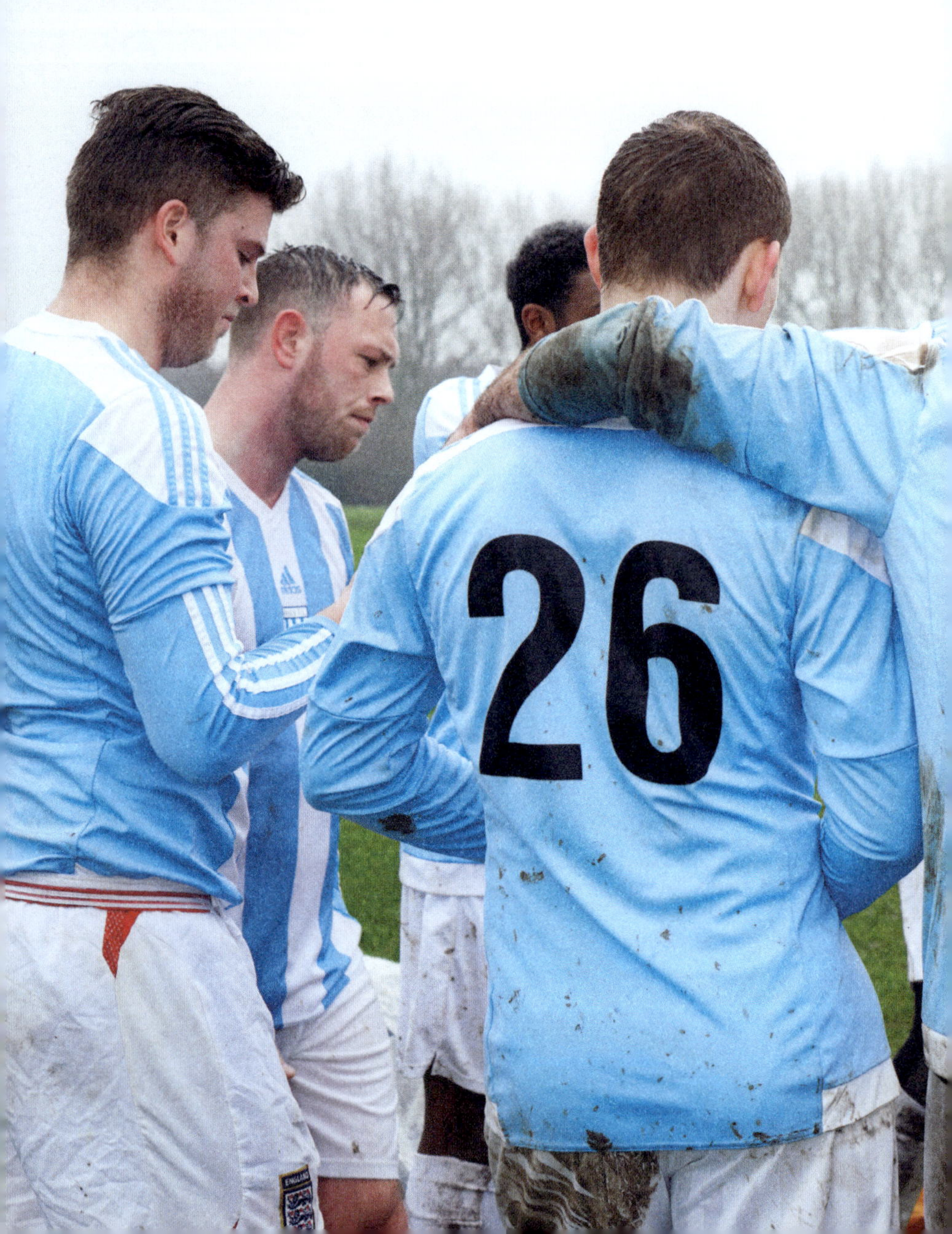

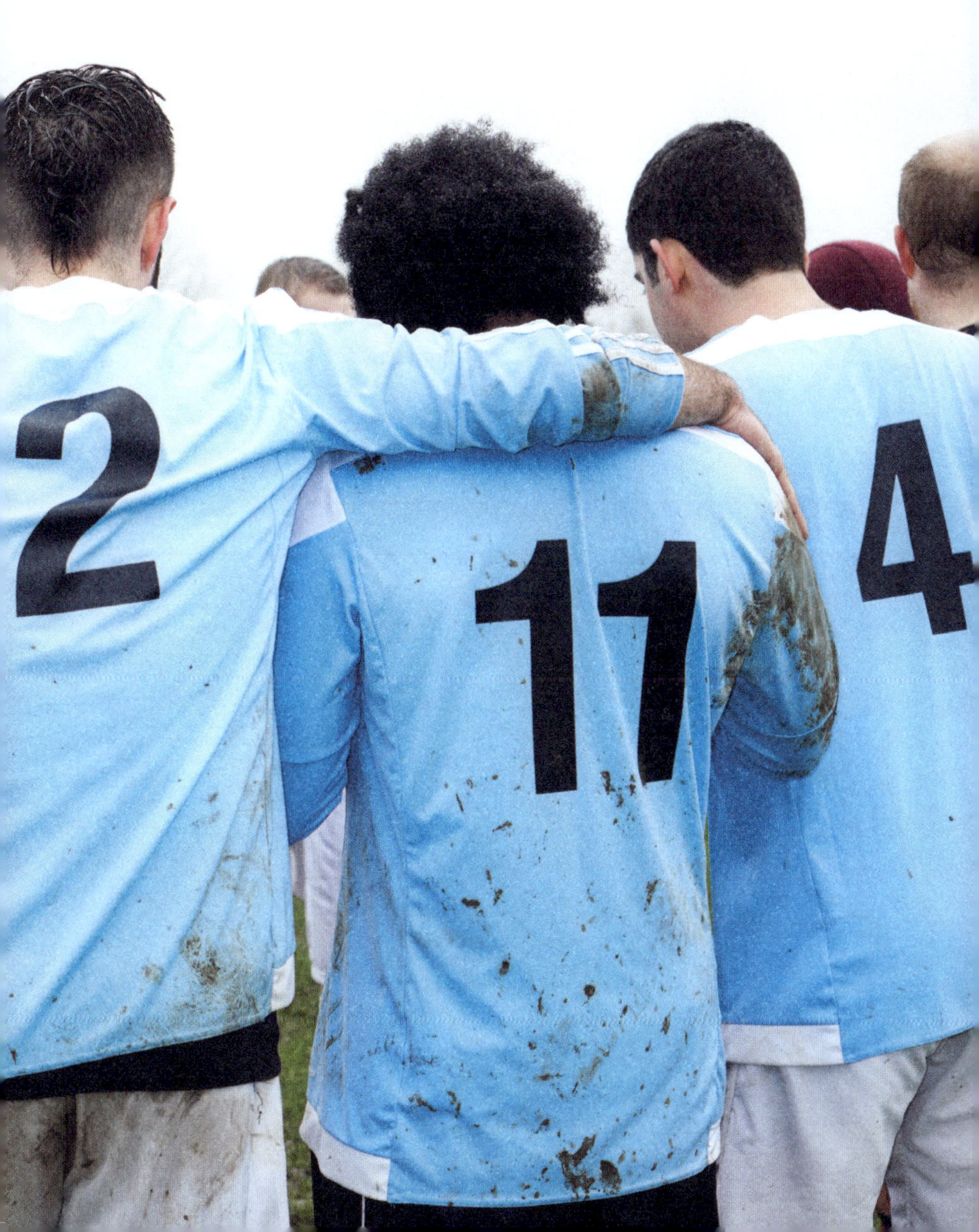

'Our old goalkeeper wore glasses but couldn't wear contacts.
This was a bit of a problem as he could only really see
a player or the ball when they reached the edge of his area.
We conceded a lot of long-range shots that year.'

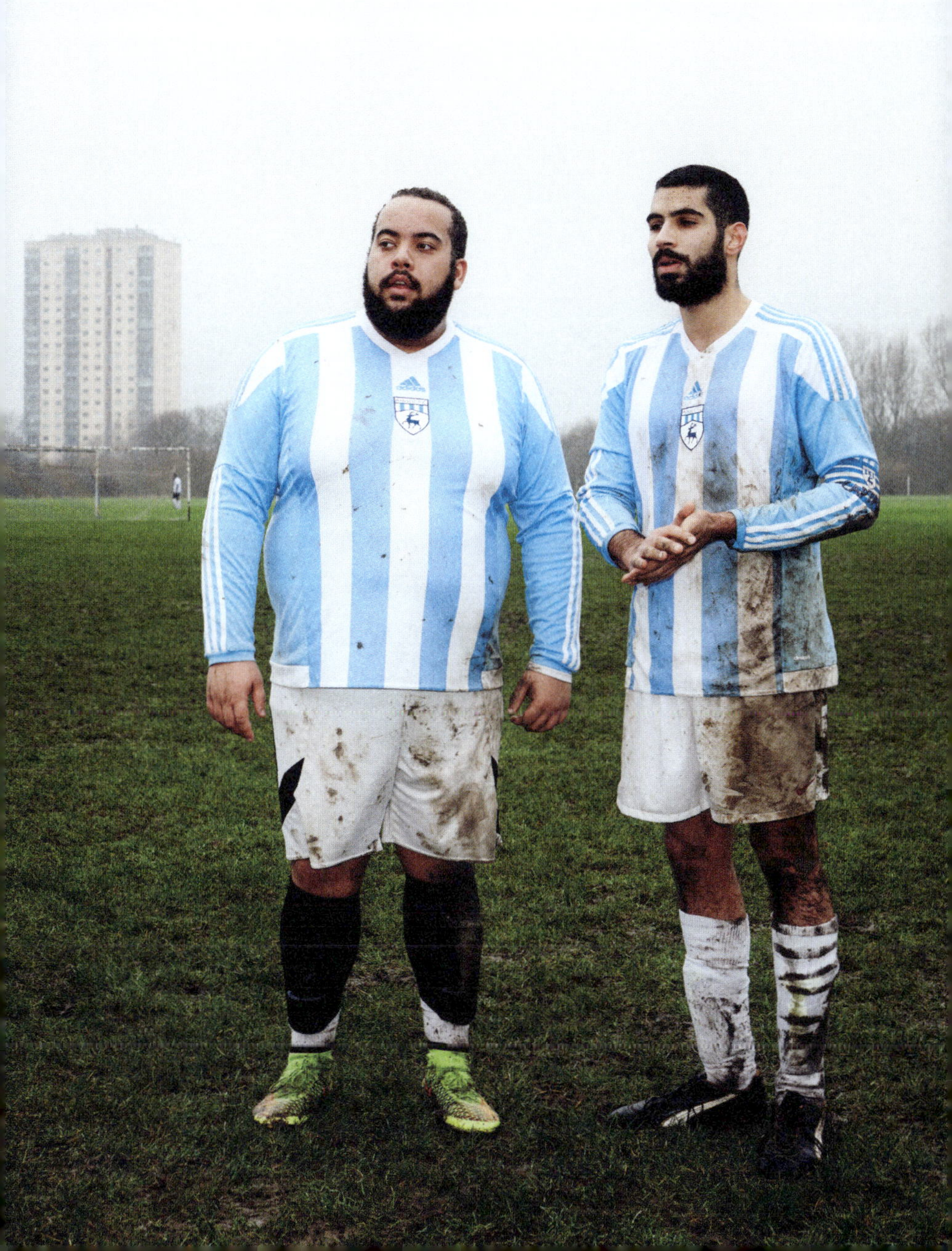

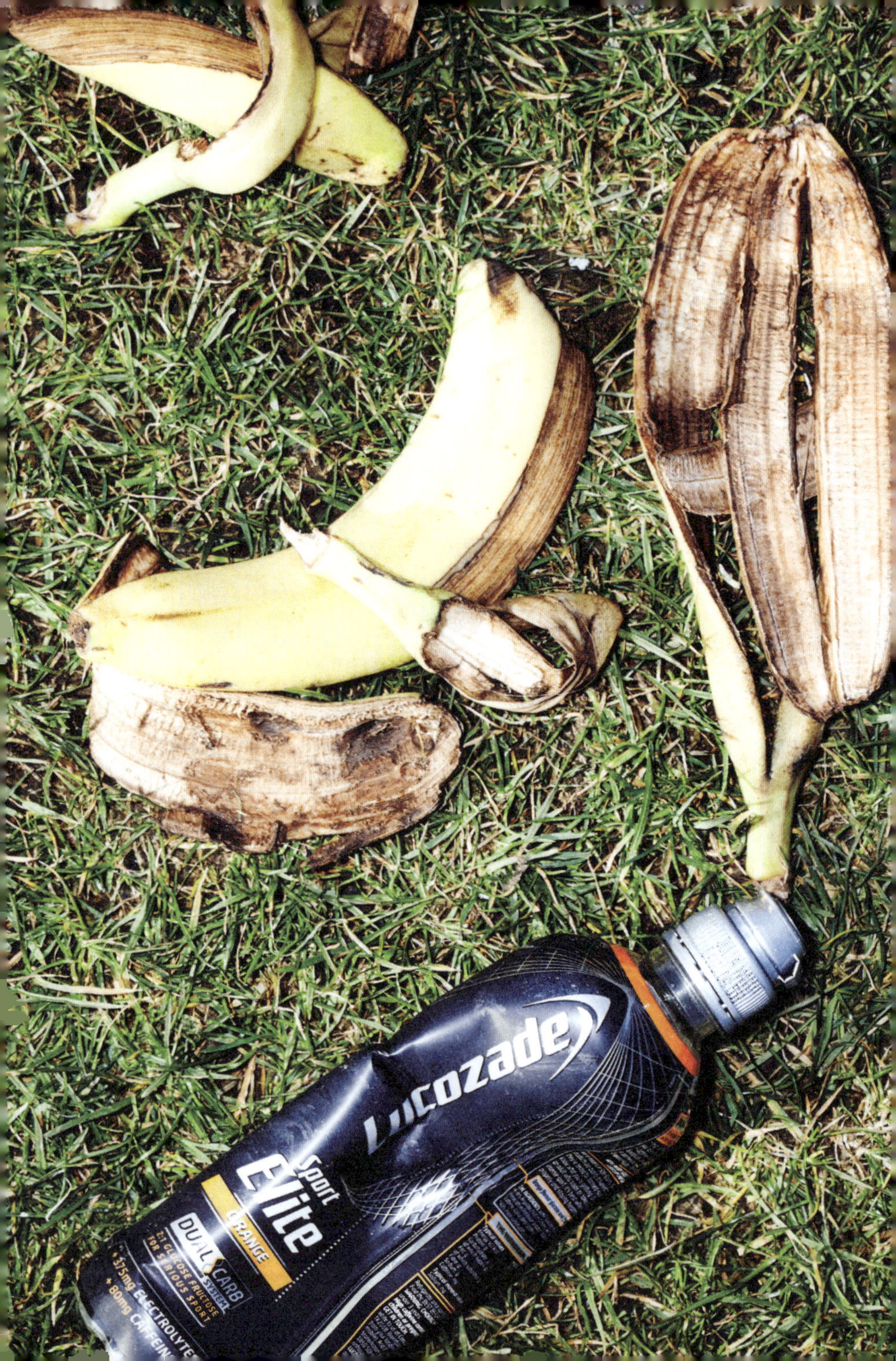

Lucozade
Sport
Elite
ORANGE
DUAL CARB
2:1 GLUCOSE : FRUCTOSE
FOR SERIOUS SPORT
375mg ELECTROLYTES
80mg CAFFEINE

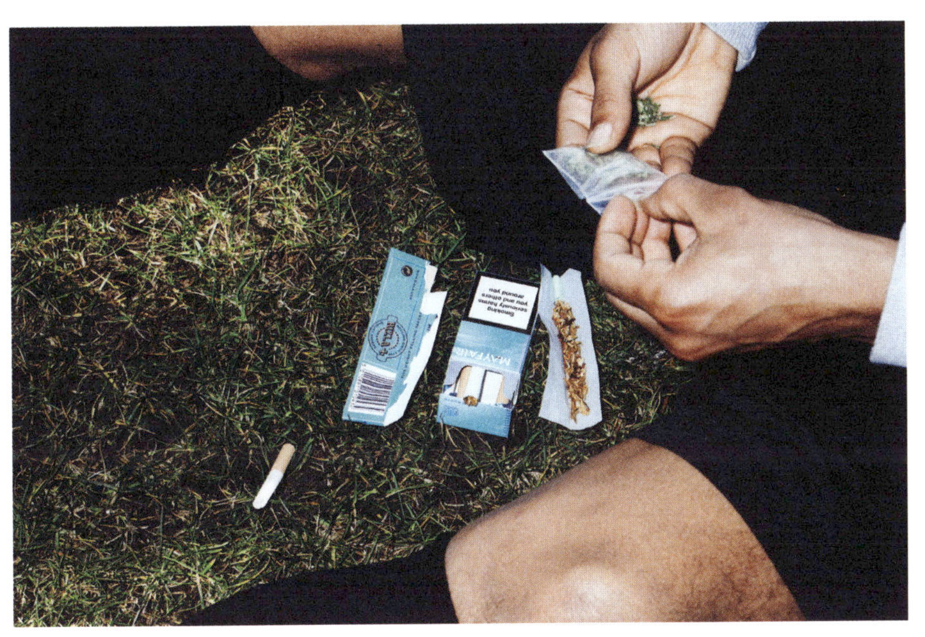

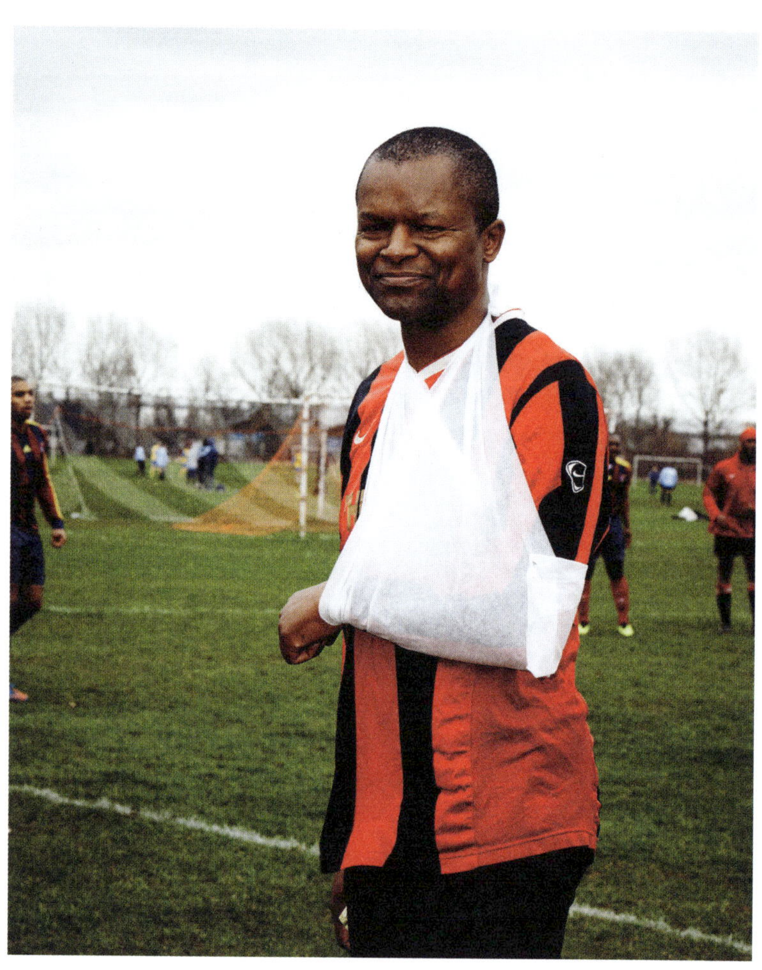

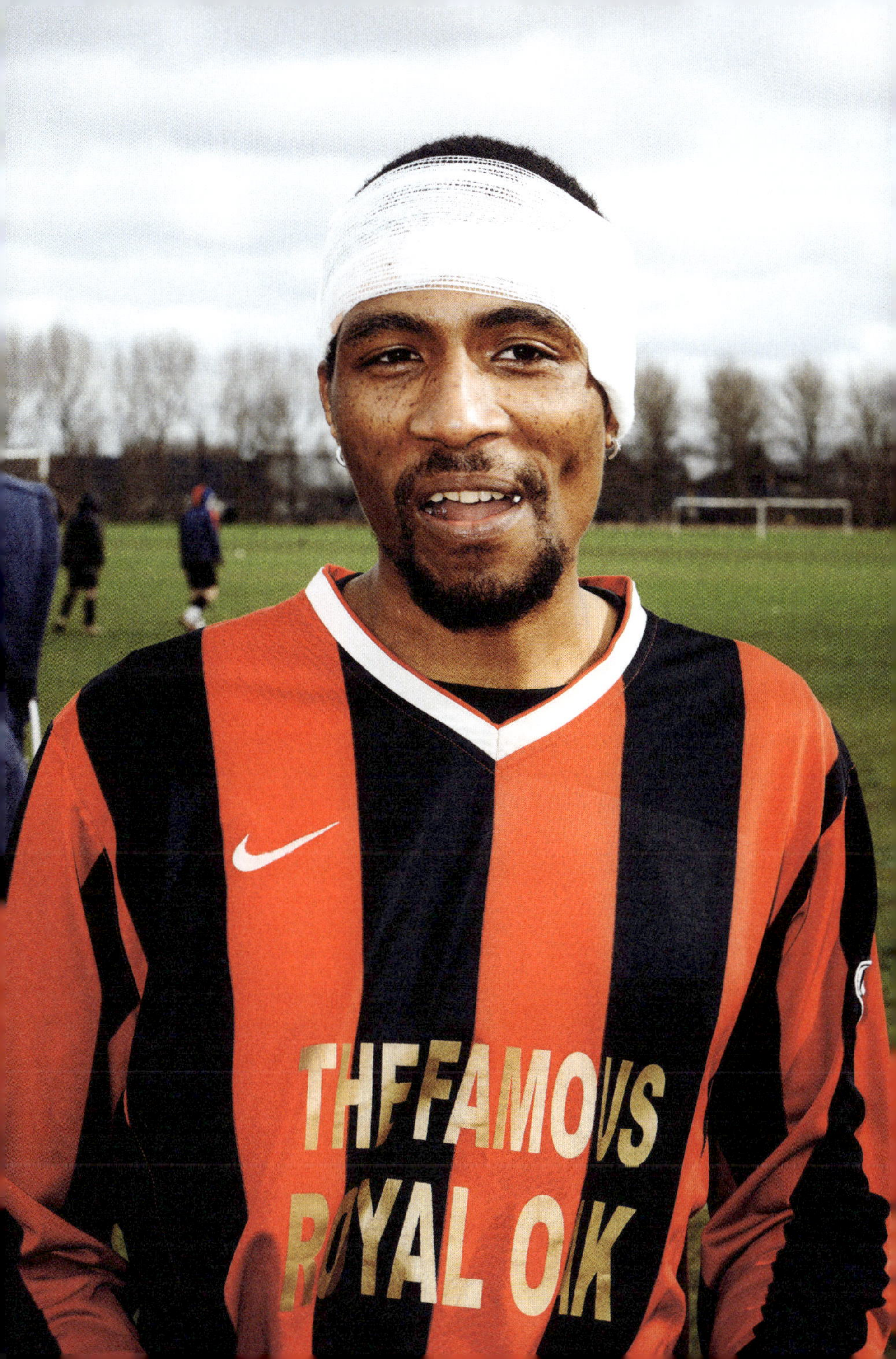

THE FAMOUS
ROYAL OK

'Football is a family tied together in knowledge and passion, where everything comes together for 90 minutes, where everything else is second to playing football.'

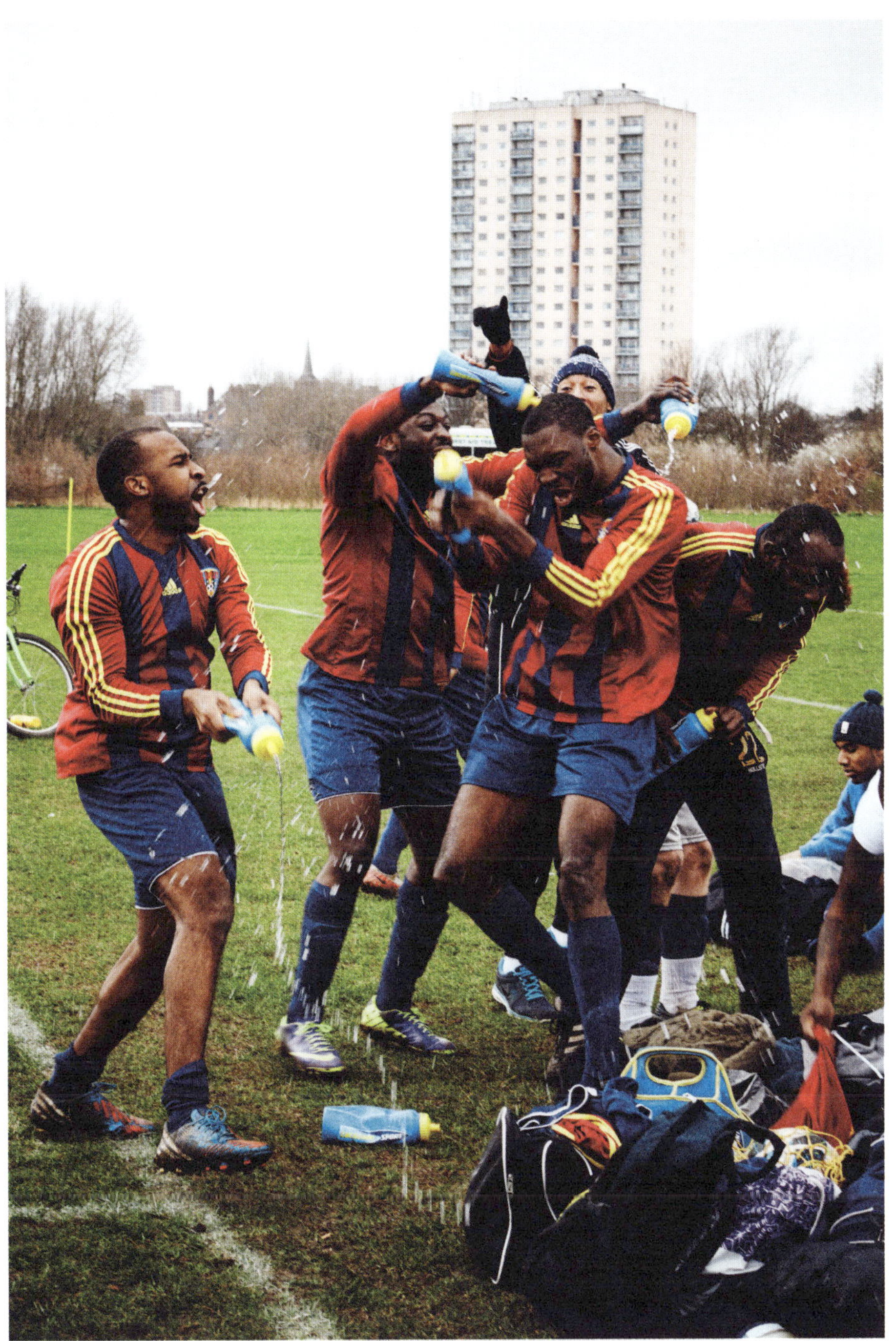

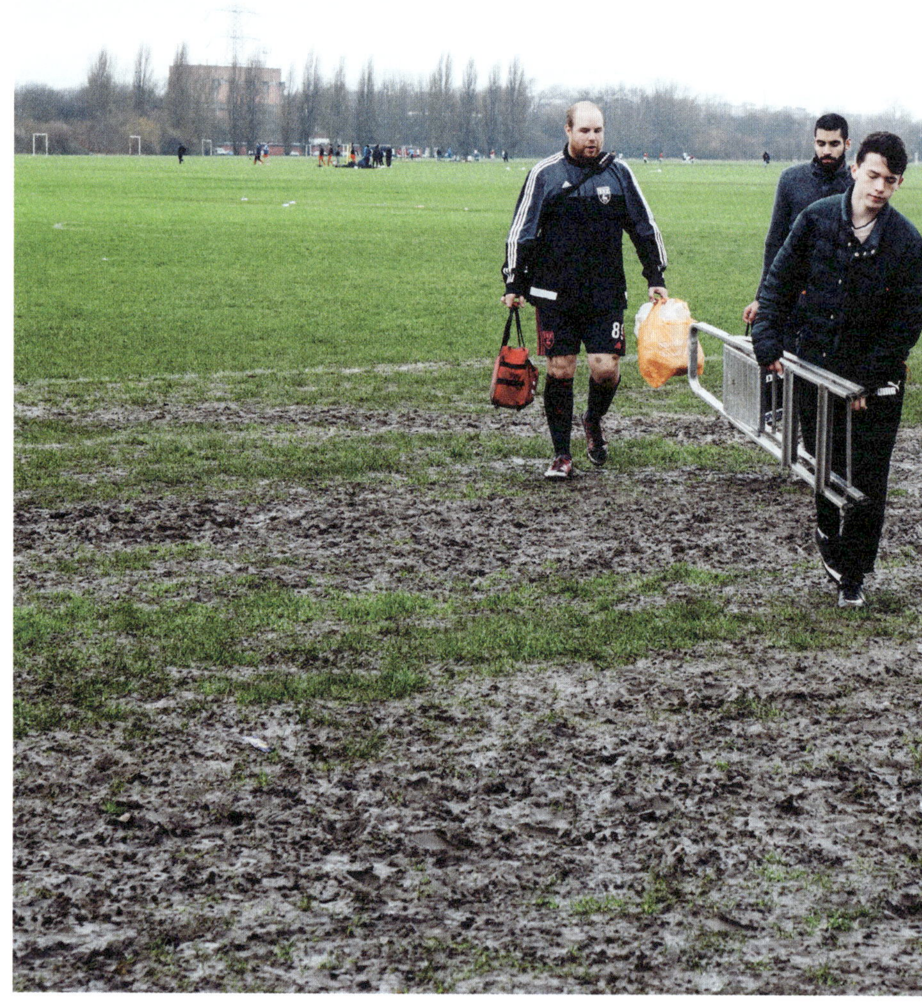

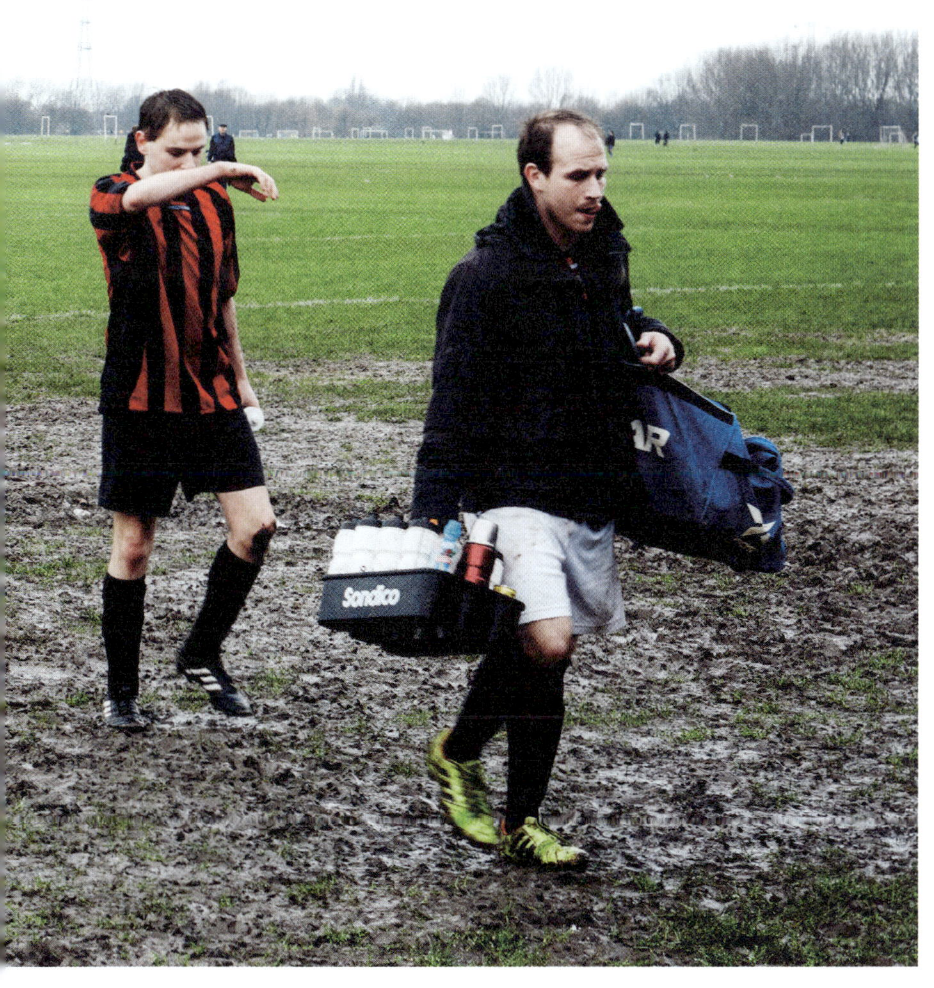
Sondico

SHOREDITCH WILD LIFE

DOUGIE WALLACE

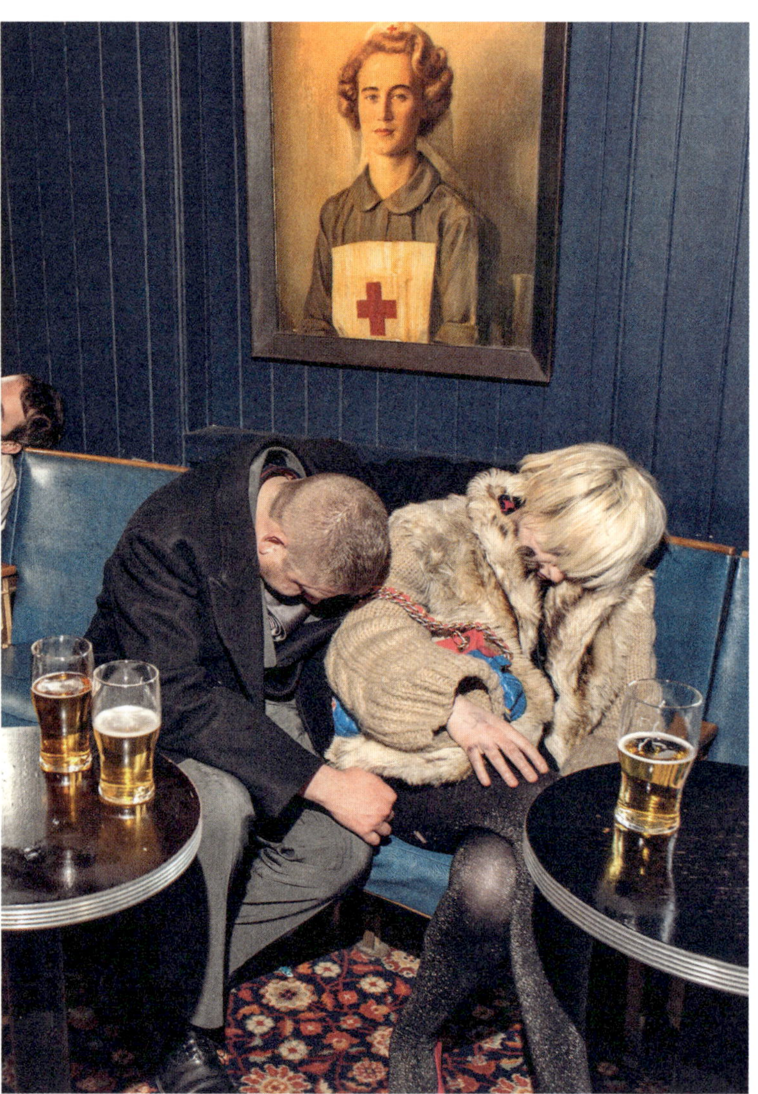

Shiny, grimy Shoreditch smacks you right in the face. It's Saturday night and you're swaying among the sweaty hipsters, faces streaked with glitter as they roll out of bars and collide in the street, falling over. Looking at Dougie Wallace's pictures, you can hear the laughter, the music, smell the second-hand weed smoke, taste the whisky. You can imagine the hangover too.

Glaswegian Wallace's route into photography was unconventional, taking in stints in the army and selling campervans. With his in-your-face manner and double-flash-gun set up, he's captured Blackpool's stag and hen scene, the super-rich of Kensington and Mumbai cabbies. People's reactions to him – the intense stares and glares down his lens, seen in *Shoreditch Wild Life* – are part of the recipe too.

In the early noughties, when Wallace started this project, there wasn't so much to see in the area – a couple of bars, the odd artist renting on the cheap. It's really during the past 12 years that it's morphed into the hedonistic club land it is today. Already, it feels a bit like we're looking at another world here, a Shoreditch that doesn't quite exist anymore. Everything feels just that bit smarter now. Although perhaps not in the wee hours of a Sunday morning.

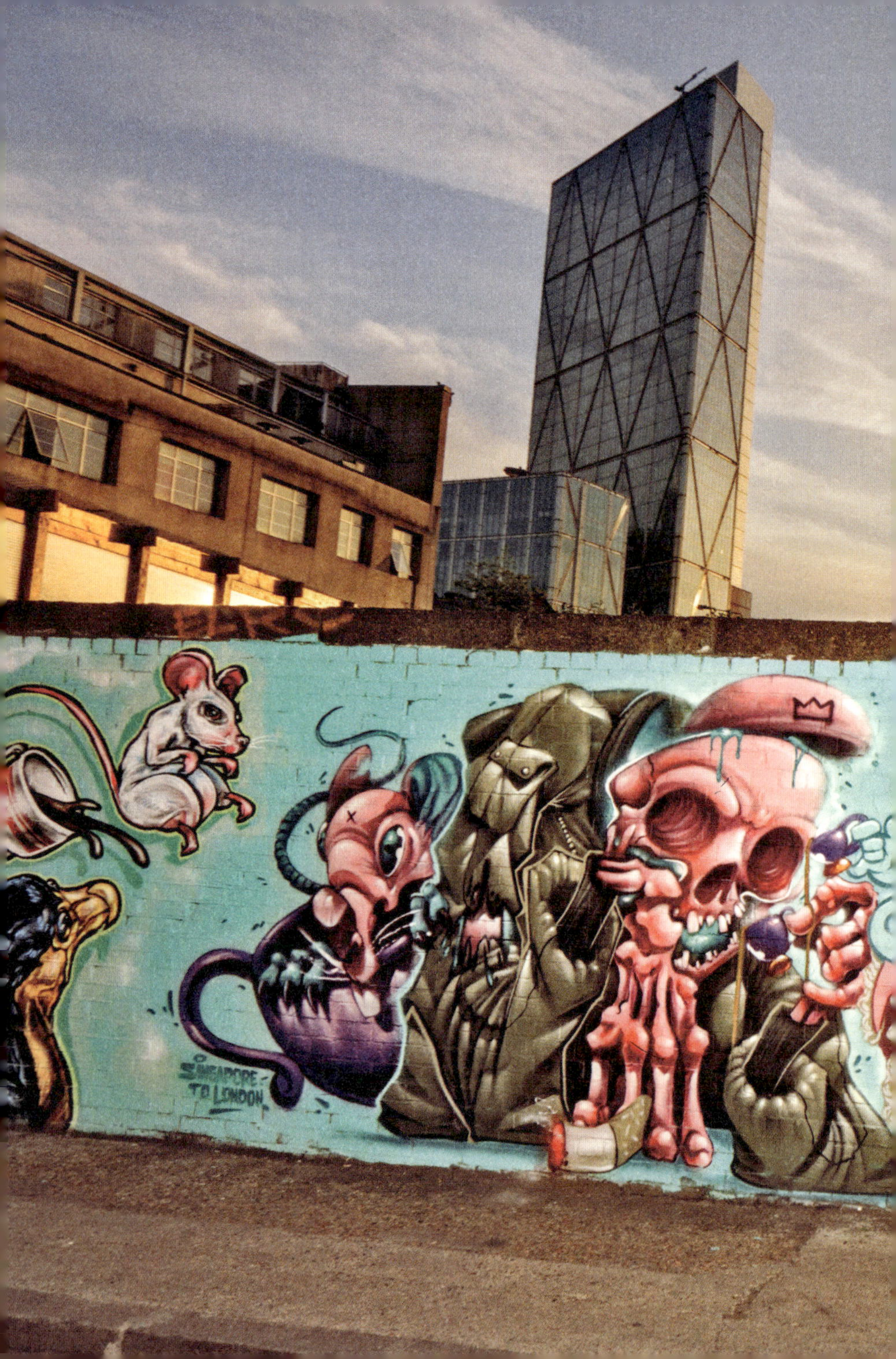
SINGAPORE
TO LONDON

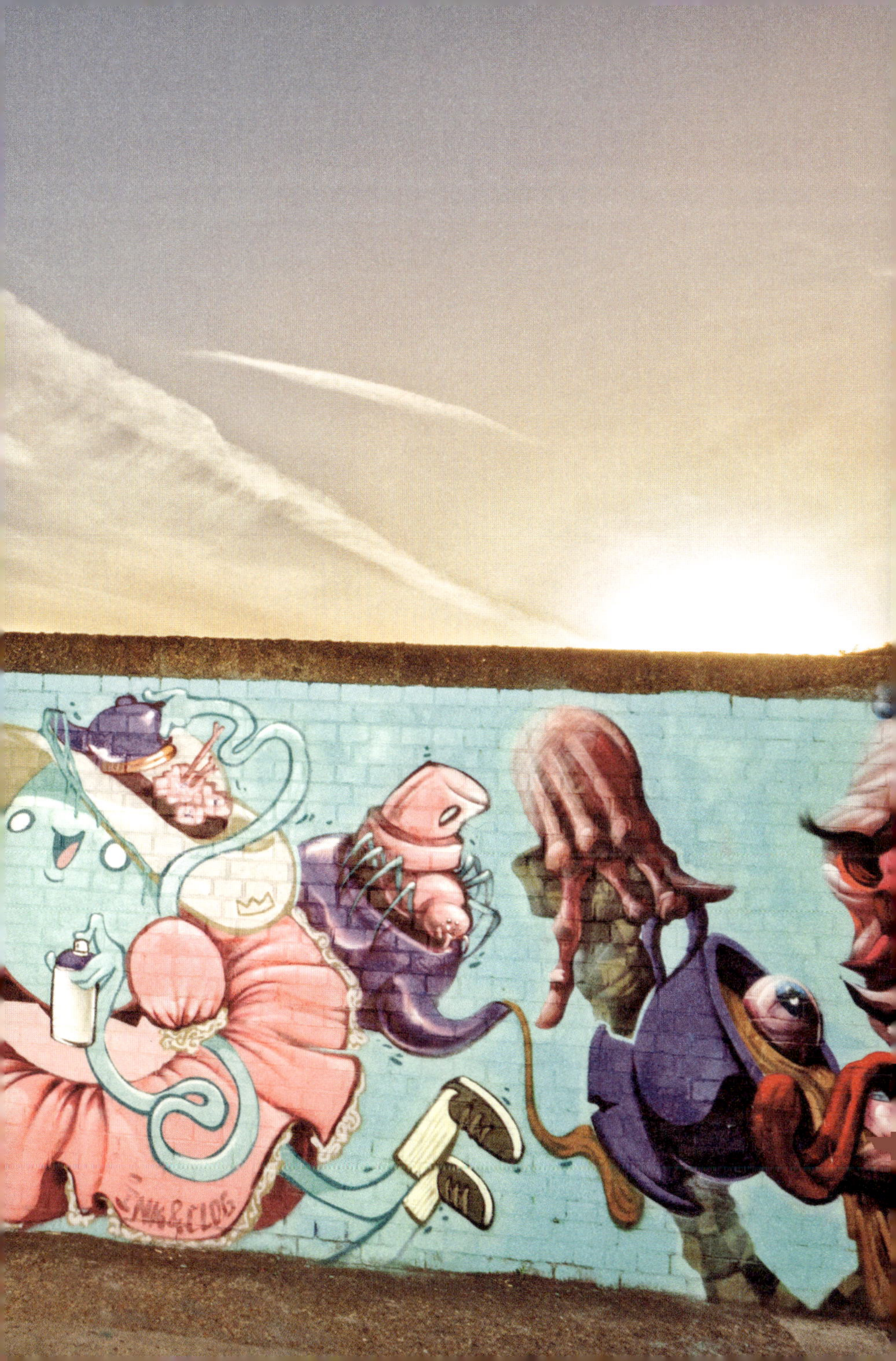

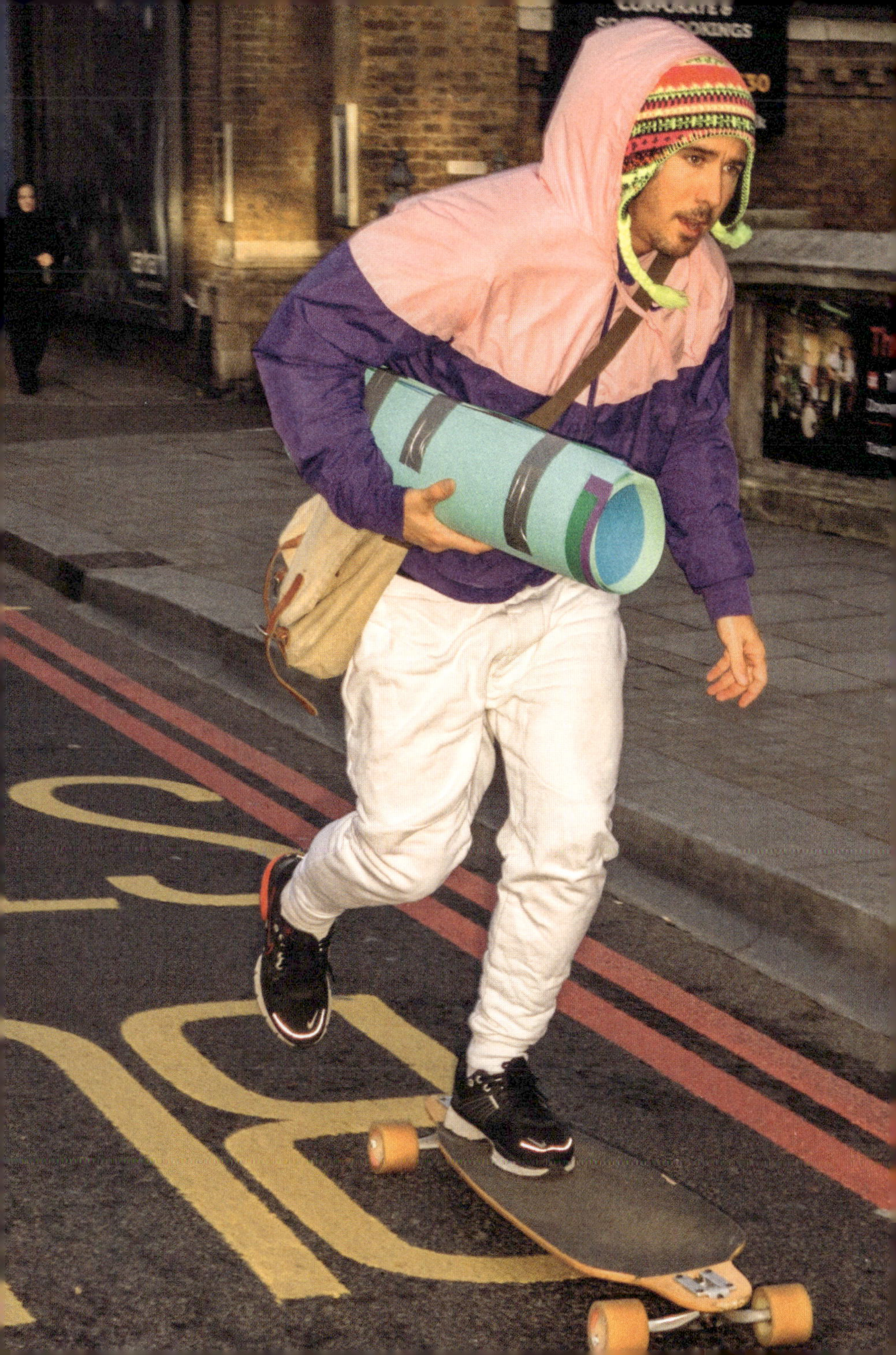

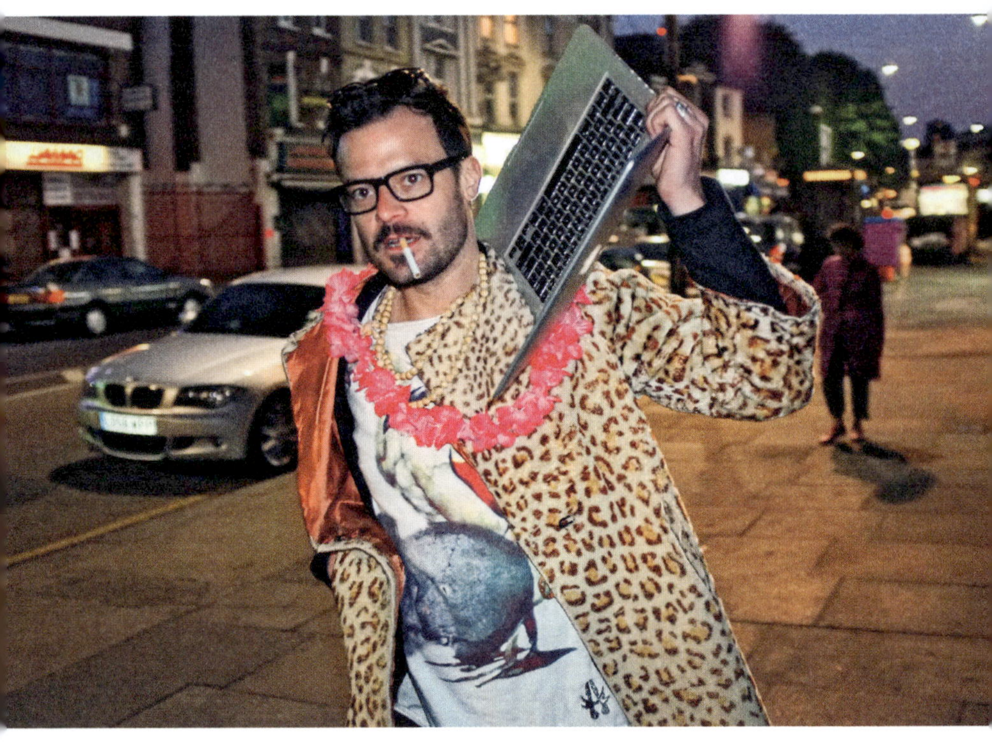

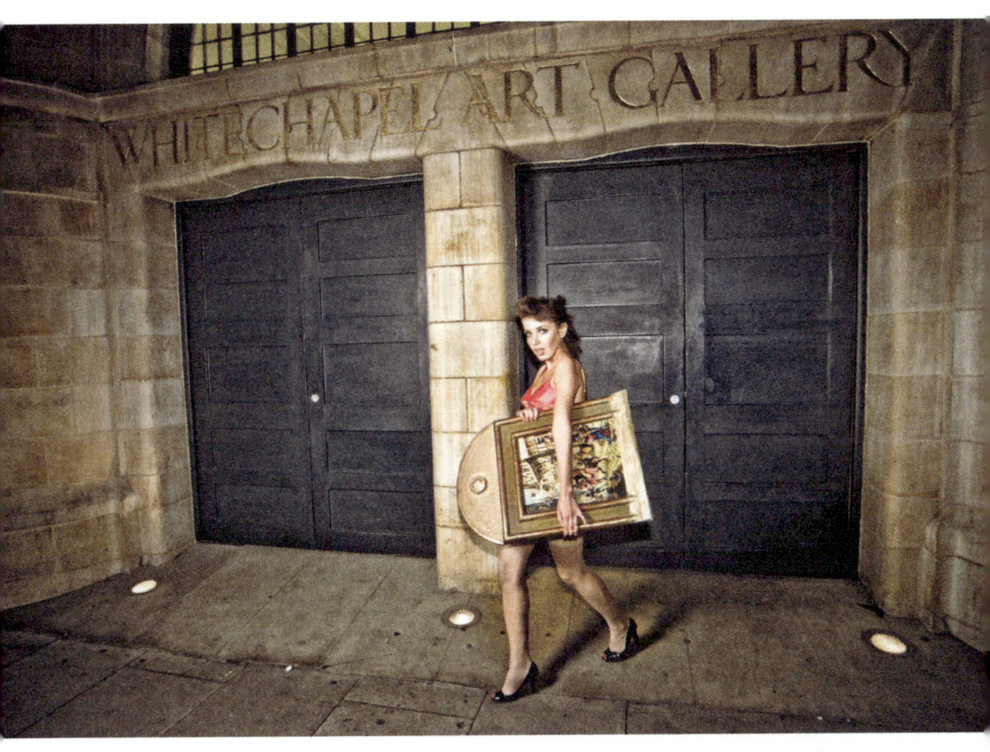

WHITECHAPEL ART GALLERY

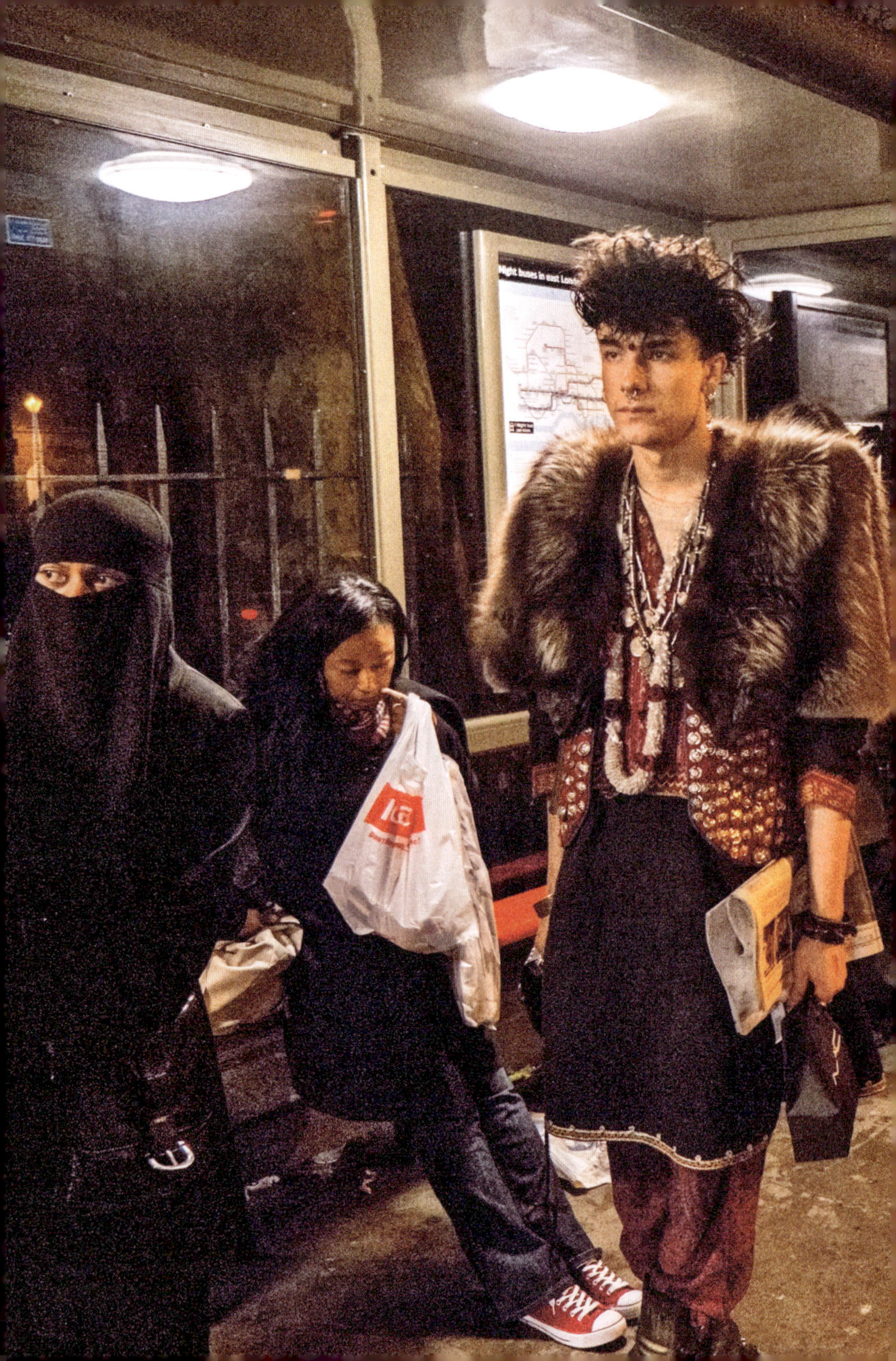

Night buses in east London

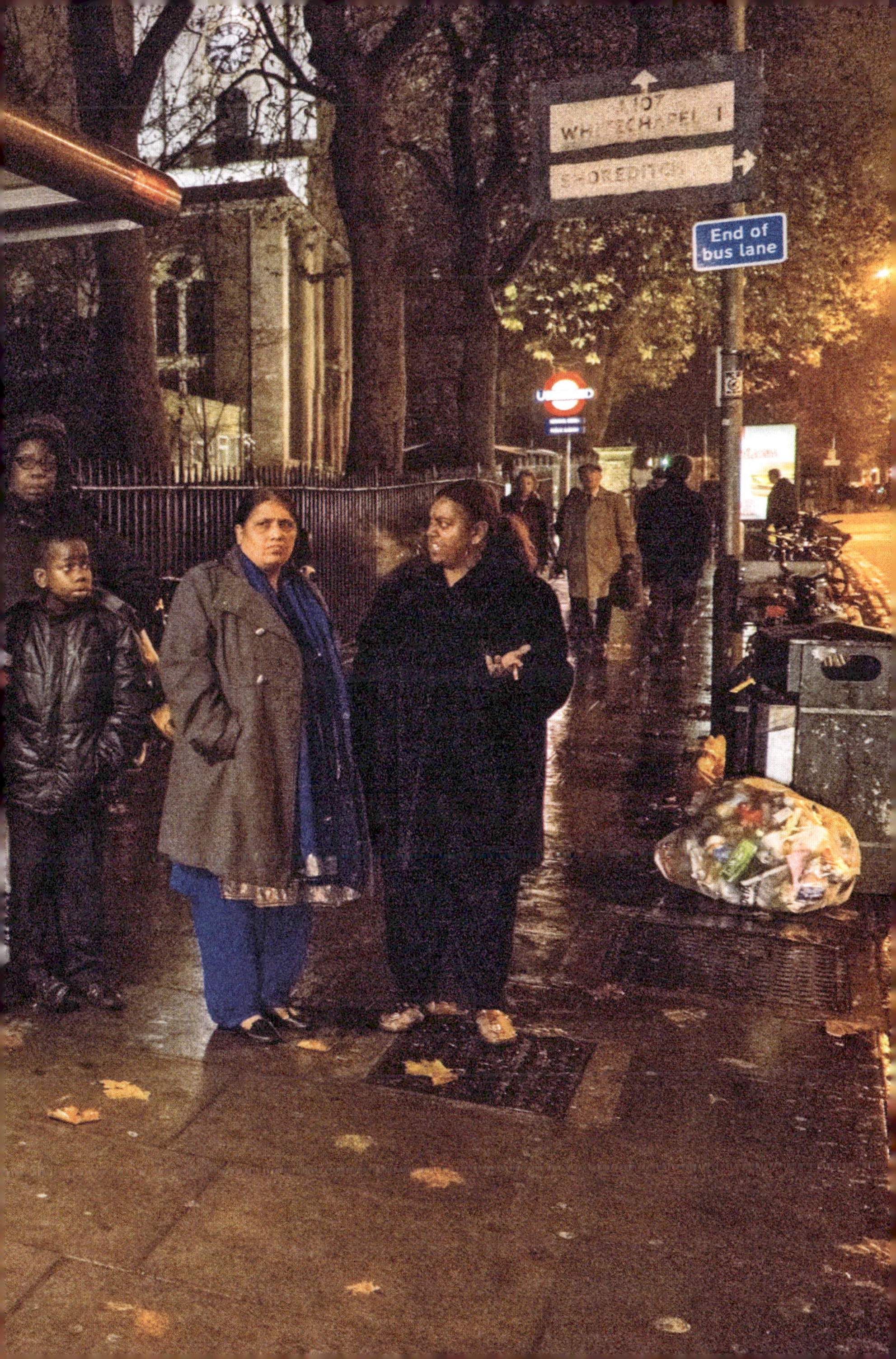

A107
WHITECHAPEL
SHOREDITCH
End of
bus lane

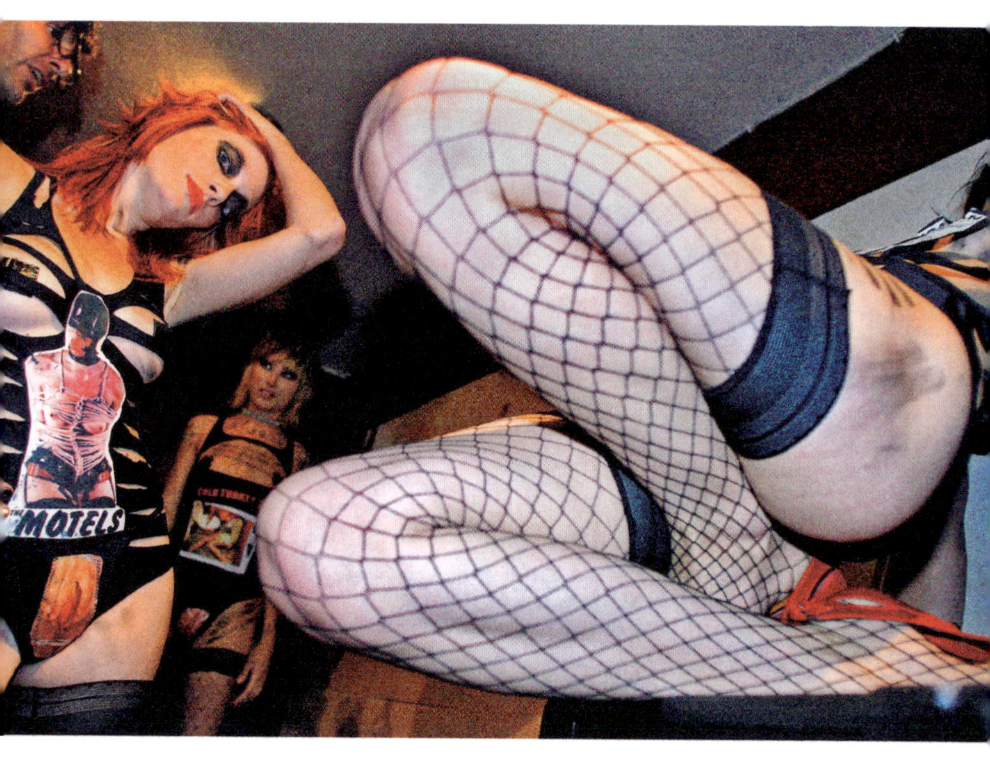

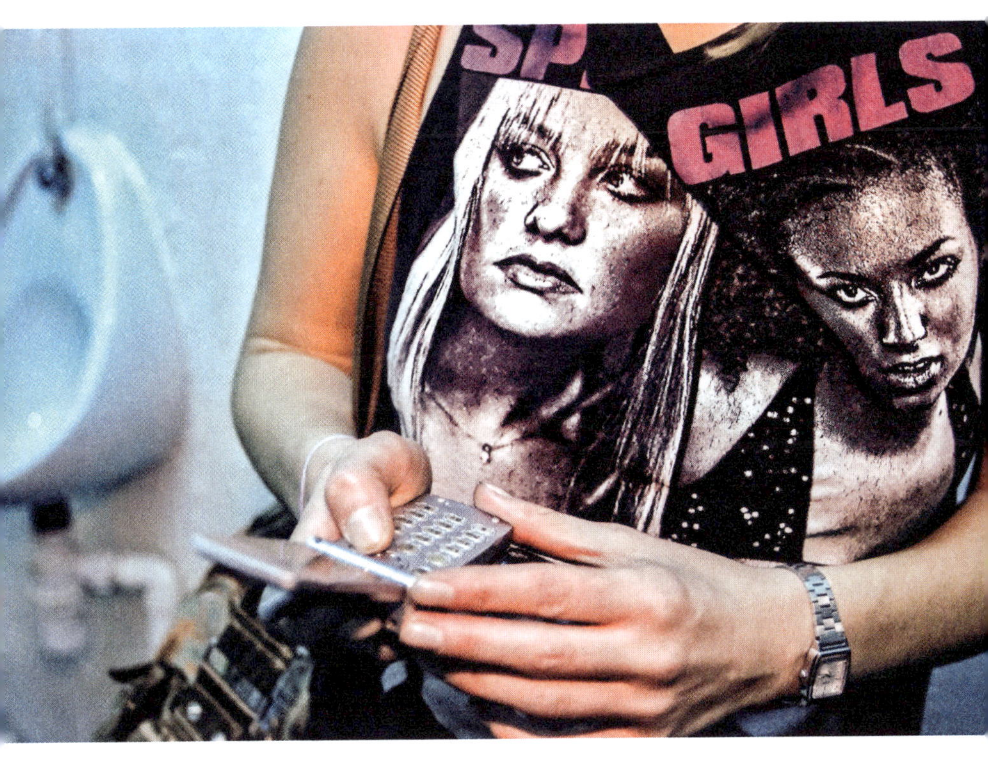
SP
GIRLS

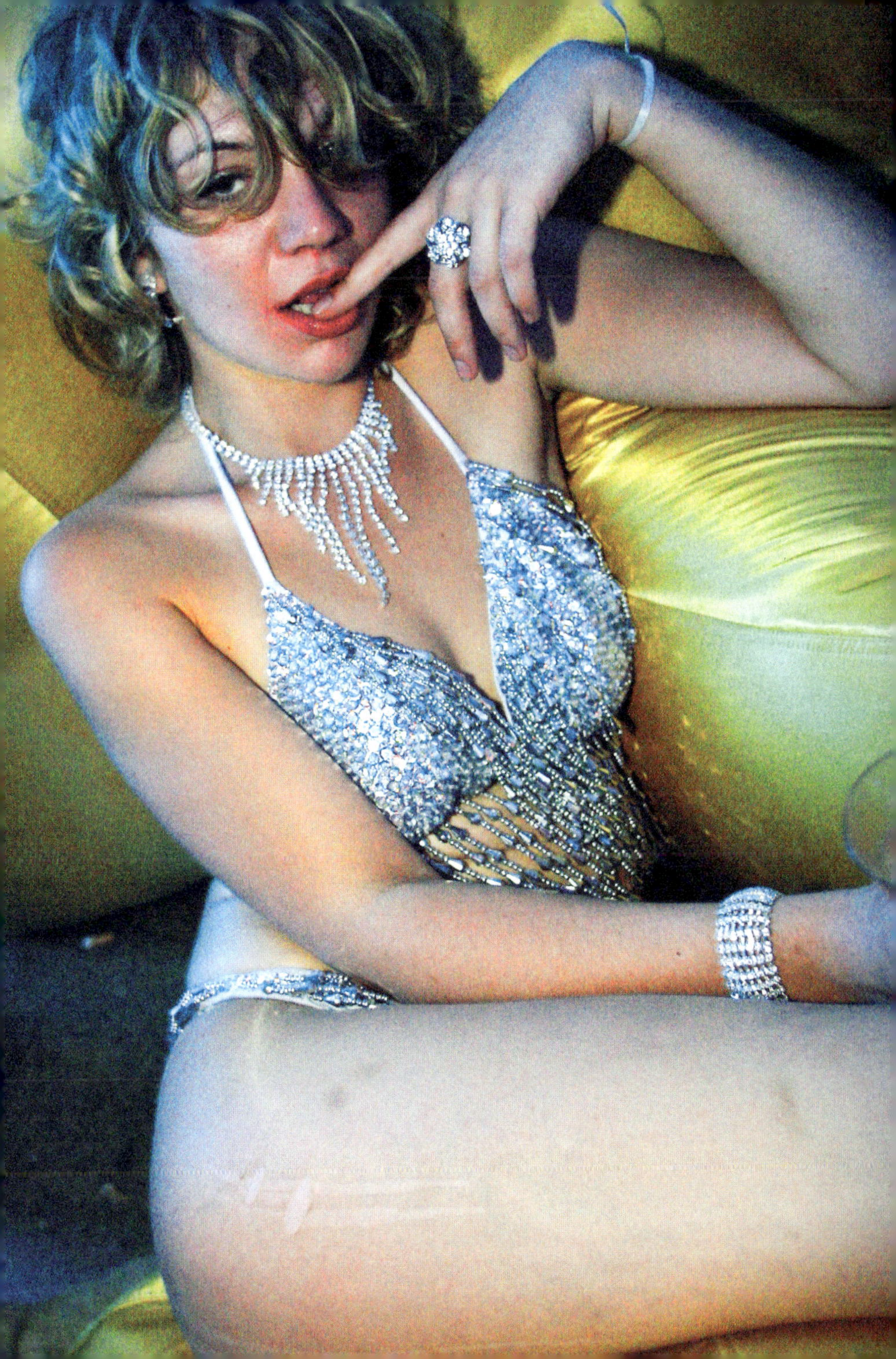

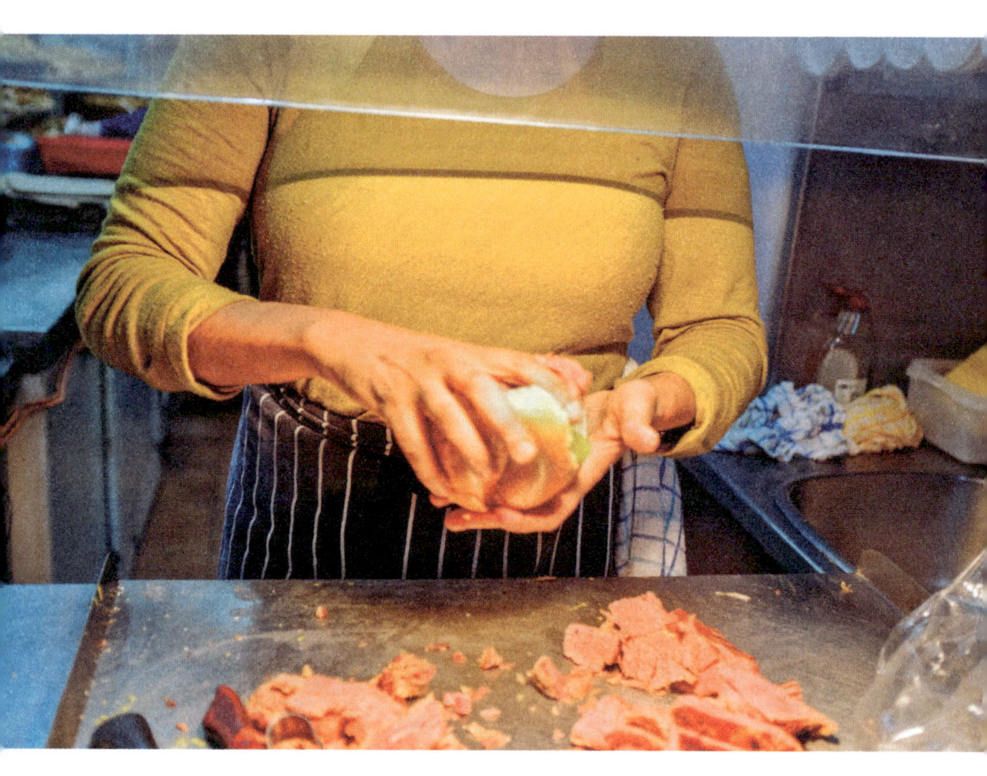

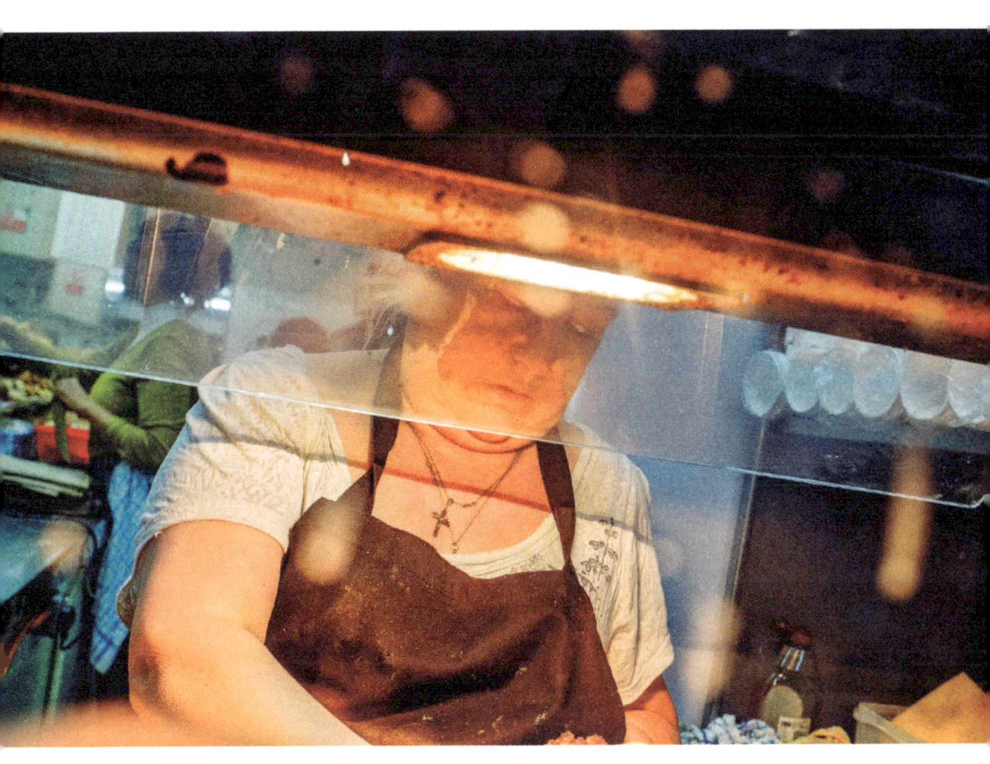

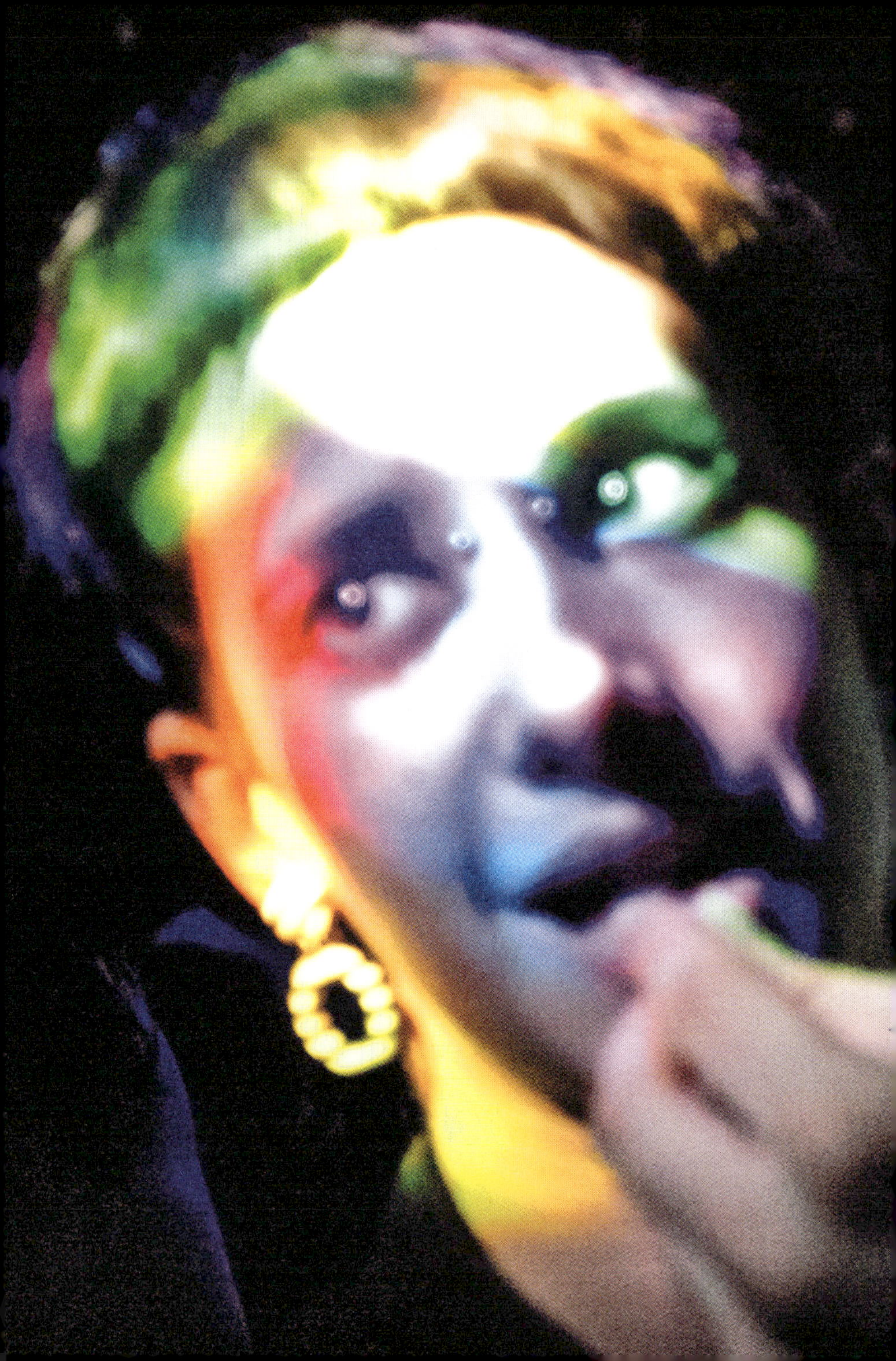

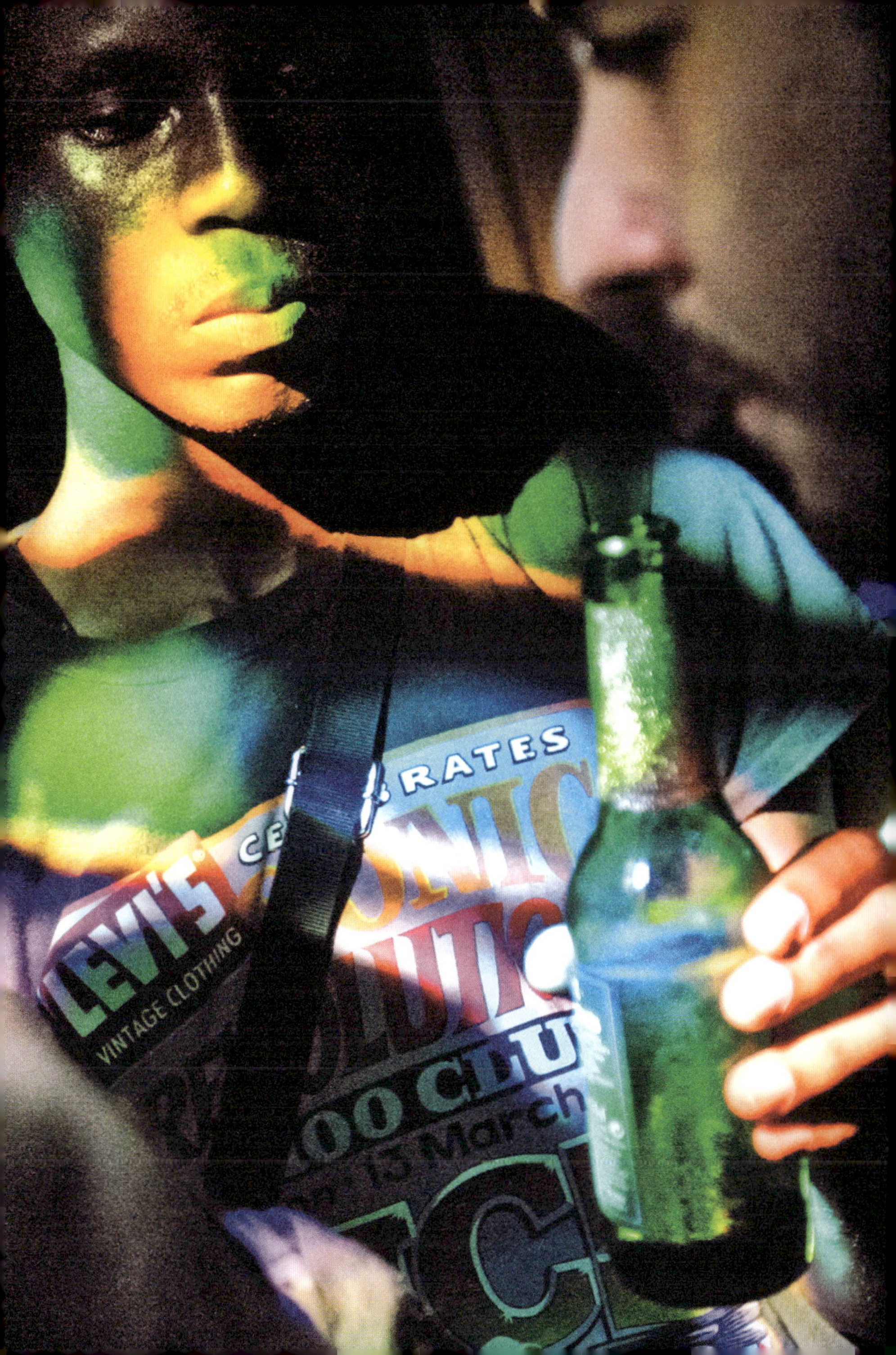

LEVI'S
VINTAGE CLOTHING
CE   RATES
ONIC
UTIO
00 CLU
15 March

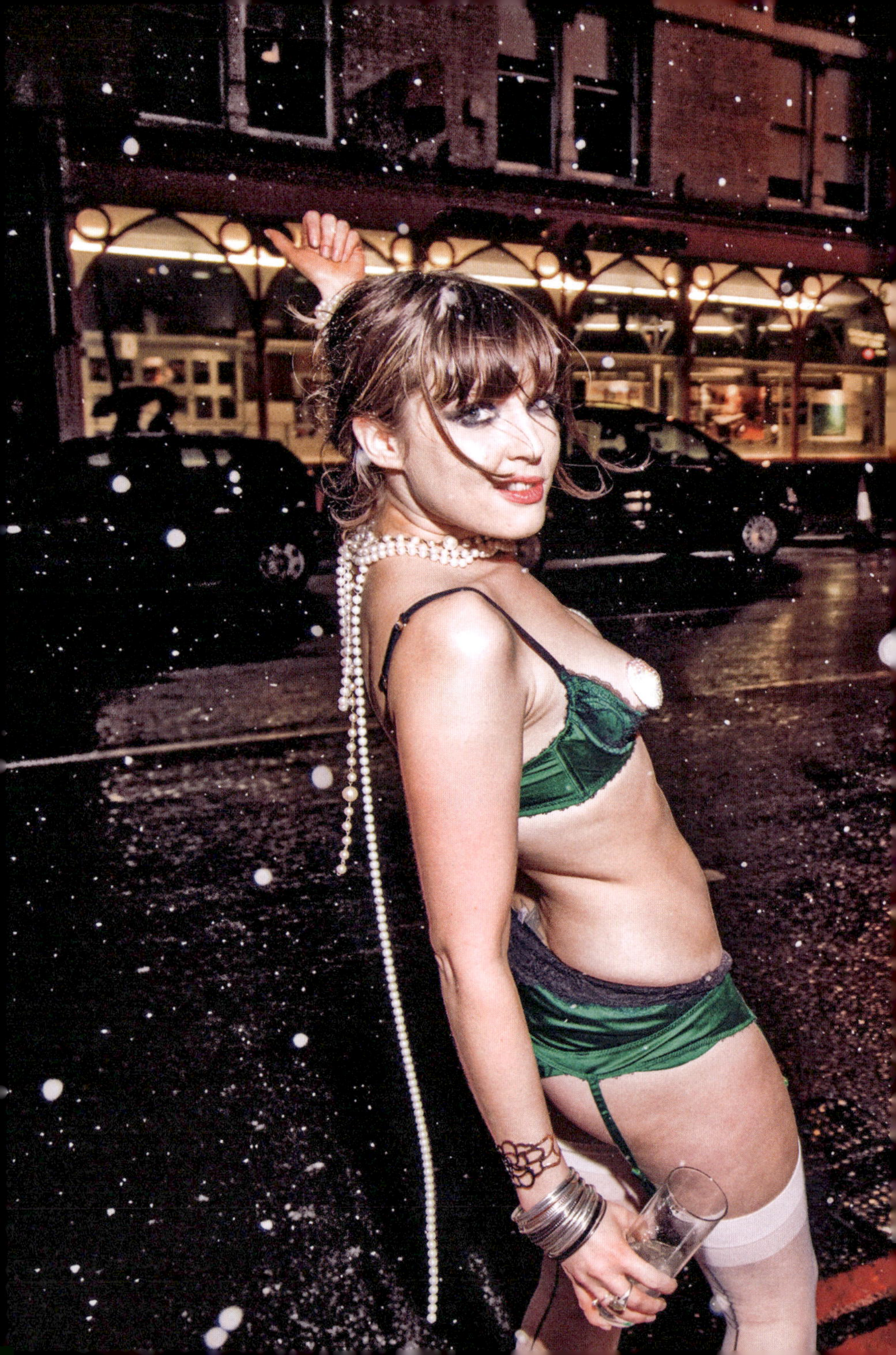

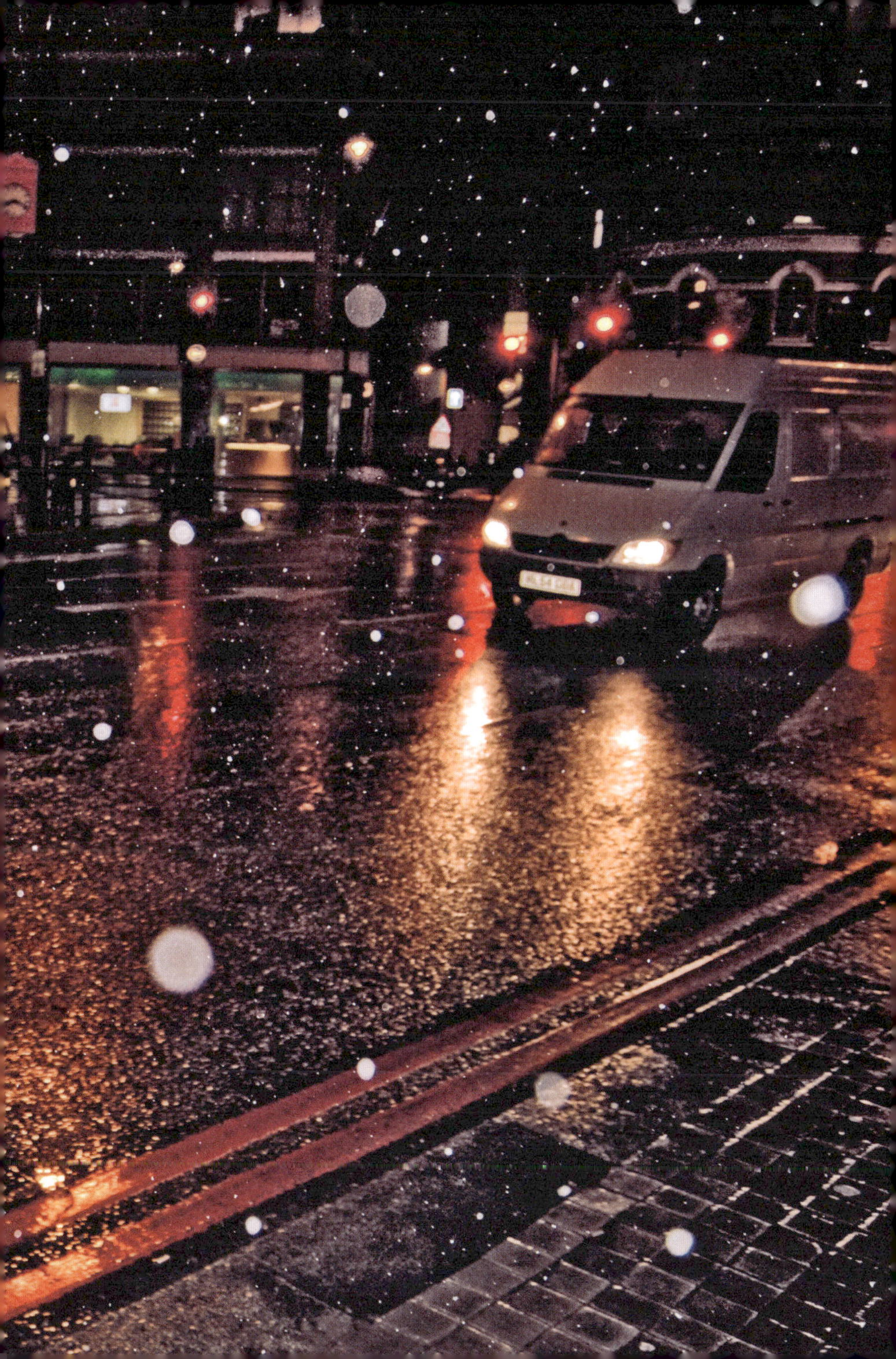

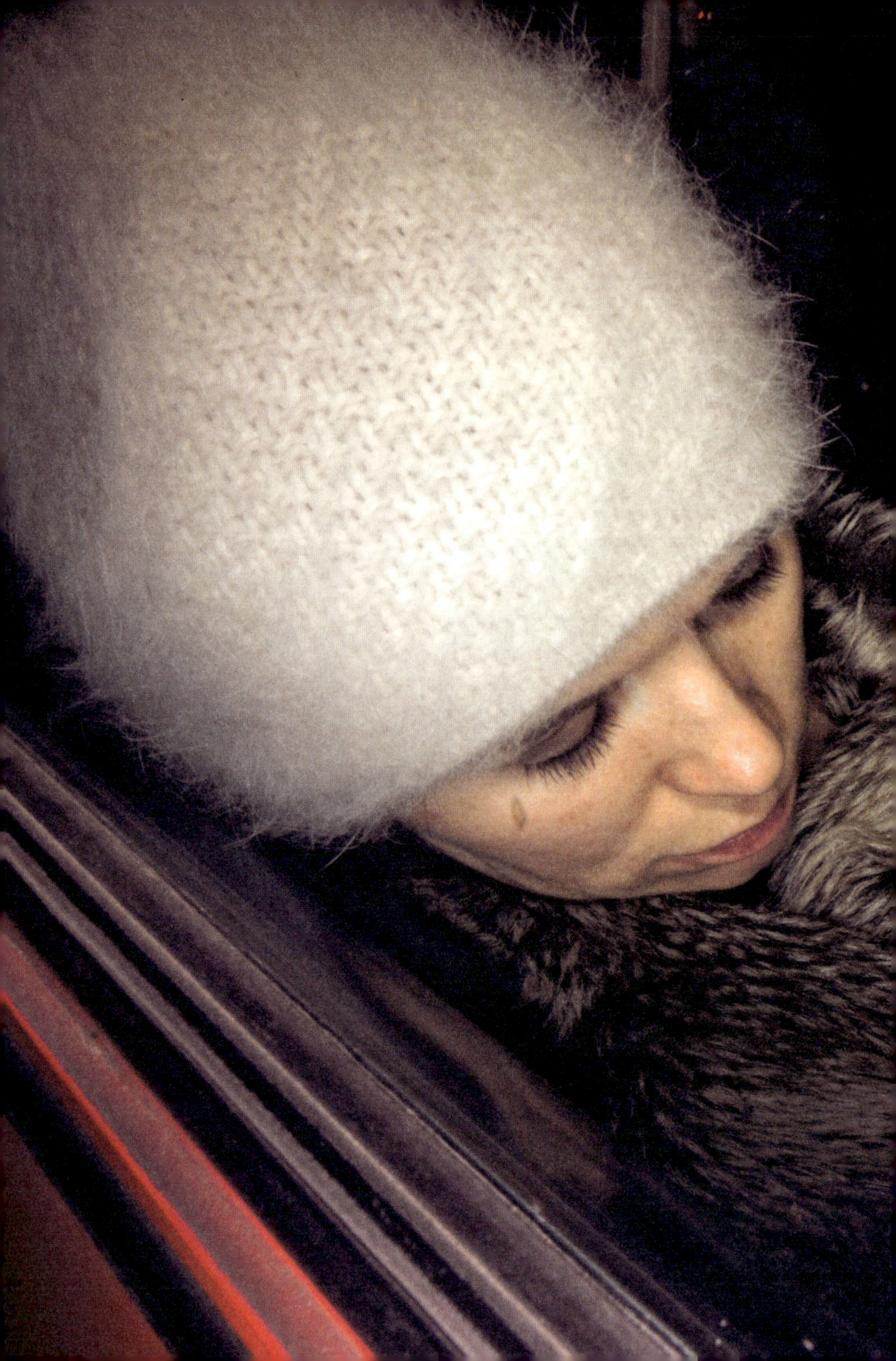

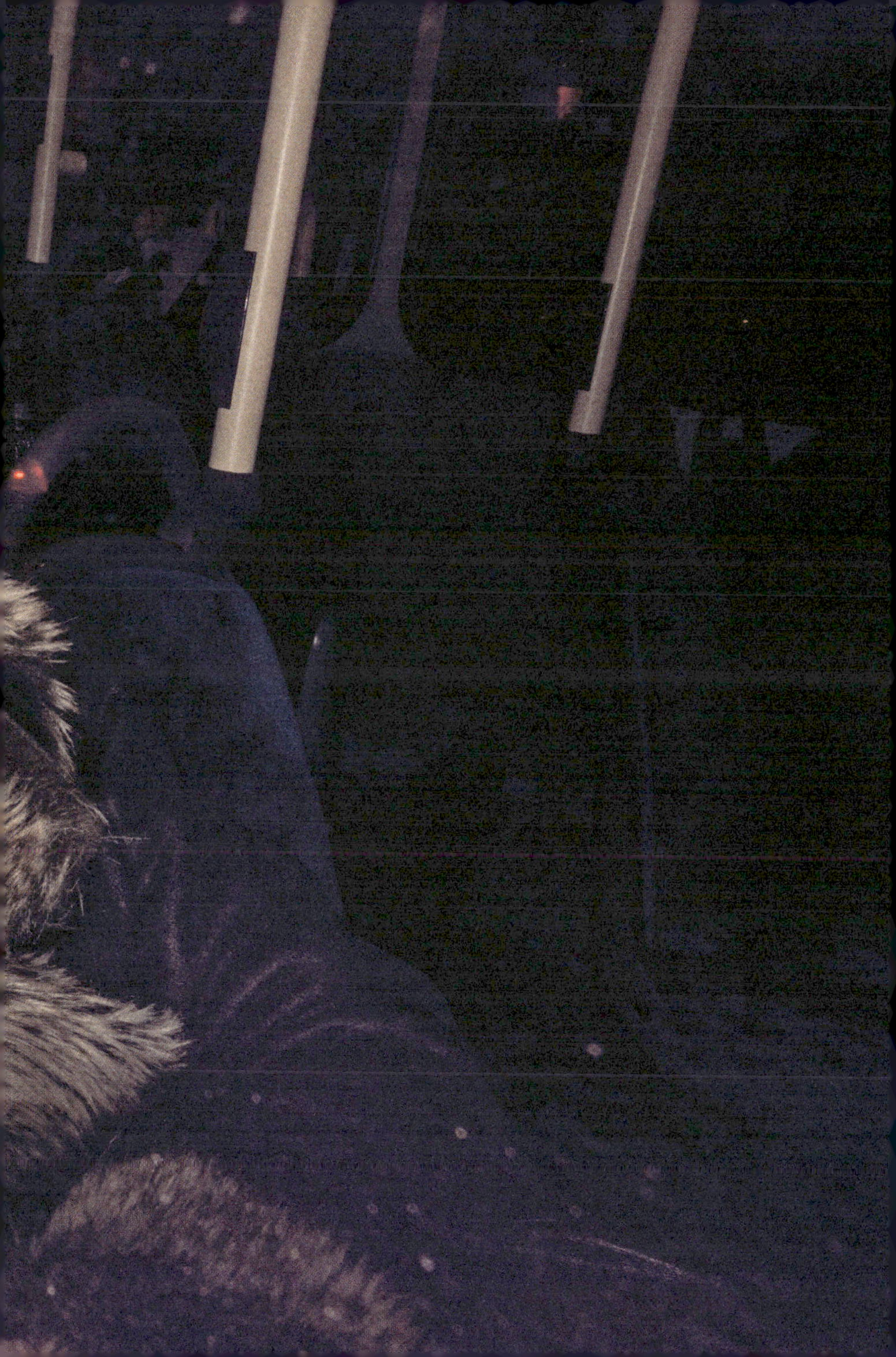

HACKNEY BY NIGHT

DAVID GEORGE

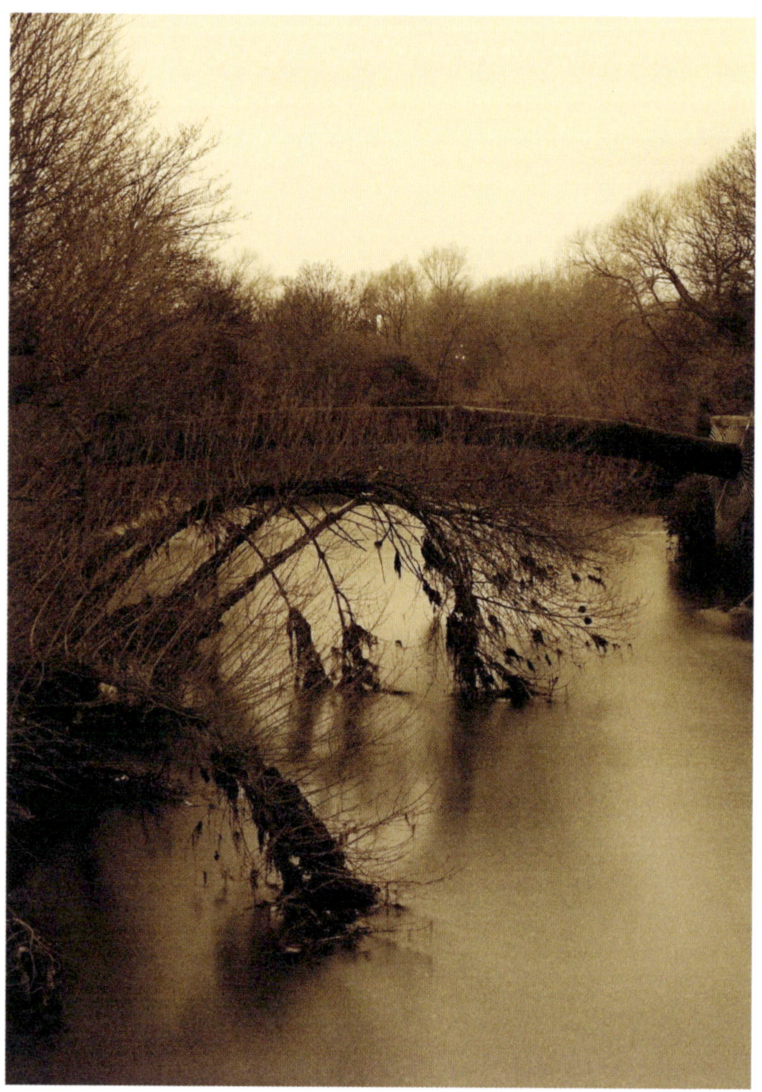

A nocturnal photographic ramble through Hackney presents the borough in a magical new light.

Can this really be Hackney? It's a question you can't help but ask yourself, looking at these ethereal, haunting scenes, some so pretty they momentarily make you stop to catch your breath. David George shot the pictures over a year between 2014 and 15, forgoing sleep for moonlit strolls in search of beauty that he froze in long exposures with his large-format camera.

What he found was another world where magical, desolate landscapes come alive in hazy shades of sepia yellow, indigo blue and emerald green, while most of Hackney slumbers. Of course there are some people still awake in Hackney at this hour – frustrated insomniacs, chemically-enhanced ravers – but you won't find them in George's economical frame.

With no human figures there to guide us, we begin to invent our own stories. What could be lurking around the corner of those shadow-strewn side streets or deserted canal paths? A wolf? Above all, it's fairytales that spring to mind. The Hackney we see in these pictures is the enchanted forests we read about as children – mysterious, full of hope, and of danger. It's a place that has always existed in our minds. And it's there every night, while we're wrapped in our dreams.

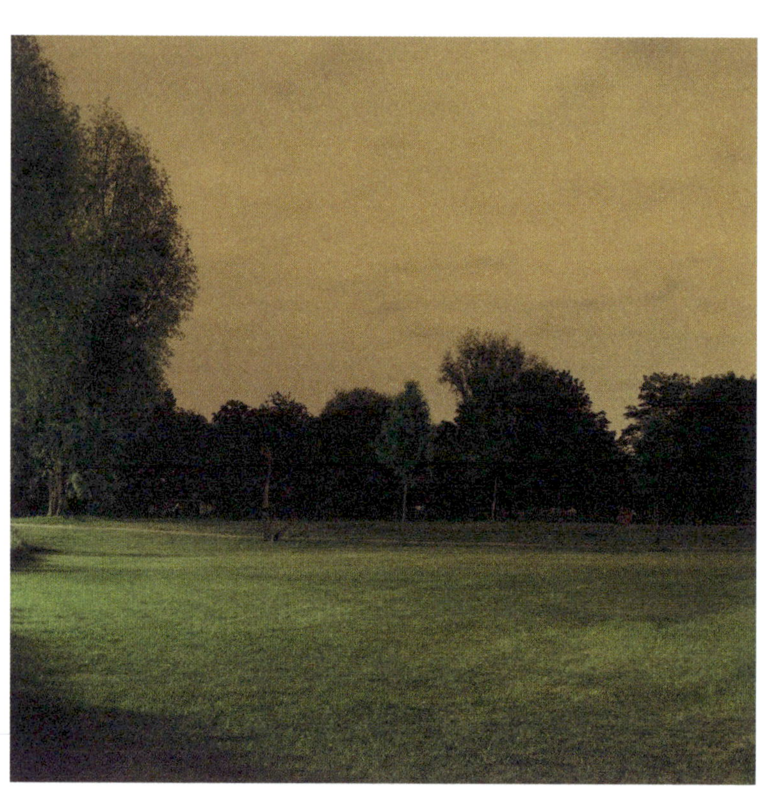

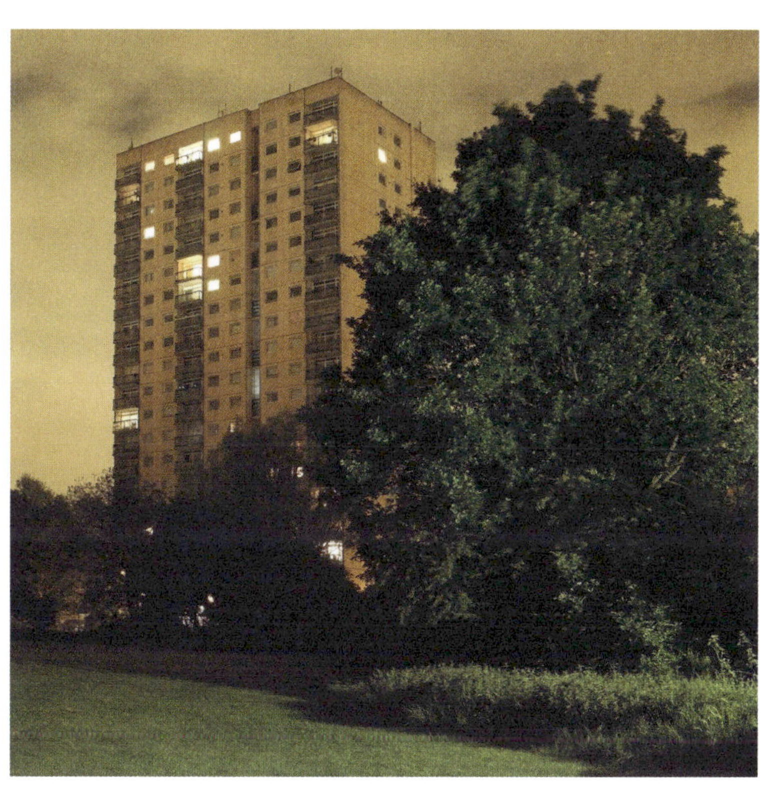

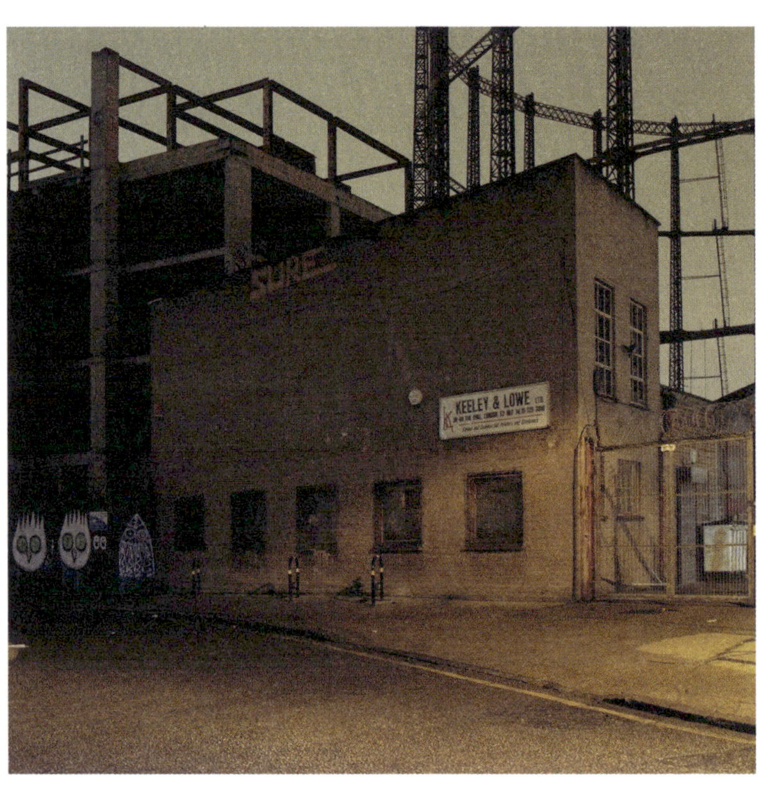

KEELEY & LOWE LTD

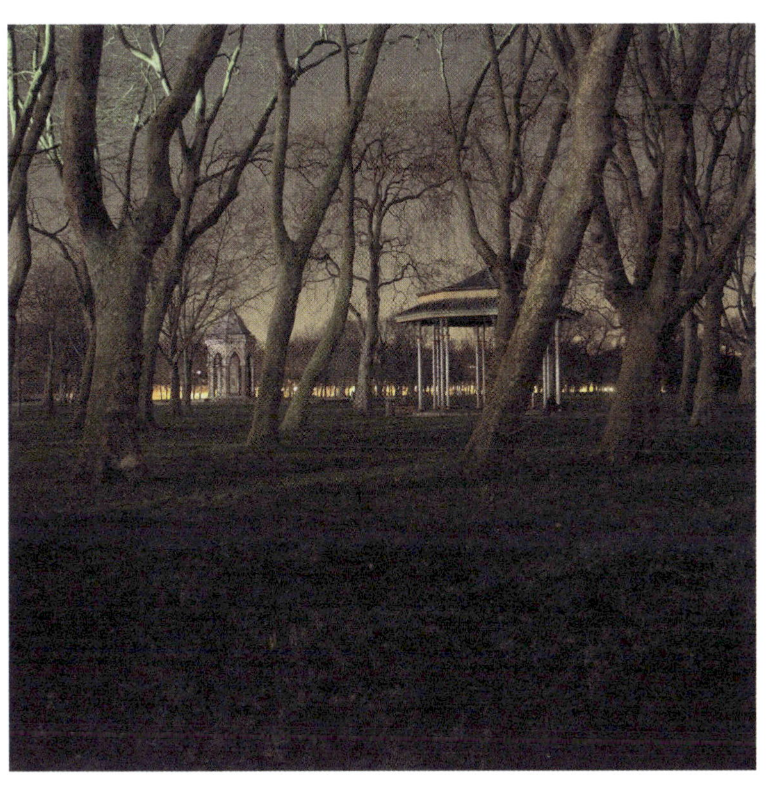

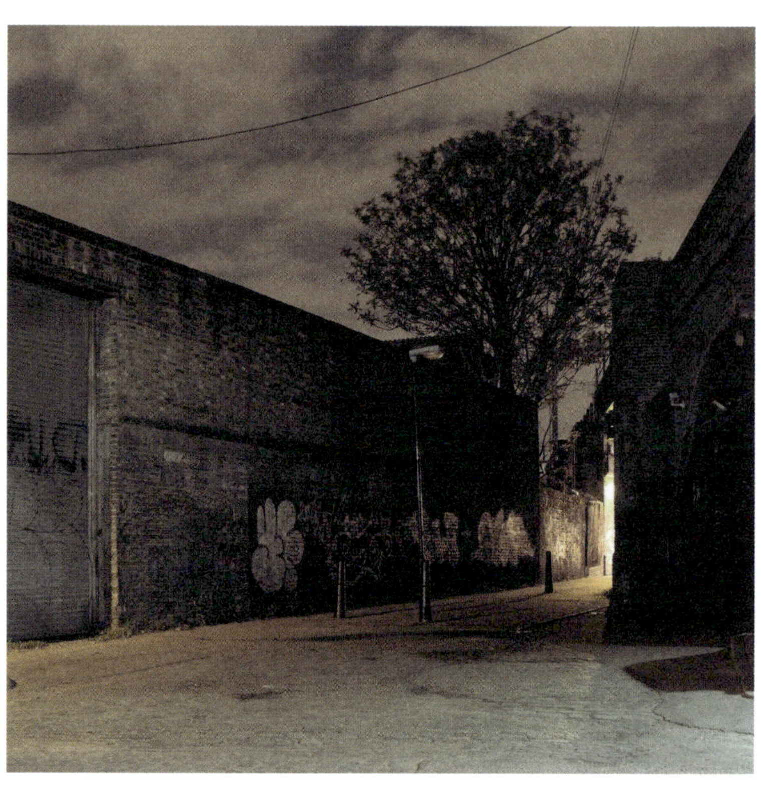

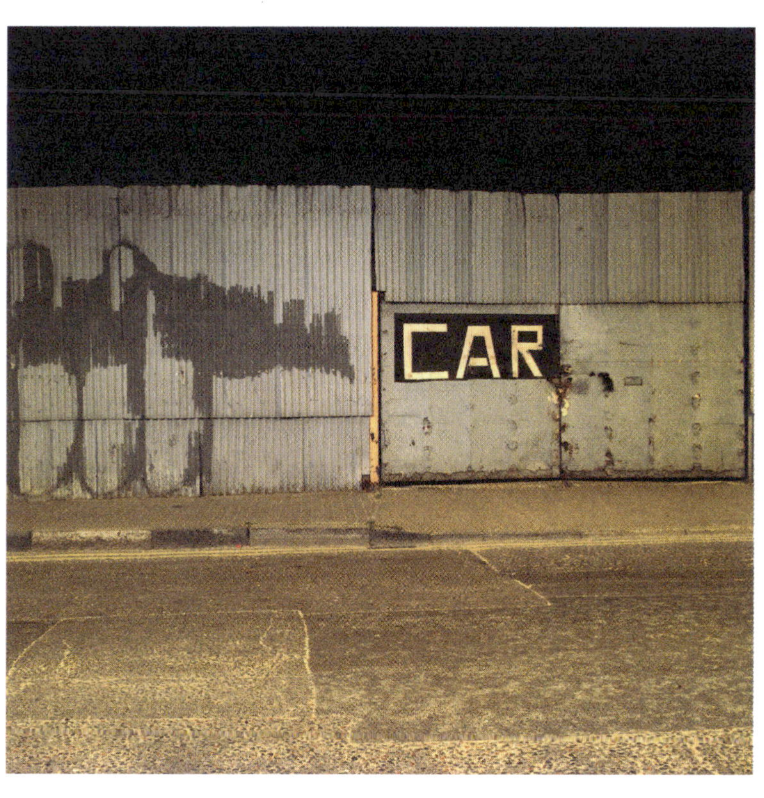
CAR

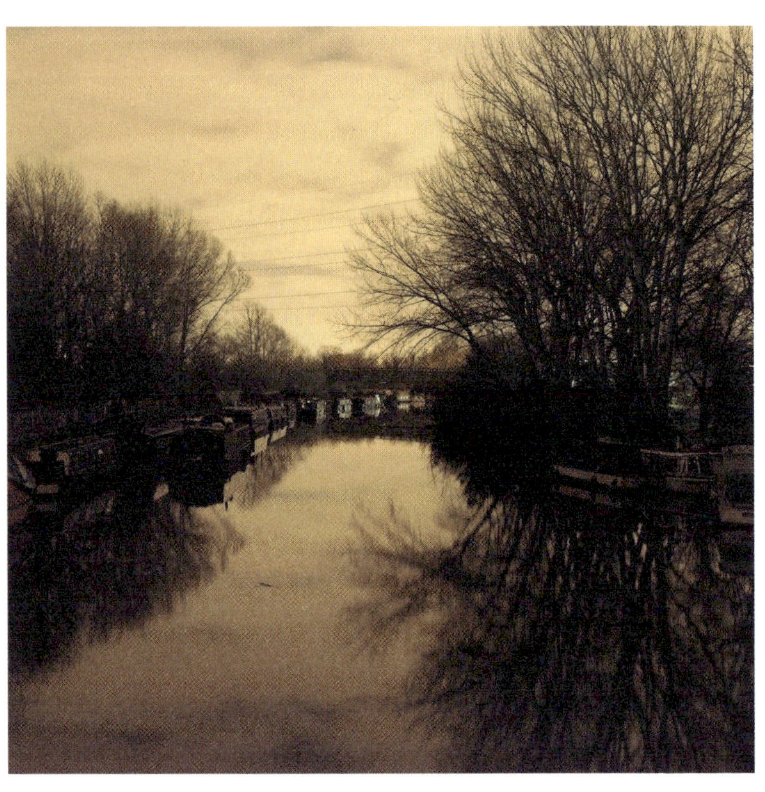

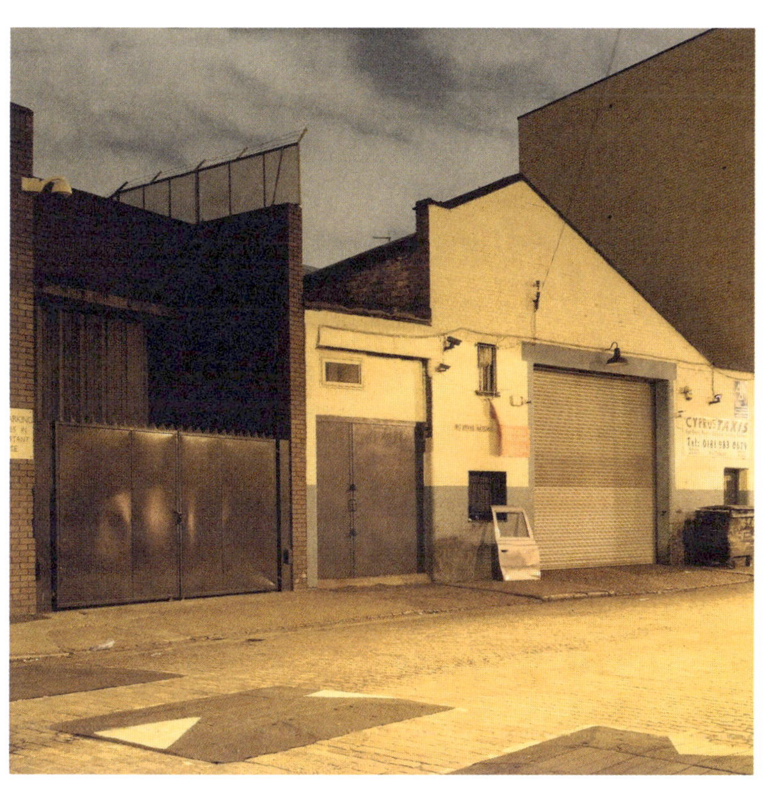

CYPRUS TAXIS
Tel: 0181 983 0679

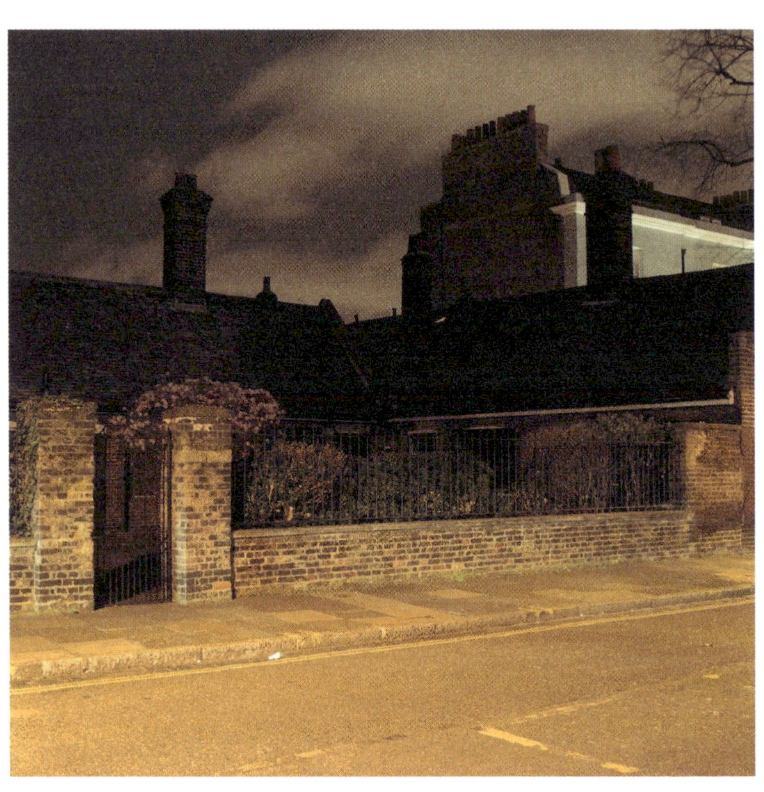

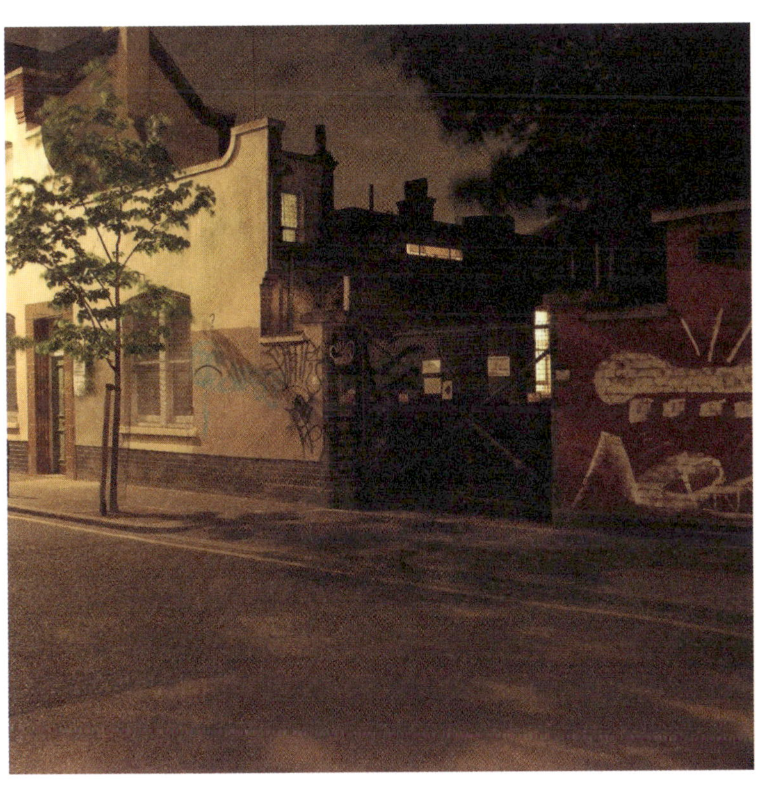

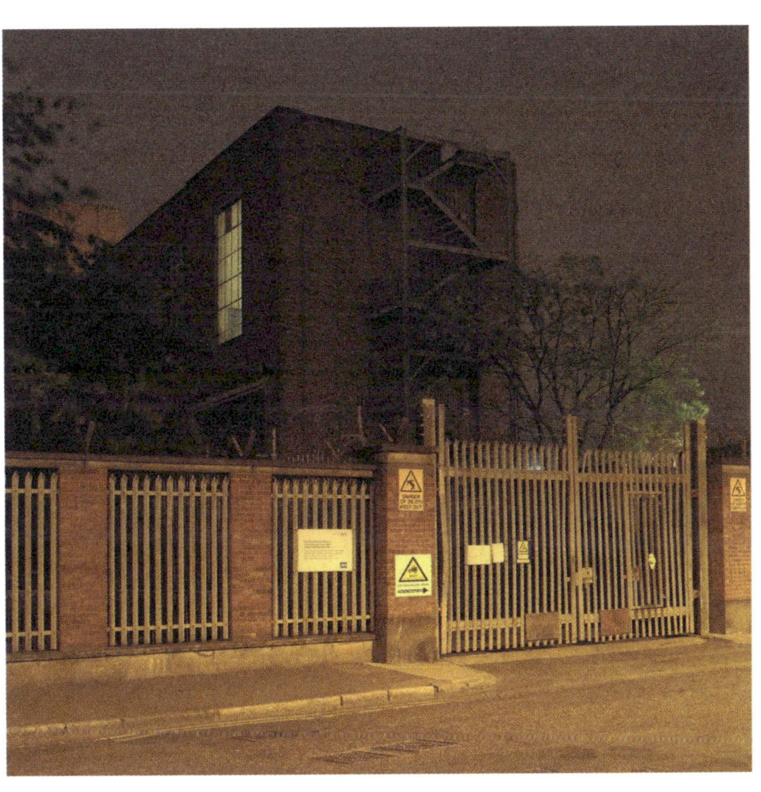

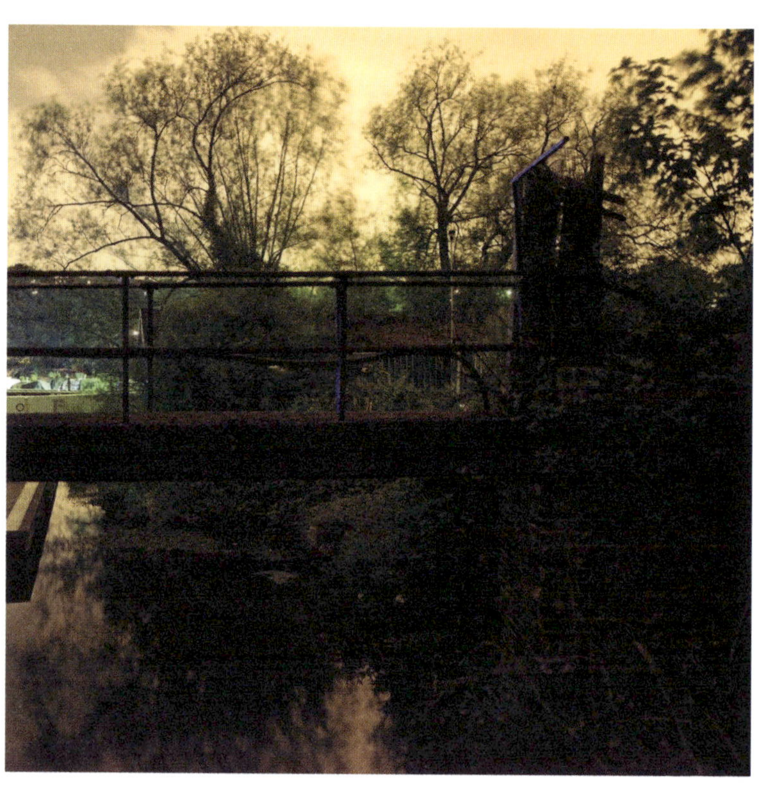

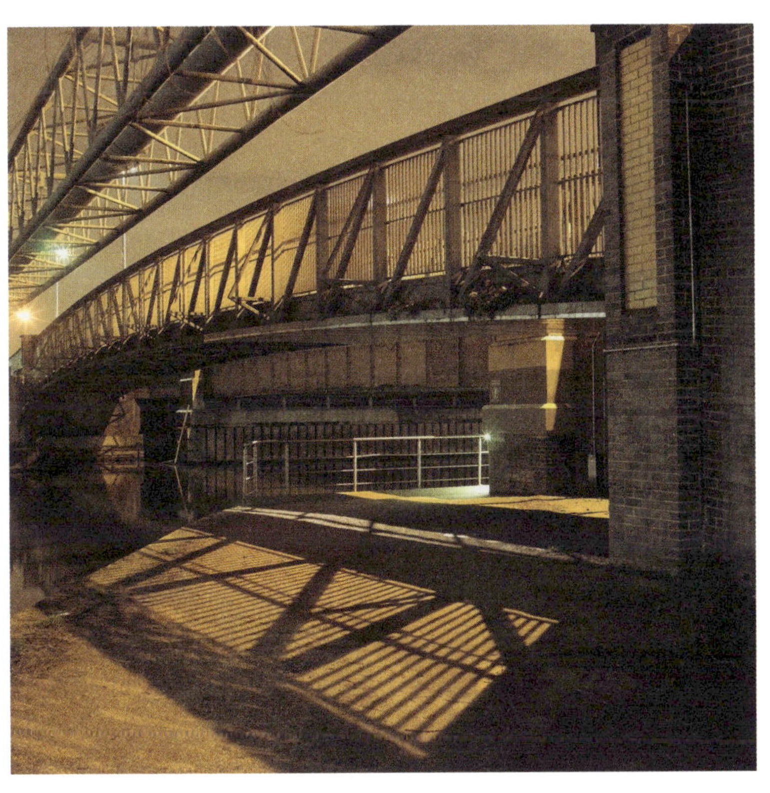

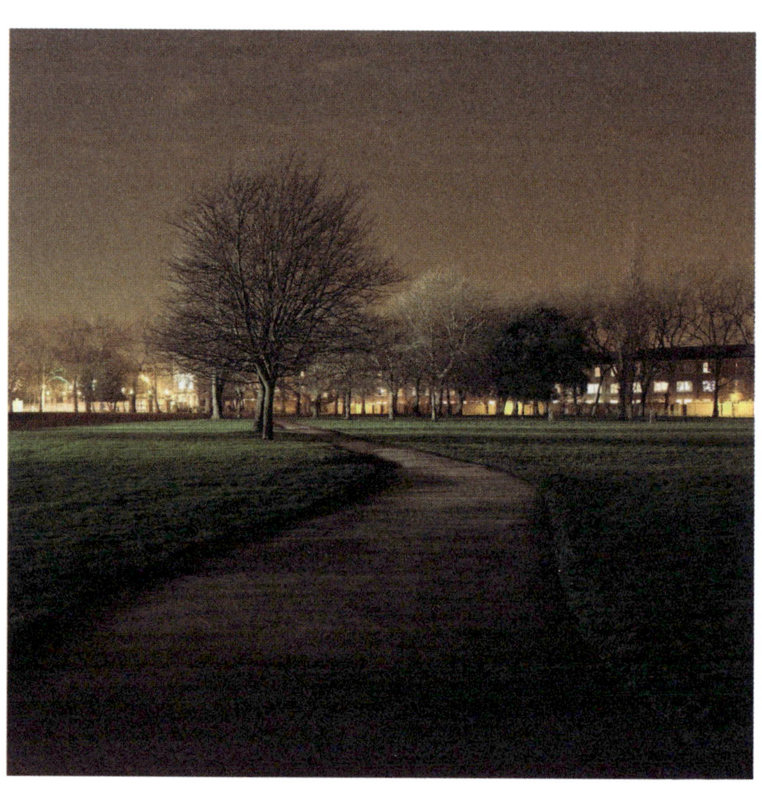

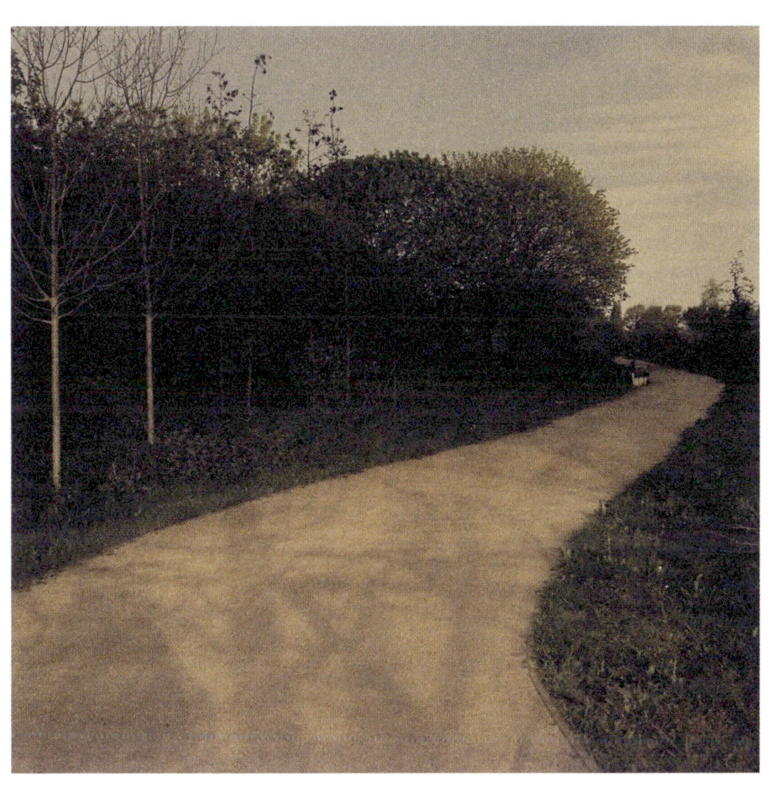

East London Photo Stories

First edition, third printing

Cover image © Zed Nelson

All photographs © The Photographers except for selected headshots on pp.6-9:
Image of Madeleine Waller © Theo Modell; Image of Jenny Lewis © Kat Green;
Image of Nicholas Sack © Timothy Cooke; Image of David Campany © Sam Contis;
Image of Chris Baker © Albert Watson

Introduction and chapter text by Rachel Segal Hamilton
Photographer biography text by Hoxton Mini Press
Design and sequence by Friederike Huber
Copy-editing by Faith McAllister

A CIP catalogue record for this book is available from the British Library

ISBN 978-1-910566-42-8

First published in the United Kingdom in 2018 by Hoxton Mini Press

Printed and bound by: Livonia Print, Latvia

To order books, collector's editions and signed prints please go to:
www.hoxtonminipress.com